C. S. LEWIS

Life, Works, and Legacy

C. S. LEWIS

Life, Works, and Legacy

Volume 3: Apologist, Philosopher, and Theologian

Edited by
Bruce L. Edwards

PRAEGER PERSPECTIVES

Westport, Connecticut
London

Library of Congress Cataloging-in-Publication Data

C.S. Lewis : life, works, and legacy / edited by Bruce L. Edwards.
    p. cm.
    Includes bibliographical references and index.
    ISBN 0–275–99116–4 (set : alk. paper)—ISBN 0–275–99117–2 (v. 1 : alk.
    paper)—ISBN 0–275–99118–0 (v. 2 : alk. paper)—ISBN 0–275–99119–9 (v. 3 : alk.
    paper)—ISBN 0–275–99120–2 (v. 4 : alk. paper)
    1. Lewis, C. S. (Clive Staples), 1898–1963—Criticism and interpretation.   I. Edwards,
    Bruce L.
    PR6023.E926Z597   2007
    823′.912–dc22   2006100486

British Library Cataloguing in Publication Data is available.

Copyright © 2007 by Bruce L. Edwards

Library of Congress Catalog Card Number: 2006100486
ISBN-10: 0–275–99116–4 (set)   ISBN-13: 978–0–275–99116–6
          0–275–99117–2 (Vol. 1)   978–0–275–99117–3
          0–275–99118–0 (Vol. 2)   978–0–275–99118–0
          0–275–99119–9 (Vol. 3)   978–0–275–99119–7
          0–275–99120–2 (Vol. 4)   978–0–275–99120–3

First published in 2007

Praeger Publishers, 88 Post Road West, Westport, CT 06881
An imprint of Greenwood Publishing Group, Inc.
www.praeger.com

Printed in the United States of America

The paper used in this book complies with the
Permanent Paper Standard issued by the National
Information Standards Organization (Z39.48–1984).

10 9 8 7 6 5 4 3 2 1

This work is dedicated to my son,

Justin Robert Edwards.

Justin's passion for life and for the life to come,
his creativity and excellence in music and movie-making,
his faith and resilience in the face of this world's challenges,
all inspire and amaze me,
and bless everyone who knows him.

Contents

Acknowledgments

The genesis of this four-volume reference set is the kind invitation I received from Suzanne Staszak-Silva of Greenwood Publishing Group in late Spring, 2005, asking me to consider creating a reference work that would comprehensively deal with the life and work of C. S. Lewis. As it was the case that I was almost literally heading out the door to Tanzania on a Fulbright-Hays Grant, we did not get to consider the project in much detail until the end of the summer when, with the help of my literary agent, Matt Jacobson, we cheerfully exchanged ideas with Suzanne that have led to the expansive volumes you now hold in your hands. Suzanne and all the capable editors and reviewers at Greenwood have been terrific to work with, and I am once again grateful to Matt Jacobson of the Loyal Arts Literary Agency for his expertise and wise counsel.

No project of this kind can, in fact, come to fruition without the help of many hands. I want to start with the contributors to this volume and the breadth and depth of C. S. Lewis scholarship they represent. Each of them, especially those contributing more than one essay, have cheerfully met my prescribed deadlines and offered both incisive and learned commentary on the topics for which they were chosen. I want to offer special thanks to busy and illustrious Lewisian colleagues and scholars, David Downing, Diana Glyer, David Bratman, Don King, Marvin Hinten, Lyle Dorsett, Colin Duriez, Victor Reppert, Devin Brown, Wayne Martindale, and Marjorie Lamp Mead, for making and taking the time to contribute their unique vantage points to this collection. Their knowledge of the Lewis canon continues to provide us with fresh insights into his legacy. The exciting thing about this particular collection, however, is not only the opportunity to recruit the already renowned scholars listed above, but also to attract new talent and younger scholars who bring their own generational insights into the issues and contexts many of us have been sifting for years.

Walter Hooper has been unfailingly kind in his support of this project, helping me arrange access to some special collections at the Bodleian Library at Oxford University. Of course, Lewis scholars everywhere are in his debt for decades of indefatigable efforts to make the letters and papers of C. S. Lewis available to the public. Likewise, Christopher Mitchell, Director, and his staff, at the Marion C. Wade Center at Wheaton College in Wheaton, Illinois, continue to operate the most outstanding resource center on C. S. Lewis and the Inklings in North America. I treasure every moment I get to spend in the beautiful Wade Center's hallowed library.

Scott Calhoun, a longtime colleague and friend from Cedarville University, Ohio, answered my call for some late counsel on the disposition of the last several essays to be included for publication, and I will always be grateful for his graceful editorial touches. (The only thing missing in this collection is an essay that I am sure Scott wishes to compose on the influence of Lewis's work on U2's Bono. Maybe next time, Scott?)

My colleagues at Bowling Green State University, especially my immediate supervisors, continue to be generous in support of my research and lecturing on C. S. Lewis. They have provided me with the writing time one needs to produce a set of volumes of this magnitude. Dr. William K. Balzer, Dean of Continuing and Extended Education and Associate Vice-President, along with Dr. Linda Dobb, Executive Vice-President, made possible a Spring 2006 trip to the Bodleian Library, Oxford, England, and a presentation at the "C. S. Lewis, Renaissance Man" Conference at Cambridge University that significantly affected the scope and accuracy of this work. My own staff headed by Ms. Connie Molnar, Director of Distance Education at Bowling Green State University, has indirectly made possible the efforts herein reflected, since their diligence and professionalism allowed me the freedom at crucial moments during the project to travel for research or to siphon off time for its final editing.

Finally, while we were completing the last stages of this volume, my wife Joan and I were trying to finish the building of a new home. As anyone who has ever tried such a foolish and audacious thing can testify, it can make for some tense (and intense) hours. Joan has been her usual patient, kind, and thoughtful self in shouldering the burden for all sorts of decisions and contingency planning for the house, liberating me to read, write, edit, and email incessantly. In the end, her contribution to this four-volume set is equal to any I can claim. These volumes are for the "Keeping Room" shelves, Sweetie. Enjoy them!

Since I have never left them out of any book I have published, I will not become inconsistent or ungrateful now. My children, Matthew, Tracey, Mary, Casey, Justin, and Michael always inspire me to reach higher and perform at my best. Their love and encouragement make all the difference on those dark and stormy nights when you wonder whether even one more word will come forth. Each of them is an artist or creator in their own right, with plenty of books (and songs and movies) of their own on the horizon. Michael specifically enhances this text further by contributing one of the most significant essays in Volume 4; I should have turned him loose on more topics! My father, Bruce L. Edwards, Sr., has always been steadfast in his support and encouragement for my work, and I sincerely thank him for continuing to take such good care of all of us. As does God Himself.

Preface

Scholars and admirers alike have long sought a full-fledged, balanced bio-critical treatment of the life and works of C. S. Lewis. They, rightly, seek a treatise that does justice to his remarkably successful, multiple careers as a Christian apologist, science fiction and fantasy writer, literary historian, poet, cultural critic, and historian of words. Such a book will be sympathetic without being sycophantic, incisive without being sensational, and comprehensive without being copious. It will illuminate his life and times, including his interesting friendships, his composing techniques, and, of course, his personal piety.

Above all, it will also help explain his enormous impact on contemporary Christianity, particularly in America, and it will set in appropriate historical context the important contribution his scholarship makes to literary culture and social and ethical discourse in philosophy and theology. Until such a book arrives, if it ever does, this current four-volume set will represent the most lucid, most dispassionate, well-informed, up-to-date, and comprehensive treatment of Lewis's life, times, and legacy to have so far been produced, exemplifying the highest standards of historical research and employing the most responsible tools of interpretation.

It has been too typical of the variety of biographies now available on Lewis for their authors to range between two extremes: (1) works furtively focused on certain presumed negative personality traits and ambiguous relationships and incidents that obscure rather than illuminate Lewis's faith and scholarship; or (2) works so enamored of Lewis that their work borders on or exceeds hagiography and offers page after page of redundant paraphrase of his putatively unique insights. The former, despite their protestations that they operate out of an objectivity missing in other treatments, or out of a respect and a healthy admiration for Lewis's "literary accomplishments," tend to be transparently premised on a rather tendentious amateur psychoanalysis and often programmatically dismiss Lewis's readership in order to discredit his literary and theological judgments. The latter evince the effects of the worshipful homage, exhausting readers and convincing them that Lewis is readily reducible to a few doctrines, a few genres, and, perhaps, a few penchants. Even so, enough of Lewis's enumerable strengths usually emerge even from these biographies to reward the Lewisian enthusiast or skeptical inquirer hungry for more informed assessment of his achievements, and his continuing impact.

It is the case, nevertheless, that the underlying theme of recent works, and among them I include biographies written by Britain's A. N. Wilson and Australia's Michael White, have been to "rescue" Lewis from the assumed cult of his evangelical idolaters, particularly in America. It is these folks who, Wilson, for one, avers in his 1991 study of Lewis, desire to create a Lewis in their own image, one they can promote as a "virginal, Bible-toting, nonsmoking, lemonade-drinking champion for Christ." But such a stance reflects a surprising naiveté about Lewis's American readership and barely disguises its contempt for the esteem accorded Lewis's scholarship, fiction, and apologetics in many diverse circles.

One aim of this present reference work is thus to correct such stereotypes of both Lewis and his readership. To accomplish this, and many more worthy goals, one must offer a thorough-going, well-researched, yet also theologically sensitive treatment of Lewis's life and times that takes into consideration not only his tumultuous upbringing but also his mature development, his successes and failures, his blind spots and prescience, his trek into and impact on both "Jerusalem and Athens" (i.e., religion and philosophy), and, the essential perspective discerning readers need to understand the key people and relationships in his life.

Consequently, assembled for this volume are contributions from the finest C. S. Lewis scholars from North America and Europe. Their essays, one and all, have been solicited to be expansive, comprehensive, informed, and self-contained prose works that contextualize each respective topic historically and deliver expository clarity to its reader. As one considers the table of contents, he or she will realize that the essays fall into four volumes slated to emphasize four distinctive areas of Lewis's life and work.

Volume 1, *C. S. Lewis: An Examined Life*, is explicitly biographical in its orientation and scope. Lewis's early life, collegiate days, military service, friendships, achievements, and ongoing impact are set in historical context, starting from his Belfast birth in 1898 to his auspicious death on November 22, 1963, the day U.S. President John Kennedy was assassinated. New essays illuminate his relationships with J. R. R. Tolkien, Owen Barfield, and his beloved wife, Joy Davidman Gresham. Volume 2, *C. S. Lewis: Fantasist, Mythmaker, and Poet*, focuses on Lewis's imaginative writing, foregrounding his achievements in fiction and poetry as one dimension of his notoriety and popularity worldwide. The provenance of his works and their significance in his times and ours are explored and defined capably. Volume 3, *C. S. Lewis: Apologist, Philosopher, and Theologian*, draws attention to the celebrity Lewis received as a Christian thinker in his radio broadcasts and subsequent renown as a defender and translator of the Christian faith among skeptics and believers alike in postwar Britain and abroad. His well-known works such as *Mere Christianity*, *Miracles*, and *Letters to Malcolm* are given close readings and careful explication. Finally, in Volume 4, *C. S. Lewis: Scholar, Teacher, and Public Intellectual*, Lewis's lesser known vocations and publications are given careful consideration and examined for the models they may provide contemporary readers and academics for responsible scholarship. This set of essays helps assess Lewis's ongoing legacy and offers an extensive annotated bibliography of secondary sources that can guide the apprentice scholar to worthy works that will further assist him or her in extending the insights this collection presents.

Within each volume, essays fall into one of three distinct categories: (1) historical, fact-based treatment of eras, events, and personages in Lewis's life; (2) expository and literary analysis of major Lewis works of imaginative literature, literary scholarship, and apologetics; (3) global essays that seek to introduce, elucidate, and unfold the connections between and among the genres, vocations, and respective receptions elicited by Lewis in his varied career.

In my original invitation letter, each essayist was told to trust his or her instincts as a scholar, and thus to be empowered to write the essay from the unique vantage point they represent from inside their discipline. Generally speaking, each kind of essay was thus written to accomplish the following:

- The *historical essays* begin with a well-documented overview of their topic, foreshadowing the era, events, personages, etc., then proceed to a chronological treatment of the particulars, interspersed with connections, informed interpretations, contextualizations that illuminate the specific era covered as well as illuminating their relationships to other historical circumstances, publications, etc. When readers finish the essay, they should have at hand all the essential facts, accurately and chronologically marshaled, with a confident sense of the significance of this period, era, or relationship for Lewis's life and work.

- *Exposition and analysis essays* focus on single works in the Lewis canon and offer the reader a comprehensive overview of the work, including coverage of its origins and place in Lewis's life and times, its historical meaning and contemporary significance, its reception among readers, scholars, academics, critics, and a reflective judgment on its enduring influence or impact. The readers of these essays will come away with a profound grasp of the value and impact of the work in itself and the reputation it creates. In cases where there may exist a range of opinions about or competing interpretations of the meaning or value of a work, the essayist articulates the varying points of view, weighing their cogency, and offering the reader an informed perspective.

• *Global essays* provide an introductory, broad contextual sweep of coverage over the main themes of an individual volume's topic areas, one per volume, focusing on the four divisions enunciated for the project.

My general exhortation to all contributors was that they try as much as it is within their power to emulate C. S. Lewis in style and substance, practicing the kind of empathetic dialogue with the subject matter that is characteristic of his own prose and poetry—as he saw it: "Plenty of fact, reasoning as brief and clear as English sunshine . . ." No easy task! But I am pleased to say that each essay does its job well—and, in my view, Lewis would not be displeased.

I want to make the distinction as clear as possible between the four volumes published here and the typical "companion to" or "encyclopedia of" approach found in other treatments of Lewis's life and work. We have not created a set of "nominalist" texts that focus on so many particulars that the "whole" is lost in the "parts." Ours is not a "flip-through" set of texts in which "key words" drive the construction of essays and the experience of the reader—but one that features holistic essays that engross and educate earnest readers seeking an inclusive view of the essay's topic area. While we enforced some general consistency of length and depth of coverage, there is no "false objectivity" or uniformity of prose style to be imposed.

No, by contrast, these essays are meant to have "personality," and serve as "stand-alone" essays that reflect an invested, personal scholarship and whose learned opinion is based on deep acquaintance with their subject matter. As independent Lewis scholars, it is important that all were granted the freedom to interpret responsibly and offer informed judgments about value, effectiveness, and significance of components of his life, times, and works, and to follow the scholarly instincts and unique insights wherever they may have led. It may be that here and there two essays will cross boundaries, and offer a different point of view on a shared topic. This is to be expected, and is not to be discouraged. Where there are controversial topics in Lewis scholarship, the task at hand was to "referee" the debate, explain the options, and gently lead us to the conclusions, if any, that best fit the facts.

The bibliography for each essay is intended to be as current as possible as we reached our publication deadline, and should reflect the span of scholarship that has emerged since Lewis's death in 1963. But, there is a major and comprehensive bibliographic essay on Lewis scholarship included in Volume 4, and we direct the reader's attention there. As in any reference set of this scope, there will be unavoidable overlap in coverage of events, people, theme, citation of works, etc., throughout the volumes, and I humbly submit this is one of its strengths.

Our contributors were attracted to this project because they saw that it offered C. S. Lewis scholars an opportunity to disseminate their work to a broader, popular audience and, consequently, offered them the potential to shape the ongoing public understanding of C. S. Lewis for a population of readers around the world for many decades. Those readers brought to C. S. Lewis through the increased visibility and popularity of *The Chronicles of Narnia*, will be especially enthused and rewarded by their sojourn in these pages.

Our common approach in writing and editing this set is "academic" in the sense that it relies on studies/research/corroborated knowledge and reflection on assigned topics, but it is also the case that we always kept our general audience in mind, avoiding as much as possible any insider jargon or technical language that tends to exclude general readers. (Of course, any well-founded disciplinary terms necessary to explain and/or exemplify the achievement of Lewis are introduced and explained in context.)

In the end, I am proud to say that our desire to present accurate and interesting information, wearing our scholarship firmly but lightly enough to invite entrance into fascinating, timely, and relevant subject matter about Lewis has been met. These essays were designed to reach, engage, and even enthrall educated and interested readers anxious to find out more about C. S. Lewis, including those who yet may not have any formal training in literary criticism or theology or apologetics per se. Indeed, these have always been Lewis's most appreciative and attentive readers, and we are most pleased to have joined him in welcoming you here.

Bruce L. Edwards

1

The Ecumenical Apologist: Understanding C. S. Lewis's Defense of Christianity

Victor Reppert

C. S. Lewis is easily the most influential Christian apologist of the twentieth century. This is remarkable in view of the fact that he only wrote three books that can be correctly said to have been devoted to Christian apologetics: *The Problem of Pain*, *Mere Christianity*, and *Miracles: A Preliminary Study*. There are, of course, a number of books and essays with considerable apologetic content, and much of even his fiction has apologetic overtones, yet if we think of what his apologetic books were, it is just those three. Moreover, those three books are short.

Nevertheless, for many people C. S. Lewis succeeded in the apologist's task, the task of showing that Christianity is worthy to be believed by modern intelligent people. I would count myself as one of those people. As an eighteen-year-old Christian with a powerful need for a faith that made sense, Lewis was immensely helpful in providing that. After going through seminary and doctoral work in philosophy, I find that Christianity is still believable for approximately the reasons that Lewis said that it was reasonable. That is not to say that I find everything equally acceptable or cogent, or that I think that Lewis has developed his arguments with sufficient precision to be defensible *as they stand* from a philosophical perspective. The word "approximately" is in that sentence for a reason. However, if I am right about what Lewis has accomplished, this is a considerable achievement.

I think there are several important elements to Lewis's success as an apologist. One contributing factor is the fact that Lewis's authorship on a wide range of topics makes it possible for those who know him in virtue of his other writings to know him as an apologist. So, for example, in the *Chronicles of Narnia* we see Professor Kirke using an argument in favor of believing Lucy's claim that she has been to *Narnia* that is similar to his famous "Mad, Bad or God" argument in *Mere Christianity*. In *That Hideous Strength* Lewis presents an account of what happens when people seriously take ethical subjectivism to heart, in *The Abolition of Man* we see these views defended by philosophical argument, and in *Mere Christianity* we find moral objectivity used as the grounds for theistic belief. Lewis brings the historical understanding of a literary scholar, the sharpened wit of a philosopher, the keen human understanding of a novelist, and the compassion of a writer of children's books, to his apologetics.

One striking feature of Lewis's writings is their persistent refusal to patronize the audience. He was firmly convinced that he could explain complex philosophical and theological concepts to a popular audience without talking over their heads, using the jargon of specialists, or by talking down to them, acting as if they would be unwilling or unable to understand the relevant concepts. In the opening chapter of *Beyond Personality*, the last of the books that comprised *Mere Christianity*, we find Lewis saying this:

Everyone has warned me not to tell you what I am going to tell you in this last book. They all say "the ordinary reader does not want Theology; give him plain practical religion." I have rejected their advice. I do not think the ordinary reader is such a fool. Theology means "the science of God," and I would think that any man who wants to think about God at all would like to have the clearest and most accurate ideas about Him which are available. You are not children: why should you be treated like children?[1]

Even in dealing with children, Lewis steadfastly refuses to insult their intelligence. In another passage in *Mere Christianity*, he says, "Most children show plenty of 'prudence' about the things they are really interested in, and think them out sensibly."[2] I think this is one reason for Lewis's success as a writer of children's fiction; he refused to insult the intelligence even of the children for whom he wrote.

Lewis also had a tremendous ability to know what the layperson did understand, and did not understand. This resulted in part from his visits to the RAF and talking with the airmen. He knew how lay audiences thought and what their obstacles were. Lewis knew what sorts of language, so familiar in church, would be unrecognizable to lay audiences, and he avoided it.

Another reason for Lewis's popularity as an apologist is that his apologetics are rational without being rationalistic. Lewis firmly believed that Christian faith is supported by reason, and was not shy about presenting arguments in favor of his Christian beliefs. At the same time, Lewis never made the assumption that human beings were purely and simply rational, and that the emotions or the will were insignificant.

The Christianity Lewis defended was traditional, historic Christianity, deeply committed to a thoroughgoing supernaturalism. He did emphasize central Christian doctrines like the Trinity, the Incarnation, the Deity of Christ, the bodily resurrection of Christ, heaven, hell, and the Second Coming. The Christianity he espoused had a miraculous element for which he did not apologize. However, with respect to other issues, the bulk of Lewis's apologetic work was neutral with respect to questions dividing Christians. I am not claiming that Lewis was completely successful in sticking to "Mere Christianity" in his apologetics and did not sometimes espouse doctrines that are at issue amongst Christians. (For example, Lewis's treatment of the problem of evil presupposes the libertarian view of free will, and his conception of hell is at odds with Calvinist theology.) But what I mean is this: that his apologetics can be readily accepted and employed by people who accept the infallibility of the pope, even though he did not. Those who accept biblical inerrancy, even though he did not, can accept it. In fact, Calvinists can accept a good deal that Lewis says, even though Lewis was not a Calvinist. Lewis is arguably the most successful ecumenist of the twentieth century, bringing together Catholics and Protestants, inerrantists and antiinerrantists, and other groups of Christians otherwise divided.

Lewis also brought the perspective of a Christian convert to his apologetics. He was an atheist, and a rather hostile one, in his teens, and came to believe in God only at the age of thirty-one. This means that he is able to look at Christianity from the non-Christian point of view. Logically, for example, there seems no good reason to suppose that the size of the universe can be used as an argument for atheism, and yet, in many minds, it does serve as such an argument (although I did see it advanced by an atheist in a debate recently), and Lewis found it necessary to respond to it.

All of these things, I believe, have contributed to Lewis's popular success as an apologist. However, Lewis has not always been equally well regarded among academics. In my own field of philosophy, his arguments are often dismissed as hardly worthy of discussion. In addition, I would have to admit that many of the things that make Lewis popular could exist in someone who, in the last analysis, offered poor reasons for being a Christian. In this essay, I will consider the question of whether the arguments found in Lewis's Christian apologetics are good ones or bad ones. In particular I will be responding to the objections of John Beversluis, who maintained in his book *C. S. Lewis and the Search for Rational Religion* that Lewis's apologetics are woefully inadequate, inconsistent, and laden with manifest fallacies.[3] I will argue, on the contrary, that even if you disagree with Lewis's conclusions, you should at least admit that his apologetics are not inconsistent and not fallacy-laden.

THE FALSE ANSCOMBE LEGEND

It is sometimes argued that not only are Lewis's apologetics woefully inadequate, but that Lewis himself recognized this and abandoned apologetics at the height of his apologetic career, as a reaction to a devastating encounter with a real philosopher. This encounter was not with an atheist; it was with the Roman Catholic Elizabeth Anscombe.

The legendary debate with Anscombe took place at the Oxford Socratic Club[4] on February 2, 1948. In his book *Miracles*, published the year before, Lewis argued that naturalism—the view that only physical reality exists—is self-contradictory. Anscombe sharply criticized the argument, claiming that it was confused and based on the ambiguous use of key terms. According to the "Anscombe legend," Lewis not only admitted that Anscombe got the better of the exchange, but recognized that his argument was wrong. Further, because of the exchange, Lewis gave up on Christian apologetics. According to Humphrey Carpenter, one of the purveyors of the Anscombe legend, "Though [Lewis] continued to believe in the importance of Reason in relation to his Christian faith, he had perhaps realized the truth of Charles Williams's maxim, 'No-one can possibly do more than decide what to believe.'"[5] In short, Lewis went from a belief in the rationality of his faith to a fideistic position, according to which belief is based on faith and should not be defended rationally.

Now it is true that, immediately following the debate, Lewis expressed disappointment to friends as to how the debate went. Further, Lewis did think that Anscombe's objections were serious enough to require him to rewrite the relevant chapter of *Miracles*. Moreover, it is true that he wrote no more explicitly apologetic books after *Miracles*. Nevertheless, we have no reason to believe that he had any apologetic books in mind that went unwritten because of the exchange with Anscombe. What we do know is that he did continue to write *essays* on apologetical subjects. In "Is Theism Important" (1952), Lewis affirms the importance of theistic arguments, and says "Nearly everyone I know who has embraced Christianity in adult life has been influenced by what seemed to him to be at least probable arguments for Theism."[6] In "On Obstinacy of Belief" (1955), Lewis defends Christianity against the charge that while scientists apportion their beliefs to the evidence, religious people do not, and are therefore irrational.[7] In "Rejoinder to Dr. Pittenger" (1958), Lewis defends his Christian apologetics against criticisms from a prominent theologian, hardly what you would expect him to do if he thought his career as an apologist had been misguided.[8] The essay "Modern Theology and Biblical Criticism" (1959) is a stinging assault on modern biblical scholarship of a skeptical variety, the sort of scholarship that is currently represented by members of the Jesus Seminar.[9] If that essay is not a piece of Christian apologetics, then I simply do not know what apologetics is.

I should note that Lewis not only revised his chapter on *Miracles*, but he also expanded the chapter. Now if you really thought that someone had proved you wrong, why in the world would you expand the very chapter that one's opponent had refuted? What is more, this revision was not just something he thought of years later; an examination of the original issue of the *Socratic Digest* in which Anscombe's article appears we find a short response by Lewis in which he lays the foundation for the subsequent revision, which appeared in 1960.[10]

One devastating blow to the Anscombe legend has come from a surprising source. In his 1985 book *C. S. Lewis and the Search for Rational Religion*, John Beversluis criticized C. S. Lewis's apologetics as a failure and in so doing referred to the psychological impact of the Anscombe incident. He also analyzed the arguments, and found that "the arguments that Anscombe presented can be pressed further, and Lewis's revised argument does nothing to meet them."[11] However, in a subsequent review of A. N. Wilson's biography of C. S. Lewis, which implied Lewis wrote Narnia because he was running away from the thumping he got from Anscombe, Beversluis, much to his credit, abandoned the Anscombe Legend entirely. He wrote:

First, the Anscombe debate was by no means Lewis's first exposure to a professional philosopher: he lived among them all his adult life, read the Greats, and even taught philosophy. Second, it is simply untrue that the post-Anscombe Lewis abandoned Christian apologetics. In 1960, he published a second edition of *Miracles* in which he revised the third chapter and thereby replied to Anscombe. Third, most printed discussions of the debate, mine included, fail to mention that Anscombe herself complimented Lewis's revised argument on the grounds that it is deeper and far more serious than the original version. Finally, the myth that Lewis abandoned Christian apologetics overlooks several post-Anscombe articles, among them "Is Theism Important?" (1952)—a discussion of Christianity and theism which touches on philosophical proofs for God's existence—and "On Obstinacy of Belief"—in which Lewis defends the rationality of belief in God in the face of apparently contrary evidence (the issue in philosophical theology during the late 1950s and early 60s). It is rhetorically effective to announce that the post-Anscombe Lewis wrote no further books on Christian apologetics, but it is pure fiction. Even if it were true, what would this

Argument from Abandoned Subjects prove? He wrote no further books on *Paradise Lost* or courtly love either.[12]

It is my contention that the Anscombe Legend is a pernicious falsehood about C. S. Lewis that richly deserves to be put to rest completely and permanently. You need to have a lot of "faith" to believe the stories Wilson and others tell about C. S. Lewis. You have to believe them even though your best reasoning tells you the weight of the evidence is against it.

DID LEWIS ABANDON HIS APOLOGETIC POSITION IN *A GRIEF OBSERVED*?

Another considerably more complex challenge to Lewis's apologetical coherence has been the claim that in the course of grieving his wife's death he retreated from some of the positions he had taken with respect to the relationship between God and goodness. Throughout his apologetic writings, Lewis had contended that when we say that God is good we mean something that is in some way continuous with the word "God" as applied to human beings. This doctrine of continuity is what Beversluis calls Platonism. The opposite view, which he calls Ockhamism, is the view that in calling God good we mean something completely different from what we mean when we call a person good. Therefore, for example, if God, before the foundation of the world, were to predestine a few people for heaven and everyone else to everlasting torture in hell, this would be good in virtue of the fact that God commanded it. The fact that this many would regard this action as cruel by any humanly conceivable moral standard would be simply dismissed as irrelevant. The fact that this is an affront to reason only shows that natural human reason is fallen and part of our desperately wicked human nature. It is not surprising that Ockhamism is popular among Calvinists, including Calvin himself.[13]

Now if this were correct, this would be a profound shift in Lewis's thinking. After all, he had written an entire book of apologetics defending the claim that it is rational to believe that God is good in some recognizable sense even though there is a great deal of evil in the world. This is necessary only if there is some commensurability between our concept of goodness as applied to us and the concept applied to God. If Ockhamism is true, then it is a full and complete answer to the problem of evil to say the words of the New Testament Book of Romans 9:22: "Who are you, O man, to answer back to God." Lewis consistently condemned this Ockhamist position, at one point even claiming that such a doctrine would reduce Christianity to devil worship.

Now in order to set the stage for our discussion of *A Grief Observed*, we should make a distinction between the intellectual problem of evil and the emotional problem of evil. Lewis directed *The Problem of Pain* at the intellectual problem posed by human suffering. In the context of the discussion of an intellectual argument, it does not matter whether the sufferers are tsunami victims in Asia, or fellow American citizens who burned to death in the 9/11 attacks, or one's nearest and dearest family members, or even one's own suffering. From an intellectual perspective, all of these instances of suffering are of equal concern, but from an emotional perspective, the nearer the suffering is to us the more difficult it is to accept. *A Grief Observed* is a piece of pastoral theology aimed at the bereaved, focusing on the emotional problem of evil.[14] However, it doesn't follow from this that, in facing the emotional problem of evil, one might not have to come to terms with some intellectual issues. However, the main issue in the book is how to deal with the emotional impact of grief, and is not primarily an attempt to solve the problem of evil from an intellectual perspective.

A *Grief Observed* is Lewis's account of his own response to his wife's death. Late in life, he married Joy Davidman, whom he knew to have cancer. Miraculously, after a prayer for healing, Joy's cancer went into remission and the couple enjoyed a period of wedded bliss that included, among other things, a trip to Greece. However, eventually she relapsed and died.

Lewis had been an atheist earlier in his life, and echoing that earlier perspective, he expressed deep anger toward God, calling him a "Cosmic Sadist," an "Eternal Vivisector," and a "very absent help in trouble." In the latter portion of the book, Lewis withdraws the charges against God and accepts God's goodness. It is Beversluis's thesis that in the early stages of the book Lewis insists on the Platonistic understanding of God's goodness, and concludes that God is a cosmic sadist. However, according to Beversluis, in the latter part of the book, he retreats to an Ockhamist position in order to escape those distressing conclusions, withdrawing the protests, but also the insistence that God be good in humanly recognizable terms.

Now although *A Grief Observed* is not primarily addressed to the intellectual issue, Lewis does pose the problem of evil in forceful terms, in the context of his own grief. He writes:

Sooner or later I must face the question in plain language. What reason have we, except our own desperate wishes, to believe that God is, by any standard we can conceive, "good"? Doesn't all the *prima facie* evidence suggest exactly the opposite? What have we to set against it?[15]

However, if we are to say that Joy's death posed an overwhelming *intellectual* problem to Lewis in his hour of grieving, it must be the case that some worldview distinct from a theism that included the commensurability of divine goodness to human goodness would have to be available to him. When we read Lewis's account of his own conversion to Christianity, we find that even though Lewis formerly defended atheism based on the problem of evil, he never said that he became a theist or a Christian because he had found excellent answers to the problem of evil. Rather, he seems to have accepted theism largely because he found alternative worldviews inadequate. If his suffering really has given him cause to doubt his faith, then there must be some worldview other than theism, which has been rendered plausible by his sufferings.

And what would that worldview be? It would certainly not be materialism. In language reminiscent of the argument from reason, he once again affirms that he finds that worldview thoroughly unbelievable.

If he "is not," then she never was. I mistook a cloud of atoms for a person. There aren't, and never were, any people. Death only reveals the vacuity that was always there. What we call the living are simply those who have not yet been unmasked. All equally bankrupt, but some not yet declared. But this must be nonsense; vacuity revealed to whom? Bankruptcy declared to whom? To other boxes of fireworks or clouds of atoms. I will never believe—more strictly I can't believe—that one set of physical events could be, or make, a mistake about other sets.[16]

Notice his argument that he cannot believe that one cloud of atoms can make a mistake about other clouds of atoms. He offers no detailed defense of this kind of argument, the way he did in the face of Anscombe's criticisms, but here he is answering himself, not Anscombe. He is indicating, in his own mind, why materialism is unbelievable.

In fact, if you think about it, Lewis's complaint against God makes sense only if you attribute a supernatural cause to Joy's recovery. If what God did was simply let nature take its course and there was no miraculous recovery for Joy, then there cannot be a case against God. If materialism were true, then both Joy's remission and her recovery would be simply a matter of nature taking its course. In *Miracles,* Lewis said that we should not expect miracles on an everyday basis. So one way for Lewis to resolve his problem with God would be to accept a "materialist" explanation of the events related to Joy's cancer. (Of course, nonmaterialists can accept materialist accounts of various phenomena without inconsistency). What Lewis seems angry with God about is that God gave him "false hopes" and "led him up the garden path." However, if God were not directly involved, there would be no problem.

So Lewis considers instead the thesis of the Cosmic Sadist. He writes:

No, my real fear is not of materialism. If it were true, we—or what we mistake for "we"—could get out, get from under the harrow. An overdose of sleeping pills would do it. I am more afraid that we are really rats in a trap. Or worse still, rats in a laboratory. Someone said, I believe, "God always geometrizes." Supposing the truth were "God always vivisects"?[17]

However, Lewis has some things to say about the thesis of the Cosmic Sadist. He writes:

I think it is, if nothing else, too anthropomorphic. When you come to think of it, it is far more anthropomorphic than picturing Him as a grave old king with a long beard. That image is a Jungian archetype. It links God with all the wise old kings in the fairy-tales, with prophets, sages, magicians. Though it is (formally), the picture of a man, it suggests something more than humanity. At the very least it gets in the idea of something older than yourself, something that knows more, something you can't fathom. It preserves mystery. Therefore room for hope. Therefore room for a dread or awe that needn't be mere fear of mischief from a spiteful potentate. But the picture I was building up last night is simply the picture of a man like S.C.—who used to sit next to me at dinner and tell me what he'd been doing to the cats that afternoon. Now a being like S.C., however magnified, couldn't invent or create or govern anything. He would set up traps and try to bait them. But he'd never have thoughts of baits like love, or laughter, or daffodils, or a frosty sunset. *He* make a universe? He couldn't make a joke, or a bow, or an apology, or a friend.[18]

Now Beversluis's commentary is as follows:

The shift occurs the moment Lewis begins to suspect that the hypothesis of the Cosmic Sadist is too anthropomorphic. According to such a view, God is like the man who tortures cats, and that is unbearable. Lewis recoils from this view and assures himself (and his readers), that when he called God an imbecile, it was "more of a yell than a thought." After that, we hear no more about the Cosmic Sadist.[19]

In short, Beversluis supposes that Lewis is recoiling from the thesis of the Cosmic Sadist for emotional reasons.

But is this all it is, an *emotional* recoil? It is at this point that my interpretation of *A Grief Observed* parts company with Beversluis's interpretation. As it happens, the thesis of the Cosmic Sadist had already surfaced in Lewis's apologetics, in his discussion of Dualism in *Mere Christianity*. Although there are many types of dualism that have been discussed in philosophy and religion, the Dualism Lewis is referring to is the kind of Dualism that says that the world was created jointly by eternally existing beings, one good and one evil. Against this, Lewis argues that the idea of an evil creator, or even an evil cocreator, is incoherent. He wrote:

If Dualism is true, then the bad Power must be a being who likes badness for its own sake. But in reality we have no experience of anyone liking badness just because it is bad. The nearest we can get to it is in cruelty. But in real life people are cruel because they have a sexual perversion, which makes cruelty cause a sensual pleasure in them, or else for the sake of something they are going to get out of it—money, or power, or safety. But pleasure, money, power, and safety are all, as far as they go, good things. The badness consists in pursuing them by the wrong method, or in the wrong way, or too much. I do not mean, of course, that the people who do this are not desperately wicked. I do mean that wickedness, when you examine it, turns out to be the pursuit of some good in the wrong way. You can be good for the mere sake of goodness, you cannot be bad for the mere sake of badness. . . . In other words badness cannot succeed even in being bad in the same way in which goodness is good. Goodness is, so to speak, itself: badness is only spoiled goodness. And there must be something good first before it can be spoiled.[20]

This argument, if correct, refutes the possibility that the world was created by an evil being, or even cocreated by an evil being. A close reading of the passage from *A Grief Observed* shows that Lewis is in that passage making exactly the same point. If Lewis is making or even referencing this argument, then it should be no surprise that we hear no more of the Cosmic Sadist. We should expect nothing else. This is why Lewis says that the name calling that he directed toward God was "more of a yell than a thought," and why he accuses himself of not thinking clearly when he criticized God in the earlier passage.

Lewis next turns to the possibility that, because of human depravity, his understanding of what is right and wrong is simply mistaken. If this is the case, then perhaps God really is a sadist, only sadistic behavior is right because it is God who does it. Lewis had attacked this position in very harsh terms in his previous writings, including *The Problem of Pain*.

It has sometimes been asked whether God commands certain things because they are right, or whether certain things are right because God commands them. With Hooker, and against Dr. Johnson, I emphatically embrace the first alternative. The second might lead to the abominable conclusion (reached, I think, by Paley), that charity is good only because God arbitrarily commanded it—that He might equally well have commanded us to hate Him and one another and that hatred would then have been right. I believe, on the contrary, that "they err who think that of the will of God to do this or that there is no reason besides his will."[21]

However, in *A Grief Observed* he presents what in my estimation is his most forceful anti-Ockhamist argument. If God's white can be our black, if our standards of good and evil mean nothing, then we cannot count upon God to do anything whatsoever, including follow through on his own threats. Thus if Ockhamism is true, and God says "Turn or burn," he could just as easily burn us after we turn (and reward all the ones who didn't turn), just because, after all, his white could after all be our black.

And so what? This, for all practical (and speculative), purposes, sponges God off the slate. The word good, applied to Him, becomes meaningless: like abracadabra. We have no motive for obeying Him. Not even fear. It is true we have His threats and promises. But why should we believe them? If cruelty is from His point of view "good," telling lies may be "good" too. Even if they are true, what then? If His ideas of good are so very different from ours, what He calls Heaven might well be what we should call Hell, and vice-versa. Finally, if reality at its very root is so meaningless to us—or, putting it the other way round, if we are such total imbeciles—what is the point of trying to think either about God or about anything else? This knot comes undone when you try to pull it tight.[22]

Rene Descartes, in order to raise skeptical doubts about even our firmest certainties, imagined that we might be under the influence of an omnipotent evil demon whose goal is to deceive us as much as possible, and more recent philosophers have speculated about the possibility of our being brains in vats. The epistemic upshot of Ockhamism is essentially the same as the upshot of these hypotheses. According to Ockhamism, we are under the complete control of a being whose motives are either wicked or incomprehensible, and we will believe the truth only if this being arbitrarily chooses that we shall believe the truth. According to Lewis, Ockhamism is every bit as self-refuting as naturalism. If it is true, then we cannot believe the truth of Ockhamism, or of anything else, in a way that gives us any rational confidence that it is true.

Beversluis argues that in *A Grief Observed* Lewis begins by insisting that God's actions be good by standards that are commensurable with the standards we use to judge human behavior. Employing those standards, according to Beversluis, Lewis rightly concluded that God would have to be a Cosmic Sadist. To escape these unpleasant consequences, however, Beversluis claims that Lewis abandoned his long-held Platonism in favor of Ockhamism, accepting God's goodness only in virtue of accepting a vacuous standard of good and evil.

However, this overlooks the fact that in *A Grief Observed* Lewis presents arguments against both the thesis of the Cosmic Sadist and the thesis of Ockhamism. Of course, Beversluis is not the only person to have overlooked these arguments; favorable commentators like Richard Purtill have overlooked them as well.

What do Lewis's critics expect; that as a safeguard against grief he should rehearse his intellectual grounds for belief? But Lewis had no intellectual doubts about his faith, and no new data which might give him intellectual grounds for doubting his faith . . . There is in fact no evidence at all that Lewis was moved to any intellectual doubts at all by his personal loss, and thus there was no need to renew or rehearse his arguments.[23]

The difficulty with Purtill's claim here is that it assumes that it is introspectively obvious to a sufferer whether the doubts are intellectual or emotional in nature. This is far from the case. One of the pastoral needs of a bereaved person might be to understand that their grief experience in no way changes the evidential situation. That is why I would not call *A Grief Observed* "a book of Christian apologetics" per se; it has other primary functions to be sure, though it did perform a kind of apologetic role. To wit, contrary to what Purtill suggests here, Lewis did rehearse at least some of the reasons he had for being a Christian, and found them to be still standing.

Given the fact that Lewis attacks the coherence of both the Cosmic Sadist theory and Ockhamism in *A Grief Observed*, what do we make of Beversluis's charge that Lewis, in understanding the pain of his own bereavement and accepting the loss in the way that he did, he implicitly accepted an Ockhamist account of God's goodness? After all, the fact that there are anti-Ockhamist arguments in *A Grief Observed* shows that Lewis never explicitly embraced Ockhamism in that work. However, perhaps his response to his own suffering was implicitly Ockhamistic, even though he did not realize it.

What I find puzzling, however, is that the actual content of what Beversluis says happens in *A Grief Observed* is very similar to his verdict on *The Problem of Pain*. In his discussion of *The Problem of Pain*, Beversluis defines Ockhamism as

[W]hen we talk about God's goodness, we must be prepared to give up our ordinary moral standards. The term *good* when applied to God *does* mean something radically different from what it means when applied to human beings. To suppose that God must conform to some standard other than his own sovereign will is to deny his ultimacy. God is bound by nothing and answerable to no one.[24]

Later on, he writes that he is not going to claim that Lewis is an Ockhamist in *The Problem of Pain*. He says:

At this point, I should perhaps allay possible suspicions that I am going to end up claiming that Lewis was really an Ockhamist. I am not. What I do insist on, however, is that by the time his argument has run its course he no longer claims that God's goodness is recognizable in any ordinary sense. On the contrary, he suggests that we can call God good only if we are willing to assign a new meaning to the term.[25]

But I thought that what it is to be an Ockhamist was that you assigned a new meaning to the term "good." Alternatively, looking at it from the opposite side, what it is to be a Platonist is to hold that our standards of good and evil must hold firm. Beversluis culminates his analysis by saying:

How is Lewis's view with its new meanings for good and love different from the Ockhamist view he deplores? In *The Problem of Pain* we are confronted with an apologist emphatically endorsing a view that he almost immediately lays aside for a position that differs only semantically from the position he claims to reject. By the time he has finished, our "black" has become God's "white," and moral standards have been reversed. What we call suffering, Lewis calls having our illusions shattered. What we call happiness, Lewis calls self-indulgence. What we call a moral outrage, Lewis calls a compliment. What we call kindness, Lewis calls indifference. What we call cruelty, Lewis calls love.[26]

When we get to *A Grief Observed*, Beversluis says

The God who knocked down Lewis's house of cards is not a Platonistically conceived deity who is good in our sense, but rather an Ockhamistically conceived being who is declared good no matter what he does. Lewis's "rediscovered" faith is a faith in a God whose goodness is unlike our own that it can bee called good only by laying aside our moral standards together with our ordinary criteria for determining who has true faith and who does not. It is in this alarming sense that Heaven is said to "solve" our problems. Good now means "whatever God wills or permits."[27]

So in his critique of *The Problem of Pain* Beversluis accuses Lewis of revising our moral standards, but this does not make him an Ockhamist; it only puts him in a position that differs only semantically from Ockhamism. In *A Grief Observed* he claims that after Lewis stops expressing anger toward God, he reverses our moral standards and in so doing, he becomes an Ockhamist. Quite honestly, the "semantic" difference between these two critiques escapes me. In order to argue for a profound transformation between *The Problem of Pain* and *A Grief Observed* Beversluis has to forget the charges that he leveled against the former work. At one point Beversluis suggests that the evil Lewis faced in his grief experience was one that was of a kind that could not be accounted for by the explanations he had used in *The Problem of Pain*, since God was directly implicated, but that won't do, since a good deal of his discussion of that book concerns his critique of Lewis's "Shattering Thesis," in which God brings us to knowledge of himself by shattering our illusions. At another point he remembers his discussion of the Shattering Thesis, but says

The Shattering Thesis of *A Grief Observed* is not, of course a hitherto unheard-of idea in Lewis's writings. It can be found in *The Problem of Pain*. What is new is not the thesis but Lewis's recognition of its logical impact on the believer.[28]

However, this will not do either, since Lewis clearly does not recognize that he has become an Ockhamist. In fact, as Beversluis himself points out, Lewis maintained that his doubts had psychological and not logical causes. In short, I find no logical way to argue for a fundamental transformation of Lewis's position between *The Problem of Pain* and *A Grief Observed*. If Lewis is open to the charge of Ockhamism in *A Grief Observed*, then he was an Ockhamist in *The Problem of Pain*. If Lewis can be acquitted of the charge of being an

Ockhamist in *The Problem of Pain*, then the same arguments can be used to show that he was not an Ockhamist in *A Grief Observed.*

THE C. S. LEWIS DEFENSE

C. S. Lewis's *The Problem of Pain* is Lewis's first full-dress book of Christian apologetics. Since it does include the claim that God uses pain as a "megaphone" to rouse a deaf world, and since he also makes the claim that God uses pain to shatter our illusions, it might be valuable to see if Beversluis can successfully make the charge that in making these statements he lapses from a Platonistic to an Ockhamistic view of the relation between God and goodness.

The problem of evil has been discussed extensively in the last forty years, and one critical distinction is the distinction between a defense and a theodicy. A defense attempts to rebut arguments from evil and does not necessarily attempt to provide a true explanation as to why suffering is permitted. A theodicy tries to account for suffering, giving the true explanations for why creatures suffer. A defense gives a possible explanation for the existence of suffering, showing the argument that God and suffering are incompatible is unsuccessful.

Alvin Plantinga developed the Free Will Defense to deal with the argument from evil. Atheist philosophers like Antony Flew and J. L. Mackie had argued that the existence of evil was logically inconsistent with the existence of God, and that anyone who believed in God and also accepted the existence of suffering in the world was contradicting himself. However Plantinga argued that at least some evil, namely, the evil that results from human action, is compatible with the existence of God, in that the freedom to act against the good was itself a good, but in creating that good God would have to open the possibility that the choices thus made were the wrong choices. However, Plantinga had to consider the fact that at least some evil is not the result of evil actions on the part of human creatures. The Asian tsunami in 2004 and Hurricane Katrina in 2005, for example, look to have not been caused by humans.

However, Plantinga responded to this by saying that it was at least possible that all the suffering in the world was caused by the actions of rebellious free agents, either human or demonic. Thus, for example, it is at least possible that while humans cause evils like murder, perhaps Satan and his minions might have caused Katrina to occur in the way that it did, in order to inflict pain and suffering on the human race. Now, if you objected that, even if possible, this wasn't very *likely*, Plantinga would argue that insofar as the atheist had begun by arguing that the theist was committed to a contradictory position in accepting the existence of both God and evil, the atheist would now be shifting ground, retreating to the probabilistic or evidential problem of evil rather than the logical problem of evil. The logic of each new variation in the argument from evil must be examined. For example, if the argument is a probabilistic argument from evil, how is probability theory being used? In Plantinga's writings on the argument from evil, the emphasis is always on showing that the arguments from evil don't work, and apart from an appeal to free will he really does little to explain exactly why evils are permitted. This approach I will call the defense strategy. It is a strategy grounded on our *expected* lack of understanding of the purposes behind God's permitting suffering.[29]

Other thinkers have gone farther in attempting to explain why God permits suffering. This strategy is called a theodicy. The idea here is that even if we are able to show that there is something wrong with every version of the argument from evil, we would like to know, as best we can, why God permits suffering. Without some explanations as to why God permits suffering, some have argued that this puts the theist at a disadvantage relative to the atheist, who argues that as a matter of course his own view would allow us to anticipate the mixed bag of good and evils that we see in the world.

It is often thought that Lewis's *The Problem of Pain* is a theodicy in the classical sense. But is it? Lewis begins the book by noting the fact that people do not typically believe in God's goodness because they infer the goodness of God from the goodness of creation; they instead believe in God's goodness for other reasons. A sense of what Rudolf Otto called the Numinous, our sense of moral obligation and moral failure, the combination of those two elements to make a moralist religion amongst the Jews, and the claims of Christ are all things that, amongst real people, cause belief in a good God. So, if for independent reasons we think that God is good, how do we account for evil in a way that makes sense? That is how Lewis construes the problem of pain.

Thomas Talbott, in his entry on *The Problem of Pain* for *The C. S. Lewis Readers' Encyclopedia*, argues that the crux of Lewis's response to the problem of evil can be found in the second chapter, entitled "Divine Omnipotence," and says that everything else in the book is ancillary. By this, he means, "even if his arguments in these subsequent chapters were substantially mistaken, his basic reply to the argument he set out to refute, the reply developed in chapter two, would stand."[30] If Talbott is correct, however, this would be a successful defense of theism against the argument from evil, but it would not be a theodicy.

Lewis's defense against the argument from evil has three steps to it. The first step is to point out that not even an omnipotent being can do the "intrinsically impossible," that is, anything that involves a contradiction. An omnipotent being cannot make $2 + 2 = 5$, or make it the case that the Apostle Paul freely repents of his sin. Lewis says, "You may attribute miracles to him, but not nonsense." Alvin Plantinga, in his Free Will Defense, argued that there were possible worlds that God did not have the power to actualize, because these worlds' actuality depends upon people freely choosing X who in fact chose Y.[31]

The second step is to argue that we are not in a position to know for sure what is and is not logically possible. Is it logically possible to go backward in time? Some people think that it is, others do not. Thus, we may think that things are logically possible when they are not, or think that they are logically impossible, when they are logically possible.

Third, the complexities involved in creating a world of free creatures that can freely choose to obey or disobey God is a good deal more complex than it looks. Thus, Lewis says:

There is no reason to suppose that self-consciousness, the recognition of a creature by itself as a "self," can exist except in contrast with an "other," a something which is not the self. It is against an environment and preferably a social environment, an environment of other selves, that the awareness of Myself stands out.[32]

Hence, a society of free souls seems on its face to require a relatively independent and "inexorable" Nature, a Nature containing objects, which could be used for mutual benefit if parties cooperate, and which can be used to harm one another if parties oppose one another. Thus, in creating a world of free persons, Lewis suggests that God may have had no choice but to open up the possibility of pain and suffering.

Lewis suggests the possibility that God might, through miracles, correct the effects of the abuse of free will, but he says that would effectively nullify the freedom of the will. He writes:

We can, perhaps, conceive of a world in which God corrected the results of the abuse of free will by his creatures at every moment: so that a wooden beam became soft as grass when it was used as a weapon, and the air refused to obey me if I attempted to set up in it the sound waves that carry lies or insults. But such a world would be one in which wrong actions were impossible, and in which, therefore, freedom of the will would be void.[33]

Imagine, for example, a world in which all virtuous actions were rewarded in short order and all vicious actions punished in short order. In such a world there would be no effective free will, because no one in their right mind would be so much as tempted to do the wrong thing. Everyone would do the right thing out of self-interest.

Nevertheless, Lewis does not claim that he knows, or that anyone knows what God could have done and what God could not have done.

As I said before, this account of the intrinsic necessities of a world is meant merely as a specimen of what they might be. What they really are, only Omniscience has the data and the wisdom to see: but they are not likely to be *less* complicated than I have suggested.[34]

Although some people think that God could clearly have made the world better by leaving cancer out of it, Talbott argues, following up on Lewis's ideas, that we are far from being in a position to know this. He writes:

Perhaps Beversluis thinks that God could have improved things immeasurably by eliminating cancer from the world. But how could anyone (who is not omniscient), possibly know that or even have reason to think it true? Try this thought experiment. Try to imagine what our world (with exactly the same persons in it), might have been in the absence of cancer. Our experiment won't be at all technically accurate, of course, and may even be incoherent, but it may also be pedagogically useful. To begin with, then we must delete from the world (in our imagination), all the pain and suffering caused by this terrible disease as well as all the psychological torment experienced by both cancer victims and those who love such victims; then we must delete all the good—such as the courageous endurance of pain—for which the cancer is a necessary condition; then we must delete all the free choices—and all the consequences of such free choices—that either would not have been made at all or would have been made differently if our world had been devoid of cancer. As one can see, things quickly get complicated. If God exists and there is an afterlife, some of the choices may be choices that result in eternal joy and happiness for some persons. But that is just the beginning of our experiment . . . Trying to figure out what a world of free persons would be like in the absence of cancer is not like calculating where the planets would be if they had been in certain specified positions last year . . . Once one begins to think through such complexities as these—which we have barely touched upon—the anti-theistic argument from evil begins to look less and less plausible.[35]

Therefore, Talbott argues, Lewis's defense of theism works not by showing that some better world would be impossible, but by showing that since we do not what worlds are and are not possible, and if they would really better worlds or whether they would not be better worlds, the argument from evil falls before the "C. S. Lewis Defense."

Now I would not be quite as confident as Talbott, in the sense that I think that the argument presupposes something that Lewis never argues for but would be denied by many defenders of the argument from evil. That is the claim that God cannot give freedom to creatures without at the same time opening the possibility that they might do wrong. If you define freedom as having the power to do what you want to do, God could create everyone in such a way that they always wanted to do the right thing, and then gave them the ability to carry out that good will at all times. If God could do that, then it seems as if He should have done that, and the argument from evil would still be unanswered. I myself do not think that this position of "compatibilism," the idea that the same action can be determined by God and free in the sense required for moral responsibility or free in the sense that God would find desirable, is one that can be defended. However, all I am pointing out here is that a complete "C. S. Lewis Defense" would require some argumentation on behalf of this crucial assumption.

If the C. S. Lewis Defense is successful, then Lewis does not have to revise our concept of goodness at all to accept the pain and suffering in the world, including his own pain and suffering as a grieving widower. All he needs to do is to maintain that he does not know that there is a world in which he does not suffer as he does that God had the power to actualize, that would be better all around that the actual world in which he does suffer because of the loss of his wife. If he can affirm that, even if he never, this side of heaven, comes to any answer as to why his wife was taken from him at that time, he cannot be said to have drifted from Platonism to Ockhamism.

LEWIS ON DIVINE GOODNESS

Lewis, of course, is not content to develop the C. S. Lewis defense, and I am not even sure he would concur with Talbott that the defense is a sufficient refutation of all arguments from evil. His next task is to develop and clarify the concept of divine goodness. On the one hand, he maintains that what we mean by good in referring to God must be commensurable with what we mean by good in creatures, and that we must not allow ourselves to say that our black is God's white. So, for example, we are not free to admit that some act of God is senselessly cruel, and then say that our black is God's white. On the other hand, our understanding of what is right or wrong may stand in need of correction. He says:

If God is wiser than we His judgment must differ from us on many things, and not least on good and evil. What seems to us good may therefore not be good in His eyes, and what seems to us evil may not be evil.[36]

Does this mean, as Beversluis charges, that at the end of the day our black really does become God's white? According to Talbott:

When considering a disagreement about the moral consequences of an act, one must distinguish carefully between two very different cases: one in which all of the relevant facts (such as the exact circumstances in which the act was performed), are known, and those in which some of the relevant facts are not known. A primitive who concludes that men in white coats bearing long needles are cruel to children need not be operating from a moral framework that differs substantially from our own; nor would it be surprising to find that a loving father in a primitive culture wants to "protect" his child from the shot of penicillin that a missionary doctor, filled with the love of God, wants to administer. The loving father simply lacks some important information.[37]

Lewis does maintain that the problem of evil will be insoluble so long as certain popular meanings are attached to the terms "good" and "love." Beversluis maintains that Lewis is redefining these terms, abandoning their ordinary usage in order to defend God against the problem of evil. However, what Lewis is in fact doing is arguing that these popular meanings are in fact corruptions of the proper uses of the terms. In fact, Lewis wrote a book entitled *Studies in Words* in which he explained how the content of some words could be damaged or weakened in popular usage, so that their meaning has been lost.[38] And Plato's Socrates was never satisfied with "popular meanings" of words, which is why he questioned people as to whether they mean what they really meant by the words they used, concluding that they not only did not know what they were talking about, but they compounded that ignorance with the further ignorance of thinking that they did.[39] About the terms "good" and "love" Lewis writes:

By the goodness of God we mean nowadays almost exclusively his lovingness, and in this we may be right. And by Love, in this context, most of us mean kindness—the desire to see others than the self happy; not happy in this way or in that, but just happy. What would really satisfy us would be a god who said of anything we happened to like doing, "What does it matter so long as they are contented."[40]

Lewis then argues that God wants to give people the only happiness that he can provide, the happiness of a life in fellowship with himself, the kind of happiness that can last for an eternity. As such, God cannot be satisfied with a creaturely "satisfaction" that does not deepen a person's connection to God. He also analyses love and discovers that the higher the love, the more the lover expects from the beloved. The higher the level of love, the "tougher" that love is on the one who is loved. However, this does not involve any alteration of what the terms "good" and "love" mean upon reflection; it is only the recognition of defective popular meanings that have been attached to these words.

Lewis then explores the human condition, arguing that the way in which humans behave is in profound need of correction, attempting to recover what he calls "the old sense of sin." Here he attempts to undermine a wide range of arguments people make for the claim that they are not such bad people after all. Why do bad things happen to good people? If Lewis had heard that question, he would argue against the supposition that such people are good. While many people are not outwardly bad compared to other people, He writes:

I have been aiming at an intellectual, not an emotional, effect: I have been trying to make the reader believe that we actually are, at present, creatures whose character must be in some respects, a horror to God, as it is, when we really see it, a horror to ourselves. This I believe to be a fact: and I notice that the holier a man is, the more fully he is aware of that fact. Perhaps you have imagined that this humility in the saints is a pious illusion at which God smiles. That is a most dangerous error. It is theoretically dangerous, because it makes you identify a virtue (i.e. a perfection), with an illusion (i.e. an imperfection), which must be nonsense. It is practically dangerous because it encourages a man to mistake his first insights into his own corruption for the first beginnings of a halo around his silly head. No, depend upon it: when the saints say that they—even they, are vile, they are recording truth with scientific accuracy.[41]

Lewis then goes on to present an admittedly speculative theory about how human beings might have gone from a state of obedience to God to one of disobedience, the doctrine of the fall of man.

It is after these preliminaries that Lewis begins to discuss human suffering and why it occurs. He first identifies the proper good of a human creature as the submission of that person's will to God, the surrender of human self-will to God's will. He points out that even non-Christian and nontheistic religions require this kind of submission, so this is not a viewpoint peculiar to Christianity. Lewis does not argue that pain is the only method God uses to bring about submission to God, but it is a significant one.

God whispers to us in our pleasure, speaks in our conscience, and shouts in our pains: it is His megaphone to rouse a deaf world.[42]

Lewis delineates three contexts in which pain may serve as the redemptive purpose of driving us toward submission to God. The first is simply an expression of the common belief that bad people ought to suffer. Although Lewis notes that some people object to the idea of retributive punishment, retribution is the only thing that makes sure that punishment is just. According to Lewis, pain "plants the flag of truth within the fortress of the rebel soul."[43]

However, if the pain of bad people shatters the illusion that all is well, pain in the lives of other people shatters the illusion that what we have is enough. Even good Christians find it difficult to turn toward God when they feel as if they have all they need. He writes:

Let me implore the reader to try to believe, if only for the moment that God, who made these deserving people, may really be right when he thinks that their modest prosperity and the happiness of their children is not enough to make them blessed; that all this must fall from them in the end, and if they have not learned to know Him they will be wretched. And therefore he troubles them, warning them in advance of an insufficiency that one day they will have to discover.[44]

In one letter Lewis asked for prayer from a Christian friend because he was going through "A Plain Called Ease."[45] If the kind of good that will make for permanent happiness requires a relationship to God, then ordinary prosperity may take that away from us.

The third role of suffering is based on the idea that God expects us to submit our wills to him, and that cannot possibly be willed by fallen creatures unless it is unpleasant. Mere obeying is intrinsically good, but given human self-will, obedience cuts against the self-centered will.

We therefore agree with Aristotle that what is intrinsically right may well be agreeable, and that the better a man is the more he will like it; but we agree with Kant so far as to say that there is one right act—that of self-surrender—which cannot be willed to the height by fallen creatures unless it is unpleasant. And we must add that this one right act includes all other righteousness, and that the supreme canceling of Adam's fall, the movement "full speed astern" by which we retrace our long journey from Paradise, the untying of the old, hard knot, must be when the creature with no desire to aid it, stripped naked to the bare willing of obedience, embraces what is contrary to its nature, and does that for which only one motive is possible.[46]

In the Book of Job Satan asks "Does Job serve God for naught?" implying that Job's righteousness can be explained by the benefit Job receives from his obedience, and he asks the question of whether Job would remain faithful and righteous if his life were wracked with suffering. Thus a faithful person, who is prospering, in one sense, is not asked to make the most profound act of self-surrender. This can only occur if the apparent link between righteousness and reward is broken.

In arguing as he does Lewis explicitly says that he is attempting to make the doctrine of being made perfect by suffering "not incredible." He does not say that he can make it palatable; in fact, he says that it is not palatable.

Now does this understanding of suffering represent a retreat from Platonism? Is it an abandonment of the idea that the standards we use in evaluating the actions of God are commensurable to the standard we use in evaluating human actions? I think pretty clearly that this is not true. There is an intended good which is a good for the creature, which is supposed to make the suffering worthwhile. Nor is it overly difficult to see how Lewis's own suffering in grief could be thought of as serving a redemptive purpose.

Since the causes of our suffering are complex, we need not presume, as Beversluis does, that the degree to which a person suffers is indicative of state of one's relationship with God. He writes:

Yet, if we accept this argument, we must conclude that those who suffer only appear to be close to God but in fact are not—otherwise, why do they suffer? We must also conclude that those who do not suffer only appear to have drifted from God but in fact have not. Furthermore, the more you suffer, the further from God you are; the less you suffer, the further from God you are. Furthermore, the more you suffer, the more God loves you, and the less you suffer, the less he loves you, since it is those we love that we punish and those to whom we are indifferent that we allow to be happy in contemptible and estranging modes.[47]

However, remember, Lewis has given three different circumstances where God might have a redemptive use for pain, and these three circumstances can occur on different spiritual levels. Remember also that Lewis has made the case that the most spiritually advanced persons are persons who recognize that they are "vile," that is, they recognize more fully than the rest of us just how far they have to go to be fully surrendered to God. Lewis's claim concerning the reasons for suffering is not a simplistic "shattering thesis," for people who are far from God, it is a complex thesis concerning how suffering works redemptively at all levels of spiritual development. The last of these uses of suffering, suffering as an opportunity to continue to serve God without the appearance of reward, involves no shattering whatsoever. As Petrik says:

The bottom line for Lewis, however, is that the business of mending souls is so complex that we can not hope to fully understand the manner in which suffering is distributed among human beings. Noting the vast discrepancy between the degree to which individuals may suffer, Lewis confesses that he is ignorant of the causes of this distribution. And of course he is right. Any speculation as to the role of suffering or its absence is playing in an individual's spiritual development will always remain fairly blind speculation . . .

In addition to this, Lewis also mentions here a redemptive use of suffering for the benefit of others. He writes:

What is good in any painful experience is, for the sufferer, his submission to the will of God, and, for the spectators, the compassion aroused and the acts of mercy to which it leads.[48]

So suffering does not merely benefit the character of the sufferer, it can also benefit the character of those who observe the suffering. As Talbott writes, "Nothing, it seems, arouses compassion and melts the heart of the arrogant and the powerful in a way comparable to the suffering of children."[49]

Another objection found in Beversluis is that if we were to inflict suffering on those we love in the way that Lewis is suggesting that God does, we would be acting wrongly. He writes:

On thing is certain in any case: if I were to become as "exacting" with (my children), in Lewis's awful sense, I am confident that they would not rejoice in their newly acquired discovery that I really loved them. Nor do I believe that such a failure would be a sign of some juvenile deficiency in them.[50]

However, someone with greater wisdom and knowledge might surely have the right to use means that someone with less wisdom and knowledge would not have the right to use. As Lewis himself says:

To turn this (the redemptive role of suffering), into a general charter for afflicting humanity "because affliction is good for them" (as Marlowe's Tamberlaine boasted himself as the scourge of God"), is not indeed to break the divine scheme but to volunteer for the post of Satan within that scheme. If you do his work, you must be prepared for his wages.[51]

So I do not think that Lewis has to violate his "professed Platonism" in order to accept his own account of suffering. Nor was Lewis wrong to see his own suffering during his grief experience as God's work in getting him to cease his reliance on earthly comforts, even the comfort of a Christian marriage.

Another difficulty, however, pressed by Erik Weilenberg, is that Lewis really does not deal with the suffering of children in his treatment of the problem of pain.[52] It is a bit odd, because he is willing to consider the suffering of another class of "special victims," that is, animals. Children are more like us than animals, and so he cannot make the comment about children's suffering that he makes about animal suffering, namely, that he really doesn't know much about the place of animals in God's plan and that whatever he says about them is going to be speculative. By way of response to this difficulty, I would make three points. One is that no treatment of the problem of evil can be expected to be comprehensive. As Daniel Howard-Snyder points out, if we could explain all of our sufferings we would be contradicting some clear biblical passages, such as what we find in the Book of Job. He goes on to say:

We do others a grievous disservice to hold out to them in private or in the pulpit any expectation to understand why God would permit so much evil or any particular instance, expectations which we have no reason to believe will be fulfilled, expectations which when left unfulfilled can become near irresistible grounds for rejecting the faith. We are in the dark here. We can't see how any reason we know of, or the whole lot of them combined, would justify God in permitting so much horrible evil or any particular horror. We need to own up to that fact.[53]

So we should see Lewis as attempting to give us a substantial understanding of much of the evil we see and experience, but I think he was not foolish enough to think that he had explained it all. But secondly, as is evident from the quote from Talbott, in the case of the suffering of children, here the case is hardest to make that it can benefit the sufferers morally, but it does have the strongest effect of all suffering on those whom Lewis calls "the spectators," it arouses their compassion in the way that nothing else in the world does. I would have liked Lewis to include more discussion of the suffering of children in *The Problem of Pain*, and I do consider it a weakness of the book that this was not included. However, that in itself is not, in my judgment, sufficient to make his book an abject failure or a tissue of fallacies.

STRAW MEN AND ETHICAL SUBJECTIVISM

The other criticisms that Beversluis makes against Lewis are that he often uses arguments that commit the straw man fallacy. In *The Abolition of Man* and in essays like "The Poison of Subjectivism" and "De Futilitate," Lewis is critical of the doctrine of ethical subjectivism, and in *Mere Christianity*, Lewis argues that objective moral values constitute the basis for an argument for theism. In "De Futilitate," Lewis writes: "A man cannot continue to make sacrifices for the good of posterity if he really believes that his concern for the good of posterity is an irrational subjective taste of his own on the same level with his fondness for pancakes and his dislike for spam." Beversluis is particularly incensed at this remark,

This unqualified rejection (of ethical subjectivism) is surprising in view of the fact that he examines only two versions of the position he opposes, and only the weakest and most carelessly formulated ones at that: the view that morality is either a "herd instinct" or a mere subjective preference on the same level as a fondness for pancakes and a dislike for spam. This is irresponsible writing. To give vent to so ill-considered an opinion is to betray either that one knows next to nothing about ethical theory or that one simply chooses to ignore inconvenient points of view.[54]

In addition, later he writes:

Ethical subjectivists do not, of course, claim that aesthetic and moral judgments are mere expressions of feelings or subjective preference. Nor do they regard such judgments as unimportant.[55]

Are these claims accurate? In *Language, Truth and Logic*, A. J. Ayer had written,

What we do not and cannot argue about is the validity of these moral principles. We merely praise and condemn them in the light of our feelings . . . For we have seen that ethical judgments are mere expressions of feelings, there can be no way of determining the validity of any ethical system, and, indeed, no sense in asking whether any such system is true.[56]

Bertrand Russell, a well-known moral subjectivist, compared moral judgments to whether one prefers oysters or does not. He wrote:

The theory which I have been advocating is a form of the doctrine which is called the "subjectivity" of values. This doctrine consists in maintaining that that, if two men differ about values, there is not a disagreement as to any kind of truth, but a difference of taste. If one man says "oysters are good" and another says "*I* think they are bad," we recognize that there is nothing to argue about. The theory in question holds that all differences as to values are of this sort, although we do not naturally think them so when we are dealing with matters that seem to us more exalted than oysters.[57]

So clearly, Lewis was not criticizing an unoccupied position.

Nor was it wrong of Lewis to criticize, as he did in *The Abolition of Man*, an English textbook that made a number of statements implying an implicitly subjectivist view of ethics and aesthetics. Often ideas really begin to show their consequences when they are taught at lower levels in education. For example, I believe that the way in which children are taught to distinguish "fact" from "opinion" in grade school has the tendency to render students insensitive to the possibility of serious reasoning about profoundly debatable issues. If something is either a "fact"(we know how to figure it out), or "opinion" (a merely subjective matter), then why reason about something so controversial and complex as, say, the existence of God?

However, does moral subjectivism *have* to be so simplistic? Even if Beversluis agrees that ethical subjectivism has sometimes been presented in just the way Lewis describes it, perhaps it does not have to have the implications Lewis says it does. Beversluis gives a number of characteristics that ethical judgments can have even though they are subjective: they guide conduct, influence choice, and express attitudes, those who make them are prepared to universalize them, and give reasons in support of them.

Now I think Beversluis's comments are somewhat anachronistic, in the sense that Lewis's discussions of moral subjectivism were written in the 1940s, but Beversluis seems to be describing a prescriptivism, which was developed in the 1950s by R. M. Hare. More seriously, however, Lewis does consider the position of many writers from his own time, which started from the claim that "traditional" morality was all subjective but then attempted to support some virtue or other on a more "realistic" basis, perhaps attempting to base ethics on "instinct" or the survival of the species. He argues that this is impossible, and that once we reject "traditional morality" by making it subjective and asking, "Why should we follow these rules?" we cannot introduce any other value without having the same question asked of the newly proffered value. The fact that someone is prepared to universalize some value judgment is no answer to somebody who simply denies the legitimacy of the value in question. So in addition to simple subjectivism, which claims that ethical judgments are like tastes in food, Lewis is prepared to consider a more complex subjectivism, which says that while ethical judgments are subjective, it has some feature X, which keeps it above the level of mere preferences. Lewis offers a general line of argument against this, which goes like this.

(Assumption for reduction):

1. Ethical judgments are subjective, but have a characteristic, X, which makes them different from mere preferences (willingness to universalize them, support for the survival of the species, and basis in instinct, etc.).
2. Either X is something that is valuable objectively, or it is only subjectively significant.
3. If X is valuable objectively, then ethical judgments are actually objective, and subjectivism is false.
4. If X is valuable only subjectively, then there is no real difference between ethical judgments and mere preferences.
5. Therefore, ethical judgments are objective, or they are not on a different level from mere preferences.

If one is going to defend moral subjectivism by denying that it puts ethical judgments on a level with mere preferences, then one must confront this line of argument from Lewis. Beversluis never comes to terms with it.

A good deal more could be said about the cogency and coherence of Lewis's apologetic arguments. It is my contention that Lewis's arguments, even if unsound, cannot be easily refuted. If they are sound, however, they require further development. I expect debate about the arguments in Lewis's apologetics to continue for years to come.

NOTES

1. C. S. Lewis, *Mere Christianity* (New York: Macmillan Publishing Company, 1952), 135.

2. Ibid., 74.

3. John Beversluis, *C. S. Lewis and the Search for Rational Religion* (Grand Rapids, MI: Eerdmans, 1985).

4. An undergraduate debating society whose purpose was to discuss issues surrounding Christian faith. Lewis was the first president of the club, a position he held at the time of the debate.

5. Humphrey Carpenter, *The Inklings: C. S. Lewis, J. R. R. Tolkien, Charles Williams, and Their Friends* (Boston, MA: Houghton Mifflin, 1979), 217.

6. C. S. Lewis, *God in the Dock* (Grand Rapids, MI: Eerdmans, 1970), 173.

7. C. S. Lewis, *The World's Last Night and Other Essays* (New York: Harcourt, Brace and Company, 1952), 13–30.

8. Lewis, *God in the Dock*, 177–183.

9. C. S. Lewis, *Christian Reflections* (Grand Rapids, MI: Eerdmans, 1967), 152–166.

10. Lewis, *God in the Dock*, 146.

11. Beversluis, *Search for Rational Religion*, 73.

12. John Beversluis, "Surprised by Freud: A Critical Appraisal of A. N. Wilson's Biography of C. S. Lewis." *Christianity and Literature* 41(2) (1992): 191–192.

13. Beversluis, *Search for Rational Religion*, 102–103; Victor Reppert, *C. S. Lewis's Dangerous Idea: In Defense of the Argument from Reason* (Downer's Grove, IL: Inter-Varsity Press, 2003), 21–28.

14. Art Lindsley, *C. S. Lewis's Case for Christ* (Downer's Grove, IL: Inter-Varsity Press, 2005), 50–65.

15. C. S. Lewis, *A Grief Observed* (New York: Bantam Books, 1961), 33.

16. Ibid., 32–33.

17. Ibid., 33.

18. Ibid., 35–36.

19. Beversluis, *Search for Rational Religion*, 150.

20. Lewis, *Mere Christianity*, 49.

21. C. S. Lewis, *The Problem of Pain* (New York: Macmillan, 1962), 100.

22. Lewis, *A Grief Observed*, 37–38.

23. Richard Purtill, "Did C. S. Lewis Lose His Faith," in *A Christian for All Christians*, ed. Andrew Walker and James Patrick (London: Hodder and Stoughton, 1990), 35.

24. Beversluis, *Search for Rational Religion*, 102.

25. Ibid., 104.

26. Ibid., 118–119.

27. Ibid., 151.

28. Ibid., 160.

29. Alvin Plantinga, *The Nature of Necessity* (Oxford University Press, 1974), 164–196.

30. Thomas Talbott, "The Problem of Pain" in *The C. S. Lewis Readers' Encyclopedia*, ed. Jeffrey Schultz and John West (Grand Rapids, MI: Zondervan, 1998), 349–350.

31. Plantinga, op cit.

32. Lewis, *The Problem of Pain*, 29.

33. Ibid., 33

34. Ibid., 34

35. Talbott, "C. S. Lewis and the Problem of Evil," in *Christian Scholar's Review* (September 1987), 41–42.

36. Lewis, *The Problem of Pain*, 37.

37. Talbott, "C. S. Lewis and the Problem of Evil," 44.

38. C. S. Lewis, *Studies in Words*, 2nd edn. (Cambridge: Cambridge University Press, 1990).

39. James Petrik, "In Defense of C. S. Lewis's Analysis of God's Goodness," *International Journal for the Philosophy of Religion* 36(1) (1994): 46–47.

40. Lewis, *The Problem of Pain*, 40.

41. Ibid., 67.

42. Ibid., 93.

43. Ibid., 95.

44. Ibid., 97.

45. Letter to Sister Penelope, June 5, 1951 in *Letters of C. S. Lewis*, ed. Hooper, 410. Quoted in Purtill, "Did C. S. Lewis Lose his Faith."

46. Lewis, *The Problem of Pain*, 101.

47. Beversluis, *Search for Rational Religion*, 117.

48. Petrik, "In Defense," 54.

49. Lewis, *The Problem of Pain*, 110.

50. Beversluis, *Search for Rational Religion*, 114.

51. Lewis, *The Problem of Pain*, 112.

52. Erik Wielenberg, "The Christian, the Skeptic, and the Atheist: C. S. Lewis, David Hume, and Bertrand Russell on God," forthcoming.

53. Daniel Howard-Snyder, "God Evil and Suffering," in *Reason for the Hope Within*, ed. Michael Murray (Grand Rapids, MI: Eerdmans, 1999), 101.

54. Beversluis, *Search for Rational Religion*, 40.

55. Ibid., 45

56. A. J. Ayer, *Language, Truth and Logic* (New York: Dover Edition, 1952), 111–112.

57. Bertrand Russell, *Science and Religion* (Oxford: Oxford University Press, 1935), 237–238.

SELECTED BIBLIOGRAPHY

Beversluis, John. *C. S. Lewis and the Search for Rational Religion*. Grand Rapids, MI: Eerdmans, 1985.

Lewis, C. S. *A Grief Observed*. New York: Seabury, 1963.

———. *The Problem of Pain*. New York: Macmillan, 1962.

Petrik, James. "In Defense of C. S. Lewis's Analysis of God's Goodness." *International Journal for Philosophy of Religion* 36(1) (1994).

Talbott, Thomas, "C. S. Lewis and the Problem of Evil." *Christian Scholar's Review* 17 (September 1987): 36–51.

2

C. S. Lewis as Allegorist: *The Pilgrim's Regress*

Mona Dunckel

C. S. Lewis's initial imaginative work, *The Pilgrim's Regress*, published in 1933, is an allegory. Although it is a veiled account of his real spiritual journey to salvation, one is moved to ask, "Why would C. S. Lewis write his first work of fiction in the form of an allegory?" While allegory had enjoyed a long and distinguished history from the Greeks through the Renaissance as a writing form, it had gradually fallen into decline and disuse in the early twentieth century. Lewis's friend J. R. R. Tolkien was notoriously opposed to allegories and clearly states his aversion in his introduction to *The Lord of the Rings*, claiming an antipathy that began with his ability to first discern the genre. His distaste stemmed from a belief that allegory afforded its author too much "domination" over the imagination of the reader. Many literary critics of the time used the term pejoratively, decrying the fact that a piece of work had "degenerated into allegory."

Lewis, however, felt differently about the genre. He was already well into his study of the medieval uses of allegory, which he would explicate in his still highly praised work of literary criticism, *The Allegory of Love*, published in 1936. The good reception of Lewis's study aided his efforts to revitalize and reestablish the position of allegory at a time when few were interested in the genre. Though the position was unlike that of many critics of his time, Lewis shared with Dorothy Sayers a belief that allegory was a natural part of man's existence and experience. Lewis also felt that allegory spoke to some basic inborn human need. Sayers had identified allegory as a genre that generally appeared as an accompaniment to great change in the thinking of an age or a culture, growing out of those changes. Lewis appears to have shared this view as well. The years following World War I could have been viewed by Lewis as an allegory-generating era. The time is marked by world–shifting changes in thought and the philosophy that forever shifted European academia as well as the worldview and behavior of the ordinary man. Perhaps Lewis saw allegory as the "time-appropriate" vehicle for his ideas? More probable, however, is that allegory seemed an appropriate medium for writing about the fundamental change that had revolutionized the foundations of his personal thinking—his conversion.

It may have further seemed like the proper vehicle for his story because allegory, at times, serves as the best manner for expressing something that is so new that one has not yet acquired the words for describing it. It is possible that Lewis had not yet found the language that would allow him to fully communicate his conversion experience. Additionally, it is not unusual in Lewis's writing to detect the influences of other writing projects he was working on at the time. While his studies and lectures, which became *The Allegory of Love*, do not seem to be a direct influence on the content of *The Pilgrim's Regress*, it certainly may have influenced Lewis's decision to choose the form of allegory for his work of fiction.

There is perhaps one further influence on Lewis's choice of allegory as the pattern for the story he wished to tell, and that is of course his familiarity with and appreciation for John Bunyan's works, *Pilgrim's Progress* and *The Holy War*. Since *The Pilgrim's Regress* was to tell Lewis's journey from unbelief to Christianity it may have seemed appropriate to replicate the form in which Bunyan earlier had written of Christian's quest. Still another possibility is that Lewis's choice of allegory as the vehicle for his story may have been aided by the fact that Lewis had already written one allegorical work, his book-length poem *Dymer*. Perhaps, like Sayers's belief that allegory serves to make some experiences clearer and more easily understood, Lewis thought allegory provided the clearest method for him to write and understand his quasiautobiographical account. *The Pilgrim's Regress* remains as Lewis's only foray into the writing of "pure" allegory, but his study and reading of the genre continued throughout his life.

LEWIS ON ALLEGORY

A brief consideration of some of Lewis's major ideas about allegory may be beneficial before going any further. Knowing how Lewis thought about the genre can only assist in the reading of *The Pilgrim's Regress*. Allegory, as Lewis explains in *The Allegory of Love*, starts when an author selects some invisible, nonmaterial reality—like truth—and creates something—a fictional character or object—to represent that nonmaterial fact in his tale. The author does this deliberately; he knows what he is doing. He expects the reader to see what is being done and to follow along in the story. From this element of Lewis's description one may define allegory as a story intentionally created by its author with two distinct levels of meaning, one found in the story itself and the other existing in the author's underlying representations.

Lewis makes several other suppositions about allegory that are also important in gaining a general understanding of the genre. First, he believed that when creating allegory, particularly if the writing was full of powerful images and word pictures, authors actually created more meanings than they were aware of. The pictures may be able to create in the mind of readers far more layers of meaning or different meanings than those the author had seen. Second, Lewis believed that the pictures that are created by allegorists use certain symbols or representations that authors expect their readers to know. If a person who doesn't know anything about the Bible reads Bunyan's *Pilgrim's Progress*, there will be many symbols that the reader simply won't be able to understand. An additionally important matter about allegory is that its meaning does not change over time. The particular meaning the author intended at the time of composition is the meaning that remains constant over time.

Lewis offers some thoughts on the reading of allegory in an essay on Edmund Spenser published more than twenty years after the publication of his *Pilgrim's Regress*. His key piece of advice for reading allegory amounts to a sort of "don't work too hard at understanding it" statement. He suggests that allegorical reading, like many other activities, is least successful when we are most consciously working at it. He would instead urge readers first to enjoy the story that they are reading, which will allow a gradual awareness of the deeper meaning.[1] More advice on reading allegory comes in the posthumously published work, *Spenser's Images of Life*. This book, an unfinished work, was completed by Alastair Fowler using Lewis's notes. This additional advice is essentially "don't translate characters into their meanings when reading the story"—in other words, one must keep the two levels of the story separate and one shouldn't mix them as he or she reads. Doing so would weaken the story on both levels.

Allegory can be difficult to read, Lewis notes, because the symbols chosen by the author, while known in his time, may no longer be part of common knowledge for the reader. When this happens the author's intended meaning may be irretrievably lost. Another obstacle to successfully reading allegory is our own preconceptions. What we expect to find and what we think we know may blind us to the meaning that the author intended. Lewis suggests that we can never be sure that we have extracted all of the intended meaning from the allegory through our reading, claiming that since the author is not fully conscious of everything included in an allegory, we as readers do not have an accurate measure of meaning to extract against which to compare our gleanings.[2] While these obstacles for reading allegory exist, they are not unconquerable; the best approach with which to combat the difficulties is practice in reading the genre, for the more time readers spend in the reading of allegory the more skillful they will become at recognizing its nuances and in unpacking the meanings within the stories.

Despite the reader's best efforts at reading allegory, Lewis realizes the author may not provide a sufficiently coherent story for the reader to follow. In an essay on John Bunyan published in 1962, Lewis explains that allegories are successful only if the author is careful to stick to his purpose and his story. Lewis contends that in the *Pilgrim's Progress*, the story breaks down at times and the reader loses sight of the author's images because Bunyan forgets his story and preaches, instead of using the story to make his point.

CONVENTIONS IN ALLEGORY

A very readable source on the conventions of allegory is Dorothy L. Sayers's essay, "On Writing and Reading Allegory." Within her short history of the form, she identifies four key elements, or conventions, generally found in allegories. First is the use of personification, in which many if not all of the characters will be what Sayers called "personified abstractions,"[3] whereby they represent some idea, vice, or virtue. One can look at any chapter of Bunyan's *Pilgrim's Progress* and find characters that embody virtues or vices. Christian, for example, travels with Faithful, meets Piety, Hopeful, as well as the giant Despair. All of these characters serve as examples of abstract ideas that have been personified.

A second common element in allegory is that the story often employs the motif of a journey. This may be a one-way or round-trip affair, but the hero is commonly a traveler or a pilgrim. This convention allows the author to introduce people or elements into the story with more ease and variety than may be achieved if the hero stays at home. The journey may also be used to introduce an overarching purpose for what takes place, particularly when the protagonist is cast as some sort of seeker or pilgrim.

A third convention of allegories is to have characters participate in informal debate, thereby allowing the author to present opinions on a wide range of topics. Lewis made extensive and excellent use of this convention in *The*

Pilgrim's Regress, but if poorly used, this device can create an undesirable tone in the story leading to its breakdown.

A final convention in many allegories is the use of a dream framework, in which a story is presented as being a dream of a narrator. In *The Pilgrim's Regress*, the author is clearly the storyteller, but it is equally clear from the first words of the novel that the story is a dream of the speaker. From the first line of Lewis's tale, there can be no doubt that the narrator is recounting his vision, and numerous other chapters remind the reader of the narrator's visionary state. For example, three of the six chapters in Book I repeat the information that the narrator is presenting what he saw as he slept, and the reminders continue to the last page of the allegory. On the final page the reader is told that the story has ended because the sleeper had awakened.

A SHORT SYNOPSIS OF *THE PILGRIM'S REGRESS*

"I dreamed of a boy who was born in the land of Puritania and his name was John."[4] So begins Lewis's story. Early in his life John learns that there are rules; he also learns that these rules were made by the steward who is the representative of the landlord, the owner of all of Puritania. John's parents took him to meet the steward who was jovial and kind, until he put on a mask and frightened John with a long lecture about the rules and the Landlord. He gave John a card on which were printed all of the rules that he must follow. John left the Steward's house confused, with two contradictory ideas about this absent Landlord: (1) he is a very kind and good person, and (2) he shuts those who do wrong in a black hole overflowing with scorpions and snakes.

Several days later, John wandered farther down the road in front of his home than he had ever been before. There he found a walled garden, and in the wall, a window. Through the window John saw a beautiful wood full of flowers. As he looked at the wood, it seemed to him as if the woodland mist had parted and he had seen a beautiful island and heard haunting music, and he felt a longing so intense that it made him forget all that had been part of his life. When the vision disappeared and the music stopped, John wept. He returned home, sure that he knew what he wanted.

When John was older he returned often to the woodland hoping for another glimpse of the island. On one visit he met a naked brown girl who convinced John that she was what he had really wanted. John tried to fulfill his desire for the island through a relationship with the girl, but his pleasure was only temporary and he came to realize that she was not what he wanted.

While John tried to follow the rules of the Landlord, he was not particularly successful. He decided that his only recourse was to run away, so that he might find his island. He left his parents' home and started out, walking all night.

As he continued his quest, he met a series of people who, after hearing of his desire, offered him their assistance.

John's first contact was with Mr. Enlightenment, who, when he learned that John was from Puritania, assertively declared that the Landlord did not exist and that the people of Puritania retained their beliefs because they were ignorant both of the real world and of the rich discoveries of science. After some time together, the two parted, but John continued his journey with great joy. He felt free from the Landlord, free of the rules, and best of all, free of the black hole.

John met Vertue next, a young man of his own age and the two became companions in the journey. John learned that Vertue, though he lacked a clear destination, traveled thirty miles daily on the main road that led west. Vertue had no set of rules from the Landlord—he had made his own rules and he faithfully followed them. The two men separated when John desired to leave the main road.

John detoured through Thrill and Eschropolis. In his detour John confronted Romanticism and Realism before being thrown into the dungeons of The Spirit of the Age. John was rescued by Reason and the two of them traveled together for a time before she put John back on the main road where he was reunited with Vertue. As night fell the two found that the road on which they were traveling ended at a precipice. While Vertue tried to convince John that they should attempt to climb down in search of a way to reach the other side, the two are visited by Mother Kirk. Her message to them was that they cannot cross on their own, they must have her assistance.

The two young men refused her offer of help and traveled North in search of a way to cross the great canyon. They spent a night with Mr. Sensible and then began their journey again, accompanied by Drudge, Sensible's servant. Although they met several other interesting characters, including warlike dwarves—the "Mussolimini," the "Marxomanni," and the "Swastici," they found no way across the gorge. As they began to retrace their way southward, Vertue fell ill and became both blind and dumb. John led him along until they came to the house of Mr. Wisdom. After some days with Mr. Wisdom, Vertue was cured. He and John were separated as they left Wisdom's house, and John found himself alone on a narrow ledge as night fell. He was given food by a mysterious man and was told where he could find water. In the morning he resumed his journey and came to a chapel where he met the Hermit, History. He spent the night in History's cave, but after awakening from a nightmare he left, intent on going back, no longer forward. He met Reason and she drove him at sword-point on in his journey until he again found Mother Kirk, who told him that he must "give himself up."[5] She further told him that the way to cure death is to die. John and Vertue were stripped of their ragged clothes and dove into the pool that Mother Kirk indicated.

The two emerged on the other side of the river, having crossed the canyon. There they were assigned a guide from whom they learned that the mountains ahead of them were the Eastern Mountains—the same ones that John as a child had seen from his home in Puritania. John also learned that his island was not an island at all; it was a part of the Eastern Mountains and that the only way to reach the mountains is by going back to where their journey began.

They traveled back with their guide. On the way each battled and killed a dragon as part of his quest, and through their battles both John and Vertue gained strength of character. On their return trip, the land appeared very different than it had seemed when they first passed through; the difference, their guide explained, was because they were now able to see things as they really are. The two travelers also found that the return trip took far less time than did their original journey. When they arrived back at the now-dilapidated cottage where John had lived as a boy, John learned that his parents had long-since "passed over the brook." He wept for all he wished he could have said to them that could not now be said. John and Vertue learned they too would cross the brook that very evening. The scene became too dark for the dreamer to see the actual crossing, but, as his dream ended, he heard the two men and their guide singing as they crossed the final brook.

A SHORT EXPOSITION OF LEWIS'S ALLEGORY

While one can find detailed explanation of the elements and characters represented in the works of several Lewis scholars, including Clyde S. Kilby and Kathryn Lindskoog, it seems fitting to discuss here at least some of the major characters and images in Lewis's allegory. This listing is not meant to be exhaustive, but it is intended to serve as an aid for stimulating the reader's own thinking and ability to understand the allegory of *Pilgrim's Regress*.

Characters

Lewis scholar Doris T. Myers, in *C. S. Lewis in Context,* describes characters in Lewis's allegory in terms of two types: humorous characters who can be recognized or identified by what they say, particularly in terms of some sort of a catch phrase that they repeated; and archetypal characters, who can be recognized by what they do.[6] Mr. Broad would be an example of a humorous character, while Mother Kirk would be an example of an archetypal character. This distinction is helpful to the beginning reader of allegory and offers one method by which characters might be cataloged. Myers also offers her opinion that Lewis was more successful with his humorous characters than with the archetypal personages, whom she sees as sometimes being underdeveloped and reduced to serving only as alternate voices for the author.[7] While this might be generally true, not all of the archetypal characters suffer from this flaw. Reason, for example, is a strong, fully developed character who plays a pivotal role in developing John's evaluative powers.

John Primary among the characters in *Pilgrim's Regress* is John, the young man who follows the call of the island that takes him ultimately to the Landlord. John is obviously a portrait of Lewis himself, but Lewis also wants the story to be potentially the story of every person, hence the typical name of John for this character. Clyde Kilby states in *Images of Salvation* that, "in terms of the longing to find the source of the vision [the quest is] everyman's."[8] Some critics go beyond this explanation and suggest that Lewis selected the name John for other reasons as well. Kathryn Lindskoog offers three additional reasons for the selection of John as the name for Lewis's traveler. She suggests that it may be related to Lewis's preference for being called Jack, a common nickname for John. She also suggests that Lewis may have chosen the name to honor John Bunyan and his allegory. Finally she suggests that Lewis may have selected John because of its meaning in Hebrew, literally "God has been Gracious."[9] However, no other scholars seem to attach such a wealth of reasons to the selection of a name for Lewis's pilgrim.

Mother Kirk One of the more misunderstood characters in the allegory is Mother Kirk, whom Lewis intends to represent Christianity itself. She describes herself as the Landlord's daughter-in-law, which would be Lewis's way of indicating the Christian tradition's view of the Church as the "bride of Christ." Many readers and critics see her, instead, as representing the Roman Catholic Church. Lewis's own words make it clear that he did not intend Mother Kirk as a representative of Catholicism.[10]

The Steward The stewards in the allegory represent ministers who are to be keepers or stewards of the things of God in this world and his representatives to the people among whom they live and serve.

The Landlord The Landlord is the character that in *Pilgrim's Regress* represents God. He is the owner of all the land and it is he who has made the rules under which those in Puritania live.

Virtue John's companion on his journey is Virtue, which represents the human conscience, or the moral element of man.

Mr. Broad This character represents the liberal church. He finds Mother Kirk out-of-date and suggests that one can perhaps better find God in the nature around him.

Sigismund The character of Sigismund seems obviously a very thinly veiled representation of Freud. Freud is but one of many thinkers who appear in the catalog of characters found in *Pilgrim's Regress*.

Reason As one of the key archetypal characters of the allegory, Reason is an explicit character; that is, her name identifies Lewis's intended reference. Although she is a powerful character—breaking the chains with which she is bound and slaying the Spirit of the Age to rescue John—her power is limited. She tells John, "I can tell you only what you know. I can bring things out of the dark part of your mind into the light part of it."[11] She also has an obvious flaw: she is without concern for John and his feelings.

Images

The Grand Canyon Lewis uses the image of the great chasm, called by locals the Grand Canyon, to represent the consequences of Original Sin.

The North This region represents the home of wrong thinking that overemphasizes what Doris Myers describes as "intellectuality and objective thought."[12] It is a region of cold, hardness, and barrenness in which feeling and emotion is repudiated as undesirable. The portrayal of the utter North as a wasteland is seen again in Lewis's map of Narnia.

The South This region represents the opposite kind of erroneous thinking, subjectivity, and elevation of the importance of the emotions. It is a region where feeling and emotion are heightened, and where the mystical and magical prevail. The land of Calormen in *The Horse and His Boy* carries this same aura of sensuality and perversion.

The Island This represents the assumed object of John's longing or desire. As the story unfolds, we find that the assumed object is not the real object of desire and cannot truly bring satisfaction to the seeker.

PUBLICATION AND RECEPTION OF *THE PILGRIM'S REGRESS*

The Pilgrim's Regress was initially published by Dent publishing and received praise in early reviews. Lindskoog reports that the reviewer for the *Times Literary Supplement*, who praised Lewis's poetry, called his allegory "arresting" and noted that it had the ability to lift "the reader up."[13] G. S. Sayer, in a review for *Blackfriars*, praised Lewis's successful "revival of the allegorical method," noting that it permitted Lewis to "treat profound and complex things in a simple way."[14] Later reviews praised the book's humor, its dialogue, and its content. Lindskoog notes that Bertrand L. Conway, in writing for *Catholic World* in 1936, called *The Pilgrim's Regress* "a caustic, devastating critique of modern philosophy, religion, politics, and art."[15]

Despite critical acclaim, initial sales of the book were disappointing. Many readers thought the book was obscure and difficult, while others found it unnecessarily combative and ill-tempered. Lewis confided to his friend Arthur Greeves in a June 1933 letter: "I think it is going to be at least as big a failure as

Dymer."[16] Sales did increase when the book became a publication of Sheed and Ward, a Catholic firm, and Lindskoog details Lewis's ire over the comments that the new publishers added, as they seemed to indicate that Lewis intended *Pilgrim's Regress* to be an endorsement of the Roman Catholic faith.[17]

CRITICAL REVIEW AND ANALYSIS

A Groundbreaking Work

The Pilgrim's Regress can be counted a groundbreaking work for Lewis on several levels. First, it marked Lewis's first venture into fictional prose as well as Lewis's inaugural publication of a book under his own name. Prior to *The Pilgrim's Regress*, Lewis had published two books of poetry: *Spirits in Bondage*, a volume of early poems, and *Dymer*, a book-length poem. Although Lewis had hoped to be a successful poet, his name was not yet well recognized because these books had been published under the pen name of Clive Hamilton. While there is evidence from Lewis's correspondence that he had begun a nonfictional autobiographical telling of his conversion before he wrote *The Pilgrim's Regress*, it was never completed. Instead, Lewis wrote the prose allegorical tale that he considered not only an account of his coming back to God, but also an apology, or a defense, of Christianity.

Secondly, *The Pilgrim's Regress* is Lewis's first work with a Christian theme. Telling the story of his conversion experience brought Lewis into contact with a new audience, one for whom he had not previously considered writing. Based on his use of a satirical style and his inclusion of a broad range of philosophies and intellectual issues, Lewis must have thought his book would appeal to only an elite, educated readership. However, it was read by some whom Lewis had not anticipated and continues to be read by a diverse audience today.

Additionally, *The Pilgrim's Regress* is Lewis's first autobiographical work. Always a private man, Lewis was not intent on drawing attention to himself at this time; this is perhaps why the book is not directly an autobiography. While the book tells of Lewis's coming to God, it lacks a one-to-one correspondence between the events in the journey of John and the events in Lewis's life. *The Pilgrim's Regress*, as an indirect autobiography, allows Lewis to convey the intellectual journey of his religious experience without all of the details of his life. Lewis's choice of allegory permitted an objective distance than a more direct telling of his own story would allow. Lewis seems to underscore this point with his claim in the Afterword to the third edition that the book is not really intended to tell his life story.

Finally, as Lewis's earliest book-length work of fiction, *The Pilgrim's Regress* serves as an introductory platform for many the themes and ideas that would resurface in his later works of both fiction and nonfiction. Joe Christopher, a biographer of Lewis's, states, "The number of motifs and ideas in the *Pilgrim's Regress* that reappear in Lewis's later works indicates how quickly his ideas matured and how little they changed."[18]

Structure and Style

The Pilgrim's Regress is organized into ten books, each of which is subdivided into several chapters. Each book is titled, as is each chapter, and an examination particularly of the chapter titles provides a window into the broad classical and cultural knowledge that Lewis possessed. While most of the titles of the books and chapters are fairly simple and without obvious connections to other writer's works, the title of Book Three, "Through Darkest Zeitgeistheim," does bring to mind the title of Henry Morton Stanley's popular travel adventure *Through the Dark Continent*, which had been a favorite selection of many readers in the late nineteenth century. Such a title provides a look at the breadth of Lewis's reading and knowledge.

Titles such as "Ichabod" (Book I, chapter 5), meaning "the glory hath departed," and "Leah for Rachel" (Book I, chapter 4), are obvious scriptural allusions. Other chapter titles, "*Quem quaertus in Sepulchro? Non est hic*" (Book I, chapter 6), (Whom do you seek in the sepulcher? He is not here.), or "*Dixit Insipiens*" (Book II, chapter 1), are portions of scripture quoted in Latin. The chapter titles reveal, however, more than merely the use of biblical allusions and quotations by Lewis. Several titles are quotations from, or titles of, works by philosophers and writers with whom educated readers would be familiar. For example, "Archtype and Ectype" (Book IV, chapter 2), refers to concepts taken up by John Locke in his 1690 work *Essay Concerning Human Understanding*, while "Esse is Percipi"—"to exist is to be perceived" (Book IV, chapter 3)—is drawn from Berkley's *Principles of Human Knowledge*. In Book Five, "Table Talk" (Book V, chapter 5), the title echoes that of a well-known book by Martin Luther. Beyond quotations and titles are also allusions to literary characters such as the title "Let Grill be Grill" (Book IV, chapter 1), which recalls a character from *The Faerie Queene*, one of Lewis's favorite works.

Another feature of Lewis's work that is visible with even a quick perusal of *The Pilgrim's Regress* is the extensive use of epigraphs. Most of the ten books begin with not merely a single epigraph, but an entire page of these carefully selected quotations. As with the sources of chapter titles, the epigraphs exhibit a wide range of sources, including everything from lengthy quotations taken from classical authors such as Plato, Homer, and Pindar, to the single sentence of a popular police maxim. A careful consideration of the epigraphic selections and their relationships to the material that they precede certainly offers tantalizing potential for mining additional riches from *The Pilgrim's Regress*.

Equally obvious to even the casual reader is the plethora of quotations contained in *The Pilgrim's Regress*. These quotations, like the epigraphs, cover a broad spectrum of writers and texts. However, not all are immediately comprehended by the contemporary reader because Lewis has introduced many of his quotations in Greek or Latin. This was, in fact, a criticism brought to Lewis's attention by his friend Arthur Greeves, who apparently suggested that all of the Greek and Latin quotations be eliminated from the book. Lewis did not, obviously, do so. There are several accessible sources that offer translations of these quotations, including Kilby's book, *Images of Salvation*. A more extensive coverage is Kathryn Lindskoog's 1995 book, *Finding the Landlord: A Guidebook to C. S. Lewis's Pilgrim's Regress*.

An additional element that can be easily identified in the reading of *The Pilgrim's Regress* is Lewis's uncanny ability to create an alternate world, complete with geography. The description of the lands through which John passed is as rich and varied as is Lewis's description of the people who John meets. A map of the lands in included with the book, printed on the endpapers. This well-formulated geography and cartography is not surprising, for even as a boy Lewis had created an elaborate geography as well as the history for his world of Boxen. Later, the topography of Narnia would not be left merely to the reader's imagination, for Lewis would again provide rich description of its geographic features and would again create a map of the land to provide full orientation for readers. Readers' responses to the so-called *Mappa Mundi* for *The Pilgrim's Regress* was not, however, entirely positive. Many complained the map included numerous places John had never visited and regions that were not mentioned in the book. Despite the complaints, Lewis defended his map and considered it appropriate because it gave the full picture of John's world and allowed readers to see additional places to which the erring pilgrim could have detoured.

An additional stylistic element that Lewis employed was the interjection of poems or a song to break the prose format. The interjections occur sixteen times within the text, usually to focus a scene more sharply or to express an emotion more clearly. Some critics point negatively to this practice as a rupture of the allegorical form, but many of the poetic interludes in no way break the story or the vehicle of the allegory. The poems occur primarily in the later books of the allegory, and while they do require a "shift of gears," most do not require the actual suspension of the story that would make them truly intrusive.

Yet another device that Lewis employs is the use of satire. Over the course of the allegory he satirizes Freudian thought, Victorian romantic thinking, numerous philosophical and literary movements, and religion, by satirizing three types of Anglican churchmen. Mr. Angular represents the Anglo-Catholic, Mr. Broad represents the Liberal, and the Steward is Lewis's portrayal of the Low-Churchman. Doris Myers succinctly describes Lewis's religious satire by stating: "Mr. Angular's futility, the Low Church Steward's hypocrisy, and Mr. Broad's lack of commitment all add up to a mordant criticism of religion."[19] Lewis's satire is at times biting and seems almost vicious, yet it shows a penetrating intellect's honest appraisal of the elements of his world.

Pilgrim's Progress and *Pilgrim's Regress*

It would be easy to look at *The Pilgrim's Regress* and quickly conclude that the novel is modeled on John Bunyan's well-known allegory, *Pilgrim's Progress*; however, this would be an inaccurate assumption. While Lewis had read and enjoyed Bunyan's work, the elements that the two works share, particularly the convention of setting the story as a dream, and the journey or quest motif are not unique to these works, but rather are common elements of Medieval and Renaissance allegories. In Lindskoog's introduction to *Finding the Landlord*, she offers a list of additional examples of what are generally called visionary allegories, including *The Romance of the Rose*, a thirteenth-century work, and Dante's *Divine Comedy*. Like Lewis biographer Joe Christopher, I believe that *The Pilgrim's Regress* probably most closely resembles the fourteenth-century poem by Langland, *Piers Plowman*. Christopher notes that both weave strands of social satire and criticism, philosophical discussion, and what he calls "religious vision," although not "in the same proportions."[20] Christopher hastens to add that he is not making "an argument of influence," but merely noting that "the similarity is one of human experience."[21] The primary similarity in the works is their recounting the human experience of seeking for and finding God.

Other Lewis scholars, particularly the late Clyde Kilby, do see a much more direct connection between *The Pilgrim's Progress* and *The Pilgrim's Regress*. In *The Christian World of C. S. Lewis*, Kilby directly identifies Bunyan's work as the model for *Pilgrim's Regress*.[22] Chad Walsh makes a similar statement regarding *Pilgrim's Progress* as a model for Lewis in *The Literary Legacy of C. S. Lewis*. U. Milo Kaufmann further explores the relationship between the work of Bunyan and that of Lewis, but his focus is primarily on their contrasting elements. Kaufmann notes that while Christian's journey in *Pilgrim's Progress* is "one way," as he flees from the world to the celestial city, John's journey is a "round-trip" as it were, in which he follows the longing that has served to call him to the Landlord, and then returns to "the community of men for witness and redemptive work."[23] Certainly this adds a new dimension to John's pursuit of the island making it more than a mere acquisition of holiness.

Themes in *The Pilgrim's Regress*

As Lewis's first religiously themed work, it seems inevitable that *The Pilgrim's Regress* should introduce concepts or thematic elements that would recur in Lewis's later writings. What follows are examples of some themes that persist and reappear with progressive sophistication in Lewis's later works.

First, *"There are none as blind as those who will not see."* While there are several passages in *The Pilgrim's Regress* to which this idea can be applied, the clearest exemplification of the concept is found in Book Four, chapter one. Reason has just slain the giant, Spirit of the Age, and now turns her attention to the prisoners who remain in his dungeon. She breaks the lock, opens the door, and invites the prisoners out, but no one comes. While the open door stands before them, the prisoners refuse to exit. They believe that what they see is not real, merely the vision of what they hope for; they do not wish to be tricked or fooled, and so they do not gain their freedom. This theme reappears in the experience of the dwarfs in Lewis's *The Last Battle*. Having decided that, "the dwarfs are for the dwarfs," and that they will not be taken in by anyone, they refuse to see the glory of Aslan's country before them. Aslan himself describes their condition saying, "Their prison is only in their minds, yet they are in that prison; and so afraid of being taken in that they cannot be taken out."[24] The dwarfs see none of the light, and experience none of the goodness that they stand within because they have closed their minds and their eyes to all but a concern for themselves.

A second theme that resonates in many of Lewis's later works is that of *Sehnsucht*, or longing. In *The Pilgrim's Regress*, this longing can be seen in John's yearning for the island. His desire is variously described as intense, thrilling, fleeting, and at times even painful because it remains unfulfilled. It becomes the driving force in his life and John desires the island so much that he leaves his home to pursue what has become his hunger and his thirst. This theme returns in *Surprised by Joy*, but the term longing has been replaced in that work by the term joy. *Sehnsucht* is identifiable in Lewis's fiction as well. One image is that of Reepicheep, who desired the "utter East" and Aslan's land all of his life. He completes his quest for them in the closing chapters of *The Voyage of the Dawn Treader*. The idea of longing is again specifically identified by using the term longing in *Till We Have Faces*. Psyche speaks of the desire created in her by the distant Gray Mountain. She describes herself as "longing, always longing . . . Everything seeded to be saying, Psyche come!"[25]

What causes a stimulation of *sehnsucht* does not remain constant throughout Lewis's works, but mountains, gardens, and islands are all used at least once to represent the source of the longing, which is one of the most important themes found in Lewis's works.

A third theme in Lewis's allegory is that we don't see the world in the same way after conversion. This theme is made clear as John and Vertue begin their journey back to Puritania after their experience crossing the Grand Canyon. Their guide tells them that although they will be traversing the same land, it will no longer look the same to them. The house of Mr. Sensible is no longer there, and the appearance of the Valley of Wisdom is significantly altered. We may observe the same theme at work in *The Lion, The Witch and the Wardrobe*. There we see it evidenced in the changed vision of Edward after he has met Aslan. Following his encounter with the lion, Edmund sees for the first time the reality of the Witch, not the illusion of a queen. Even the land itself looks different to a changed boy. The same difference of perspective can be seen in *Out of the Silent Planet* and *Perelandra* as well, but in those works it is best observed by contrasting the vision of Ransom, a "new" man, with the vision of an "old" man, Weston. Where Ransom sees beauty and gentleness, Weston sees ugliness and threat. The world does indeed look different to those who have been given a new vision.

Yet another theme that can be traced from its origins in *The Pilgrim's Regress* is that we cannot change ourselves. We must give ourselves up to another in order to be changed. John comes finally to Mother Kirk and admits that he can do nothing. He gave himself up for a fundamental alteration that required nothing more on his part than letting go. When he stripped away his rags it caused some pain, and "a little skin came with them."[26]

How like the experience of Eustace Scrubb in *The Voyage of the Dawn Treader*. Eustace, who had become a dragon, had no hope of returning to what he had been—a boy. Aslan effectively "undragons" Eustace by peeling off the dragon scales that cover him. The experience is not without pain, but it is necessary if there is to be any change in his condition. He too had to let go, and as he lay down before Aslan to let himself be descaled he did what was necessary for his healing.

Lewis also presents us with the idea that God uses our desires to draw us to Him and we do not seek Him on our own. John had no interest in seeking the Landlord or in knowing him. Once he knew longing for the island, John gradually came to the place where all he could do was pursue his longing. He was willing to give up everything else to reach the island. Once he followed his quest, he ultimately learned that what he was truly seeking was God. The longing had served to awaken in John a desire that drew him to the Landlord. Lewis describes this same kind of drawing in *Surprised by Joy*. There he speaks again of a longing that was stirred in him that served to begin his movement toward God. Similarly, Jill Pole learns in *The Silver Chair* that she had not been brought to Narnia because she had called to Aslan, but that rather she called to Aslan because he had called to her.[27]

The theme of redemption is certainly central to *The Pilgrim's Regress*, as it also is in *The Chronicles of Narnia* and other of Lewis's works. John and Vertue are redeemed in their crossing over the Grand Canyon—they have their characters transformed. The evidence of their change is in part the new vision they have acquired and the new courage that each will use as he battles his own dragon. The theme of redemption resurfaces many times in Lewis's later works, but a classic example of the theme as it occurs in the *Chronicles of Narnia* is Edmund's redemption in *The Lion, the Witch and the Wardrobe.* Edmund is both redeemed from the power of the White Witch by Aslan's sacrifice and he is redeemed thematically as he repents of his evil and matures over the course of the adventure. Mark Studdock, the primary character in *That Hideous Strength,* offers yet another example of the redemption theme as he is saved from N.I.C.E. The struggle for Mark's redemption is the central element of the story, and when he at last is convinced of the evil of Belbury he undergoes a thematic redemption similar to that of Edmund. Mark, too, matures and develops over the course of Lewis's novel and ultimately becomes willing to die for what is right, as he obviously has changed from the arrogant young man he was at the beginning of the novel.

A final theme to consider here is that our first steps of obedience make the way to God easier. John experiences this truth as he is confronted with a trail that offers no other option, and so he takes it on his descent to the floor of the canyon. As he climbed down, he found that the rock offered more handholds than he had expected and that the way down was easier than he had expected. Kilby describes this theme as a "first token move toward godly obedience and its resultant heavenly encouragement."[28] Jill Pole, in *The Silver Chair*, finds a similar ability to face her fears and a similar "heavenly encouragement" when she must pass by the lion if she is to satisfy her thirst at the stream. As she talks with the lion she takes her first steps toward the stream, then, although still fearful, she finds she is able to walk to the stream and drink before she answers the lion's summons to come before him. Lewis seems to delight in reminding his readers that God always honors and encourages the steps that a seeker takes toward him.

Critical Treatments of *The Pilgrim's Regress*

A contemporary criticism of Lewis's work focuses on his choice of imagery. In Book One, he introduces the "brown girls," who serve as John's earliest substitute for the real object of his desire. The brown girl in the wood becomes John's first sexual partner. Later another woman, named Media Halfway, entices John sexually during his visit to Thrill and is revealed to be merely another of the brown girls. In Book Two, John also refers to black girls as another unsuccessful substitute for "joy." Some critics have seen Lewis's choices of *brown* and *black* girls as both racist and imperialist. Certainly the imagery, like that of his *dark* Calormen villains, does not "play well" in the contemporary climate of tolerance and political correctness. Those who are embarrassed by Lewis's imagery would do well to remember that it was an appropriate symbol at the time in which he wrote. One can only concur with Lindskoog that if Lewis were writing today it is likely that he would have chosen a different symbol for sexual desire, and that his choice would have been made out of a true sensitivity for what is right. We can assume that his choice made today would carefully avoid intolerance and prejudice.[29]

Chad Walsh levels a criticism at *The Pilgrim's Regress* that is rooted in Lewis's choice of his literary form. Walsh believes that all allegories suffer from characters that fail to "live" or which in some way do not come across to the reader as "real." He would attribute this to the fact that the reader knows that each character merely represents something else, often an abstract idea, and that the reader's knowledge makes it impossible to see the characters as compelling. The criticism seems to stem more from an antipathy on the part of Walsh toward allegory than in the reality of readers responses to Lewis's characters, but it is certainly a potential problem, particularly among readers who do not have a taste for allegory.

Doris Myers identifies what she sees as a significant weakness in *The Pilgrim's Regress*, which she describes as "Lewis's apparent refusal to face the woundedness of society between the [world] wars."[30] She considers John's response to the Clevers, when they identify "the War" as the source of their disillusionment, to be harsh and cruel. John's reply to them is, "That war was years ago. It was your fathers who were in it."[31] Myers argues that in light of the publication date, merely fourteen years after the war that many of his readers would have been veterans of, Lewis should have refrained from satirizing them. She believes that the weakness she finds in the work can possibly be traced to Lewis's own ambiguity about his war experiences. While some of Lewis's writings do indicate ambiguous feelings about the World War I and his experiences in it, it seems more likely that Lewis's choice of words in John's discussions with the Clevers is more the forcefulness of one who has found his life newly come right (the book was written after Lewis's conversion), which can produce a sometimes unreasonable impatience with those who have not yet found their way past their experiences.

An additional criticism may be described as the book's "datedness." Much of Lewis's rich imagery is lost on those of today's generation who do not read widely and who thus lack experience with the thoughtful reading required by allegory. This is further compounded by this generation's lack of experience with classical languages, which makes Lewis's Greek and Latin quotations interrupters rather than well-fitted elements that move his intended image forward. However, even though the book is in some ways a "snapshot" of thought in a particular era, the themes are certainly timeless; they would resonate as well with someone who is seeking God today as with the audience for whom Lewis wrote in the 1930s.

A final criticism of *The Pilgrim's Regress* is its breadth. There are so many images, so many characters, and so much that is satirized that the reader can be overwhelmed. The book might have proven more successful with a more narrow focus. Limiting the incidents would have allowed a greater depth of character development and produced an easier landscape for the reader to cross. This particular weakness is not surprising when one remembers that this was Lewis's first work of fiction. Over time Lewis seemed to have learned to keep his stories more focused.

The Continuing Value of *The Pilgrim's Regress*

In a society that often describes the value of a book by its continued popularity, there should be little argument that *The Pilgrim's Regress* is a book of value. The most recent paperback edition was published by Eerdmans in 1992, nearly sixty years after the book's initial publication. Another indicator of a book's value is its "rereadability." Can readers go back to the work and in rereading it find additional truth or wisdom? Lewis's book most certainly seems to pass this test as well. The more readers return to this work the more they have been rewarded with increased understanding of and appreciation for the ideas that Lewis introduced.

But what specific values does *The Pilgrim's Regress* offer to the contemporary reader? First, the work is invaluable as a social history. Lewis draws a rich and full portrait of the "spirit of the times," of the post-World War I years—morally, intellectually, and religiously, cataloging the ideas that shaped thought and the men who had created the ideas. Because of the detail of Lewis's writing, the catalog of characters is particularly rich. Although it is focused toward the world of academics, Lewis's allegory raises within its context questions and issues that extend throughout popular culture. Reading the work as a cultural history will allow readers to return imaginatively to the interwar period and see what was taking place.

Second, the work is invaluable as an autobiography. Although Lewis seeks to make John representative of everyone, it clearly remains his personal story throughout. It provides, ultimately, the story of Lewis's own spiritual journey through the intellectual landscape of his times by which he finds faith, and in faith, the joy he was seeking. When read in tandem with *Surprised by Joy*, the book offers a richer vision of Lewis's passage from unbelief to belief.

Pilgrim's Regress also offers an invaluable research tool for scholars who would investigate the development of an author's prose style. As Lewis's first novel, it provides a benchmark against which his later use of language, fluidity of expression, and ideas can be compared. While it allows scholars and ordinary readers to trace the development of themes first introduced by Lewis here and then later developed in his subsequent works, it also permits the study of his stylistic maturation. It gives us a measure of the thinking of Lewis as a new convert and as such provides an amazing picture of spiritual thought well underway to maturity.

Although the story can be relatively quickly read, reaping the richness of the satire and the allegory requires more effort. But the depth of the riches that lie within *The Pilgrim's Regress* will continue to be sought by future readers, especially those who, like John, have heard the call of the island and are determined to find the satisfaction of the longing it has created within them.

NOTES

1. C. S. Lewis, "Edmund Spenser," in *Studies in Medieval and Renaissance Literature*, ed. Walter Hooper (Cambridge: Cambridge University Press, 1966), 137–139.

2. Ibid., 140–143.

3. Dorothy Sayers, "The Writing and Reading of Allegory," in *The Whimsical Christian: 18 Essays* (New York: Macmillan, 1978), 208.

4. C. S. Lewis, *Pilgrim's Regress* (Grand Rapids, MI: Eerdmans, 1992), 3.

5. Ibid.

6. Doris T. Myers, *C. S. Lewis in Context* (Kent, OH: Kent State University Press, 1994), 22.

7. Ibid., 22–24.

8. Clyde S. Kilby, *Images of Salvation in the Fiction of C. S. Lewis* (Wheaton, IL: Harold Shaw Publishers, 1978), 101.

9. Kathryn Lindskoog, *Finding the Landlord: A Guidebook to C. S. Lewis's Pilgrim's Regress* (Chicago, IL: Cornerstone Press, 1995), 2.

10. For the full content of Lewis's remarks see the final paragraph of "Afterword to Third Edition," *The Pilgrim's Regress*.

11. Lewis, *Pilgrim's Regress*, 58.

12. Myers, *C. S. Lewis in Context*, 13.

13. Lindskoog, *Finding the Landlord*, 136.

14. Ibid., 135.

15. Ibid., 136.

16. C. S. Lewis, *They Stand Together: The Letters of C. S. Lewis to Arthur Greeves (1914–1963)*, ed. Walter Hooper (New York: Macmillan, 1979), 454.

17. Lindskoog, *Finding the Landlord*, xxix.

18. Joe R. Christopher, *C. S. Lewis* (Boston, MA: G. K. Hall & Co., 1987), 14.

19. Myers, *Lewis in Context*, 44.

20. Christopher, *C. S. Lewis*, 10.

21. Ibid.

22. Clyde S. Kilby, *The Christian World of C. S. Lewis* (Grand Rapids, MI: William B. Eerdmans Publishing, 1964), 36.

23. U. Milo Kaufmann, "The Pilgrim's Progress and The Pilgrim's Regress: John Bunyan and C. S. Lewis on the Shape of the Christian Quest," in *Bunyan in Our Time*, ed. Robert G. Collmer (Kent OH: Kent State University Press, 1989), 194.

24. C. S. Lewis, *The Last Battle* (New York: Collier Books, 1970), 148.

25. C. S. Lewis, *Till We Have Faces: A Myth Retold* (New York: Harcourt, 1984), 74.

26. Lewis, *Pilgrim's Regress*, 167.

27. C. S. Lewis, *The Silver Chair* (New York: Collier Books, 1970), 19.

28. Kilby, *Images of Salvation in the Fiction of C. S. Lewis*, 101.

29. Lindskoog, *Finding the Landlord*, 27–28.

30. Myers, *C. S. Lewis in Context*, 24.

31. Lewis, *Pilgrim's Regress*, 41.

BIBLIOGRAPHY

Bunyan, John, *The Pilgrim's Progress from This World to That Which Is to Come.* Uhrichsville, OH: Barbour, 1990.

Carnell, Corbin Scott. *Bright Shadow of Reality: C. S. Lewis and the Feeling Intellect.* Grand Rapids, MI: William B. Eerdmans Publishing, 1974.

Christopher, Joe R. *C. S. Lewis.* Boston, MA: G. K. Hall & Co., Twayne, 1987.

Duriez, Colin. *The C. S. Lewis Handbook: A Comprehensive Guide to His Life, Thought, and Writings.* Grand Rapids, MI: Baker Books House, 1990.

Glover, Donald E. *C. S. Lewis: The Art of Enchantment.* Athens, OH; Ohio University Press, 1981.

Green, Roger Lancelyn, and Walter Hooper. *C. S. Lewis: A Biography.* New York: Harcourt Brace Jovanovich, 1974.

Kaufmann, U. Milo. "The Pilgrim's Progress and The Pilgrim's Regress: John Bunyan and C. S. Lewis on the Shape of the Christian Quest." In *Bunyan in Our Time.* Edited by Robert G. Collmer. Kent OH: Kent State University Press, 1989, 186–199.

Kilby, Clyde S. *The Christian World of C. S. Lewis*. Grand Rapids, MI: Eerdmans, 1964.

———. *Images of Salvation in the Fiction of C. S. Lewis*. Wheaton, IL: Harold Shaw Publishers, 1978.

Lewis, C. S. *The Allegory of Love: A Study in Medieval Tradition*. New York: Galaxy, 1958.

———. *The Last Battle*. New York: Collier Books, 1970.

———. *The Lion, the Witch and the Wardrobe*. New York: Collier Books, 1970.

———. *The Pilgrim's Regress*. Grand Rapids, MI: Eerdmans, 1992.

———. *Selected Literary Essays*. Edited by Walter Hooper. Cambridge: Cambridge University Press, 1969.

———. *The Silver Chair*. New York: Collier Books, 1970.

———. *Spenser's Images of Life*. Edited by Alistair Fowler. Cambridge: Cambridge University Press, 1967.

———. *Studies in Medieval and Renaissance Literature*. Edited by Walter Hooper. Cambridge: Cambridge University Press, 1966.

———. *That Hideous Strength: A Modern Fairy Tale for Grown-Ups*. New York: Macmillan, 1965.

———. *They Stand Together: The Letters of C. S. Lewis to Arthur Greeves (1914–1963)*. Edited by Walter Hooper. New York: Macmillan, 1979.

———. *Till We Have Faces: A Myth Retold*. New York: Harcourt, 1984.

———. *The Voyage of the "Dawn Treader"*. New York: Collier Books, 1970.

Lindskoog, Kathryn. *Finding the Landlord: A Guidebook to C. S. Lewis's Pilgrim's Regress*. Chicago, IL: Cornerstone Press, 1995.

Manlove, C. N. *C. S. Lewis: His Literary Achievement*. New York: St. Martin's Press, 1987.

Myers, Doris T. *C. S. Lewis in Context*. Kent, OH: Kent State University Press, 1994.

Piehler, Paul. "Visions and Revisions: C. S. Lewis's Contributions to the Theory of Allegory." In *The Taste of the Pineapple*. Edited by Bruce L. Edwards. Bowling Green, OH: Bowling Green Popular Press, 1988, 79–91.

Sayers, Dorothy. "The Writing and Reading of Allegory." In *The Whimsical Christian: 18 Essays*. New York: Macmillan, 1978, 205–234.

Schakel, Peter J. *Reason and Imagination in C. S. Lewis: A Study of "Till We Have Faces."* Grand Rapids, MI: Eerdmans, 1984.

Walsh, Chad. *The Literary Legacy of C. S. Lewis*. New York: Harcourt Brace Jovanovich, 1979.

3

Mere Christianity: Uncommon Truth in Common Language

Joel D. Heck

INTRODUCTION

"Ever since I became a Christian I have thought that the best, perhaps the only, service I could do for my unbelieving neighbors was to explain and defend the belief that has been common to nearly all Christians at all times."[1] That's how C. S. Lewis explains his purpose in writing one of the most influential Christian books of the twentieth century, *Mere Christianity*, the most important work of Christian apologetics he ever produced. This purpose helped to create "the supreme example of C. S. Lewis's ability to make profound truths clear to everyone."[2]

The term "mere Christianity" comes from the Protestant theologian Richard Baxter (1615–1691),[3] a chaplain in one of Oliver Cromwell's regiments. Lewis explains the meaning of *Mere Christianity*: "Measured against the ages 'mere Christianity' turns out to be no insipid interdenominational transparency, but something positive, self-consistent, and inexhaustible."[4] In other words, Lewis was referring to historic Christianity, centered in the Incarnation of Jesus Christ. By avoiding denominational distinctives, Lewis provides a guide to that common core of beliefs that nearly all Christian denominations have held since the first century A.D. Consequently, he avoids topics where there are differing views among Christians, such as the Sacraments, the Second Coming, worship, or the Virgin Mary. He uses the word

Christian, not in the popular sense of a good person, but to refer to someone who accepts the teaching of the original disciples of Jesus[5] and "one who accepts the common doctrines of Christianity."[6]

In 1993, a *Christianity Today* poll named *Mere Christianity* the single most influential book for Christians, other than the Bible. Heading a list that included works by Oswald Chambers, John Bunyan, Francis Schaeffer, and Dietrich Bonhoeffer, *Mere Christianity* was listed first for having the most significant impact on the Christian life. It drew more than twice as many votes as any other book.[7] *Mere Christianity* is the first "good Christian book" that John Stott recommends in his book, *Basic Christianity*, and it is the most frequently mentioned work that influenced members of the Evangelical Theological Society and the Wesleyan Theological Society, though Lewis was neither an evangelical nor a Wesleyan.[8] In the book *Indelible Ink: 22 Prominent Christian Leaders Discuss the Books That Shape Their Faith* (Colorado Springs, CO: WaterBrook Press, 2003), General Editor Scott Larsen puts *Mere Christianity* as the top book and Lewis as the top Christian author with Lewis mentioned more than three times more frequently than the next author, Fyodor Dostoyevsky. Obviously, what Lewis once wrote about his own feelings toward apologetics does not apply to his readers. On August 2, 1946, he wrote to Dorothy Sayers, "My own frequent uneasiness comes from another source—the fact that apologetic work is so dangerous to one's own faith. A doctrine never seems dimmer to me than when I have just successfully defended it."[9]

The book has sold more than eleven million copies and helped turn around the lives of such well-known public figures as Charles Colson, author, founder of Prison Fellowship, and former legal counsel to an American President, and Thomas Monaghan, founder of Domino's Pizza.[10]

Mere Christianity gives us an introduction both to the thought and the writing style of Lewis. The thought is profound and the writing style plain English, the product of a skilled writer, a Christian layman, and a student of the English language. That, of course, is the necessary approach for material that was first written for radio. The radio listener does not have the opportunity to consult the dictionary, if a word is unfamiliar, so the speaker must use common language that will be understood by all. A good radio producer can detect those places where the writer is likely to lose his audience, and Lewis benefited in this way from the BBC's Eric Fenn, Assistant Director of Religious Broadcasting. For the purpose for which *Mere Christianity* was written, then, the medium of radio served as a support.

In 1946, Lewis wrote an essay later published by the Student Christian Movement under the title "Man or Rabbit?" In it Lewis argued that one of the distinctive characteristics of a human being was the desire to know things, particularly their truth claims. The question asked by some people of the day was whether they could live a good life without believing in Christianity. Lewis pointed out the fact that being good is not the essence of Christianity, but being remade, taking on the Divine Life, being transformed into a real person, a son or daughter of God, "drenched in joy." People should not ask how helpful Christianity is, but how *true* it is! And if true, then the Materialist view, which places the good of civilization in prime position (since individuals live only a few decades), will be replaced by the Christian view, which places the good of the individual in prime position (since individuals actually live forever). And, in fact, the person who isn't really interested in knowing about the truth of Christianity is afraid of considering that question because he is afraid that he will find out that it is true. Then he would have to change both his way of thinking and his behavior.[11] *Mere Christianity* is not simply a book written in the common language; it is a book about truth.

The book is autobiographical in the sense that it contains much of the thought process Lewis himself used in arriving at the conclusion that Christianity is true. For example, he used to believe, when he was an atheist, that most of the human race was wrong about the existence of God. Later, as a Christian, he didn't have to believe that all other religions were completely wrong.[12] Lewis's argument against the existence of God when he was an atheist created a problem for him. Where had he gotten the idea that the universe was unjust? If the universe was senseless, why was he so opposed to it?[13] Lewis's own awareness of the problem of justice forced him to conclude that he must have gotten an idea of justice from some source outside of himself. "If the whole universe has no meaning, we should never have found out that it has no meaning."[14] Later, Lewis alludes to what he calls "good dreams," particularly those of a dying and rising god.[15] This allusion takes us back to the time prior to Lewis's conversion to Christianity, when he had accepted the position of Sir James George Frazer, whose twelve-volume work, *The Golden Bough*, argued that Christianity was simply one myth among the many religions that taught of a dying and rising god. Late in *Mere Christianity*, Lewis talks about his own situation, where he realizes that the most obvious sin in his life is a sin against charity. He has sulked or stormed that day when he did not need to. And the best evidence for the kind of person you are is how you act when you are taken off guard.[16]

The book reflects another aspect of Lewis's life in that Lewis uses in his apologetic writings the training that he received especially from W. T. Kirkpatrick. That training was substantially a relentless search for truth, and it influenced Lewis for the rest of his life. Conversation frequently became disputation, whether that conversation took place with friends or opponents. Former student John Lawlor once wrote, "One quickly felt that for him dialectic supplied the place of conversation."[17] Such an approach prepared Lewis for apologetics, the defense of the Christian faith and a task that is in essence disputative.

AT THE BBC DURING WORLD WAR II

The book *Mere Christianity*, published in 1952, originated as four series of broadcasts over the BBC from 1941 to 1944 (see the Appendix to this chapter). When Lewis was invited to speak over the BBC, the British Broadcasting Company was less than twenty years old. Founded in 1922 and incorporated in 1927, "the early BBC fully adopted Christian values."[18] This would explain their willingness during World War II to invite such a noted Christian speaker as Lewis.

Under Reverend F. A. Iremonger, Director of Religious Broadcasting, the BBC had begun to introduce into its religious programming lay speakers during the 1930s, including such leading lights as New Testament scholar, C. H. Dodd.[19] Rather than simply broadcasting worship services and church music, the BBC wanted to provide the listening audience with relevant, Christian programming. Then Germany invaded Poland on September 1, 1939, and Great Britain declared war on September 3. During the war the BBC was also anxious to raise the morale of the people. Lewis was one of those who could speak in his rich baritone voice with power, clarity, and relevance, becoming the second most well-known radio voice in England after Winston Churchill.

In a setting where television, cinema, theater, and other places of entertainment closed because of the war and where newspapers became scarcer due to paper shortages, radio became the most important and strategic method for delivering information to the British people and for maintaining the nation's morale. The only restriction on radio time was the broadcast plans of the programmers, which had to be censored in order not to lower the morale of the country or inadvertently give valuable information to the enemy.[20] This created a situation that made the BBC the voice of the entire nation during the war, which writer J. B. Priestley described as "something as important to us in this war as an army or navy or air force."[21] Justin Phillips wrote, "It was not just a battle for the mind and morale of a nation at war. For the religious broadcasters, it was a battle for the soul."

Reverend James Welch, Director of Religious Broadcasting at the BBC, read Lewis's book, *The Problem of Pain*, which was published in 1940, and was impressed by the lucid mind, the clarity of writing, and the powerful ideas. This led him to contact Lewis about appearing on the BBC, especially in view of the topic of Lewis's book. The book was published at an opportune time. In

July 1940, Hitler had given Reichsmarschall Goering orders to destroy British air power, and in August the Battle of Britain had begun. On September 7, German bombers attacked London. The Blitz struck London over the next nine months and, at one point, for fifty-seven consecutive days. The Blitz ended on the night of May 10–11, 1941, the worst night of the Blitz and just a few days after Lewis had his microphone test in preparation for his first series of BBC broadcasts.[22] It's no wonder that Lewis could write, "Most of us have got over the pre-war wishful thinking about international politics."[23]

The war informed Lewis's broadcasts, not only in providing a part of the motivation for raising the nation's morale, but also in his choice of language. The broadcasts contain numerous words from the battlefield, on average more than one such reference per page. The Christian life involves the believer in spiritual warfare, so the comparison is apt. For example, Lewis uses the word *war* eighty times in his broadcasts, the word *surrender* eight times, the word *soldier* sixteen times, and a total of more than two dozen different terms in all.[24]

Welch wrote to Lewis at Magdalen College on February 7, 1941, inviting him to do a series of talks from a Christian perspective on either the underlying assumptions of modern literature or the Christian faith as Lewis saw it. The smaller number of undergraduates at Oxford University during the war seems to have made it possible for Lewis to accept, but the larger number of students as the war drew to a close made it hard for Lewis to accept future invitations to speak over the BBC. Lewis responded positively on February 10, preferring a series of talks during his summer vacation on the topic of the Law of Nature, that is, an objective standard of right and wrong. The New Testament assumes an audience that believes in the Law of Nature, but we can't assume that for modern England. His hope was "to create, or recover, the sense of guilt" that was mostly absent in England.[25]

The person in charge of producing religious talks, Eric Fenn, Assistant Director to James Welch, booked Lewis for four weeks, starting on August 6, the date that became the first of twenty-five broadcast talks that Lewis would give. They settled on the title, "Right and Wrong: A Clue to the Meaning of the Universe?" Lewis sent the first two scripts to Fenn by June 3, and Fenn replied, "I think they are excellent and there is very little that any of us wish to suggest about them."[26] Though the talks were well-written, Fenn still wanted Lewis to do a script rehearsal and read-through, so he wrote to Lewis on July 31 with an invitation to do so. His concern was that Lewis might speak too quickly or too slowly, and he wanted to be prepared. Lewis had never broadcast before,[27] and the medium of radio allows for no dead time.

The day of the first broadcast arrived, and Lewis faced the unenviable position of following the 7:30 P.M. news broadcast in Norwegian! While the

Norwegian broadcast provided an important public service to a part of the listening audience, apparently no one had thought about the sequence of the programs. The problem was solved later, and Lewis never again followed the news in Norwegian. In spite of the schedule, Lewis's rich voice, fluency, command of the English language, passion for his topic, and the powerful content of his ideas all combined to produce an excellent broadcast. Listeners apparently agreed, for many letters began to pour in to the BBC.[28] A request from Fenn for a second series of five talks had arrived before the first series was over.

As soon as the four series were completed, a request came to the Overseas Religious Broadcasting Officer of the BBC from Australia for Lewis to rebroadcast all of his talks.[29] Several years later, a request originating with Charles Taft, President the Federal Council of Churches (FCC), came from the United States. A BBC officer in their New York office, Lillian Lang, wrote, "Apparently his new approach to religious subjects is causing considerable interest in this country."[30] She was requesting a script of one of his talks and a list of topics he had covered in the hope of being able to include a talk by Mr. Lewis in a network program of the FCC. But Lewis never did rebroadcast any of his talks.

THE APPROACH

In spite of the tremendous influence his writings have had, Lewis downplayed his role, stating, for example, about his BBC talks, "Mine . . . attempt to convince people that there is a moral law, that we disobey it, and that the existence of a Lawgiver is at least very probable and also (*unless* you add the Christian doctrine of the Atonement) that this imparts despair rather than comfort."[31] His role was to convince the skeptic that there was a moral law and that the existence of the moral law suggested a deity behind that law.

He saw his writings as only a shadow of God's work. In his Preface to *The Pilgrim's Regress*, Lewis spoke of God's work in nature when he wrote that narrow anti-Christian dogmatism ". . . exaggerates the distinctness between Grace and Nature . . . and . . . makes the way hard for those who are at the point of coming in."[32] In other words, Lewis argues as Paul argues in his Epistle to the Romans that "the natural man" knows certain things about God by nature and sees those truths echoed in nature. Consequently, to understand Lewis as an apologist, in *Mere Christianity* and elsewhere, we must see the connection between his role and the role of nature. For Lewis, nature will point people to God. Lewis's role is to make that connection more explicit, to nudge the sleeping imagination, to point out the vague longing for something greater than oneself.

But there is more that Lewis does with this vague longing. Not only does he point it out, but he also sharpens that longing so that people might see the one thing that satisfies, Jesus Christ. He had found in his own life that only Christ could satisfy his longings, and a biblical theology affirms the same thing. Writes Lewis, "Has not every object which fancy and sense suggested for the desire, proved a failure, confessed itself, after trial, not to be what you wanted? Have you not found by elimination that this desire is the perilous siege in which only One can sit?"[33]

But first, the reader, or listener, has to understand that things are not right between him and God. Lewis writes, "We have to convince our hearers of the unwelcome diagnosis before we can expect them to welcome the news of the remedy."[34] In England in the 1940s, Lewis felt, "A sense of sin is almost totally lacking."[35] He chose to use the common language to communicate truth. "My task was therefore simply that of a *translator*—one turning Christian doctrine, or what he believed to be such, into the vernacular, into language that unscholarly people would attend to and could understand."[36] He believed that if speakers and writers could not translate their thoughts into common language, then their thoughts were confused.[37] In some places, he would use the vehicle of storytelling. "The inhibitions which I hoped my stories would overcome in a child's mind may exist in a grown-up's mind too, and may perhaps be overcome by the same means."[38] And he would allow the story to do its own work. "I am aiming at a sort of pre-baptism of the child's imagination."[39] His strategy was no different for adults than for children. These stories, he hoped, would awaken the Law of Nature in both children and adults.[40]

Story allows the storyteller to convey profound truth in easily understood concrete language, which is not the natural language of the apologist. Around 1955, Lewis wrote the essay, "The Language of Religion" in which he argued that there was no specifically religious language, as there was a scientific language or a poetic language. He explained one of the reasons for his effective use of analogy in apologetic writings such as *Mere Christianity*, stating that the apologist cannot do effective apologetic writing in concrete language, but must use the abstract. This creates a problem, since most people have difficulty with abstract language. Lewis solved this problem in *Mere Christianity*, not by the use of stories, but by the use of analogy.[41] Analogies have the same ability that stories have, enabling the writer to set aside abstract language in favor of concrete terms.

Though primarily an apologist, Lewis at times takes on the role of an evangelist, for example, when he tells his readers that the biblical message can start to make a difference for them tonight.[42] Likewise, when he invites readers to imagine themselves standing in the presence of God,[43] he wants them to think of the importance of their relationship to Him.

BOOK ONE: "RIGHT AND WRONG AS A CLUE
TO THE MEANING OF THE UNIVERSE"

After three unsuccessful attempts,[44] Lewis and the BBC finally settled on a title for the first series of broadcast talks, later known as Book One of *Mere Christianity*. The title was "Right and Wrong as a Clue to the Meaning of the Universe." In short, when Welch invited Lewis to speak on the BBC, Lewis proposed as his topic the Law of Nature. He wanted to awaken a consciousness of sin in the listener, something that could not be taken for granted in the England of the 1940s. Christianity would be mentioned only at the end.[45]

In chapter one, "The Law of Human Nature," Lewis presents two basic ideas, that there is a Moral Law that people know they should obey and that they break that Law. Chapter two, "Some Objections," deals with the fact that this Moral Law, or Law of Human Nature, is neither instinct nor social convention. In chapter three, "The Reality of the Law," Lewis argues that the Law of Human Nature is not to be compared to the law of gravitation, which is only a description of what always happens when something is dropped. The Law of Human Nature is a law that is real and that tells us what humans *ought* to do rather than what they in fact do. Lewis writes, "A man occupying the corner seat in the train because he got there first, and a man who slipped into it while my back was turned and removed my bag, are both equally inconvenient. But I blame the second man and do not blame the first. I am not angry—except perhaps for a moment before I come to my senses—with a man who trips me up by accident; I am angry with a man who tries to trip me up even if he does not succeed."[46] Chapter four, "What Lies Behind the Law," addresses the two major views of the universe—the materialist view and the religious view. The matter of the Moral Law is not materialistic and therefore not subject to science, for it is not a scientific question. The religious view has the advantage that we are able to look inside ourselves. We can observe our conviction that there is a moral law, which we should obey; and that there is Something behind the law, which is directing the universe and urging us to obey that law. That Something is more like a mind than anything else. Chapter five, "We Have Cause to be Uneasy," encourages the reader to turn back if she is going in the wrong direction. It offers two pieces of evidence about the Something behind the universe, that is, the universe itself and the Moral Law. They tell us that this Something is a great artist, since the universe is beautiful, and that He is interested in right conduct. It is best to recognize our failure to obey this law, and Christianity will make no sense to people who do not realize that. We must go back to go forward.

As the first series of broadcasts concluded, Fenn wrote a letter of thanks to Lewis:

My dear Lewis,

I warned you as I bade good-bye that we should make a more formal expression of our gratitude to you by post, and this is meant to be it!

We should like you to know how extremely grateful we are for these five talks and for your promise of further talks at a later date if we can find a suitable time.

I do think the talks were really good. The only one that seemed to me to be turgid was the second, which was in many ways the most difficult. Last night's I thought was an excellent finish.[47]

BOOK TWO: "WHAT CHRISTIANS BELIEVE"

When Fenn read the scripts for the second series, he wrote to Lewis, "I think they are quite first class—indeed I don't know when I have read anything in the same class at all. There is a clarity and inexorableness about them, which made me positively gasp!"[48] The third broadcast, entitled "The Shocking Alternative," more than any other, "established Lewis's reputation as a Christian apologist of the first rank."[49]

In a section later removed from the published talk, Lewis provided an introduction to the second series, since he was unable to assume that listeners remembered his first series, which had ended four months earlier:

It's not because I'm anybody in particular that I've been asked to tell you what Christians believe. In fact it's just the opposite. They've asked me, first of all because I'm a layman and not a parson, and consequently it was thought I might understand the ordinary person's point of view a bit better. Secondly, I think they asked me because it was known that I'd been an atheist for many years and only became a Christian quite fairly recently. They thought that would mean I'd be able to see the difficulties—able to remember what Christianity looks like from the outside. So you see, the long and the short of it is that I've been selected for this job just because I'm an amateur not a professional, and a beginner, not an old hand. Of course this means that you may well ask what right I have to talk on the subject at all.

Well, when I'd finished my scripts I sent them round to various people who *were* professionals: to one Church of England theologian, one Roman Catholic, one Presbyterian, and one Methodist. The Church of England man and the Presbyterian agreed with the whole thing. The Roman Catholic and the Methodist agreed in the main, but would have liked one or two places altered. So there you've got all the cards on the table.

What I'm going to say isn't *exactly* what all these people would say; but the greater part of it is what all Christians agree on. And the main reason why I couldn't alter it so as to make them agree completely was that I've only got 15 minutes for each talk.

That doesn't give you time to make many subtle distinctions. You've got to go at it rather like a bull in a china shop or you won't get through.

One thing I can promise you. In spite of all the unfortunate differences between Christians, what they agree on is still something pretty big and pretty solid: big enough to blow any of us sky-high if it happens to be true. And if it's true, it's quite ridiculous to put off doing anything about it simply because Christians don't fully agree among themselves. That's as if a man bleeding to death refused medical assistance because he'd heard that some doctors differed about the treatment of cancer. For if Christianity is true at all, it's as serious as that. Well, here goes . . .[50]

The four clergymen to whom Lewis sent these scripts were probably former student Dom Bede Griffiths (Roman Catholic), RAF friend Reverend Joseph Dowell (Methodist), his BBC producer Reverend Eric Fenn (Presbyterian), and Reverend Austin Farrer (Anglican), chaplain of Trinity College, Oxford University.[51]

In the first chapter of Book Two, "The Rival Conceptions of God," Lewis divides all of humanity into those who believe in God or gods and those who don't. Christianity is in the majority by maintaining a belief in God. Then Lewis divides those who believe in God according to the sort of God they believe in—the Pantheists and the Theists. In the latter category, he includes Jews, Muslims, and Christians. If one adopts a pantheistic view of the world, Lewis argues, then one can't complain about injustice. For the Pantheist, God is a part of the world, God permeates the world, and God almost *is* the world. That drives one to the conclusion that what we call evil really can't be evil; after all, it's God. If there truly is a good and a bad, then "you must believe that God is separate from the world and that some of the things we see in it are contrary to His will."[52]

Chapter two, "The Invasion," whose title shows the influence of World War II, addresses the Incarnation. The rightful king has landed in enemy-occupied territory, but in disguise, and He is inviting us to join Him in a campaign of sabotage. That is the Christian view. The other view that Lewis also addresses, and demolishes, is Dualism, the view that there are two equal powers, one of them good and the other bad. The universe is the battlefield, and these two powers are at war with one another. The moment you judge one of these powers "good" and the other "bad," you are using a standard above both powers and saying that one power conforms to that standard while the other does not. And the source of that standard is God. Furthermore, goodness can be experienced for its own sake, while badness cannot. No one likes badness just because it is bad, but because of something they can gain by it. Badness is parasitic, only able to function by corrupting that which is good. Therefore, badness looks much more like it came from an originally good, but now fallen, creature than from an eternally existent being that is on a par with goodness.

The Principal of Manchester College at Oxford University, Nicol Cross, a Unitarian, didn't like the logic of Lewis in one of his talks. He said at a meeting of the Socratic Club on November 11, 1946 that "he must allude to the 'vulgar nonsense' that 'a man who said the things that Jesus said, and was not God would be either a lunatic or a devil.'"[53] He was quoting Lewis's BBC address, entitled "The Shocking Alternative," first delivered on February 1, 1942, an address that later became chapter three of Book Two in *Mere Christianity*. Elton Trueblood, professor of philosophy and chaplain at both Stanford University and Earlham College, had a much different and more accurate perspective on this most powerful chapter: "In reading Lewis I could not escape the conclusion that the popular view of Christ as being a Teacher, and only a Teacher, has within it a self-contradiction that cannot be resolved. I saw, in short, that conventional liberalism cannot survive rigorous and rational analysis."[54] In this chapter, Lewis presents what is often referred to as the Free Will Defense. God could not create a world of love and goodness without creating creatures that could freely give or withhold such love. To eliminate free will would be to create robots instead of people. Lewis addresses the fall of Satan, the flaw in human beings, and God's solutions—He gave us a conscience, good dreams (stories that seem to anticipate the Christian religion), and the Jewish people. One of those Jewish people claimed to forgive sins, and that leads us to the shocking alternative: either Jesus was a liar, a lunatic, or the Son of God.

Chapter four, "The Perfect Penitent," describes fallen mankind in need of repentance, and in this chapter Lewis pictures repentance as a kind of death. The problem is that only a bad person needs to repent, but only a good person can. The worse a person is, the less capable she is of repenting. But God has solved that problem for us in sending His Son to endure death in our place so as to pay our debt of sin. The fifth and last chapter in this book, "The Practical Conclusion," tells us that the suffering and death of Christ have made possible a new kind of person for those who believe in Him. Baptism, belief, and the Lord's Supper convey that Christ-life to us. And one day, in the practical conclusion of all things, God will land in force rather than in disguise.

BOOK THREE: "CHRISTIAN BEHAVIOR"

In chapter one, "The Three Parts of Morality," Lewis describes moral rules as "directions for running the human machine" rather than attempts on God's part to spoil people's fun. Then he discusses the three aspects of morality as: (1) relations between people, (2) what's inside an individual, and (3) the purpose of human life, or relations between people and God. Most people think of morality as the first part, relations between people, but the second and third parts need to be considered also. The third aspect of morality, rarely discussed in most circles, is important because people will last forever while civilizations will not.

"The Cardinal Virtues," or pivotal virtues, are four—prudence, temperance, justice, and fortitude. God wants a child's heart but a grownup's head, so He wants prudence, or common sense. He wants people to take the path of moderation rather than excess, so He wants temperance. He wants fairness, or justice, and He wants courage, or fortitude. Why? For three reasons, which correspond to the three aspects of morality from chapter one: (1) so that we will learn to do the right thing for the right reason, (2) so that we will develop into the right sort of person, and (3) because these virtues are necessary for the next life as well.

Chapter three, "Social Morality," presents the Golden Rule, "treat others as you wish to be treated." Christianity does not provide a particular political program, but a sense of direction and a source of energy. God wants everyone to pull their own weight, no manufacturing of unnecessary luxuries, no advertisements to convince us that we need those luxuries, obedience to authority, giving to the poor, sacrificial giving, and a development of the inner self through a relationship with God.

In chapter four, "Morality and Psychoanalysis," Lewis agrees that Freud was correct in attributing some of our behavior to the subconscious. When Freud became an amateur philosopher, however, and espoused a particular worldview, Lewis disagreed. Morality has to do with choices people make, but psychoanalysis has to do with the feelings and impulses that sometimes cause our choices to go wrong and not at all with the moral choices we make. Most important of all, however, Lewis argues that every choice we make changes us from what we are, causing us to become either more of a heavenly creature or more of a hellish creature.

Chapter five, "Sexual Morality," is not the center of Christian morality, in spite of what some people think. Christianity thoroughly approves of the body, for God took on a human body in the person of Jesus of Nazareth, and Christianity has produced nearly all of the great love poetry. Sexuality is part of God's creation, so God is in favor of the appropriate practice of our sexuality. Given our warped natures, however, propaganda has convinced many that we are sexually starved and need to indulge our senses. The evidence around us is that the sexual appetite grows by indulgence, just as any other appetite does. The evidence of jealousy, lies, deceit, disease, impotence, and other problems suggests that the indulgence of the past has not solved any problems of the sexual instinct, but has actually made them worse. Therefore, the Christian practice of marriage, or complete faithfulness to your spouse, or abstinence is the best road to sexual health.

Chapter six, "Christian Marriage," discusses three types of "love": (1) infatuation, (2) the initial sense of "being in love," and (3) the deep unity and commitment that lasts. This third type of love is the engine by which the marriage runs, while "being in love" is the explosion that starts the marriage. Lewis correctly places sexuality within marriage as one type of union that should not be isolated from the other types of union that come with marriage. Few have accepted his view that there be two kinds of marriage, one governed by the State and the other governed by the Church, but Lewis attempts to recognize that Christians make a different commitment in marriage than those who are not Christian.

Chapter seven addresses the topic of "Forgiveness," a topic that Lewis calls even more unpopular than chastity. How does one forgive one's enemies? How can a Pole or a Jew forgive the Gestapo? Two things make it easier—start by forgiving a member of your family and learn the meaning of loving your neighbor. One can hate bad actions without hating the person, or, as Lewis writes, "hate the sin but not the sinner." Lewis tells us that we do that to ourselves all the time, loving the self while disliking our pride, or our greed, or our cowardice. Christians realize that each thought or action changes the central part of us and moves us more toward being a heavenly creature or a hellish creature. To love our enemy is not to feel fond of the enemy or to be nice to the enemy, but to wish good to the enemy. After all, God loves us, and we don't really have much in us that is lovable.

"The Great Sin" is the topic of chapter eight. That sin is pride, the center of Christian morals, and its opposite is humility. Few see the problem in themselves, and most detest it in others. Pride is "the complete anti-God state of mind." Pride is competitive by nature, and that is why it is the chief cause of misery in people's lives, but also the chief reason why people turn away from God. "As long as you are looking down, you cannot see something that is above you." Lewis also addresses misconceptions about pride: (1) Pleasure at being praised is not pride, provided that the praise doesn't result in causing you to think how wonderful a person you are to have done what you did. (2) Being proud of others is a step away from pride, which is a very self-centered thing. (3) God is not concerned about His dignity, so He does not forbid pride for His own sake. He forbids pride because He wants us to know Him. (4) Humility does not result in a smarmy person, but in someone who is truly interested in you.

Chapter nine, "Charity," covers the first of the three theological virtues, faith, hope, and charity. While the term now means giving to the poor, it originally meant something much wider, that is, "Love, in the Christian sense." Charity is a state of the will, that of willing good to someone else. We need not fear that we don't feel loving; we must simply act as if we did. The feelings will follow the actions. The same is true of our love for God. We must act as if we did, and we will find that we soon feel the same way. But although our feelings for God may come and go, God's love for us is always steadfast.

Chapter ten, "Hope," addresses the second theological virtue with this stunning statement: "the Christians who did most for the present world were just those who thought most of the next." Hope is not escapism or wishful thinking; it is "a continual looking forward to the eternal world." "Aim at Heaven and you will get earth 'thrown in': aim at earth and you will get neither."[55] Our tendency is to think of this world and to fail to notice the longings that point to another world. The fool blames people and things, the disillusioned person learns not to expect too much, but the Christian understands that these longings, or desires, which cannot be satisfied by anything in this world, mean that we were made for another world.

In chapter eleven, "Faith," Lewis addresses faith in its first sense, that of believing or regarding as true the teachings of Christianity. Lewis says that his faith is based on reason, but people don't always make decisions on the basis of reason. Reason and faith are often opposed by emotion and imagination. The habit of faith needs to be developed so that we learn to hold on to our faith in spite of our changing moods. Before Lewis addresses the second sense of faith, he wants us to know that the idea that most people have at one point or another—that we might be able to earn a passing mark on God's exam or somehow put God in our debt—will never happen.

In chapter twelve, "Faith," talks about faith in the second sense. When we despair of our own efforts and leave our spiritual condition in the hands of God, we put our trust in Christ and discover that He offers something for nothing, in fact, that He offers everything for nothing. Lewis goes on to discuss the relationship between faith and good actions, attempting to chart a middle course between them, thereby avoiding the heart of the issue and arguing that we need both to lead us home. It would have been best for him to say that it is not faith *plus* works that saves, but a faith *that* works.

BOOK FOUR: "BEYOND PERSONALITY: OR FIRST STEPS IN THE DOCTRINE OF THE TRINITY"

Chapter one, "Making and Begetting," compares theology to a map. While doctrines are not God, nor the experience of God, they are a map that is based on the experiences of many people who knew God. Therefore, theology has the very practical value of being able to provide directions. It provides directions that avoid the popular idea that Jesus Christ was merely a great moral teacher. Christ is the Son of God, who can enable us to become sons of God, but in a different sense than He is. Begetting results in something of the same kind, because a human being begets a human being and God begets God. When God enables us to become sons and daughters of God, He is making us, not begetting us, into sons and daughters of God, which Lewis compares to statues or pictures of God. We become like God, as a statue is like a person. This making us into sons and daughters of God occurs because God adds spiritual life (*Zoe*) to our biological life (*Bios*).[56] We are thereby changed, as a statue would change if it became a real person. "This world is a great sculptor's shop. We are the statues and there is a rumor going round the shop that some of us are some day going to come to life."[57]

Chapter two, "The Three-Personal God," explains the doctrine of the Trinity as God being *more than* personal rather than *less than* personal, or impersonal. The illustration of a three-dimensional figure serves as "a sort of faint notion" of a super-personal God, that is, Father, Son, and Spirit. That biblical picture of God isn't anything we could have made up, because people would have made a simpler picture. For us to know God, He has to take the initiative. And He has.

Chapter three, "Time and Beyond Time," is a chapter that Lewis invites the reader to skip, if the reader has no interest in the topic. He addresses the problem of how God can answer the prayers of millions of people at the same time. His answer? God is not in time and therefore has all of eternity to answer the millions of prayers that come to Him at any given moment. God is like a novelist who leaves a story he is writing to answer the door. The character's action stops when the novelist lays down the pen or when the reader lays down the book. Time has stopped for the character at that moment, and that is similar to God's state of timelessness. All moments are now for God.

Chapter four, "Good Infection," explains how God makes people into little Christs. This happens by the work of the third person, the Holy Spirit, who delivers to us spiritual life, *Zoe*, much like a germ or virus infects us with disease, except that this infection is a good infection. This infection allows us to share in the life of Christ.

In chapter five, "The Obstinate Toy Soldiers," Lewis compares the making of sons of God to the turning of a tin soldier into a real person. The problem is that we are self-centered and don't want to be turned into sons of God. A tin soldier would be self-centered also, not wanting to become a flesh and blood person because he would see that as killing him. He would cease to be made of tin and would then be made of flesh. God solved this problem in the Incarnation when God became an actual human being, thereby becoming what all people were intended to be. He not only showed us what we could become; He made it possible for us to become sons and daughters of God by being killed and then rising again. If we open ourselves to the possibility of being transformed, then God will turn our biological life (*Bios*) into a spiritual life (*Zoe*) with that "good infection" mentioned in the previous chapter.

Chapter six, "Two Notes," answers two questions raised as a result of the previous chapter. The first question: If God wanted sons and daughters instead of toy soldiers, why didn't He just make lots of sons and daughters in the first place? After all, the process of becoming sons and daughters is so difficult and painful. The first answer to this question is that our turning away from God long ago made this becoming of sons and daughters into a difficult process. People could turn away because God made us with a free will. He made us with a free will because to do otherwise was to create robots instead of people capable of love and, therefore, of infinite happiness. The second answer to this question states that it is nonsensical to ask, when talking of God, if it could have been otherwise. We will never know, and the speculation does no good.

In response to the second question, which had to do with the value of the individual versus the value of the whole, Lewis argues both that we do belong to the whole human race and that individual differences do matter. Christianity wants individuals to share their uniqueness with others and complement them in the same way that the different bodily organs complement one another. That's one of the reasons for differences. These differences do not allow us to ignore someone else's problems because they aren't our business; in fact, they belong to the same organism, the human race. Therefore, we should avoid both errors—neither becoming an Individualist who ignores the human race nor becoming a Totalitarian who ignores individual differences.

In chapter seven, "Let's Pretend," Lewis opens with the story of a man who wore a mask to make himself look nicer than he really was. After many years of wearing the mask, the man took off the mask and discovered that his face had taken the shape of the mask and was now quite handsome. In the same way, living like a son of God is pretending, because we know at the time that we really aren't sons of God. So we dress up as Christ. Pretending can be either good or bad. It is bad if it is a sham or a pretence, designed to cover up the real thing; it is good if the pretence leads to the real thing and actually helps us to get there. The real Son of God is gradually turning us into real sons and daughters of God. He concludes the chapter with two points—what we are is more important than what we do, since our deeds flow from our character, and God is the one who actually does the pretending, since He is at work in us.

Chapter eight expresses its purpose by its title, "Is Christianity Hard or Easy?" The answer is "both." It is hard because Christ tells us to take up our cross, and it is easy because Christ says that His yoke is easy and his burden is light. The hard thing is that our natural self is constantly looking to have its own way, while God wants to kill that natural self and give us a brand new self.

Chapter nine, "Counting the Cost," builds on chapter eight by telling us that the only help that Christ wishes to give is help to enable us to become perfect. God is like the dentist who wants, not to ease the pain of a toothache, but to eliminate the problem. Lewis cites George MacDonald who wrote, "God is easy to please, but hard to satisfy."[58] God will be delighted with our first feeble steps, much like the parent is with the young child. But God will not stop there. Where we think that He wants to remodel us just a bit, God wants to do a great work in our lives and reshape us into palaces. And that hurts, but it's a good hurt.

In chapter ten, "Nice People or New Men," Lewis responds to the objection that all Christians should be obviously nicer than all non-Christians. Christianity makes people nicer, but you can't divide all people into two camps. Although most would disagree with Lewis, he argues that some are in the process of coming to Christianity, and others are leaving it. Furthermore, some people have niceness because of their upbringing or their innate God-given temperament. Consequently, some non-Christians will be nicer than some Christians. However, the Christian will be nicer than she would have been without Christianity, and the non-Christian will not be as nice as he could have been with Christianity. The real problem is that this entire discussion suggests that the essence of Christianity is niceness, or that Christianity is something that nasty people need and nice people do not. That's not true. The crucial thing is whether people will offer their natures to God. The crucifixion of Christ made that possible, but we can turn away from giving our natures to God. The paradox is that only those things that we give to God are the things that really belong to us.

Chapter eleven, "The New Men," concludes the book. God wants transformation rather than improvement. How does He accomplish that? Not through some evolutionary or gradual process, not through sexual reproduction, but through the good infection of the nature of Christ into us. This is voluntary, Lewis writes, not because we choose it but because we have the opportunity to refuse it. And it comes like a flash of lightning. New men and women are all over the world right now. When the One who is beyond personality takes over our lives, we become more truly ourselves. "Look for Christ and you will find Him, and with Him everything else thrown in."[59]

PUBLICATION AND REVIEWS

Before *Mere Christianity* was published, the individual BBC talks were published in separate volumes. The first two series of talks, "Right and Wrong: A Clue to the Meaning of the Universe" and "What Christians Believe," were published as *Broadcast Talks* (Bles, 1942),[60] the third as *Christian Behavior*

(Bles and Macmillan, 1943), and the fourth as *Beyond Personality* (1944 in the United Kingdom by Bles, 1945 in the United States by Macmillan).

Reviews appearing in 1942 demonstrate the general opinion of the listening, or reading, public to the first two series of talks. *The Tablet* wrote, "We have never read arguments better marshaled and handled so that they can be remembered, or any book more useful to the Christian . . . who finds himself called upon to argue briefly from first premises, to say why morality is not herd-instinct, why there is a special and unique character attached to the sense of obligation, why the conviction that there is a law of right and wrong and a transcendent morality is only intelligible if there is a God." *The Times Literary Supplement* said, "No writer of popular apologetics today is more effective than Mr. C. S. Lewis." *The Clergy Review* carried G. D. Smith's opinion: "The author shows himself a master in the rare art of conveying profound truths in simple and compelling language."[61]

When *Christian Behaviour* was published, reviewers were equally enthusiastic. Robert Speaight wrote for *The Tablet*, "Mr. Lewis is that rare being—a born broadcaster; born to the manner as well as to the matter. He neither buttonholes you nor bombards you; there is no false intimacy and no false eloquence. He approaches you directly, as a rational person only to be persuaded by reason. He is confident and yet humble in his possession and propagation of truth. He is helped by a speaking voice of great charm and a style of manifest sincerity." A reviewer for *The Guardian* wrote, "His learning is abundantly seasoned with common sense, his humor and his irony are always at the service of the most serious purposes, and his originality is the offspring of enthusiastically loyal orthodoxy."[62]

The reviewers of *Beyond Personality* were just as effusive as those who reviewed the previous publications of portions of *Mere Christianity*. A reviewer wrote for *The Times Literary Supplement*, "Mr. Lewis has a quite unique power of making theology an attractive, exciting and (one might almost say) an uproariously fascinating quest . . . Those who have inherited Christianity may write about it with truth and learning, but they can scarcely write with the *excitement* which men like . . . C. S. Lewis show, to whom the Christian faith is the unlooked-for discovery of the pearl of great price."[63]

CONCLUSION

Mere Christianity contains uncommon truth in common language. It is uncommon truth because of the power of Lewis's ideas, all of them reflecting biblical teaching, and it was common language because of the style in which Lewis wrote, his drawing upon universal human longing, and his use of analogy and the war in which Europe was at the time engaged. Few writers have the capability of presenting profound truth in exceedingly clear language, but Lewis is one of those. As Lewis wrote in his essay, "Christian Apologetics," "Our business is to present that which is timeless (the same yesterday, today, and tomorrow) in the particular language of our own age."[64] The timeless is uncommon truth, and the language of the age is common language.

APPENDIX

This table provides a quick overview of the original broadcast dates and themes Lewis performed that became the work known as *Mere Christianity*.

BBC Broadcast Title	Date	Chapter Title in *Mere Christianity*

Series 1: "Right and Wrong: A Clue to the Meaning of the Universe" (Wednesdays from 7:45 to 8:00 P.M., August 6 through September 6, 1941). This became Book 1 in *Mere Christianity*, and the chapter numbers are designated after the chapter titles.

Common Decency	August 6, 1941	The Law of Human Nature, chapter 1
Scientific Law and Moral Law	August 13, 1941	The Reality of the Law, chapter 3
Materialism or Religion	August 20, 1941	What Lies Behind the Law, chapter 4
What Can We Do about It?	August 27, 1941	We Have Cause to Be Uneasy, chapter 5
Answers to Listeners' Questions	September 6, 1941	Some Objections, chapter 2

Series 2: "What Christians Believe" (Sundays from 4:45 to 5:00 P.M., January 11 through February 15, 1942). This became Book 2 in *Mere Christianity*.

First Talk	January 11, 1942	The Rival Conceptions of God, chapter 1
Second Talk	January 18, 1942	The Invasion, chapter 2
Third Talk	February 1, 1942	The Shocking Alternative, chapter 3
Fourth Talk	February 8, 1942	The Perfect Penitent, chapter 4
Fifth Talk	February 15, 1942	The Practical Conclusion, chapter 5

Series 3: "Christian Behavior" (Sundays from 2:50 to 3:00 P.M., September 20 through November 8, 1942). This became Book 3 in *Mere Christianity*. Some of the chapters in *Mere Christianity* were never broadcast (chapters 2, 6, 9, and 10).

(*continued*)

BBC Broadcast Title	Date	Chapter Title in *Mere Christianity*
First Talk	September 20, 1942	The Three Parts of Morality, chapter 1
		The "Cardinal Virtues," chapter 2
Second Talk	September 27, 1942	Social Morality, chapter 3
Third Talk	October 4, 1942	Morality and Psychoanalysis, chapter 4
Fourth Talk	October 11, 1942	Sexual Morality, chapter 5
		Christian Marriage, chapter 6
Fifth Talk	October 18, 1942	Forgiveness, chapter 7
Sixth Talk	October 25, 1942	The Great Sin, chapter 8
		Charity, chapter 9
		Hope, chapter 10
Seventh Talk	November 1, 1942	Faith, chapter 11
Eighth Talk	November 8, 1942	Faith, chapter 12

Series 4: "Beyond Personality: The Christian View of God" (Tuesday evenings from 10:20 to 10:35 P.M., February 22 through March 30, 1944). This became Book 4 in *Mere Christianity*. Some of the chapters in *Mere Christianity* were never broadcast (chapters 3, 6, 9, and 10).

Making and Begetting	February 22, 1944	Making and Begetting, chapter 1
The Three-Personal God	February 29, 1944	The Three-Personal God, chapter 2
		Time and Beyond Time, chapter 3
Good Infection	March 7, 1944	Good Infection, chapter 4
The Obstinate Toy Soldiers	March 14, 1944	The Obstinate Toy Soldiers, chapter 5
		Two Notes, chapter 6
Let's Pretend	March 21, 1944	Let's Pretend, chapter 7
Is Christianity Hard or Easy?	March 28, 1944	Is Christianity Hard or Easy? chapter 8
		Counting the Cost, chapter 9
		Nice People or New Men, chapter 10
The New Man	April 4, 1944	The New Men, chapter 11

NOTES

1. C. S. Lewis, *Mere Christianity* (New York: HarperCollins 1980), viii.

2. Walter Hooper's comment in the Foreword to Justin Phillips, *C. S. Lewis at the BBC* (London: HarperCollins *Publishers*, 2002), vi.

3. See Baxter's *Church History of the Government of Bishops*, published in 1680. For more information, see N. H. Keeble, "C. S. Lewis, Richard Baxter, and 'Mere Christianity,'" in *Christianity and Literature* XXX(3) (Spring 1981), 27–44.

4. C. S. Lewis, "On the Reading of Old Books," 203.

5. Lewis, *Mere Christianity*, xv.

6. Ibid., xii.

7. Michael G. Maudlin, "1993 Christianity Today Book Awards," *Christianity Today* (April 5, 1993): 27f.

8. Mark Noll, "C. S. Lewis's 'Mere Christianity' (the Book and the Ideal) at the Start of the Twenty-first Century," *SEVEN, An Anglo-American Literary Review* 19 (2002): 35.

9. C. S. Lewis, *Collected Letters*, 2, 730.

10. Justin Phillips, *C. S. Lewis at the BBC*, 295.

11. C. S. Lewis, "Man or Rabbit?" 108–110, 112.

12. Lewis, *Mere Christianity*, 35.

13. Ibid., 38f.

14. Ibid., 39.

15. Ibid., 50.

16. Ibid., 192.

17. John Lawlor, *C. S. Lewis: Memories and Reflections*, Dallas, TX: Spence Publishing Company, 1998, 3.

18. Phillips, *C. S. Lewis at the BBC*, 15.

19. Ibid., 21.

20. Ibid., 6, 33.

21. Ibid., XI.

22. Ibid., 86.

23. Lewis, *Mere Christianity*, 32.

24. By my count Lewis uses the following words: battle (4x), invasion/invade (4x), force (20x), Allies (once), march (2x), Gestapo (2x), army (4x), blow to bits (3x), soldier (16x), war (80x), ration (21x), battle/battlefield (4x), enemy (22x), fight (16x), struggle (once), German/Germany (4x), Nazi (3x), infantry (once), sabotage (once), rebel/rebellion (9x), surrender (8x), arms (7x), conquest (2x), conquer (2x), Jews (7x), smuggle (2x), and military (once) for a total of 247 World War II references.

25. Lewis, *Collected Letters*, 2, 470.

26. Phillips, *C. S. Lewis at the BBC*, 88.

27. Ibid., 111f.

28. Ibid., 124.

29. Mr. R. S. Lee wrote to Lewis about this on October 3, 1944. Phillips, *C. S. Lewis at the BBC*, 262.

30. This request came to the BBC in London on June 16, 1948. Phillips, *C. S. Lewis at the BBC*, 272.

31. Lewis, *Collected Letters*, 2, 484f.

32. C. S. Lewis, *The Pilgrim's Regress*, 207.

33. Ibid., 155.

34. C. S. Lewis, "God in the Dock," 244.

35. C. S. Lewis, "Christian Apologetics," 95. See also "God in the Dock," 243.

36. C. S. Lewis, "Rejoinder to Dr Pittenger," 183.

37. C. S. Lewis, "Christian Apologetics," 98.

38. C. S. Lewis, "Sometimes Fairy Stories May Say Best What's to Be Said," 38.

39. George Sayer, *Jack: A Life of C. S. Lewis*, Wheaton, IL: Crossway Books, 1988, 318.

40. For more information on this topic, see my chapter, *"Praeparatio Evangelica,"* in *C. S. Lewis: Lightbearer in the Shadowlands*.

41. C. S. Lewis, "The Language of Religion," 136, 141.

42. Lewis, *Mere Christianity*, 187.

43. Ibid., 217.

44. First, Lewis suggested "The Art of Being Shocked," or "These Humans," then "Inside Information." Phillips, 85, 91.

45. A letter dated February 10. 1941, *Collected Letters*, 2, 470.

46. Lewis, *Mere Christianity*, 18.

47. Written on September 4, 1941. Phillips, *C. S. Lewis at the BBC*, 129.

48. Ibid., 141.

49. Ibid., 147.

50. Walter Hooper, *C. S. Lewis: A Companion & Guide*. New York: HarperCollins Publishers, 1996, 306f.

51. Phillips, *C. S. Lewis at the BBC*, 142.

52. Lewis, *Mere Christianity*, 37.

53. *The Socratic Digest*, 4, 103.

54. Elton Trueblood, *While It Is Day: An Autobiography*, New York: Harper & Row, 1974, 99.

55. Lewis, *Mere Christianity*, 134.

56. *Zoe* and *Bios* are Greek words for "life," with the former denoting a spiritual kind of life and the latter denoting biological life.

57. Lewis, *Mere Christianity*, 159.

58. Ibid., 203.

59. Ibid., 227.

60. Bles, 1942. Published by Macmillan in the United States as *The Case for Christianity* (1943).

61. Hooper, *C. S. Lewis: A Companion & Guide*, 327.

62. Ibid., 327.

63. Ibid., 328.

64. Lewis, "Christian Apologetics," 93.

BIBLIOGRAPHY

Heck, Joel D. *"Praeparatio Evangelica."* In *C. S. Lewis: Lightbearer in the Shadowlands*. Edited by Angus Menuge. Wheaton, IL: Crossway, 1997, 235–37.

Hooper, Walter. *C. S. Lewis: A Companion & Guide.* New York: HarperCollins Publishers, 1996, 303–328.

———. ed. *C. S. Lewis: Collected Letters, Volume 2. Books, Broadcasts, and War 1931–1949.* London: HarperCollins Publishers, 2004.

Lawlor, John. *C. S. Lewis: Memories and Reflections.* Dallas, TX: Spence Publishing Company, 1998.

Lewis, C. S. "Christian Apologetics." In *God in the Dock.* Grand Rapids, MI: Eerdmans, 1970, 89–103.

———. "God in the Dock." In *God in the Dock.* Grand Rapids, MI: Eerdmans, 1970, 240–44.

———. "The Language of Religion." In *Christian Reflections.* Grand Rapids, MI: Eerdmans, 1967, 129–141.

———. "Man or Rabbit?" In *God in the Dock.* Grand Rapids, MI: Eerdmans, 1970, 108–113.

———. *Mere Christianity.* New York: HarperCollins Publishers. Copyright 1980.

———. "On the Reading of Old Books." In *God in the Dock.* Grand Rapids, MI: Eerdmans, 1970, 200–207.

———. *The Pilgrim's Regress.* Grand Rapids, MI: Eerdmans, 1992.

———. "Rejoinder to Dr Pittenger." In *God in the Dock.* Grand Rapids, MI: Eerdmans, 1970, 177–83.

———. "Sometimes Fairy Stories May Say Best What's to Be Said." *Of Other Worlds: Essays and Stories.* New York: Harcourt Brace & Company, 1966, 35–38.

Maudlin, Michael G. "1993 Christianity Today Book Awards," *Christianity Today* 37(4) (April 5, 1993), 27f.

Noll, Mark. "C. S. Lewis's 'Mere Christianity' (the Book and the Ideal) at the Start of the Twenty-first Century." *SEVEN: An Anglo-American Literary Review* 19 (2002), 31–44.

Phillips, Justin. *C. S. Lewis at the BBC.* London: HarperCollins, 2002.

Sayer, George. *Jack: A Life of C. S. Lewis.* Wheaton, IL: Crossway Books, 1988.

———. *The Socratic Digest.* Oxford: Oxonian Press and Basil Blackwell, 1942–1952.

Trueblood, Elton. *While It Is Day: An Autobiography.* New York: Harper & Row, 1974.

4

The Sermons of C. S. Lewis: The Oxford Don as Preacher

Greg M. Anderson

"Where God gives the gift, the 'foolishness of preaching' (I Corinthians 1:21) is still mighty."

—C. S. Lewis[1]

Their outstanding qualities as sermons or addresses are more easily catalogued than imitated. The clear distinctions, careful arguments, pellucid clarity, fertility of illustrations, pithy epigrams, the deep wisdom and insight into the will of God and the nature of man, the candidness that is piercing, the presentation of central themes and abiding issues, as well as the loyal exposition of ageless and unpopular religious and moral truth, are some of the eminent characteristics.

—Horton Davies on Lewis's sermons[2]

Few preachers have their inaugural sermon printed in a book called *Famous British Sermons*.[3] During World War II, a reluctant preacher and a full-time Oxford don, C. S. Lewis, pushed preaching to the highest levels of artistic and aesthetic discourse. Ralph Turnbull, in *A History of Preaching*, noted that C. S. Lewis's occasional sermons "were given rapt attention" because he was a "devout layman whose intelligence matched his spirituality."[4] Lewis preached sermons that deserve a place in any study of great twentieth century preaching. James Como writes, "Lewis delivered only a handful of sermons, but they made history in their day."[5]

In his first broadcast talk, Lewis was careful to point out that "I am not preaching."[6] Horton Davies wrote that "Lewis is cast more congenially in the role of apologist than of preacher."[7] But Lewis's longtime friend Owen Barfield noted that Lewis took on different roles over his career as tutor, scholar, apologist, and fiction writer, and we might best understand Lewis by recognizing that there were actually three "Lewises," or possibly even five.[8] Lewis "the preacher" could be a contender for the sixth Lewis. Most of the attention to the genius of Lewis has been paid to his roles as a writer, a critic, and an apologist. Lewis was a polymath, but in the midst of everything else he did he was also a preacher. Any comprehensive treatment of Lewis needs to make room for his sermons.

Great preaching is rarely found. Seldom do sermons attract attention as great artistic expression. What was it about Lewis that made him such an exceptional preacher? To answer that question, we will look at the place of preaching in the life and work of Lewis and consider some of his key sermons. Most of his sermons were composed and delivered during what I call Lewis's "Fabulous Forties," from around 1939 to 1946. Only one sermon will be examined after this period, and we will notice how the feast of the Forties became a "Fifties Famine," as Lewis came to compose and deliver fewer new sermons.

LEWIS'S PREPARATION FOR PREACHING

Lewis developed his speaking and debating ability during his childhood years in school and especially under the exacting rigor of his private tutor William Thompson Kirkpatrick, whom Lewis famously called "The Great Knock." His tutorials at University College, Oxford, as well as membership in the "The Martlets," the literary society at Oxford, further developed his speaking skills. As his career unfolded as a don at Oxford, he was expected to deliver a yearly schedule of university lectures, which afforded him the opportunity to hone his public delivery techniques.

When his religious writings propelled him into the public eye, there were ample opportunities for Lewis to give Christian talks to public societies, Royal Air Force stations surrounding Oxford, and eventually on the BBC radio. It is clear that the lessons he learned by speaking to a university audience carried over into his preaching before public audiences. Charles Gilmore, the head of the RAF chaplain's school, recalls the first time Lewis spoke to a room of future chaplains:

At first, however, my worst fears looked as if they were being confirmed. To these men, probing life in the raw and trying to do something about it, [Lewis] chose to speak on "Linguistic Analysis and Pauline Soteriology." Worse, if you can imagine it, he seemed to be feeling for words. Clive Staples Lewis feeling for words! He hummed, and the ill-mannered coughed. A future bishop secretly got on with *The Times'* crossword. But Lewis knew his men. He suddenly said something about prostitutes and pawnbrokers being "Pardoned in Heaven, the first by the throne," and the rest of the morning was full of the clang of steel on steel and the laughter of good fellows, and answers that belonged to life.[9]

Though Lewis accepted invitations to speak as a Christian explaining the beliefs and practices of Christianity, he did not see himself as a preacher. A strong case can be made that Lewis considered preaching his war work. In the preface to his 1944 sermon "Transposition," he bemoaned the "too numerous addresses I was induced to give during the late war."[10] As almost all of his sermons were preached during World War II and its immediate aftermath, Erik Routely reminds us that "Lewis's main work was not preaching: he would do it if asked, but what he probably did more comfortably was more informal."[11] Comfortable or not, as the war began, Lewis began to receive more and more invitations to speak, and he did not turn them down.[12] His friend J. R. R. Tolkien thought Lewis took up wartime speaking as a sort of penance:

He took it up in a Pauline spirit, as a reparation; now the least of Christians (by special grace) but once an infidel, and even if [Lewis] had not persecuted the faithful, he would do what he could to convert men or stop them from straying away. The acceptance of the RAF mission, with its hardship of travel to distant and nasty places and audiences of anything but the kind he was humanly fitted to deal with, lonely, cheerless, embarrassed journeys leaving little behind but doubt whether any seed had fallen on good soil; all this was in its way an imitation of St. Paul.[13]

Lewis and Tolkien shared similar standards for what constituted a good sermon. Tolkien's idea was that "good sermons require some art, some virtue, some knowledge. Real sermons require some special grace which does not transcend art but arrives at it by instinct or 'inspiration'; indeed the Holy Spirit seems sometimes to speak through a human mouth providing art, virtue and insight he does not himself possess: but the occasions are rare."[14] Lewis's view, as expressed in *The Screwtape Letters*, was that in a successful sermon there was a partnership between divine revelation and human listening, which "lays itself open in uncommenting, humble receptivity to any nourishment . . . This attitude, especially during sermons, creates this condition . . . in which platitudes can become really audible to a human soul."[15] But like Tolkien, Lewis found that great preaching rarely happened. Through a humorous caricature of two preachers in *The Screwtape Letters*, we glimpse Lewis's lamentation on the dearth of adequate preaching in his day:

Vicar is a man who has been so long engaged in watering down the faith to make it easier for a supposedly incredulous and hard-headed congregation. . . . In order to spare the laity all "difficulties" he has deserted both the lectionary and the appointed psalms and now, without noticing it, revolves endlessly round the little treadmill of his fifteen favourite psalms and twenty favourite lessons. We are thus safe from the danger that any truth not already familiar to him and to his flock should ever reach them through Scripture.

At the other church we have Fr. Spike. The humans are often puzzled to understand the range of his opinions—why he is one day almost a Communist and the next not far from some kind of theocratic Fascism[16]

Lewis was a perceptive consumer and critic of sermons. When attending his parish church, Holy Trinity, in Headington, Lewis and his brother Warren listened to good and bad sermons. In 1939, when Warnie was away, Lewis would score the preaching of the curate from "a really excellent discourse" to "a sermon by Blanchett not all at his best."[17] Any preacher would dread hearing this description from "The Sermon and the Lunch":

as he spoke I noticed that all confidence in him had departed from every member of the congregation who was under thirty. They had been listening well up to this point. Now the shuffling and coughing began. Pews creaked; muscles relaxed. The sermon, for all practical purposes was over; the five minutes for which the preacher continued talking were a total waste of time—at least for most of us.[18]

We could say that Lewis had a traditional and high view of preaching and the role of the sermon, and that when communicating the faith, Lewis strove to have his sermons encompass both apologetics and preaching. Though Lewis was much more comfortable as a writer, broadcaster, debater, and as a religious lecturer, in effect he was an apologist for the Christian faith in a variety of media. James Como reminds us that "not all preaching is necessarily apologetic, of course, but all (Christian) apologetic has about it an aspect of preaching."[19] Lewis was an eloquent defender of the faith, but it may be that he saw himself as more of a "pre-preacher" or a "para-preacher," as one who offered intellectual and imaginative assistance to the preacher who could also get at his listener's emotions. While participating on a roster with some of the great preachers in England during a September, 1945, Tom Rees's "This Is the Victory" Crusade, which attracted three thousand people a night,[20] Lewis noticed in some sermons "an appeal of a much more emotional and also more 'pneumatic' kind has worked wonders on a modern audience. But best of all is a team of two: one to deliver the preliminary intellectual barrage, and the other to follow up with a direct attack on the heart."[21] Proclamation of Christianity requires both an appeal to the head and the heart, and it became clear to Lewis that his job was to provide the intellectual softening of the head that would work in tandem with a more spiritual and emotional appeal to the heart.

A PROPOSITIONAL AND PICTORIAL PREACHER

What is puzzling in Lewis's preaching is his lack of explicit biblical references. He was biblical in his theology but the biblical texts seldom made it into his sermons. If one is looking for biblical exegesis and exposition as the core content of competent preaching, Lewis fails the test. Horton Davies compares C. S. Lewis to the other great university preacher of his day, Bernard Word Manning: "Manning is convinced that the only right that he has to proclaim the Gospel is by submitting himself to the discipline of understanding, obeying, and expounding the Revelation of God in Holy Scripture. His sermons are all expository, whereas Lewis's are topical."[22] Lewis saw himself as the person speaking to those on the fringes of the faith. These occasions required propositional argumentation, rather than Scriptural proof-texts. However this argumentation has echoes and paraphrases of Scripture at every turn.

Lewis also saw the need for imaginative and ethical appeals to reach the will as well as the mind of his audience. Lewis is well known for his rational defense of the faith and also for his imaginative and creative works and his most rational works contain word pictures, analogies, and artistic use of language that complement what is rather standard or "mere" Christian orthodoxy. Lewis was able to combine the propositional and the pictorial in a way that few preachers have before or since. He did not discard rational and logical discourse and adopt the irrational and illogical world of super-subjectivity.

Jolyon Mitchell, a former BBC producer who now teaches homiletics at the University of Edinburgh, builds a case for "a discourse which engages the listener multi-sensorially." He develops the theological justification for such discourse around the "embodiment principle" and the "translation principle."[23] It is small surprise that he uses the radio addresses of C. S. Lewis as an illustration of visual, pictorial preaching. Mitchell is a representative of what has become known as the "New Homiletics," with its move away from rhetoric to poetics, and from persuasion to art. The shift from propositional and rational argument has been an emphasis on narrative and homiletical moves that create discourse, which pushes preaching beyond the proverbial "three points and a poem." The "New Homiletic" might be in response to a failure of nerve in preachers in postmodernity, or it might be an attempt to compete with a media-sated audience.

Lewis, however, would not find himself in comfortable company with the New Homilecticians. He believed in both proposition and picture, both rhetoric and poesis, both persuasion and story. It was what made him so distinctive. He combined reason, imagination, passion, ethics, and an uncanny sense of audience. A later examination of his sermons will demonstrate how this gifted part-time preacher used the "foolishness of preaching" with a mighty power.

SOME COMPLICATIONS WHEN CONSIDERING LEWIS'S SERMONS

This essay limits itself to the addresses Lewis preached in churches in the context of a worship service. Most of the sermons to be considered can be classified as apologetic in nature, but it will be helpful to bear in mind that Lewis was a genre-jumper when composing his sermons. Lewis roamed widely among a variety of verbal genres, from lecture, to debate, to sermon, to eulogy, and would sometimes mix the Aristotelian genres of deliberative, judicial, and ceremonial oratory all into one address. Bryan Hollon finds that "the literary category, 'Christian apology,' transcends the definition of apology found in [classical] rhetorical handbooks. A second-century Christian apology does not necessarily take the form of judicial defence. Rather, second-century Christian apologies . . . are united in their concern to justify and clarify Christian beliefs and practices in the midst of a culture that misunderstands them."[24] Historians of rhetoric and preaching find that the Christian sermon is derived from the Jewish Midrash and the Greek funeral oration. Chaim Perelman claimed, "the funeral sermon of the Greeks was transformed by Christianity into a means of edification."[25] The sermon is a blended or hybrid genre from the start and Lewis further blurred rhetorical and homiletical distinctions in his practice. As a twentieth-century apologist, Lewis found himself using all three classical genres as he defended the faith. He asked people to make decisions and choices and raised ceremonial appeals to a new level in sermons such as "The Weight of Glory." Like his early Christian forbears, he sought "to justify and clarify Christian beliefs and practices in the midst of a culture that misunderstands them."

No one seems to know how often Lewis preached. Even with the paper trail Lewis left behind, it is difficult to find out the exact number of times he preached. Douglas Gresham, when asked how often his stepfather gave a sermon, responded, "Lots."[26] Personal accounts of the frequency and locales for Lewis's preaching differ. Fred Paxton, Lewis's handyman and chauffeur, claimed that when Lewis "preached at Quarry Church, it was always packed."[27] However, the church administrator at St. Mary's, the Quarry Church, did not think that Lewis had ever preached there. The rector thought that he might have but the parish record had been turned over to the county and could not be inspected.

In his diary, dated March 31, 1946, Warren Lewis wrote, "To Evensong in our own Church, where [Lewis] preached an excellent sermon, illuminating for me an old difficulty of my own. He began by speaking of the doubts which some of us feel about the wording of the *Book of Common Prayer*."[28] Lewis's brother's account confirms that he preached there and tells something about what Lewis spoke about.[29] A little more detective work determines that Lewis addressed this same concern the next Sunday. On April 7, 1946, he preached "Miserable Offenders" at St. Matthew's Church, Northampton, and it was later published in a booklet, *Five Sermons for Laymen*.[30]

A cryptic comment Lewis made in a letter to Alec Vidler dated August 17, 1941, shows that Lewis himself was not in full command of his speaking schedule:

Dear Vidler,

I preached two sermons in St. Mary's and can't remember which was on which date. If the one you've got is on Rev. ii 26–28 beginning 'If you asked twenty good men' I shd. be glad for it to be printed in Theology. *The Weight of Glory* was the title. If on t'other hand it is a sermon on Faith beginning 'We are all quite familiar', then I fear it already bespoke.[31]

Lewis himself could not reconstruct his preaching so soon after the event, and it has remained just as difficult to do so some sixty years later. "The Weight of Glory" is Lewis's most famous sermon, but what about the "bespoken" sermon on faith? We have the text to the sermon "Religion: Reality or Substitute," but we don't know where it was it preached.[32] The leading candidate would be at St. Mary's church, yet there is no record of Lewis ever preaching at the university church, since the Register of Service book from St. Mary's from 1938–1944 is missing.[33]

Lewis preached at least four times at his parish church but we have no manuscript for his March 29, 1942 sermon "Religion and _____" or even a title to his February 18, 1945 sermon.[34] There is a possibility that "Religion: Reality or Substitute" was the later title for "Religion and _____" preached first at St. Mary's and then later at his parish church. As there is no exhaustive list of his sermons, we will restrain ourselves from further pining for Lewis's lost preaching.

LEWIS'S FORTIES PREACHING FEAST

Though we are not able to reconstruct Lewis's sermon manuscripts, many of them were transformed into essays. On at least two occasions, and much later in life, Lewis added more material to the essays than was in the sermons. As we look into the biographical context of his life, we find that he was working on many writing projects at the time he was preaching. In effect, Lewis used sermons as trial balloons. The most obvious one is the sermon "Miracles," which was ultimately transformed into a book by that same title.

It is clear that ideas from his sermons were to find more permanent expression in his later writings. In the preface to *Transposition*, he understates, but at least states, the case: "In one or two places they seem to repeat, though they really anticipated, sentences of mine which have already appeared in print."[35]

What follows are discussions of some of Lewis's sermons. For each sermon, indicated by its title and the date on which Lewis delivered it, I will provide some context for the work and then consider the text of the sermon itself, followed by a brief discussion of its reception.

Learning in Wartime, December 22, 1939

Context

Lewis's inaugural sermon was preached at St. Mary's the Virgin in Oxford on October 22, 1939.[36] The vicar of St. Mary's, the Reverend Theodore Milford, had read Lewis's *The Pilgrim's Regress* and was impressed. Because of the uncertainty facing Oxford undergraduates during the war, Milford capitalized on the facts that Lewis was an Oxford don who had fought in World War I. Milford arranged for everyone present to have a mimeographed copy of the sermon bearing the title "None Other Gods: Culture in War-Time."[37] Erik Routley was present at the service and gives this account:

But on the second Sunday of the first term of the war, in October, 1939, I saw that he was billed to preach in the University Church. It was odd enough in those days to have a preacher who wasn't a clergyman of the Church of England, and I thought I would go along. The service was to begin at 8:00 P.M., and I supposed I arrived at about ten minutes before eight. There was hardly a seat to be had. The one I got was right under the pulpit. I could see the preacher only when he was going up the steps. And I said to myself, "So *that's* Lewis!" The church was dim. Only minimal lighting was allowed. Most of us had to sing the hymns from memory. But Lewis gave us the sermon called "Learning in Wartime," which was, I suppose, his debut as a preacher. "A Syrian ready to perish was my father," from Deuteronomy 26, was his text.[38]

Routley is right, as far as existing evidence indicates, that this sermon was Lewis's debut as a preacher. Several weeks before he preached the sermon, Lewis revealed in a letter to his brother his determination to continue as a scholar, even though he lost his university lectureship because of the war. He claimed to have found "the perfect summing up of [his] personal war aims" in an Anglo-Saxon chronicle: "During all this evil time Abbot Martin retained his abbacy."[39]

Text

The goal of the sermon was to encourage the young scholars of Oxford to continue their studies despite the war, and at the same time to use the war to put larger spiritual issues in focus. The critical question he posed was: "What is the use of beginning a task which we have so little chance of finishing?"[40] Lewis continues to ask how scholars can continue their "placid occupations when the lives of our friends and the liberty of Europe are in the balance. Is it not like fiddling while Rome burns?"[41] Horton Davies, in the best commentary on this sermon, finds it "jeweled with witty epigrams."[42] His example is Lewis's turning the table on Nero: "But to a Christian the true tragedy of Nero must be not that he fiddled while the city was on fire but that he fiddled on the brink of hell."[43]

Lewis claims that the heaven or hell question puts the war in a proper puny perspective. "The war creates no absolutely new situation: it simply aggravates the permanent human situation so that we can no longer ignore it. Human life has always been lived at the edge of a precipice. Human culture has always had to exist in the shadow of something infinitely more important than itself."[44] He claims that "life has never been normal" and gives historical examples of good work done in extreme situations: "They propound mathematical theorems in beleaguered cities, conduct metaphysical arguments in condemned cells, make jokes on scaffold, discuss the last new poem while advancing to the walls of Quebec."[45]

He made a case for culture, even in times of crisis, but only in the sense of Christian vocation. "The work of Beethoven, and the work of a charwoman, become spiritual on precisely the same condition, that of being offered to God, of being done humbly 'as to the Lord.' "[46] He went on to admit "we are all members of one body, but differentiated members, each with his own. A man's upbringing, his talents, his circumstances, is usually a tolerable index of his vocation." He then pointed out that since his listener's parents had sent them to Oxford, and the country had allowed them to stay, "the life which we, at any rate, can best lead to the glory of God at present is the learned life."[47]

After making a case for the learned life, Lewis listed three distractions that could keep the scholar from fulfilling his vocation: excitement, frustration, and fear. He ends by noting that the war has shattered false ideas about human culture and that "the life of learning, humbly offered to God, was, in its own small way, one of the appointed approaches to the Divine reality and the Divine beauty which we hope to enjoy hereafter."[48]

Reception

Ashley Sampson, one of Lewis's publishers, remarked that Lewis "put out a feeler for that light which is all that we can see as yet of the world that is ahead of us" in this sermon "preached at a dramatic moment in the world's history."[49] The sermon was a paean to Christian vocation in general and scholarship in particular. Several years after Lewis gave the sermon, Sampson remarked:

There can be no doubt that Dr. Lewis is a phenomenon. His "arrival" among intellectual starts at a moment when Europe had plunged into a Second World War was rather like a fairy-tale ... Our hopes had been changed to bitterness and men were asking themselves what God was doing when C. S. Lewis (a lay don of literary reputation who had once been a rather cynical atheist) preached a sermon in the University Church that set all Oxford, and later all England, talking.[50]

The sermon's original title was changed to "Christians in Danger" and first published as a pamphlet by the Student Christian Movement in 1939, and was included in anthology entitled *Great English Sermons.* In a February 18, 1940, letter to his brother, the new preacher's pride and wit are both at work:

Did I tell you that someone wants to include that St. Mary's sermon of mine in a collection of (save the mark) *Famous Sermons?* I am divided between gratification and a fear that I shall be merely made a fool of by appearing in the same book as Bede, Latimer, Donne, Taylor, etc. However, I hope that I shall be divided from them by some good 19th century duds![51]

Sampson was in no small measure responsible for getting the word out. He was Lewis's publisher of *The Problem of Pain* and he would include the sermon in a sermon anthology. The sermon was first a mimeographed sheet, then a SCM pamphlet, and with a few changes,[52] a chapter in a book. Lewis included it, in his *Transposition and Other Addresses* and it has been reprinted in a variety of collections ever since.

The Weight of Glory, June 8, 1941

Context

On Sunday, June 8, 1941, Lewis made his second foray as a preacher at St. Mary's[53]; the result was a sermonic masterpiece, based on 2 Corinthians 4:17. He mounted the pulpit where John Wesley started the Methodist movement and Newman the Tractarian. "The Weight of Glory," was preached at an evensong at the Oxford University church, St. Mary the Virgin to "one of the largest crowds assembled there in modern times."[54]

Lewis never learned to drive, so his handyman Fred Paxton drove him to the church and managed to find a place to park and to sit. Paxton recounted the sermon to Walter Hooper, "Gor Blimey! Mr. Jack didn't give half of it to em."[55] Rosamund Rieu Cowen wrote: "I was in St Mary's the night he gave his address on 'The Weight of Glory.' It was marvelous. But you see when I was a young student at Oxford although I knew he was a remarkable man of exceptional mind, I didn't realize his greatness."[56]

Also in the throng of students was again, Erik Routley, who was preparing for ministry at the Congregational theological college, Mansfield. He remembered:

I think the next time he preached was in June, 1941, and the sermon was entitled "Weight of Glory." This time it was a summer evening. Lighting was no problem. But the place was packed solid long before the service began. The last hymn was "Bright the Vision that Delighted." The sermon took three-quarters of an hour to deliver. Just to read it now is to be captivated by its uncanny combination of sheer beauty and severe doctrine. Here, you will feel when reading, and you felt it ten times more when listening, was a man who had been laid hold of by Christ and enjoyed it.

Lewis had a superbly unaffected delivery: a deep voice which went well with his cheerful and bucolic appearance (all pictures of him that I know are good ones). It was a voice that really did vindicate the saying that the medium is the message. No rhetorical tricks: he read every word. Yet the way he used words as precision tools, the effortless rhythm of the sentences, the scholarship made friendly, the sternness made beautiful— these things all made it impossible for the listener to notice the passing of time.

In this sermon there was a stunning blend of the three skills that made Lewis such an able Christian communicator. It was a precursor to all his later work. The romantic strains in his *Chronicles of Narnia*, the reasoned argument of *Mere Christianity*, and his relational concern that would later be evidenced in his letters, were to coalesce and whistle through the pages of the sermon he preached that evening. Here on display was the rational defender of the faith, an imaginative and romantic streak, and the emotional burden for his fellow human beings, which he felt especially strongly during wartime and which compelled him to speak.

Text

Lewis began the sermon with his "turning the tables" rhetorical trick. He knew his audience saw Christianity negatively rather than positively. Hence "self-denial" rather than "love" was posited as the highest Christian virtue. After putting self-denial in its proper subordinate place, Lewis made an astounding claim:

It would seem that our Lord finds our desires, not too strong, but too weak. We are half-hearted creatures, fooling about with drink and sex and ambition when infinite joy is offered to us, like an ignorant child who wants to keep on making mud pies in a slum because he cannot imagine what is meant by a holiday at the sea. We are far too easily pleased.[57]

One can almost imagine the Oxford undergraduates wondering where he was going with this line. He continued by describing Christian reward and desire by the analogy of a general and a schoolboy.

He talked of a "transtemporal, tranfinite good" as our "real destiny," a "desire for our own far-off country" that we call "Nostalgia and Romanticism and Adolescence." He claims we try to label this desire "beauty" and attacks "any rhetoric that comes to hand to keep out of your mind" that elusive and eternal desire that he labels *Sehnsucht* or better yet, "surprised by joy."[58]

Peter Kreeft writes, "There are three places in C. S. Lewis's work where the argument from desire is stated at length, though *Sehnsucht* itself seeps out from many pages in Lewis, most perfectly in "The Weight of Glory.""[59] Kreeft has cleverly labeled the romantic rhetorical device that Lewis used to introduce his sermon as the "argument from desire." The argument has a history running from St. Augustine to Blaise, from Pascal to Lewis, and on to Jacques Derrida.[60] A "proof" that focuses on desire rather than design is an effective theological and rhetorical move. Lewis the theorist claimed that "[rhetoric] works to produce in our minds some practical resolve" and "it does so by calling the passions to the aid of reason."[61] In so doing he hearkens back to Aristotle's concept of *pathos*. The result is that he has unleashed a romantic longing that needs some sort of object.

Lewis concludes the first major section of the sermon with a claim, "We remain conscious of a desire which no natural happiness can satisfy."[62] In the middle of the sermon Lewis makes his case. He summed up the biblical answer in five points: "It is promised, firstly, that we shall be with Christ; secondly, that we shall be like Him; thirdly, with an enormous wealth of imagery, that we shall have 'glory'; fourthly, that we shall, in some sense, be fed or feasted or entertained; and, finally, that we shall have some sort of official position in the universe."[63] After a discussion of symbols, he turned to his explication of the notion of "glory," which can mean being noticed, not being pitied by God, and "glory as brightness, splendour, luminosity."[64] He then brings the longing of the first part of his sermon to fulfillment: "Our lifelong nostalgia, our longing to be reunited with something in the universe . . . the healing of that old ache" is realized in the God who was in Christ. Lewis states that it is not reason but rather revelation that ultimately leads one to God. He put it in a more poetic way than would a more prosaic preacher: "But all the leaves of the New Testament are rustling with the rumor that it will not always be so."[65]

On a deeper level, Lewis was recognized as an authority able to speak for God, yet he chose not to highlight his own status but rather developed an *ethos* based on the *pathos* of desire and the *logos* of its Scriptural fulfillment. He gently reminded his listeners, "Meanwhile, the cross comes before the crown and tomorrow is Monday morning."[66] His extended discussion of glory ended with the corrective:

It may be possible for each to think too much of his own potential glory hereafter; it is hardly possible for him to think too often or too deeply about that of his neighbour. The load, or weight, or burden of my neighbour's glory should be laid daily on my back, a load so heavy that only humility can carry it . . .[67]

He goes on to warn that in this society of people on the way to becoming a glorious or horrendous eternal being, "we are . . . helping each other to one of these destinations."[68]

In what is one of the most quoted passages in the sermon if not in all his writing, he preached:

The load, or weight, or burden of my neighbour's glory should be laid daily on my back, a load so heavy that only humility can carry it . . . It is a serious thing to live in a society of possible gods and goddesses, to remember that the dullest and most uninteresting person you talk to may one day be a creature which, if you saw it now, you would be strongly tempted to worship, or else a horror and a corruption such as you now meet, if at all, only in a nightmare. All day long we are, in some degree, helping each other to one or other of these destinations. It is in the light of these overwhelming possibilities, it is with the awe and the circumspection proper to them, that we should conduct all our dealings with one another, all friendships, all loves, all play, all politics. There are no ordinary people. You have never talked to a mere mortal.[69]

Lewis had a very transcendent ethical urge. Culture, society, and other constructions of modernity were less important to Lewis than character and ultimate destination. As Wesley Kort reminds us, Lewis stated his basis for his choice between culture and character clearly in a famous sermon, "The Weight of Glory." Culture, even in the form of its most magnificent monuments . . . is of secondary importance when compared to the nature and destiny of persons.[70]

Lewis ends with the famous claim that there are "no ordinary people," no "mere mortals":

Next to the Blessed Sacrament itself, your neighbour is the holiest object presented to your senses. If he is your Christian neighbour he is holy in almost the same way, for in him also Christ *vere latitat*—the glorifier and the glorified, Glory Himself, is truly hidden.[71]

Homiletical historian David Larsen speaks for all who have studied the sermon: "The sermon is biblical, theologically sound and aptly and personally applied."[72]

Theologian J. I. Packer describes Lewis this way: "he was a Christian communicator without peer on three themes; the reasonableness of and humanity of the Christian faith; the moral demands of discipleship; and heaven as *home*, the place of all value and contentment."[73] All three of the themes: reason, moral demand, and heaven as home are present in this sermon, in perhaps their most poignant and profound expression.

Reception

Alan Jacobs judges that "The Weight of Glory" is Lewis's "greatest sermon."[74] Peter Kreeft goes even further when he claims that "The Weight of Glory" is "the best sermon I have ever read."[75] Walter Hooper writes, " 'The Weight of Glory' is so magnificent that not only do I dare to consider it worthy a place with some of the Church Fathers, but I fear I should be hanged by Lewis's admirers if it were not given primacy of place."[76] The sermon and the essay it became provide the best single example of how Lewis blended his rational, romantic, and relational case for Christ. Passages from this sermon have been included in other people's sermons ever since. Most of us in the preaching profession read this, compare it to our efforts, and realize, to borrow from Lewis, "We are far too easily pleased."

Lewis's autobiography, *Surprised by Joy*, would take up the theme and demonstrate how crucial the search for joy or longing was to all that Lewis was and wrote. Yet this sermon summed up the ache and beauty of life as well as it could be said. At the graveside funeral of theatrical genius Kenneth Tynan, a former student of Lewis, words from this sermon were read by his daughter. Alan Jacobs uses the same words to close his biography of Lewis:

The books or the music in which we thought the beauty was located will betray us if we trust to them; it was not *in* them, it only came *through* them, and what came through them was longing. These things—the beauty, the memory of our own past—are good images of what we really desire; but if they are mistaken for the thing itself, they turn into dumb idols, breaking the hearts of their worshippers. For they are not the thing itself; they are only the scent of a flower we have not found, the echo of a tune we have not heard, news from a country we have not yet visited.[77]

Religion . . . , March 29, 1942

Context

Lewis was invited to preach at the Evensong service at the Quarry Church by its vicar, T. E. Bleiben. This was the first of four Lenten services that he was to preach to his home congregation. A notation in the Register of Services states that it was a "National Day of Prayer." This is the first time that Lewis is recorded as preaching at the Quarry Church. The register is signed by Lewis and he, in almost illegible penmanship in a tiny space, wrote the title of the sermon as "Religion . . ." There must have been great excitement that evening. Fred Paxford, caretaker of the Kilns and possible model for the character of Puddleglum in *The Silver Chair*, remembered: "When he preached at Quarry Church, it was always packed. He had a full clear voice which could be heard all over the church; and he nearly always brought a bit of humor into the sermon; and people seemed to like this."[78]

Besides the intrinsic value Lewis brought to his home congregation, the extrinsic factors, such as his reputation as the author of *The Screwtape Letters*, published a mere month before,[79] *Out of the Silent Planet*, and most of all the as man in the midst of the broadcast talks that captivated the nation, must have made the atmosphere electric.

Text

There are not too many extant essays with "religion" in the title. "Religion: Reality or Substitute?" is a possible candidate. There is no way Lewis could have fit that title into the allotted slot in the service book. Perhaps he used a different—and shorter title—out of necessity. This essay reads like a sermon, and was later expanded, as was "Transposition" and also "Miracles." It has the hallmarks of a sermon on that has been transformed into an essay.

The key concept, that experience can fool us into thinking the spiritual is the substitute, rather than the reality, has some vivid illustrations. He used the wartime substitution of margarine for butter and his childhood preference for a gramophone rather than a real orchestra. He used an example from Milton, which is interesting, since Lewis was turning the University College of North Wales Mathews Lectures into the book *A Preface to Paradise Lost* within the time period of the mystery sermon. Until more evidence is unearthed, "Religion: Reality or Substitute" is the most likely full title.

Miracles, September 27, 1942

Context

St. Jude's-on-the- Hill sits in the center of Hampstead Garden Suburb, an imposing church designed by the great architect, Sir Edwin Lutyens. For their 1942 third series of "Voice of the Laity," the committee invited John G. Winant, the American Ambassador to the Court of St. James, who turned them down for health reasons. Undeterred, they asked Hugh Lyon, the headmaster of Rugby, C. S. Lewis, who was to speak on September 27, and E. Leitberger from the Polish Embassy. Friedrich Hertz, a refugee economist substituted for the American ambassador, and the whole series culminated with the visit of the Archbishop of Canterbury, William Temple, on October 18, 1942. The talks were given during the Evensong conducted by the Vicar, W. H. Maxwell Ronnie.

The parish magazine introduced Lewis as:

One of the most brilliant and provocative lay voices in the Church today. His recent book, *The Problem of Pain*, is still a best-seller and was one of the most widely-discussed books of recent years. The *Spectator* described it as "a really remarkable book." Since then he has written *The Screwtape Letters*, which has gone through many editions . . . Mr. Lewis broadcasts frequently and has been a guest of the Brains Trust. His subject of "Miracles" offers opportunities for an unusually notable address.[80]

Lewis came to the service after his stop at BBC Broadcasting House where he gave his afternoon live broadcast, "Social Morality." The service was crowded and the largest offering of the series, save for the Archbishop's visit, was taken.

Text

The sermon started with one of his most effective audience-captivating introductions: "I have known only one person in my life who claimed to have seen a ghost." He followed that up with a reversal of a truism, "Seeing is not believing. This is the first thing we must get clear in talking about miracles."[81] He then used reasoning and more biblical citations than in any of his other sermons, to make the case that "experience by itself proves nothing." He posited that there are two conditions necessary; belief in the normal stability of nature and that there is some reality beyond nature. He found that most moderns dislike the idea of the miraculous and they confuse "the laws of nature and the laws of thought." He turned to George Macdonald and to Athanasius to make the case that miracles "do small and quick what we have already seen in the large letters of God's universal activity."[82] He labeled that the first class of miracle and went on to a second class of miracles that "foretell what God has not yet done, but will do, universally."[83]

At this juncture, he admitted, "My time is nearly up and I must be very brief with the second class of people . . . those who mistake the laws of nature for the laws of thought."[84] He did not develop the argument fully but showed how both nature and thought seek to explain through use of sign and symbol to recall us back to reality.

He ended on a sacramental note, declaring: "Common bread, miraculous bread, sacramental bread—these are distinct but not separated. Divine reality is like a fugue. All his acts are different, but they all rhyme or echo to one another."[85] "This vast symphonic splendour" reminded him of Julian or Norwich's vision of Christ holding a small hazelnut. His last sentence made the most of this enigma: "And it seemed to her so small and weak that she wondered how it could hold together at all."[86] Likewise, Lewis tried to hold difficult theological and philosophical abstractions together in this sermon.

Reception

A letter written by an unbelieving listener gave Lewis some valuable feedback: "I knew beforehand that I should be much moved by your address tonight, and I knew from experience that I should sit entranced, but I never dreamed that I should approach so remotely near to believing in the subject of your talk." She went on to criticize that the sermon was dependent on "the tacit agreement of the main structure of the Christian faith" and asked. if his "arguments could in any way apply or be of value if they did not assume Christianity." She decided that they were of "true value to those who already believe."[87]

Rosamund Rieu's letter is invaluable on many fronts. As earlier noted, it helped establish when and where the sermon was preached. It demonstrates the sway Lewis had over the audience. And it raises the thorny issue of whether Lewis was an apologist for the unbeliever or simply an intellectual exhibit that believers could hold up as proof that smart people can believe in God.

Lewis responded to the letter with a clarity that wasn't always present in the sermon itself:

Dear Miss Rieu,
Speaking in a Church, I assumed:
1. Belief in the divinity of Jesus.
2. Belief in the general historicity of the New Testament and hence,
3. That if *any* miracles *could* be true, these ones would be. My argument only attempted to prove that the existence of supernatural was certain and its irruption into the Natural Order not improbable.[88]

The sermon, along with an adapted article, demonstrates that Lewis was pondering the subject of miracles. Biographers Hooper and Green make a good case that Dorothy L. Sayers provoked him into writing a full-length book on the subject. In a letter to Lewis of May 13, 1943, she complained that "there are not any up-to-date books on miracles."[89] He replied to her on May 17 to say he was writing a book and included a copy of the St. Jude's sermon.[90]

Lewis's sermon serves as a précis of his booklength treatment of the subject of miracles. It is hard to establish an exact source for the book or a trail of influence, but it is clear that Lewis used this sermon as a trial rhetorical run as he examined the nature of miracles and their defense before a skeptical world.

Forgiveness, April 1, 1943

Context

On April 1, 1943, Lewis preached his second annual Lenten Evensong sermon. The "Register of Services" noted that it was the fourth Sunday in Lent, and included Lewis's signature and the title, "Forgiveness."

Text

Walter Hooper writes in the "Preface" to *Fern-Seed and Elephants*: "[the] manuscript of "On Forgiveness" came to light while this book was in preparation. The essay was written in 1947 and has never been published anywhere before."[91] One possibility is that it was actually written in 1942 and it was the sermon Lewis preached at the Quarry Church in 1942. The other possibility is that the sermon preached on forgiveness was an early draft of the broadcast talk titled "Forgiveness," which Lewis gave on October 18, 1942, which later became chapter seven in Book III of *Mere Christianity*. In either case, we have a key example how Lewis used preaching to work out ideas that would later appear in print. We have a sermon before it was transformed into something else. In his preface to *Transposition*, Lewis disingenuously claimed: "All were composed in response to personal requests and for a particular audience, without thought of subsequent publication." Even if he didn't realize it, he was working out key ideas that would later find fuller and more permanent expression. Lewis continued in the preface, "As a result, in one or two places they seem to repeat, though they really anticipated, sentences of mine which have subsequently appeared in print."[92]

Lewis builds the sermon around a phrase in the Apostles' Creed and implicitly on the words Jesus used in the Lord's Prayer in Matthew 6:12. Lewis claimed that "we often make a mistake both about God's forgiveness of our sins and about the forgiveness we are told to offer to other people's sins."[93] We have a mistaken concept of God's forgiveness that we want God "not to forgive" but "to excuse."[94] He found that most people are too satisfied with excuses. The remedy to this misconception is to first realize that God knows all the excuses and then to "really and truly believe in the forgiveness of sins," from God's perspective rather than ours.[95]

Lewis then turns to the question of forgiving other people. He again reminded his listeners that forgiving is not excusing. He contrasted the willingness to believe one's own excuses and the unwillingness to believe the excuses of others by beginning his conclusion with a poignant observation: "To be a Christian means to forgive the inexcusable, because God has forgiven the inexcusable in you. This is hard." He claimed it was "not so hard to forgive a single great injury. But to forgive the incessant provocations of daily life," and here he mentioned "the bossy mother-in-law, the bullying husband, the nagging wife." He then closed: " 'Forgive our trespasses as we forgive those who trespass against us.' We are offered forgiveness on no other terms. To refuse it is to refuse God's mercy for ourselves. There is no hint of exceptions and God means what he says."[96]

Reception

There is not enough evidence to trace the sources and influence of this sermon. But his published works and private letters demonstrate his preoccupation with helping people who too facilely say "forgiveness is a lovely idea, until they have something to forgive."[97]

Unknown Sermon at Mansfield College, February 1944

Lewis's reputation as a preacher led "Peterborough" in *The Daily Telegraph* of February 26, 1944, to call him "Modern Oxford's Newman":

Ascetic Mr. C. S. Lewis, Magdalen's English Literature tutor and author of *The Screwtape Letters,* is becoming ever more of a power in Oxford. Though a layman, he often occupies one or other of the pulpits in the University. An elderly Oxford don remarked to me the other day that there had been no preacher with Mr. Lewis's influence since Newman. He more than fills the University church of St. Mary's. Preaching on a recent Sunday in Mansfield College, to a congregation in which there were many senior members of the University, including the Warden of All Souls, he made a deep impression.[98]

The fact that the Anglican layperson Lewis attracted so many of the Oxford worthies to a Congregational college upset some Anglican chaplains who resented the reduced attendance at their own services. They were not the only ones upset. J. R. R. Tolkien complained about the column in a letter to his son Christopher, dated March 1, 1944:

Lewis is as energetic and jolly as ever, but getting too much publicity for his or any of our tastes. "Peterborough," usually fairly reasonable, did him the doubtful honour of a peculiarly misrepresentative and asinine paragraph in the *Daily Telegraph* of Tuesday last. It began "Ascetic Mr. Lewis"—! I ask you! He put away three pints in a very short session we had this morning, and said he was "going short for Lent."[99]

It seems that Lewis cut down on ale and added preaching to his Lenten discipline. Most of his sermons were preached during Lent. This may be a coincidence, although it adds more proof to Tolkien's penitential preaching theory discussed earlier in this essay.

Transposition, May 28, 1944

Context

Nathaniel Micklem, the principal of Mansfield College, Oxford, wrote in his biography, "I can think of four preachers who in their day could be relied upon to 'fill the chapel'; Russell Maltby, T. R. Glover, C. S. Lewis, and George Macleod."[100] Micklem invited Lewis back for a second sermon, this time on the Feast of Pentecost, May 28, 1944. This sermon, called "Transposition," is important as the explication of his view of communication. It is also an important sermon because it was the one that Lewis almost didn't finish. *The Daily Telegraph* of June 2, 1944, reported in an article titled, "Modern Oxford's Newman" that "in the middle of the sermon Mr. Lewis, under stress of emotion, stopped, saying 'I'm sorry,' and left the pulpit." After assistance from Nathaniel Micklem and a hymn, he was able to conclude the sermon "on a deeply moving note."[101]

Text

Lewis preaching on Pentecost introduced his sermon with a discussion of speaking in tongues. He used the story of Pentecost to frame the central question of apologetic, "Our problem is that the obvious continuity between things which are admittedly natural and things which, it is claimed, are spiritual."[102] How does the preacher convey God's glory and message to the natural world that cannot comprehend the supernatural? The "reasoning from below" model didn't work for Lewis. What one person might think as emotion, another might think as a chemical reaction to something she ate. He stressed "revelation from above." That revelation needs to be translated, or to borrow a term from music, "transposed." There is no one-to-one correspondence between the supernatural and the natural. Lewis continued, "We are all quite familiar with this kind of transposition or adaptation from a richer to a poorer medium. The most familiar example of all is the art of drawing. The problem here is to represent a three-dimensional world on a flat sheet of paper."[103] He proceeded to develop this "Transposition from above" to dispel notions of "mere natural" answers to spiritual questions: "At the worst, we know enough of the spiritual to know that we have fallen short of it."[104]

At that moment he said, "I'm sorry," and he disappeared from the pulpit. After a brief respite, he regained his composure and finished the sermon.

He concluded with four points:

1. Transposition is not development.
2. Transposition helps with the doctrine of the incarnation.
3. Don't see all facts and miss the meaning—a "nothing but" fallacy.
4. Transposition throws new light on the resurrection.

Reception

Lewis seems to not have been satisfied with this sermon as it was when he delivered it. He apparently did nothing with it for several years. Walter Hooper writes:

My guess is that at sometime, but not necessarily in 1944, he may have felt that he had not succeeded as well as he might have with "Transposition." Though he was quite ill during the spring of 1961 when Jock Gibb, his publisher at Geoffrey Bles, was pressing him to edit a volume of his essays, something wonderful happened. With a simplicity that is perhaps an instance of Heaven coming to its own rescue, Lewis was shown what glories are involved by the corruptible putting on the incorruptible, and there came from his pen an additional portion that raises that sermon to an eminence all its own. This new portion begins on p. 68 with the paragraph "I believe that this doctrine of Transposition provides . . ." and concludes on p. 69 with the paragraph ending, "They are too transitory, too phantasmal." This extended version of the sermon first appeared in Lewis's *They Asked for a Paper* (London, 1962).[105]

When a fan of Lewis's named Rhonda Bodle wrote with a question about the incarnation, Lewis sent her a copy of the recently published book *Transposition* and recommended the essay based on the sermon.[106]

Miserable Offenders, March 31, 1946 and April 7, 1946

Context

This sermon was preached first at the Quarry Church and on the next Sunday the same sermon was preached at St. Matthew's Church, Northampton. St. Matthews invited "five distinguished laymen who are members of the Church of England" to preach on Sunday nights in April and May 1946. Lewis inaugurated the series, followed by his former student, the poet John Betjeman, two military men, and Sir Eric Maclagan of the Victoria and Albert Museum.[107]

The sermons continued Lewis's string of Lenten preaching.

Text

Warnie Lewis served as a critic when he wrote in his diary on Sunday March 31, 1946:

He began by speaking of the doubts which some of us feel about the wording of the Book of Common Prayer: e.g. the confession before Communion, when we say of our sins, "The burden of them is *intolerable*." Not having this feeling, I always leave this sentence out; but J's theory is that the matter of feeling does not arise—the sense of the phrase is that, whether we are aware of it emotionally or not, we are carrying a load of sin which unless we get rid of it, will ultimately break us as an excessive load will break a bridge: and in this sense our sin *is* intolerable.[108]

Lewis once again used his old turning-the-table trick:

Does Christianity encourage morbid introspection? The alternative is much more morbid. Those who do not think about their own sins make up for it by thinking incessantly about the sins of others. It is healthier to think of one's own . . . A serious attempt to repent and really to know one's own sin is in the long run a lightening and relieving process.[109]

The final sentence sums up the sermon: "It is the difference between the pain of the tooth about which you should go to the dentist and the simple straightforward pain which you know is going to get less and less every moment when you have had the tooth out."[110]

Untitled March 9, 1947

This would be Lewis's last Lenten Evensong service at the Quarry Church. The Register of Service notes that it was the Third Sunday in Lent.[111] There is no further information on the title of the sermon.

LESS PREACHING, MORE WRITING

There was, as far as the existing records indicate, an almost decade long hiatus in Lewis's preaching. The most logical explanation is that the war was over and he felt his obligations to speak were over. There was also the matter of his commitment to finish a raft of other writing projects. He began to commute from Oxford to his new professorial chair at Cambridge University in 1954. Then there were family demands of an aging Mrs. Moore, whom he had been taking care of since he made a World War I promise to her son to do so should her son not live through the war, his alcoholic brother Warnie, and of course Joy Davidman Gresham and her two sons.

Douglas Gresham remembers that Lewis "preached every now and then by invitation" so there may be more sermons yet to be discovered. However, he highlights several reasons why Lewis cut back on his preaching: "First, he was very busy from 1954 to 1960 looking after my mother and spending what little time he had with her in the care and enjoyment of their short marriage, and secondly, Jack would not speak unless he had something to say."[112]

It seems that he had more and more to write and less and less to preach. Whatever the reason, his preaching career was over, except for a brief and brilliant reprise. When Lewis left Oxford to take up his chair at Cambridge, he became a fellow at Magdalene College. The chaplain of the college invited him to preach at Evensong, on January 29, 1956. The tiny chapel was overflowing with over a hundred people who came to hear what turned out to be Lewis's last sermon, "Slip of the Tongue." The introduction provides one of the secrets of his preaching success: "When a layman has to preach a sermon I think he is most likely to be useful, or even interesting, if he starts exactly from where he is himself; not so much presuming to instruct as comparing notes."[113] Rather than using a Scriptural text, Lewis admitted that he slipped up in the collect for the fourth Sunday after Trinity and prayed, "so to pass through things eternal that I finally lost not the things temporal."[114] He admitted that his temptation is to "guard the things temporal," not to "get out of my depth and holding on to the lifeline that connects me with my things temporal."[115] He used amusing stories and Trollope's Archdeacon to make his case against shallow spirituality.

He continued to develop the shore metaphor and claimed, "that the lifeline is really a death-line but 'our real protection is to be found elsewhere . . . Swimming lessons are better than a lifeline to shore.'"[116] He continued in elegant aphorism: "He will be infinitely merciful to our repeated failures; I know no promise that he will accept deliberate compromise. For he has, in the last resort, nothing to give us but himself."[117]

Lewis ended the sermon with the emphasis on transformation: "What God does for us, he does in us." He encouraged his listeners to prayer, "Grant me to make an unflawed beginning today, for I have done nothing yet."[118] As Lewis encouraged his listeners to pray each morning, I cannot think of a better way to close than to encourage meditation upon Lewis's "The Apologist's Evening Prayer," from whose opening and closing lines one glimpses the humility and perspicacity of Lewis, reflecting on his true vocation and the perils therein:

From all my lame defeats and oh! Much more
. . . .
Thou, who wouldst give no sign, deliver me.
. . . .

Lord of the narrow gate and the needle's eye,
Take from me all my trumpery lest I die.[119]

NOTES

1. C. S. Lewis, "Modern Man and His Categories of Thought," *Essay Collection and Other Short Pieces* (London: HarperCollins, 2000), 260.

2. Horton Davies, *Varieties of English Preaching 1900–1960* (London: SCM Press, 1963), 187.

3. C. S. Lewis, "The Christian in Danger," in *Famous English* Sermons, ed. Ashley Sampson (London: Thomas Nelson, 1940).

4. Ralph G. Turnbull, *A History of Preaching*, vol. 3 (Grand Rapids, MI: Baker, 1974), 466–467.

5. James Como, *Branches to Heaven* (Dallas, TX: Spence Publishing, 1998), 148.

6. C. S. Lewis, *Mere Christianity* (London: Geoffrey Bles, 1952), 6. The talk that formed the basis for the first chapter of the book was given on August 6, 1941. See Justin Phillips, *C. S. Lewis at the BBC* (London: HarperCollins, 2002) for a brilliant history of Lewis's radio speaking.

7. Horton Davies, *Varieties of English Preaching 1900–1960* (London: SCM Press, 1963), 186.

8. Barfield first described Lewis this way in his Preface to *The Taste of the Pineapple: Essays on Lewis as Reader, Critic, and Imaginative Writer*, ed. Bruce Edwards (Bowling Green, OH: Bowling Green State University Popular Press, 1988).

9. Charles Gilmore, "To the RAF," in *C. S. Lewis at the Breakfast Table*, ed. James Como (New York: Macmillan, 1979), 189.

10. C. S. Lewis, *Transposition and Other Essays* (London: Geoffrey Bles, 1949), 5. This same preface is included in all further editions of what in America was published as *Weight of Glory*.

11. Erik Routley, "Striking Effect," in *In Search of C. S. Lewis*, ed. Stephen Schofield (South Plainfield, NJ: Bridge Publishing, 1983), 99.

12. Phone conversation with Walter Hooper, June 12, 2006.

13. Unpublished letter cited in A. N. Wilson, *C. S. Lewis: A Biography* (London: Collins, 1990), 179.

14. Humphrey Carpenter, ed. *The Letters of J. R. R. Tolkien* (London: George Allen and Unwin, 1981), 75.

15. C. S. Lewis, "Letter XVI," *The Screwtape Letters* (London: Geoffrey Bles, 1942), 82.

16. Ibid., 82–83.

17. November 19, 1939 and September 18, 1939 letters in C. S. Lewis, *Collected Letters Vol. II*, ed. Walter Hooper (London: HarperCollins, 2004), 290, 277.

18. C. S. Lewis, *Essay Collection and Other Short Pieces* (London: HarperCollins, 2000), 341.

19. James Como, *Branches to Heaven* (Dallas, TX: Spence Publishing, 1998), 147.

20. Paul Sangster, *Doctor Sangster* (London: Epworth, 1960), 303. Dr. Sangster outlines his father's participation. W. E. Sangster was joined by evangelist Gypsie Smith and a host of other prominent Christians. See the program to *Westminster 1945: The Westminster Central Hall Campaign Programme and Hymns.*

21. C. S. Lewis, "Modern Man and His Categories of Thought," *Essay Collection and Other Short Pieces* (London: HarperCollins, 2000), 260.

22. Horton Davies, *Varieties of English Preaching 1900–1960* (London: SCM Press, 1963), 178.

23. Jolyon P. Mitchell, *Visually Speaking: Radio and the Renaissance of Preaching* (Edinburgh, Scotland: T and T Clark, 1999), 6–7.

24. Bryan C. Hollon, "Is the Epistle to Diognetus an Apology? A Rhetorical Analysis." *Journal of Communication and Religion* 29 (March 2006): 142.

25. Chaim Perelman and L. Olbrechts-Tyteca, *The New Rhetoric: A Treatise on Argument* (Notre Dame, IN: University of Notre Dame Press, 1969), 50.

26. Personal e-mail from Douglas Gresham on June 19, 2006.

27. Fred W. Paxford, "He Should Have Been a Parson," in *We Remember C. S. Lewis*, ed. Douglas Graham (Nashville, TN: Broadman and Holman, 2001), 127.

28. Warren H. Lewis, *Brothers and Friends: The Diaries of Major Warren Hamilton Lewis*, ed. Clyde S. Kilby and Marjorie L. Mead (San Francisco, CA: Harper and Row, 1982), 189.

29. The Register of Services (from April 23,1944 to March 26, 1947) contains Lewis's signature as the preacher at the 6 p.m. Evening Prayer service at Holy Trinity, Headington Quarry. PAR127/1/R7 10 at Oxfordshire County Archives.

30. The history of the published sermon, except for the fact that it was first preached at the Quarry Church, is found in Lesley Walmsey's Introduction to the sermon in C. S. Lewis, *Essay Collection and Other Short Stories* (London: HarperColllins, 2000), 461.

31. C. S. Lewis, *Letters of C. S. Lewis*, ed. W. H. Lewis (London: Collins, 1966), 490.

32. This sermon became an essay eventually published in *World Dominion*, vol. XIX (September–October 1943), and expanded and published in *Christian Reflections* (London: Bles, 1967), 37–43.

33. The Oxfordshire County archives contain the service books before and after. The archives have term cards listing preachers starting in 1947 as well as the sermon texts from 1947 to 1997. Alas, the Lewis sermons were preached before that.

34. The Register of Services from 1 November 1940-19 April 1944," PAR 127/1/R7/9 contains Lewis's signature and the Title "Religion & _____," which looks like the word "Pleasure." There is no essay by that title but Walter Hooper told me that it is a phrase Lewis uses in a letter (Phone conversation, June 2, 2006). The later sermon, without a title, is found in Register of Services from 23 April 1944–26 March 1949." PAR/127/1/R7/10

35. C. S. Lewis, *Transposition and Other Essays* (London: Geoffrey Bles, 1949), 5.

36. Not December 1939 as claimed by Lesley Walmsley in her introduction to "Learning in Wartime" in C. S. Lewis, *Essay Collection and Other Short Pieces* (London: HarperCollins, 2000), 579.

37. Walter Hooper interviewed Milford and shares the results in his "Introduction," C. S. Lewis, *The Weight of Glory: Revised and Expanded Edition*, ed. Walter Hooper (New York: Macmillan, 1980), xxi.

38. Erik Routley, "A Prophet," in *C. S. Lewis and the Breakfast Table*, ed. James T. Como. (New York: Macmillan, 1979), 34, 33–37.

39. C. S. Lewis, *C. S. Lewis: Collected Letters: Brooks, Broadcast and War 1931–1949, vol. 2*, ed. Walter Hooper (London: HarperCollins Publishers, 2004), 280.

40. C. S. Lewis, *Transposition and Other Essays* (London: Geoffrey Bles, 1949), 45.

41. Ibid.

42. His chapter entitled "Distinguished Lay Preaching: B. L. Manning and C. S. Lewis," in Horton Davies, *Varieties of English Preaching 1900–1960* (London: SCM Press, 1963) is stunning. The quote is from page 172.

43. Lewis, *Transposition and Other Essays*, 45; Horton Davies, *Varieties of English Preaching*, 172.

44. Lewis, *Transposition and Other Essays*, 46.

45. Ibid., 46–47.

46. Ibid., 50.

47. Ibid.

48. Ibid., 54.

49. Ashley Sampson, ed., *Famous English Sermons* (London: Thomas Nelson, 1940), xvi.

50. Robert Lancelyn Green and Walter Hooper, *C. S. Lewis: A Biography* (London: HarperCollins, 2002), 286.

51. C. S. Lewis, *Collected Letters, vol. 2*, ed. Walter Hooper (London: HarperCollins, 2004, 353.

52. For example, the first line "A university, as you all know, is a society ..." becomes "A university is a society for the pursuit of learning."

53. James Como, *Branches to Heaven* (Dallas, TX: Spence Publishing, 1998), 148. Como claims that "Lewis delivered only a handful of sermons, but they made history in their day."

54. Walter Hooper, "Introduction," in C. S. Lewis, *The Weight of Glory: Revised and Expanded Edition*, ed. Walter Hooper (New York: Macmillan, 1980), xxi.

55. "God blind me (or good heavens), Jack gave them both barrels" is the way an English colleague translated the sentence for me. The remark is recorded in Robert Lancelyn Green and Walter Hooper, *C. S. Lewis: A Biography* (London: HarperCollins, 2002), 244.

56. Rosamund Cowen, "With Women at College," in *In Search of C. S. Lewis*, ed. Stephen Schofield (South Plainfield, NJ: Bridge Publishing, 1983), 63.

57. C. S. Lewis, *Transposition and Other Essays* (London: Geoffrey Bles, 1949), 21.

58. Lewis's autobiography, *Surprised by Joy* (London: Geoffrey Bles, 1955), is the best source for an expansion of this sense of longing.

59. Peter Kreeft, "C. S. Lewis's Argument from Desire," in *G. K. Chesterton and C. S. Lewis: The Riddle of Joy*, ed. M. H. Macdonald and A. A. Tade (Grand Rapids, MI: Eerdmans, 1989), 252.

60. Frank Burch Brown makes the case for Derrida as a "poetic philosopher" who is an "unlikely" witness to this apologetical move in *Good Taste, Bad Taste, and Christian Taste* (New York: Oxford University Press, 2000), 90ff.

61. C. S. Lewis, *Preface to Paradise Lost* (London: Oxford University Press, 1942), 53.

62. C. S. Lewis, *Transposition and Other Essays* (London: Geoffrey Bles, 1949), 25.

63. Ibid., 26.

64. Ibid., 30.

65. Ibid., 31.

66. Ibid., 32.

67. Ibid.

68. Ibid.

69. Ibid.

70. Wesley A. Cort. *C. S. Lewis: Then and Now* (New York: Oxford University Press, 2001), 100.

71. C. S. Lewis, *Transposition and Other Essays* (London: Geoffrey Bles, 1949), 33.

72. David L. Larsen, *The Company of the Preachers* (Grand Rapids, MI: Kregel, 1998), 762.

73. J. I. Packer, "What Lewis Was and Wasn't," in *We Remember C. S. Lewis*, ed. Douglas Graham (Nashville, TN: Broadman and Holman, 2001), 8.

74. Alan Jacobs, *The Narnian* (San Francisco, CA: HarperSanFrancisco, 2005), 231.

75. Peter Kreeft, "C. S. Lewis's Argument from Desire," in *G. K. Chesterton and C. S. Lewis: The Riddle of Joy*, ed. M. H. Macdonald and A. A. Tade (Grand Rapids, MI: Eerdmans, 1989), 252.

76. Walter Hooper, "Introduction," in C. S. Lewis, *The Weight of Glory: Revised and Expanded Edition*, ed. Walter Hooper (New York: Macmillan, 1980), xxi.

77. Alan Jacobs, *The Narnian* (San Francisco, CA: HarperSanFrancisco, 2005), 314.

78. Fred W. Paxford, "Observations of a Gardener," in *We Remember C. S. Lewis*, ed. David Graham (Nashville, TN: Broadman, and Holman, 2001), 127.

79. Walter Hooper, *C. S. Lewis: A Companion and Guide* (London: HarperCollins, 1996), 803. It was published on February 9, 1942.

80. Anonymous, "Voice of the Laity, Third Series," *St. Jude's Gazette* 72 (September, 1942): 4.

81. C. S. Lewis, "Miracles," *Essay Collection and Other Short Pieces* (London: HarperCollins, 2000), 107.

82. Ibid., 113.

83. Ibid.

84. Ibid., 115

85. Ibid., 117.

86. Ibid.

87. September 27, 1942, letter to Lewis from Rosamund Rieu, "With Women at College," in *In Search of C. S. Lewis*, ed. Stephen Schofield (South Plainfield, NJ: Bridge Publishing, 1983), 64.

88. Lewis responded to Rosamund Rieu, who was at St. Hilda's and one of his first women students on September 28, 1942. It is found in Scofield's *In Search of C. S. Lewis*, 66.

89. Robert Lancelyn Green and Walter Hooper, *C. S. Lewis: A Biography* (London: HarperCollins, 2002), 285.

90. C. S. Lewis, *Collected Letters, vol. II*, ed. Walter Hooper (London: HarperCollins, 2004, 573.

91. C. S. Lewis, *Fern-seed and Elephants and Other Essays on Christianity* (London: William Collins, 1975), 8.

92. C. S. Lewis, *Transposition and Other Essays* (London: Geoffrey Bles, 1949), 5.

93. C. S. Lewis, *Essay Collection and Other Short Pieces* (London: HarperCollins, 2000), 184.

94. Ibid.

95. Ibid., 185.

96. Ibid., 186.

97. C. S. Lewis, *Mere Christianity* (London: Geoffrey Bles, 1952), 91.

98. Walter Hooper, *C. S. Lewis: A Companion and Guide* (London: HarperCollins, 1996), 37–38.

99. Humphrey Carpenter, ed. *The Letters of J. R. R. Tolkien* (London: George Allen and Unwin, 1981), 68.

100. Nathaniel Micklem, *The Box and the Puppets (1883–1953)* (London: Geoffrey Bles, 1957), 122.

101. Walter Hooper, "Introduction," in C. S. Lewis, *The Weight of Glory: Revised and Expanded Edition*, ed. Walter Hooper (New York: Macmillan, 1980), xxii.

102. C. S. Lewis, *Transposition and Other Essays* (London: Geoffrey Bles, 1949), 10.

103. Ibid., 14.

104. Ibid., 17.

105. Walter Hooper, "Introduction," in C. S. Lewis, *The Weight of Glory: Revised and Expanded Edition*, ed. Walter Hooper (New York: Macmillan, 1980), xxii–xxiii.

106. C. S. Lewis, *Collected Letters, vol. 2*, ed. Walter Hooper (London: Harper-Collins, 2004), 926.

107. The sermons were collected in C. S. Lewis, John Betjemen, Oliver Leese, R. J. R. Scott, and Eric Maclagan, *Five Sermons by Laymen* (Northampton, Northamptonshire: St. Matthews, 1946).

108. Warren H. Lewis, *Brothers and Friends: The Diaries of Major Warren Hamilton Lewis*, ed. Clyde S. Kilby and Marjorie L. Mead. (San Francisco, CA: Harper and Row, 1982), 188.

109. C. S. Lewis, "Miserable Offenders," *Essay Collection and Other Short Pieces* (London: HarperCollins, 2000), 464–465.

110. Ibid., 465.

111. PAR 127/1/R7/10 Register of Services April 23, 1944–March 26, 1949.

112. Personal e-mail from Douglas Gresham on June 19, 2006.

113. C. S. Lewis, "Slip of the Tongue," *Essay Collection and Other Short Pieces* (London: HarperCollins, 2000), 384.

114. Ibid., 384.

115. Ibid., 385.

116. Ibid., 386.

117. Ibid.

118. Ibid.

119. C. S. Lewis, *Poems* (London: Geoffrey Bles, 1964), 129.

BIBLIOGRAPHY

Anonymous. "Voice of the Laity, Third Series." *St. Jude's Gazette* 72 (September, 1942): 4.

Babbage, Stuart Barton. "To the Royal Air Force." *C. S. Lewis: Speaker and Teacher.* Edited by Carolyn Keefe. Grand Rapids, MI: Zondervan, 1971, 85–102.

Ceccareli, Leah. *Shaping Science with Rhetoric.* Chicago, IL: University of Chicago Press, 2001.

Como, James. *Branches to Heaven: The Geniuses of C. S. Lewis.* Dallas, TX: Spence Publishing, 1998.

Cort, Wesley A. *C. S. Lewis: Then and Now.* New York: Oxford University Press, 2001.

Cowen, Rosamund. "With Women at College." *In Search of C. S. Lewis.* Edited by Stephen Schofield. South Plainfield, NJ: Bridge Publishing, 1983, 61–66.

Davies, Horton. *Varieties of English Preaching 1900–1960.* London: SCM Press, 1963.

Gilmore, Charles. "To the RAF." *C. S. Lewis at the Breakfast Table and Other Reminiscences.* Edited by James T. Como. New York: Macmillan, 1979, 186–191.

Goffar, Janine. *C. S. Lewis Index: Rumours form the Sculptor's Shop.* Carlisle, UK: Solway Press, 1997.

Graham, D., ed. *We Remember C. S. Lewis*. Nashville, TN: Broadman and Holman, 2001.

Green, Robert Lancelyn and Walter Hooper. *C. S. Lewis: A Biography*. Fully Revised and Expanded Edition. London: HarperCollins, 2002.

Griffin, William. *Clive Staples Lewis: A Dramatic Life*. New York: Harper and Row, 1986.

Hollon, Bryan C. "Is the Epistle to Diognetus an Apology? A Rhetorical Analysis." *Journal of Communication and Religion* 29 (March 2006), 127–46.

Hooper, Walter. *C. S. Lewis: A Companion and Guide*. London: HarperCollins, 1996.

———, ed. "Introduction." *The Weight of Glory and Other Address: Revised and Expanded Edition*. New York: Macmillan, 1980.

Jacobs, Alan. *The Narnian: The Life and Imagination of C. S. Lewis*. San Francisco, CA:HarperSanFrancisco, 2005.

Jenkins, Simon. *England's Thousand Best Churches*. London: Penguin Press, 1999.

Kreeft, Peter. "C. S. Lewis's Argument from Desire." *G. K. Chesterton and C. S. Lewis: The Riddle of Joy*. Edited by M. H. Macdonald and A. A. Tade. Grand Rapids, MI: Eerdmans, 1989.

Larson, David L. *The Company of Preachers: A History of Biblical Preaching from the Old Testament to the Modern Era*. Grand Rapids, MI: Kregel, 1998.

Lewis, C. S. *C. S. Lewis: Collected Letters: Brooks, Broadcast and War 1931–1949*, vol. 2. Edited by Walter Hooper. London: HarperCollins, 2004.

———. *C. S. Lewis: Collected Letters: Family Letters 1905–1931*, vol. 1. Edited by Walter Hooper, London: HarperCollins, 2000.

———. "The Christian in Danger." In *Famous English Sermons*. Edited by Ashley Sampson (London: Thomas Nelson, 1940), 368–382.

———. *The Christian in Danger*. London: SCM, 1939.

———. *Essay Collection and Other Short Pieces*. London: HarperCollins, 2000.

———. *Fern-Seed and Elephants and Other Essays on Christianity*. Edited by W. Hooper. London: William Collins, 1975.

———. *Letters of C. S. Lewis*. Edited by W. H. Lewis. London: Collins, 1966.

———. *Mere Christianity*. London: Geoffrey Bles, 1952.

———. "Miracles." *St. Jude's Gazette* 73 (October 1942): 4–7.

———. "None Other Gods: Culture in War Time." Church of St. Mary the Virgin: Oxford, December 22, 1939.

———. *Preface to Paradise Lost*. London: Oxford University Press, 1942.

———. *Poems*. London: Geoffrey Bles, 1964.

———. *The Screwtape Letters*. London: Geoffrey Bles, 1942.

———. *Transposition and Other Essays*. London: Geoffrey Bles, 1949.

———. *Undeceptions: Essays on Theology and Ethics*. Edited by Walter Hooper. London: Geoffrey Bles, 1971.

———. *The Weight of Glory*. London: SPCK, 1942.

———. *The Weight of Glory and Other Addresses: Revised and Expanded Edition*. Edited by Walter Hooper. New York: Macmillan, 1980.

Lewis, Warren H. *Brothers and Friends: The Diaries of Major Warren Hamilton Lewis*. Edited by Clyde S. Kilby and Marjorie L. Mead. San Francisco, CA: Harper and Row, 1982.

Micklem, Nathaniel. *The Box and the Puppets (1883–1953)*. London: Geoffrey Bles, 1957.

Mitchell, Jolyon P. *Visually Speaking: Radio and the Renaissance of Preaching*. Edinburgh, Scotland: T and T Clark, 1999.

Packer, J. I. "What Lewis Was and Wasn't." In *We Remember C. S. Lewis*. Nashville, TN: Broadman and Holman, 2001, 8.

Paxford, William W. "He Should Have Been a Parson." In *We Remember C. S. Lewis*. Nashville, TN: Broadman and Holman, 2001, 207.

Perelman, Chaim and L. Olbrechts-Tyteca. *The New Rhetoric: A Treatise on Argument*. Notre Dame, IN: University of Notre Dame Press, 1969.

Pettegree, Andrew. *Reformation and the Culture of Persuasion*. Cambridge: Cambridge University Press, 2005.

Phillips, Justin. *C. S. Lewis at the BBC. Messages of Hope in the Darkness of War*. London: HarperCollins, 2002.

Rees, Tom. *Westminster 1945: The Westminster Central Hall Campaign Programme and Hymns*. London: Westminster Hall Campaign, 1945.

"Register of Services Advent IV 1938-16 April 1944." St. Jude-on-the-Hill, Hampstead Garden Suburb.

"Register of Services, 1 November 40–19 April 44." Holy Trinity Church, Headington Quarry. PAR 127/1/R7/9. Oxfordshire Record Office.

"Register of Services 23 April 1944- 26 March 1949." Holy Trinity Church, Headington Quarry. PAR 127/1/R7/10. Oxfordshire Record Office.

Routley, Erik. "A Prophet." *C. S. Lewis and the Breakfast Table*. Edited by James T. Como. New York: Macmillan, 1979, 33–37.

———. "Striking Effect." *In Search of C. S. Lewis*. Edited by S. Schofield, South Plainfield. NJ: Bridge Publishing, 1983, 97–102.

Sangster, Paul. *Doctor Sangster*. London: The Epworth Press, 1962.

Simpson, Ashley. "An Anglican Picture Gallery." *Church of England Newspaper* (October 4) (1946): 7.

———, ed. *Famous English Sermons*. London: Thomas Nelson, 1940.

Tolkien, J. R. R. *The Letters of J. R. R. Tolkien*. Edited by Humphrey Carpenter. London: George Allen and Unwin, 1981.

Turnbull, Ralph G. *The History of Preaching*, vol. 3. Grand Rapids, MI: Baker Book House, 1974.

Wilson, A. N. *C. S. Lewis: A Biography*. London: Collins, 1990.

5

The Abolition of Man: C. S. Lewis's Philosophy of History

Michael Travers

The Abolition of Man (1943) is the published version of the three Riddell Memorial Lectures sponsored by the University of Durham. C. S. Lewis ("Jack") and his brother Warren ("Warnie") traveled from Oxford to the university and cathedral town of Durham, arriving on February 24, 1943. Jack delivered the three lectures on the evenings of February 24, 25, and 26 in Newcastle-upon-Tyne.[1] Warnie records in his diary that the event was "a little oasis in the dreariness"[2] of their lives at the time. It was the middle of World War II, food was rationed, and life was grim for everyone in Britain. Jack and Warnie loved the beautiful cathedral and university town of Durham and enjoyed the three-day respite immensely.[3]

The Riddell Memorial Lectures were founded in 1928 in memory of Sir John Walter Buchanan-Riddell. These lectures were established to address "a subject concerning the relation between religion and contemporary development of thought."[4] Lewis delivered the Fifteenth Series of these lectures, and Oxford University Press published the lectures immediately, as it did in a number of the other Riddell Memorial Lectures in the years surrounding Lewis's lectures.[5] A quick look at some of the titles shows the subjects addressed in the lectures at that time,[6] with topics ranging from science to psychology, philosophy, politics, and history. Issues related to religion and culture marked the common ground for all of the Riddell Memorial

Lectures. Lewis's 1943 Riddell Memorial Lectures addressed the decline in modern times of belief in an objective natural law and a correspondence epistemology.

CONTEXT IN C. S. LEWIS'S LIFE

The stage of Lewis's life when he published *The Abolition of Man* (1943) was a prolific time of writing and publication. The years from 1938 to 1947 embody the early stage in a two-decade period of writing in a wide range of genres extending from apologetics to adult fiction, children's fantasy, theology and more. The early 1940s were also the war years when many Britons faced difficulties brought about by the war and were forced to consider the serious metaphysical and ethical questions raised by Nazi aggression. Beginning in 1938, Lewis published *Out of the Silent Planet*, the first in the Ransom trilogy or "science fiction" novels, and in 1940, *The Problem of Pain*, his first sustained attempt at apologetics. In August of 1941, he began the British Broadcasting Corporation (BBC) radio broadcasts, which he delivered live in four series lasting through 1944 and published in 1952 as *Mere Christianity*. These talks were immediately popular, so much so they must have hit a nerve much deeper than the war itself, for they addressed universal issues of the human condition. In 1941 the popular Socratic Club, an open weekly forum at Oxford University to discuss "the *pros* and *cons* of the Christian Religion,"[7] was initiated with Lewis as its first president and a major debate participant. In 1942 Lewis published *The Screwtape Letters*, another immensely popular work, and *A Preface to Paradise Lost* in which he "rehabilitates" the misunderstood poet, John Milton, for the modern academy. Along with *The Abolition of Man* in 1943, Lewis published an essay that amounts to something of a summary of *The Abolition of Man*, "The Poison of Subjectivism," and also *Perelandra*, the second in the Ransom Trilogy novels. In 1945, he published *The Great Divorce*, a theological fantasy on heaven and hell, and *That Hideous Strength*, the final Ransom novel in which he says he wrote a "tall story" about the "serious 'point'" he made in *The Abolition of Man*.[8] Finally, in 1947, Lewis published *Miracles*, the last of this series of works written during this period. These same years saw a sudden increase in his popularity (because of *The Screwtape Letters* and the BBC Radio Talks) and a sharp increase in his correspondence. It was in this context that Lewis published *The Abolition of Man*, a book that he later claimed was "almost my favourite among my books but in general has been almost totally ignored by the public."[9] Lewis was not alone in this assessment, for his literary executor Walter Hooper states that *The Abolition of Man* is "an all but indispensable introduction to the entire *corpus* of Lewisiana."[10]

A BRIEF SUMMARY OF *THE ABOLITION OF MAN*

The occasion for *The Abolition of Man* was the publication of two English textbooks that, inadvertently or otherwise, espoused a moral relativism that Lewis found untenable. To save the authors embarrassment, Lewis used fictional names for these books. The first book, which he calls "The Green Book" by "Gaius and Titius," is in fact *The Control of Language* by Alex King and Martin Ketley, published in 1940.[11] The second offending textbook, for which Lewis identifies only an "author" ("Orbilius"), is *The Reading and Writing of English* by E. G. Biaggini, published in 1936.[12] It does not take long for the reader of *The Abolition of Man* to understand that Lewis is not simply admonishing English schoolmasters to correct a pedagogical error. He is, rather, writing to tackle nothing less than the hegemony of relativism in modern western culture. For Lewis, this subjectivism was most apparent and dangerous in epistemology and ethics. Consequently, *The Abolition of Man* is a book about ethics, with roots in history and metaphysics. It is a trenchant critique of modernity, specifically its subjectivism in morals and epistemology, its abuse of scientific thinking, and its belief in "unilinear progression," which Lewis considered simply unrealistic.[13] In *C. S. Lewis in Context,* Doris T. Myers states that Lewis knew that the ideas in *The Control of Language,* carried to their logical conclusions, "would lead to the destruction of everything that makes human beings truly human"[14]—or, in other words, to the "abolition of man." King and Ketley's little schoolbook may have seemed harmless to many, but Lewis understood that its convictions were dehumanizing,[15] and so worked to refute them in the Riddell Memorial Lectures and *The Abolition of Man.*

The Abolition of Man has three chapters corresponding to the three lectures delivered at the University of Durham. In the first chapter, "Men without Chests," Lewis identifies the problem in modern culture as a radical subjectivity that has undermined everything that makes us human. Throughout the history of the West until modern times, people have held that there is a universal moral law and that our understanding of reality is reliable because our knowledge corresponds to reality as it is—in short, a correspondence epistemology. Lewis cites Plato and Augustine, among others, as examples of this long-standing and nonsectarian understanding of "the way things are." In *Mere Christianity*, Lewis calls the universal moral code "the law of human nature" or simply "natural law," and in *The Abolition of Man* he calls it the "Tao."[16] While *The Tao* may seem amorphous and unnecessarily Asian to many readers, Lewis thought it was sufficient for his case.[17] He defines *The Tao* as "the doctrine of objective value, the belief that certain attitudes are really true, and others really false, to the kind of thing the universe is and the kind of things we are."[18] In the twentieth century, however, intellectuals turned away from the traditional view of values and knowledge to a subjectivist perspective, and for Lewis, this shift is lethal to fundamental humanity. What is the antidote to the subjectivism of modern culture? For Lewis, the antidote is for us to reassert the objectivity of traditional values and order our behavior accordingly. And as he concludes, "The head rules the belly through the chest"[19]—that is, the intellect (the "head") rules the appetites (the "belly") through justly educated sentiments (the "chest"). Lewis's point is that objective values based in natural law distinguish us from angels on the one hand and animals on the other. Reason aligns us with the angels, passion with the animals. A proper education in Lewis's view trains right virtues in children and teaches them to behave according to the traditional moral code of western civilization. "Men without chests"? These are people whose loss of traditional values (the "chest") renders them something other than what we have understood historically by the word "human."

In chapter two, "The Way," Lewis defends traditional values in large measure by demonstrating the inconsistencies in the opposing subjectivist position. For example, Lewis argues against the idea that values are based on instincts and therefore relative. "Our instincts," he writes, "are at war" and do not in themselves provide a moral imperative.[20] How can they? Defining one instinct as "good" and another as "bad" requires an appeal to a third standard, which is neither one of the two instincts so called. It is to invoke the universal moral code.[21] No logic can draw a value judgment from factual propositions.[22] No matter how hard we try, we simply cannot step outside of the moral law. It alone provides the basis for all value judgments. Lewis's unflinching commitment to universal, objective moral standards in face of the subjectivist drift in modern culture is his great contribution to ethical thinking in the modern world. He knew we can neither refute natural law nor raise a new system of value in its place. It is simply impossible to do so.[23] Or, at least, it is impossible to do so, according to Lewis, and remain human.

Chapter three, "The Abolition of Man," looks to the future of humankind without traditional moral values, a "brave new world" where rulers do not believe in objective truth, reality, or values (such as "truth and mercy" and "beauty and happiness"),[24] but rather follow their own subjective impulses. Part of Lewis's concern in this chapter is that the rejection of natural law will result in the unprincipled rule of a few men over the billions,[25] with these men subject only to their own "irrational impulses" as the only guide for their behavior.[26] They will have rejected all objective morality in natural law and stepped outside the mainstream of western history to legislate their own preferences as a "new" morality. In *The Restitution of Man: C. S. Lewis and the Case against Scientism*, Michael D. Aeschliman captures both the idea and the tone of Lewis's concern about this trend toward subjectivism. Aeschliman writes, "The triumph of personal desire over objective validity as a standard of behavior creates what is tantamount to a moral vacuum into which will rush disordered passions bloated in their abnormal freedom from any constraint."[27] Without an objective moral code, we put ourselves at risk. Humans are by nature ethical creatures and cannot live in moral nihilism for long. Aeschliman's imagery of "disordered passions [that are] bloated . . ." expresses Lewis's fears well, for passion is tyrannical. To state it more baldly, power cut off from moral rectitude inevitably leads to desire, not obligation, on the part of those who rule. And without the *Tao*, what is to stop the leaders who have the power at their disposal from using their citizens to satisfy their own desires? Machiavelli understood society and its rulers this way.

One of the tools these "Conditioners," as he calls these new leaders, will use is scientific knowledge and advances. Now, Lewis is not opposed to science and the many benefits it offers,[28] but he is opposed to the abuse of science to gain raw power. He calls this abuse "scientism." Lewis distinguishes between science and scientism by comparing the modern scientist with the magician of earlier ages. He states, "For the wise men of old the cardinal problem had been how to conform the soul to reality, and the solution had been knowledge, self-discipline, and virtue. For magic and applied science alike the problem is how to subdue reality to the wishes of men: the solution is a technique.[29] The magicians of earlier times have been replaced by the conditioners of modern times, but both seek dominance over nature and humankind alike.[30] A world ruled by such amoral conditioners and their lackey scientists is a world in which raw desire grasps raw power. It is a world in which we will have 'abolished' mankind. A fool's bargain it would be, to sell the soul for tyranny and slavery."[31] Doris T. Myers understands the high stakes. She writes, "If the absolute standards of the Tao are . . . built into human nature, then any attempt to study or control human nature apart from these standards is dehumanizing."[32] Subjectivism in values, scientism, and the control of human nature—these are the objects of Lewis's attack in *The Abolition of Man*. At bottom, they all deny reality, destroy all virtue and value in human life, lead us away from our essential humanity, and result in social tyranny and slavery. Lewis's concerns, expressed in the context of Nazi aggression and the Soviet revolution, seem terribly prophetic of the postmodern culture of the early twenty-first century.

HELP FROM HISTORY

For Lewis, it was clear that, if we were to preserve our essential humanity in the face of subjectivism and scientism, we would have to do so from the grounds of objective truth and morality. To regain a proper understanding of objective truth and morality, Lewis knew that we must study history. Accordingly, *The Abolition of Man* develops an implicit philosophy of history as an important part of the context within which he sees the issues in modern culture. The remainder of this chapter will consider Lewis's philosophy of history and what he thinks history has to offer us if we are to recover our abolished humanity.

In the essay entitled "Historicism" published originally in 1950, Lewis lists six senses of history, in part to demonstrate how difficult it is to claim that we can understand history with any ultimate authority. The term *history*, Lewis says, may refer to (1) all of time—past, present, and future; (2) all of the events of the past; (3) as much of the past as we can discover from evidence; (4) the events of the past discovered by cutting-edge researchers; (5) the events made available to the general populace by great historians; and (6) the vague picture of the past the educated man has in his mind.[33] Now it is obvious that we cannot make any serious claims to understand history in the first two senses; it is clear that we can never have a complete picture of history in the third sense; it is evident that only a few will know history in the fourth sense, while most people will think of the fifth sense when they think of history at all. Lewis considers the sixth sense in this essay, specifically when historians attempt to generalize about "meanings" of historical periods. When they do so, Lewis claims, they cease being historians and become historicists. "The mark of the Historicist," Lewis writes, "is that he tries to get from historical premises conclusions which are more than historical; conclusions metaphysical or theological or (to coin a word) atheo-logical."[34] At best this is a flaw in logic, at worst sectarianism and even propaganda.

Even apart from the problems historicist readings of history bring, Lewis expresses serious reservations about the possibility of developing a philosophy of history at all. Peter Kreeft states that Lewis "disbelieves in the philosophy of history."[35] In his inaugural address at Cambridge University on November 29, 1954, "De Descriptione Temporum," Lewis announced he was a "desperate skeptic" about "everything that could be called 'the philosophy of history.'"[36] *Contra* Hegel, he doubted whether historians could identify the spirit or meaning of a given period of history with accuracy.[37] It is true that we can know certain facts from the past, though we will never be certain that they are representative and complete. What troubled Lewis was the all-too-common attempt to interpret history in such a way as to assign a given period an essential meaning or identity. All such futile attempts he calls "historicism," which he defines as "the belief that men can, by the use of their natural powers, discover an inner meaning in the historical process."[38] For Lewis, the historian can describe events of the past, albeit in an incomplete manner, but he cannot interpret events in such a way as to characterize the "meaning" of a period with any certainty. To try to do so would be to change from being a historian to becoming a historicist. The problem is that we live in "an untidy world," which "as Lewis experiences it," Gilbert Meilaender states, "resists complete systematization."[39] It is simply impossible to speak with any authority of what the character of an age might have been. Historicist renderings are a *non sequitur* in Lewis's view, a process of drawing metaphysical or theological (or even "atheo-logical," to use Lewis's coined term) conclusions from historical premises, and are therefore illogical and specious.[40]

THE GREAT TRADITION IN WESTERN HISTORY

His "desperate skepticism" about the philosophy of history notwithstanding, however, Lewis stands squarely within the mainstream of classical western thinking that there is a "great tradition" in history. This tradition rests on the conviction that reason used as it was intended leads us to God. It is the "common sense" heritage of people throughout the ages, or in Michael D. Aeschliman's words, "the great central philosophical/metaphysical tradition of the West in which Lewis enlisted his own mind and pen."[41] Aeschliman identifies the great thinkers in this central western tradition as Plato, Aristotle, St. John, Augustine, Aquinas, Richard Hooker, Samuel Johnson, and G. K. Chesterton—all men who shared a common morality at bottom, despite whatever differences they may have had.[42] In "Is Progress Possible?" Lewis adds that the "key-conceptions" of this tradition are "natural law, the value of the individual, [and] the rights of man."[43] These virtues fall in the center of the tradition of "natural law," which Lewis identifies in *The Abolition of Man*,[44] and "The Law of Human Nature" in *Mere Christianity*. John Warwick Montgomery understood rightly that for Lewis "the main function of literary as of historical study is to make contact with that great tradition which for the first time since ancient classical times has been broken" in modern times.[45] *The Abolition of Man* attempts to reconnect its readers with this great tradition in western history—the tradition of objective and universal moral standards and the acceptance of an objective reality and the correspondence epistemology that accompanies it.

The cornerstone of Lewis's analysis of western history in *The Abolition of Man* is the tradition of natural law, or the *Tao*. For Lewis, the nature of man as created by God provides the foundation of this traditional morality; it is not grounded in any specifically Christian or New Testament understanding of morality but is rather an innate moral code shared by everyone, everywhere.[46] In *The Abolition of Man* Lewis states that the *Tao* "is the reality beyond all predicates, the abyss that was before the Creator Himself. It is Nature, it is the Way, the Road."[47] While we might disagree with the idea that moral law precedes the existence of God [that is, God *qua* Creator], the important point in Lewis's statement is that natural law is a universal moral code. It is, in Meilaender's words, constituted by "the primeval moral platitudes," which all humans in all cultures share[48] and, in John G. West's words, the "ethical first principles shared by all human beings."[49] Natural law is archetypal. It is universal and objective, and it regulates and judges all actions of all people everywhere—even those who deny it.

This universal natural law does not contradict the Christian view of ethics, but rather supports it. The classical New Testament expression of natural law is found early in the book of Romans, quoted here in the translation of the Bible which Lewis used, the King James or Authorized Version. Paul writes, "For when the Gentiles, which have not the law, do by nature the things contained in the law, these, having not the law, are a law unto themselves: Which show the work of the law written in their hearts, their conscience also bearing witness, and their thoughts the mean while accusing or else excusing one another."[50] Lewis agrees with Paul's argument that all people everywhere have a moral conscience, and that conscience is grounded in an objective moral law. In "Men without Chests" Lewis declares that there is an objective reality in which objects inherently demand certain responses from human beings based on a correspondence epistemology.[51] To affirm that such virtues as "truth and mercy and beauty and happiness"[52] are good is simply to admit what is inherently true with or without our affirmation. What is more, it is to do so from within the tradition of natural law—the only position from which we can understand reality and truth.[53] Of the absolute necessity of living, thinking, and behaving from within the *Tao*, Meilaender writes, "If the *Tao* is the reality within which human life must be lived, it is destructive of one's humanity to claim autonomy over against its maxims. It is, in fact, *self-destructive*."[54] This is the foundational teaching and burden of *The Abolition of Man*. Humans are by nature ethical creatures, and their ethics are objective and universal in essentials.

While Lewis thinks that natural law does not depend on any sectarian philosophy of life, not even the Christian or Judeo-Christian views, he does see a Christian shape to the larger narrative of human history. It is perhaps in this way that his addresses at the University of Durham in 1943 best fit the founding purpose of the Riddell Memorial Lectures. There is for Lewis a Christian metahistory that frames the events of human life and gives shape to them. In *The Discarded Image*, Lewis states that Christians will see history as "a story with a divine plot."[55] Its central event for Lewis is the Incarnation of Jesus Christ,[56] and it will come to an end someday in God's time, whether by the H-bomb or some other means.[57] There is teleology to history for

Lewis, even a specifically Christian one, though he makes no claims that we can use even a Christian metahistory as a tool to understand any particular "trend in the world depicted."[58] To do so would be to shift from history to historicism, albeit with a "Christian" moniker, which is no better than any other type of historicism. Still, the big picture of history is clear when seen from a Christian perspective, and it is important to realize that it is this understanding that gives ethical and metaphysical significance to the events of human history. Christianity teaches that God created man in his own image; mankind fell in the form of Adam and Eve in the garden of Eden, introducing sin and a sinful nature into humanity; Jesus Christ died to pay the price of sin, was resurrected, and ascended into heaven; and he is coming again to bring history to its conclusion. Surely the Christian understanding of the metapattern to history assigns significance to human actions, for they reflect, as it were, on their creator. Human actions are significant as well because they have consequences in eternity. While Lewis writes of a universal moral law, he does so from within a Christian framework that informs his analysis.

"UNILINEAR PROGRESS" OR "FATAL SERIALISM"?

Despite its Christian metahistory and teleology, one thing history does not demonstrate in Lewis's view is any clearly defined sense of progress in which things are improving over the ages. It would be a naïve person indeed who can look at the history of the modern era and see moral progress. Technology has progressed at a rapid rate in modern times, but no complementary moral advance has accompanied the technological advances. Simply because something is new does not mean that it is better, and Lewis makes it clear in *The Abolition of Man* that he has no tolerance for the popular modern notion of out-and-out progress. Lewis gladly acknowledges that Owen Barfield, a fellow Inkling and the "wisest and best of [his] unofficial teachers,"[59] taught him "not to patronize the past"[60] by valorizing the present. In *Surprised by Joy*, Lewis calls the naïve belief in unmitigated progress "chronological snobbery," and he defines it as "the uncritical acceptance of the intellectual climate common to our own age and the assumption that whatever has gone out of date is on that account discredited."[61] Chronological snobbery reflects arrogance toward ourselves and a corollary disdain for those who have gone before us—and who, ironically, share the same essential humanity we possess and which provides the foundation of modern advances. At bottom, it is unrealistic and does not square with the facts of history.

Unfortunately in Lewis's view, the paradigm in which many modern people think is precisely this one of naïve progress. In *The Abolition of Man* Lewis calls such a view "the fatal serialism of the modern imagination—the image of infinite unilinear progression which so haunts our minds."[62] Such naïve faith in progress was the ruling paradigm in Lewis's day, and it is yet today. Perhaps because of the obvious evidence of progress in technology, modern people find it difficult to understand that what is new is not on that account necessarily better. Technological progress makes it easy to think there is a similar progress in ethics as well. But such a view does not square with reality, as even a cursory consideration of the history of the twentieth century would demonstrate. Two world wars, countless bloody coups, Soviet gulags, ethnic cleansing in the Baltics and Africa, and the terrorism of the twenty-first century—progress? History is not a linear march upward. For Lewis any such view of history is a myth.[63]

One reason why we cannot expect a "unilinear progression" in history is that human nature remains essentially the same in all places and at all times. Are we not made in the image of our parents[64] as well as in the image of God?[65] In *The Allegory of Love*, Lewis uses the image of a train to remind us that one reason why we study old poetry is because we share a common humanity with the old poets. "Humanity does not pass through phases as a train passes through stations," Lewis writes; "being alive, it has the privilege of always moving yet never leaving anything behind. Whatever we have been, in some sort we are still."[66] If humans did not remain essentially the same, there would be no ground for natural law, and Lewis's Appendix to *The Abolition of Man* would be a mere curiosity about historical coincidences. As it is, however, natural law is universal and objective. The unchanging essence of human nature is one of those assumptions we must make if we are to think at all. "If nothing is self-evident," Lewis declares in *The Abolition of Man*, "nothing can be proved."[67] We must accept the fact of an essentially unchanging humanity as a premise if we are to enter the arena of logic or ethics and, if we accept such a premise, it is impossible to see history as a story of progressive improvement. In fact, if we accept Lewis's premise that human nature is essentially constant, we concede the conclusions of *The Abolition of Man* and the Appendix becomes an indictment of modern culture as the first civilization to normalize a wholesale subjectivism.

A second reason why history is not progressing is that "the doctrine of the Second Coming is deeply uncongenial to the whole evolutionary or developmental character of modern thought."[68] The Christian revelation of history in the New Testament "foretells a sudden, violent end imposed from without."[69] There is no suggestion in the New Testament that humankind improves with time and will one day enter a peaceful millennium on the basis of humanitarian and benevolent efforts. To be sure, Lewis goes well beyond his own understanding of natural law when as a Christian he adopts the New Testament account of the *eschaton*, for he regards natural law to be innate in all people and not a specifically Christian ethic.[70] Perhaps the best way to understand Lewis's apparent shift here is to remember that this is another one of those self-evident premises that make thought possible. While Lewis does not think that the Christian revelation can speak to particular incidents or even periods in history, it most emphatically does speak to the end of history. It may well be that for Lewis the Christian paradigm of history speaks most authoritatively to the fall and apocalypse, rather than to the events of nation-states, which occur between those two book-ending events in human history. In John's Apocalypse a sovereign God judges that humans have not improved since the days of Noah or Christ and therefore brings history to a cataclysmic close.[71] There is no hope in the Book of Revelation for redemption from within humankind.

In the same way, hopes for a better future on the basis of political ideology or economic improvement are vain in Lewis's view as well. Both Fascism and Communism lead to tyranny on the one hand and slavery on the other. In this regard, Aeschliman writes in *The Restitution of Man* of "Marxist scientism" and its "scientific socialism" and states that it is nothing but an "empty promise of historical inevitability and its tragically real tyranny and barbarism."[72] The ideologies of progress are thinly veiled tyrannical dystopias, and this is so because of human sin and greed. Lewis is quite clear in *The Abolition of Man* when he writes, "what we call Man's power over Nature turns out to be a power exercised by some men over other men with Nature as its instrument," and again, "Man's conquest of Nature . . . means the rule of a few hundreds of men over billions upon billions of men."[73] While this may be the future as Lewis thought of it in 1943, it is not a desirable one, and he wrote in order to forestall that possibility.

MAN'S SELF-ABOLITION

As Lewis took stock in the 1940s, he saw the moral trajectory of modernity as a downward one. He said so publicly in the Riddell Memorial Lectures in February 1943. In December of the same year, he wrote to Arthur C. Clarke that a human race concerned only with technological power and with no regard for ethics would be "a cancer on the universe."[74] He had not changed his mind some fifteen years later when he wrote "Religion and Rocketry" and stated, "Man destroys or enslaves every species he can. Civilized man murders, enslaves, cheats, and corrupts savage man."[75] In the first two Ransom Trilogy books, Weston and Devine are obvious examples of the dehumanizing and acquisitive nature of humankind. So too are most of the "scientists" in the N.I.C.E. [the "National Institute of Coordinated Experiments"] in *That Hideous Strength* (the third in the trilogy and published in 1945). The

"Progressive Element" at Belbury in *That Hideous Strength* includes such former human beings as Frost, Wither, Straik, and Fairy Hardcastle, whose names alone are enough to intimate Lewis's attitude toward them. Wither, the Deputy Director of the Institute, is a frightening portrait of a man who has jettisoned the *Tao* and, along with it, his essential humanity. The lesbian Fairy Hardcastle in her Gestapo boots and smoking her cigar is in the final throes of perverted femininity. And Straik is theologically obtuse enough to think that the N.I.C.E. will usher in the Kingdom of God on this earth. All of these "educated" people bow down to "the Head"—a human head apparently kept alive at Belbury by blood transfusions. Here is a brave new world indeed. Lewis knew that a culture that jettisoned the *Tao* and allowed a group of elite rulers—the conditioners—to rule without recourse to a common morality would ultimately bow before the irrational impulses of its leaders.[76] Under these circumstances we should not expect improvement, but decline. Many would argue that in fact this has been the history of the west in the last half of the twentieth century and into the beginning of the new millennium.

The decline Lewis perceived in the culture of his day is nothing less than man's self-abolition. If humans can change their morality in some substantive way—if they can step outside of the *Tao*, to use Lewis's terms—then they become something other than human. Lewis is explicit in "The Poison of Subjectivism," where he writes, "Out of this apparently innocent idea [to 'improve our morality'] comes the disease that will certainly end our species (and, in my view, damn our souls) if it is not crushed; the fatal superstition that men can create values, that a community can choose its 'ideology' as men choose their clothes."[77] In what way would forming a new morality bring an "end to our species" and even "damn our souls"? The idea of forming a new morality is simply a disguise for the desire for power. It transforms the human subject of government into the object of control, the end (human beings) into the means (that is, to establish power for the elite). In *The Narnian: The Life and Imagination of C. S. Lewis*, Alan Jacobs states, "Modern humanists, like the scientists and magicians of the Renaissance, seek power and control rather than wisdom. That is how they have cut themselves off from the moral law—what Lewis calls the *Tao*—and are contributing, not to the enrichment of humanity, but to its abolition."[78] By abolishing the traditional morality that has survived throughout history until modern times, they abandon wisdom and opt for power. In the past, "rulers" generally ruled for the good of the people, their subjects. In the future, "leaders" who are outside the *Tao* will rule people as "domestic animals" for their own purposes and use their own "morality" to justify their tyranny.[79] Machiavellian? Yes. Nietzschean? Certainly. Inevitable? Only if we do not hold ourselves to the objective standard of natural law. If we reject natural law, we become "men without chests" or "mere artifacts," in Lewis's words.[80] This is the trajectory in modern life that so concerns Lewis in *The Abolition of Man*.

What makes the threat of man's self-abolition so significant a threat to civilization in the 1940s is the fact that prior to the twentieth century, no civilized state had been able to change the moral thinking of the masses of its people. There had been tyrants in the past, to be sure, and they certainly imposed their will on their people. And this is precisely the point—they imposed their will on a people against accepted moral codes. But with a tyrant like Hitler, all that changed. Lewis makes very few references to Hitler in *The Abolition of Man*, choosing rather to address the metaphysical and moral issues he sees in modern life. At the same time, however, Hitler's rise to power represents one example of a change in the rules of engagement for civilized societies. "'Good' and 'bad,' applied to [leaders like Hitler] are words without content," Lewis says, "for it is from them that the content of these words is henceforward to be derived."[81] Leaders like Hitler define the rules of engagement in a Machiavellian way to enable their own desires to be met. Hitler faced little opposition to his plan to exterminate Jews and use them in hideously inhumane experiments, for he was forming "the master race" in the Germany of the Third Reich. In the case of Hitler it is that too few people called his actions immoral and took a stand against them. Dietrich Bonhoeffer raised the alarm, but there were not enough Bonhoeffers in Germany or in Western Europe at large in the 1930s and early 1940s to stop Hitler's advance. By the time the Churchills of the world had the public ear, Hitler was occupying foreign territories in Europe and the rest of Europe awaited what appeared to be inevitable. In *The Abolition of Man*, however, Hitler is a symptom, not a cause.

The cause, in Lewis's view, for why a Hitler was able to rise to power and mobilize such a vast war machine was the hitherto unthinkable nexus of a decade of brainwashing of the German people and Hitler's access to "the powers of an omnicompetent state" with "irresistible scientific technique."[82] It is the union of eugenics and technology that makes man's self-abolition possible, and the Third Reich represented that possibility all too obviously for Lewis in 1943. Lewis's concern is clear in the last chapter of *The Abolition of Man*:

The final stage is come when Man by eugenics, by pre-natal conditioning, and by an education and propaganda based on a perfect applied psychology, has obtained full control over himself. *Human* nature will be the last part of Nature to surrender to Man. The battle will then be won. We shall have "taken the thread of life out of the hand of Clotho" and be henceforth free to make our species whatever we wish it to be. The battle will indeed be won. But who, precisely, will have won it?[83]

The lack of an objective moral code, the presence of effective psychologizing, eugenics, education, and the political power to make it happen—these are the ingredients in man's abolition of himself. It is this nexus that presented the philosophical and ethical dilemma Lewis addresses in *The Abolition of Man*.

Nor is this nightmare limited to the Third Reich of Germany or even Europe in the 1940s alone; it can happen in any modern state that wishes it to happen. Not even an international state, or a megastate, would change the picture substantively. The same conditioning can go on across national lines as well as within them. Lewis expresses his anxieties about a global state in the context of his apprehension about the abuse of science. In "Is Progress Possible," he writes:

We must give full weight to the claim that nothing but science, and science globally applied, and therefore unprecedented Government controls, can produce full bellies and medical care for the whole human race: nothing, in short, but a world Welfare State. It is a full admission of these truths which impresses upon me the extreme peril of humanity at present.[84]

Unless there is an agreed-upon moral code, there are no grounds on which to condemn the Third Reich or any regime like it—or even a world Welfare State. All that remains is our subjective preferences, which simply happen to digress from those of others. Hitler would grant that and take the same privilege for himself, and leaders of a world state, along with their scientist lackeys, would do the same.

Lewis raised the alarm on one other front in the last chapter of *The Abolition of Man*, and that is the effects of the engrained subjectivism in modern life on future generations of people. A culture that allows its leaders to create their own moralities and so condition people in society—as at the worst modern media and "politicians" (not "statesmen") are guilty—exercises power over later generations, a power that they have not conceded and likely would not concede. As each generation modifies the environment and the rules of engagement, it "exercises power over its successors."[85] It limits the options of later generations by making choices for its own benefit, rather than passing on the heritage of traditional morality that so many generations of human beings have passed on to their children. The conditioners will not pass on what they received from the *Tao* as their ancestors did for them. It will no longer be "grown birds" teaching "young birds" to fly, as Lewis puts it.[86] Rather, the conditioners will pass on a new understanding of morality, and this is a redefinition of humanity—or, more properly, the abolition of humanity as we know it.

The effect of a reality without the *Tao* is to make successive generations the patients of the power of the present Conditioners. "There is therefore no question of a power vested in the race as a whole steadily growing as long as the race survives. The last men, far from being the heirs of power, will be of all men most subject to the dead hand of the great planners and conditioners and will themselves exercise least power upon the future."[87] The Nietzschean bargain of power without obligation proves to be fool's gold, for the power so acquired contains the seeds of its own destruction. No natural law? Lewis asks; no ultimate power either. There is simply a law of diminishing returns inherent in the subjectivist position that makes each of man's conquests over nature a conquest of nature over man.[88] Seen along the axis of time no less than in the modern period on its own, the subjectivists make a fool's bargain, simply inviting the next strong leader to subjugate them the way they subjugated others. As Lewis said in another context, "Where is the rot to end?" to which he answers, "We must never allow the rot to begin."[89]

CONCLUSION: THE GREAT TRADITION IN WESTERN HISTORY

In a society where the rot has already begun, and is even well advanced, how do we stem the tide, and perhaps turn it back? Does Lewis offer any hope in the face of advancing subjectivism in ethics and metaphysics? It has to be said that he sees no solutions from governments and politicians. In "C. S. Lewis in the Public Square," Richard John Neuhaus states that Lewis had a "studied skepticism toward the search for political or legal fixes for human problems."[90] Public policy applied from the outside is not likely to solve human problems that are, finally, internal and ethical. Legislation cannot solve the problems either, for social problems are the results, not the causes, of ethical problems. Political and legal matters are simply manifestations of the human problem. Likewise, Lewis does not trust the "empowered elite"[91] to resolve social and legal problems. In fact, in a society divested of natural law, the leaders are the ones who arrogate power to themselves for their own ends no matter how they may frame "moral" arguments to defend their actions. For such a society, Lewis can offer no panaceas to anesthetize the lazy "trousered ape"[92] who simply wants the government to do his ethical thinking for him. At the same time, however, Lewis does offer hope if we have the moral courage to shoulder our responsibility toward our children.

The hope Lewis offers rests in our passing along the great tradition of western culture to our children. Lewis begins *The Abolition of Man* with concern over what education two English school textbooks give to their readers. At first glance, the issue appears modest enough, and perhaps too insignificant for a major university lecture like the Riddell Memorial Lectures at the University of Durham. Lewis knows, however, how important the matter is and understands that the problem and the solution share the same provenance—education. The hope for the future, in Lewis's view, is to teach our children objective values and objective truths. The hope lies in right ethics and right metaphysics.

Right Ethics

In a practical sense, the best education we can give our children is training in right ethics based on natural law, or the *Tao*. In the face of modern subjectivism in morals, teaching right morals is the burden of *The Abolition of Man*, and it is fitting that Lewis would begin the first chapter of the book with an apparently harmless school textbook, which nevertheless inculcates the unwary and ignorant schoolchild with a thorough-going subjectivism in values. In the second chapter, Lewis challenges the reader to restore the "chest," by which he means rightly educated virtues and sentiments—in short, to reverse the drift toward subjectivism in values. And in the final chapter, he teases out the frightening implications of not teaching our children proper ethical thinking. Gilbert Meilaender is certainly correct in his recognition of the emphasis Lewis places on moral education. Meilaender writes, "This stress on moral education could be said to be the strongest and most permanent theme of Lewis's ethic."[93] If we do not have the courage to teach our children the virtues that are their birthright, we surrender the future to leaders like Hitler, Stalin, Saddam Hussein, and any petty technocrat who can foist his personal values on people who will not know enough to rebel. Educate the chest, Lewis says, for the chest is what makes us human.

We educate the chest by teaching children the eternal verities and the eternal values. To return to Lewis's illustration from Coleridge early on in *The Abolition of Man*, the waterfall is inherently sublime. "Sublimity," when applied to the waterfall in question, is not a feature of the observer's emotions; it is a characteristic of the waterfall itself. Because sublimity is a characteristic of the waterfall, it is "eternal" in the sense that it does not change as an observer's emotions will. Whatever is true is true eternally. The same goes for values, for they too are eternal. Whatever is inherently virtuous is eternally and universally virtuous, and whatever is inherently evil is eternally and universally evil. Cowardice, theft, tyranny, and lust are all inherently evil; courage, honor, self-sacrifice, and love are all inherently good. No amount of subjectivist "rot" will change this objective state of affairs. In truth and values rightly understood, there is something eternal; it is "the way things are." In *Not a Tame Lion*, Bruce L. Edwards notes that Lewis "adopted the perspective of eternity"[94] in his apologetics throughout the Narnian stories, and he adopts the eternal point of view in *The Abolition of Man* as well (and in all of his writings, for that matter). In writing of God's love for us and the love for him we should develop in this life and most certainly will experience in heaven, Lewis himself states in *The Four Loves*, "all that is not eternal is eternally out of date."[95] Lewis's comments on God's love in *The Four Loves* are particularly helpful in our analysis of *The Abolition of Man* because they remind us that love is an action, a moral choice to put another first. In love, as in all ethical behavior, the eternal enters the temporal. Meilaender says it well in "The Everyday C. S. Lewis," where he writes about "This sense that eternal issues are at stake in the mundane choices of our every day life."[96] To train our children in natural law is to give them eternity's perspective. Educate the chest—the eternal values.

Right Metaphysics

We end with Lewis's view of right metaphysics, and to do that we return to Lewis's understanding of the Christian metanarrative of human history. Lewis's Christian perspective of history is grounded in two important considerations—natural law and historicism. First, Lewis insists that natural law is not a narrowly Christian moral code, but rather a universal moral law inherent in all human beings. Were the Appendix the only part of *The Abolition of Man* he had written, it would be evident that he believed natural law to be universal and objective. But we have the whole book, and its three chapters spell out the reality of natural law and the moral and epistemological dangers of rejecting that innate moral code. Second, Lewis does not think that historians can identify the character of an era in history or discover the meaning of a particular period of history. For Lewis, all such claims are neither objective nor historical; they are merely subjective and historicist. At the same time, however, there is an obvious metanarrative or metapattern, if we can call it that, to the trajectory of history that allows us to see significance in human actions. And this metanarrative coincides with the Christian understanding of human history, at least in the broad picture. Within the framework of these two caveats Lewis exhorts us to reclaim the great tradition of western culture from the past and lay hold of the future for our children.

The great tradition in western civilization provides continuity and allows for development. There is a tension, to be sure, between progress and stability, but understood from within the *Tao* the tension is healthy. At the end of the second chapter of *The Abolition of Man*, Lewis insists that it is impossible for us to invent a new system of morality by stepping outside of the tradition of natural law and still remain human. As we have seen, this is what he means by "men without chests"—men who have adopted a subjective morality and have become something other than men. In the context of this claim, however, Lewis states that some progress is not only possible, but is also necessary. "Some criticism [of current social mores, for instance], some removal of contradictions," Lewis writes, "is required."[97] In other words, we can develop the moral law from within its own framework and bring about moral advances.[98] In this way we can improve our understanding and application of natural law, as long as we do not attempt to redefine it in any essential or substantive manner. In "C. S. Lewis on Mere Science," Michael Aeschliman states that Lewis was "a believer in the essential sanity and continuity of Western Civilization,"[99] and the *Tao* is certainly one of the primary ways in which western civilization remains stable and progresses—and even survives, for that matter.

In the end, we must counter the subjectivism in metaphysics and ethics in modern culture with the thoroughgoing objectivism of the great tradition in western civilization. Reality is real. Right is right. Wrong is wrong. The apostle Paul had it correct when he spoke of creation revealing the deity,[100] and the conscience "accusing and excusing" all human beings on the basis of their actions.[101] The antidote to the decline in modern society is to reassert the great tradition that is our heritage from our fathers. In *The Restitution of Man*, Aeschliman states, "To the debilitating modernism which counts nothing sacred, Lewis juxtaposed the health of vital tradition, which he strove to enrich and transmit."[102] This is the burden of *The Abolition of Man*— to transmit to our children the great tradition of natural law. We must, in Richard Neuhaus's words, make "the very best arguments we can. . . . And we should tell better stories that winsomely, even seductively, reintroduce the Great Story."[103] In his apologetic books, *Mere Christianity* and *The Abolition of Man*, C. S. Lewis makes the "best arguments" to modern man by providing a logical defense of natural law in a culture where many saw values subjectively. In stories like *The Chronicles of Narnia*, the Ransom Trilogy, and *Till We Have Faces*, Lewis tells "better stories" by writing well-told narratives that point to the moral responsibility of all human beings and the good news of the great rescue that is available to all. "The task of the modern educator," Lewis writes, "is not to cut down jungles but to irrigate deserts."[104] Lewis did so at the University of Durham on those three days in February 1943, and he does so to those of us who come after in the pages of *The Abolition of Man*.

NOTES

1. Walter Hooper, *C. S. Lewis: A Companion and Guide* (New York: HarperSan Francisco, 1996), 330–331.

2. Warren Lewis, *Brothers and Friends: The Diaries of Major Warren Hamilton Lewis*, ed. Clyde S. Kilby and Marjorie Lamp Mead (San Francisco, CA: Harper and Row, 1982), 178.

3. Ibid., 179.

4. At http://www.ncl.ac.uk/calendar/pdf/public_lectures.pdf (accessed July 30, 2006).

5. Oxford's publications of the Riddell Memorial Lectures prior to Lewis's series included Oliver Chase Quick's 1930 lectures, *Philosophy and the Cross*; William Ralph Inge's 1932 series, *The Eternal Values*; J. L. Stocks's, *On the Nature and Grounds of Religious Belief* (1933); the tenth series by F. M. Powicke on *History, Freedom and Religion* in 1938 (a significant topic given the state of affairs on the continent at the time); and the 1940 Riddell Lectures by Robert Henry Thouless entitled, *Conventionalization and Assimilation in Religious Movements as Problems in Social Psychology*. Subsequent to Lewis's address, Oxford published the 1945 lectures by John Baillie, *What is a Christian Civilization?* The 1946 lectures were *Science, Faith and Society* by Michael Polanyi, and the 1947 series by Arthur David Ritchie was *Science and Politics*.

6. The author acknowledges the assistance of Laura Schmidt, Archivist at the Marion E. Wade Center at Wheaton College, Illinois, for the names of the authors and titles of the Riddell Memorial Lectures in the years before and after C. S. Lewis's 1943 talks.

7. Hooper, *C. S. Lewis: A Companion and Guide*, 786.

8. C. S. Lewis, Preface to *That Hideous Strength* (New York: Simon and Schuster, 1996), 7.

9. C. S. Lewis, Letter to Mary, February 20, 1955, *Letters to an American Lady*, ed. Clyde S. Kilby (Grand Rapids, MI: Eerdmans, 1967), 37.

10. Walter Hooper, note 1 to "On Ethics" in *Christian Reflections*, ed. Walter Hooper (Grand Rapids, MI: Eerdmans, 1996), 47.

11. John G. West, Jr. Essay on *The Abolition of Man* in *The C. S. Lewis Readers' Encyclopedia*, ed. Jeffrey D. Schultz and John G. West, Jr. (Grand Rapids, MI: Zondervan, 1998), 68.

12. Ibid., 68.

13. C. S. Lewis, *The Abolition of Man* (New York: Simon and Schuster, 1996), 86.

14. Doris T. Myers, *C. S. Lewis in Context* (Kent, OH: Kent State University Press, 1994), 73.

15. Ibid., 74.

16. C. S. Lewis, *The Abolition of Man*, 30.

17. Cf. Myers, *C. S. Lewis in Context*, 78: "Apparently Lewis uses the term to get away from the associations the term 'natural law' has with Christian ethics, for he is attempting to write nontheistically rather than from a Christian viewpoint."

18. C. S. Lewis, *The Abolition of Man*, 31.

19. Ibid., 35.

20. Ibid., 49.

21. C. S. Lewis, 49; cf. *Mere Christianity*, Foreword by Kathleen Norris (New York: HarperSanFrancisco, 2001), 9–10.

22. C. S. Lewis, *The Abolition of Man*, 52. Cf. 45, where Lewis argues that "sentiments," such as "society ought to be preserved," are in themselves rational principles and premises. It is only on the basis of these accepted premises that we can draw conclusions about value.

23. Compare "On Ethics," 53 and "The Poison of Subjectivism" in *Christian Reflections*, ed. Walter Hooper (1996), 75.

24. C. S. Lewis, *The Abolition of Man*, 77.

25. Ibid., 67. In *Beyond Freedom and Dignity*, B. F. Skinner states that the rule of the few over the many is "inevitable in the nature of cultural evolution" and that Lewis's concern here amounts to something on the order of paranoia. See B. F. Skinner, *Beyond Freedom and Dignity* (New York: Alfred A. Knopf, Inc., 1971), 206.

26. Ibid., 76. *Contra* Lewis, B. F. Skinner writes of the "autonomous man—the inner man, the homunculus, the possessing demon, the man defended by the literature of freedom and dignity" as one who needs to be "abolished" as soon as possible. See Skinner, 200.

27. Michael D. Aeschliman, *The Restitution of Man: C. S. Lewis and the Case against Scientism* (Grand Rapids, MI: Eerdmans, 1998), 76.

28. Ibid., 82–83. Lewis even writes of a "regenerate science" that would apply scientific advances in a humane and charitable way (p. 85). Compare Lewis's comments in a letter to Arthur C. Clarke, December 7, 1943, *The Collected Letters of C. S. Lewis*, vol. 2, ed. Walter Hooper (New York: HarperSanFrancisco, 2004), 593–594. The whole of this letter considers the issue of scientism.

29. Ibid., 83–84.

30. Ibid., 82–85.

31. Ibid., 81.

32. Myers, *C. S. Lewis in Context*, 82.

33. C. S. Lewis, "Historicism" in *Christian Reflections*, ed. Walter Hooper (Grand Rapids, MI: Eerdmans, 1996), 105.

34. Ibid., 100–101.

35. Peter Kreeft, *C. S. Lewis for the Third Millennium* (San Francisco, CA: Ignatius Press, 1994), 12.

36. C. S. Lewis, "De Descriptione Temporum" in *Selected Literary Essays* (London: Cambridge University Press, 1979), 3.

37. C. S. Lewis, *English Literature in the Sixteenth Century, Excluding Drama* (Oxford: Clarendon Press, 1954), 63.

38. C. S. Lewis, "Historicism" in *Christian Reflections* (Grand Rapids, MI: William B. Eerdmans Publishing Company, 1967), 100.

39. Gilbert Meilaender, *The Taste for the Other: The Social and Ethical Thought of C. S. Lewis* (Vancouver, OR: Regent College Publishing, 2003), 5.

40. Ibid., 101.

41. Aeschliman, *The Restitution of Man: C. S. Lewis and the Case against Scientism*, 3.

42. Ibid., 3. John G. West makes the point that Lewis rejected the idea of "a peculiarly 'Christian' morality' in favor of a 'natural moral law known by all through human reason.'" John G. West, "Finding the Permanent in the Political: C. S. Lewis as a Political Thinker," at http://www.discovery.org/scripts/viewDB/index.php?command=view&id=457&printer, 3. (Accessed July 30, 2006)

43. C. S. Lewis, "Is Progress Possible?" in *God in the Dock: Essays on Theology and Ethics*, ed. Walter Hooper (Grand Rapids, MI: Eerdmans, 1996), 314.

44. C. S. Lewis, *The Abolition of Man*, 77: Lewis lists truth, mercy, beauty, and happiness as examples of the virtues found in Natural Law, or the *Tao*.

45. John Warwick Montgomery, *The Shape of the Past: A Christian Response to Secular Philosophies of History* (Minneapolis, MN: Bethany House Publishers, 1975), 55–56, n.3.

46. John Randolph Willis, *Pleasures Forevermore: The Theology of C. S. Lewis* (Chicago, IL: Loyola University Press, 1983), 104.

47. Lewis, *The Abolition of Man*, 30.

48. Meilaender, *The Taste for the Other: The Social and Ethical Thought of C. S. Lewis*, 200.

49. John G. West, "C. S. and the Materialist Menace" at http://www.discovery.org/scripts/viewDB/index.php?command=view&id=458&printerFri, 5. (Accessed July 30, 2006)

50. Rom. 2:14–15 (Authorized—King James—Version)

51. C. S. Lewis, *The Abolition of Man*, 28–30, 31.

52. Ibid., 77.

53. Ibid., 31.

54. Meilaender, *The Taste for the Other: The Social and Ethical Thought of C. S. Lewis*, 210, Lewis's emphasis.

55. C. S. Lewis, *The Discarded Image: An Introduction to Medieval and Renaissance Literature* (Cambridge: Cambridge University Press, 1998), 176.

56. C. S. Lewis, "The Grand Miracle," in *Miracles: A Preliminary Study* (New York: Simon and Schuster, 1996), 143, 144. Essentially the same chapter is found in *God in the Dock: Essays on Theology and Ethics*, ed. Walter Hooper (Grand Rapids, MI: Eerdmans, 1996), 80–88.

57. C. S. Lewis, "Is Progress Possible?" in *God in the Dock: Essays on Theology and Ethics*, 312.

58. Ibid., 176.

59. C. S. Lewis, Dedication to *The Allegory of Love* (New York: Galaxy Book, 1958), np.

60. Ibid.

61. C. S. Lewis, *Surprised by Joy: The Shape of My Early Life* (New York: Harcourt Brace, 1955), 207.

62. C. S. Lewis, *The Abolition of Man*, 86.

63. C. S. Lewis, "The World's Last Night" in *The World's Last Night and Other Essays* (New York: Harvest Books, 1960), 101.

64. Gen. 5:3.

65. Gen. 1:26–27.

66. C. S. Lewis, *The Allegory of Love*, 1.

67. C. S. Lewis, *The Abolition of Man*, 53. Compare "On Ethics," 55.

68. C. S. Lewis, "The World's Last Night," 100. Lewis goes to some pains in this article to establish the fact that his comments on evolution relate to the "popular" understanding of evolution as naïve progress, not to the scientific Darwinian thinking (about which he has particular views as well). In other words, Lewis is not deriding science but the superficial interpretation of evolution as progressive improvement.

69. Ibid., 101.

70. See note 34.

71. See for instance Rev 9:20–21; 11:15b; 18:1–3; 20:11–5.

72. Aeschliman, *The Restitution of Man: C. S. Lewis and the Case against Scientism*, 32.

73. C. S. Lewis, *The Abolition of Man*, 67, 69.

74. C. S. Lewis, Letter to Arthur C. Clarke, December 7, 1943, *The Collected Letters of C. S. Lewis*, vol. 2, 594.

75. C. S. Lewis, "Religion and Rocketry" in *"The World's Last Night" and Other Essays* (New York: Harvest, 1959), 89.

76. C. S. Lewis, *The Abolition of Man*, 76.

77. Lewis, "The Poison of Subjectivism," in *Christian Reflections*, 73.

78. Alan Jacobs, *The Narnian: The Life and Imagination of C. S. Lewis* (New York: HarperCollins, 2005), 186. Lewis makes the same point in *The Abolition of Man*: "For the wise men of old the cardinal problem had been how to conform the soul to reality, and the solution had been knowledge, self-discipline, and virtue. For magic and applied science alike the problem is how to subdue reality to the wishes of men: the solution is technique . . ." (pp. 83–84).

79. Lewis's distinction between "rulers" and "leaders" is that rulers rule *for* the people, while leaders rule *over* the people and it is found in "Is Progress Possible," in *God in the Dock: Essays on Theology and Ethics*, 314.

80. C. S. Lewis, *The Abolition of Man*, 74.

81. Ibid., 73.

82. Ibid., 71.

83. Ibid., 69–70, italics the author's.

84. C. S. Lewis, "Is Progress Possible?" in *God in the Dock: Essays on Theology and Ethics*, 315.

85. Ibid., 68.

86. C. S. Lewis, *The Abolition of Man*, 34.

87. Ibid., 68–69.

88. Ibid., 79–80.

89. C. S. Lewis, "Meditation in a Toolshed" in *God in the Dock: Essays on Theology and Ethics* (Grand Rapids, MI: Eerdmans, 1996), 215.

90. Richard John Neuhaus, "C. S. Lewis in the Public Square," *First Things* 88 (December 1998), 30.

91. Aeschliman, *The Restitution of Man: C. S. Lewis and the Case against Scientism*, 76.

92. C. S. Lewis, *The Abolition of Man*, 23.

93. Meilaender, *The Taste for the Other: The Social and Ethical Thought of C. S. Lewis*, 199.

94. Bruce L. Edwards, *Not a Tame Lion: Unveil Narnia through the Eyes of Lucy, Peter, and Other Characters Created by C. S. Lewis* (Wheaton, IL: Tyndale House Publishers, 2005), 189.

95. C. S. Lewis, *The Four Loves* (New York: Harcourt Brace, 1960), 188.

96. Gilbert Meilaender, "The Everyday C. S. Lewis," *First Things* 85 (August/September 1998): 29.

97. C. S. Lewis, *The Abolition of Man*, 56.

98. Ibid., 57.

99. M. D. Aeschliman, "C. S. Lewis on Mere Science," *First Things* 86 (October 1998), 17.

100. Rom. 1:19–20.

101. Rom. 2:15.

102. Aeschliman, *The Restitution of Man: C. S. Lewis and the Case against Scientism*, 7.

103. Neuhaus, "C. S. Lewis in the Public Square," *First Things* 88 (December 1998): 35.

104. C. S. Lewis, *The Abolition of Man*, 27.

BIBLIOGRAPHY

Aeschliman, M. D. "C. S. Lewis on Mere Science," *First Things* 86 (October 1998), 16–18.

———. *The Restitution of Man: C. S. Lewis and the Case against Scientism*. Grand Rapids, MI: Eerdmans, 1998.

Edwards, Bruce L. *Not a Tame Lion: The Spiritual World of C. S. Lewis*. Wheaton, IL: Tyndale House Publishers, 2005.

Hooper, Walter. *C. S. Lewis: A Companion and Guide*. New York: HarperSan Francisco, 1996.

———. *The Collected Letters of C. S. Lewis*, vol. 2. Edited by Walter Hooper. New York: HarperSanFrancisco, 2004.

————. Ed. *God in the Dock: Essays on Theology and Ethics.* Grand Rapids, MI: Eerdmans, 1996.

Jacobs, Alan. *The Narnian: The Life and Imagination of C. S. Lewis.* New York: HarperCollins, 2005.

Kreeft, Peter. *C. S. Lewis for the Third Millennium.* San Francisco, CA: Ignatius Press, 1994.

Lewis, C. S. *The Abolition of Man.* New York: Simon and Schuster, 1996.

————. *The Allegory of Love.* New York: Galaxy Books, 1958.

————. *Christian Reflections.* Edited by Walter Hooper. Grand Rapids, MI: Eerdmans, 1996.

————. "De Descriptione Temporum." In *Selected Literary Essays.* London: Cambridge University Press, 1979.

————. *The Discarded Image: An Introduction to Medieval and Renaissance Literature.* Cambridge: Cambridge University Press, 1998.

————. *English Literature in the Sixteenth Century, Excluding Drama.* Oxford: Clarendon Press, 1954.

————. *The Four Loves.* New York: Harcourt Brace, 1960.

————. "The Grand Miracle." In *Miracles: A Preliminary Study.* New York: Simon and Schuster, 1996, 143, 144. Essentially the same chapter is found in *God in the Dock: Essays on Theology and Ethics.* Edited by Walter Hooper. Grand Rapids, MI: Eerdmans, 1996, 80–88.

————. "Historicism." In *Christian Reflections.* Edited by Walter Hooper. Grand Rapids, MI: Eerdmans, 1996.

————. "Is Progress Possible?" In *God in the Dock: Essays on Theology and Ethics.* Edited by Walter Hooper. Grand Rapids, MI: Eerdmans, 1996, 314.

————. *Letters to an American Lady.* Edited by Clyde S. Kilby. Grand Rapids, MI: Eerdmans, 1967.

————. "Meditation in a Toolshed." In *God in the Dock: Essays on Theology and Ethics.* Grand Rapids, MI: Eerdmans, 1996.

————. *Mere Christianity.* Foreword by Kathleen Norris. New York: HarperSanFrancisco, 2001.

————. "Religion and Rocketry." In *"The World's Last Night" and Other Essays.* New York: Harvest, 1959, 83–92.

————. *Surprised by Joy: The Shape of My Early Life.* New York: Harcourt Brace, 1955.

————. *That Hideous Strength.* New York: Simon and Schuster, 1996.

————. "The World's Last Night." *The World's Last Night and Other Essays.* New York: Harvest Books, 1960.

Lewis, Warren. *Brothers and Friends: The Diaries of Major Warren Hamilton Lewis.* Edited by Clyde S. Kilby and Marjorie Lamp Mead. San Francisco, CA: Harper and Row, 1982.

Meilaender, Gilbert. "The Everyday C. S. Lewis." *First Things* 85 (August/September, 1998): 27–33.

———. *The Taste for the Other: The Social and Ethical Thought of C. S. Lewis.* Vancouver, OR: Regent College Publishing, 2003.

Montgomery, John Warwick. *The Shape of the Past: A Christian Response to Secular Philosophies of History.* Minneapolis, MN: Bethany House Publishers, 1975, 55–56, n.3.

Myers, Doris T. *C. S. Lewis in Context.* Kent, UK: Kent State University Press, 1994, 73.

Neuhaus, Richard John "C. S. Lewis in the Public Square." *First Things* 88 (December 1998): 30–35.

Skinner, B. F. *Beyond Freedom and Dignity.* New York: Alfred A. Knopf, Inc., 1971, 206.

West, John G. "*The Abolition of Man.*" *The C. S. Lewis Readers' Encyclopedia.* Edited by Jeffrey D. Schultz and John G. West, Jr. Grand Rapids, MI: Zondervan, 1998, 68–70.

———. "C. S. and the Materialist Menace," http://www.discovery.org/scripts/viewDB/index.php?command=view&id=458&printerFri. Accessed July 30, 2006.

———. "Finding the Permanent in the Political: C. S. Lewis as a Political Thinker," http://www.discovery.org/scripts/viewDB/index.php?command=view&id=457&printerFri. Accessed July 30, 2006.

Willis, John Randolph. *Pleasures Forevermore: The Theology of C. S. Lewis.* Chicago, IL: Loyola University Press, 1983, 104.

6

The Great Divorce: Journey to Heaven and Hell[1]

Wayne Martindale

INTRODUCTION

I begin with a confession: I have not always wanted to go to Heaven. I can see now that many myths had unconsciously crowded into my mind: fuzzy logic conspired with pictures of stuffy mansion houses and ghosts walking on golden (therefore barren and cold) streets. Perhaps my biggest fear, until some time after my undergraduate years, was that Heaven would be boring. I knew I *should* want to go to Heaven, but I didn't. I would have said that I want to go to Heaven when I die, but mainly, I just didn't want to go to Hell. My problem was a badly warped theology and a thoroughly starved imagination. I knew that in Heaven we would worship God forever. But the only model I had for worship was church, and frankly, I wasn't in love with church enough to want it to go on through ages of ages, world without end. My mental image was of Reverend Cant droning on forever and ever.

Somewhere in the back of my mind, quite unconsciously, Heaven was an extended, boring church service like those I had not yet learned to appreciate on earth—with this exception: you never got to go home to the roast beef dinner. What a way to anticipate my eternal destiny. But then I read C. S. Lewis's *The Great Divorce.* It awakened in me an appetite for something better than roast beef. It aroused a longing to inherit what I was created for: that which would fulfill my utmost longings and engender new longings and fulfill those, too. After reading *The Great Divorce*, for the first time in my life, I felt Heaven to be both utterly real and utterly desirable. It was a magnificent gift. Small wonder, then, that *The Great Divorce* has always been one of my favorite books because when I read it, it awakened me to my spiritual anorexia. I was starving for heavenly food and didn't even know I was hungry.

Since then, I've read everything Lewis has written—at least everything published—and that reading has only expanded both my understanding of Heaven and Hell and my desire for Heaven, but none of that reading has bumped *The Great Divorce* from first place in thinking about eternity. To borrow a phrase from Lewis, it "baptized my imagination." Few writers bring to any subject Lewis's theological sophistication, historical grasp, imaginative range, and clarity of expression. My hope for this study is to advance Lewis's agenda: not only to enhance the reader's understanding, but to awaken or energize the sense of wonder and desire for our eternal home, and to eagerly anticipate that glorious day when we leave the shadowlands for good.

CONTEXT AND DESIGN

The Great Divorce was read in 1944, as it was being written, to the Inklings, an auspicious group of writers including Lewis, Tolkien, and Lewis's brother Warnie, among others. By the time he published *The Great Divorce* serially in a magazine called *The Guardian* in 1945 and then as a separate volume in 1946, Lewis had already written the book that catapulted him onto the cover of *Time* Magazine (1947) and won a large American following, *The Screwtape Letters* (1942); this work plus *The Problem of Pain* (1940), which contains key chapters on Heaven and Hell, provide important background to *The Great Divorce*. But the work that made his the most well-known voice in England (only after Winston Churchill's) was the BBC broadcasts from 1941 to 1944 that were eventually published as *Mere Christianity* (1952). He had also published the first two volumes of the Space or Ransom Trilogy, *Out of the Silent Planet* and *Perelandra*, and had finished writing the third, *That Hideous Strength*.

All of these works are in one way or another about choices and their consequences, a major theme carried forward in *The Great Divorce*, which he took up immediately on the heels of the Trilogy. But as with many of Lewis's books, the idea had been on his mind for a decade, which we know from his brother Warren's notation in his diary for April 16, 1933: "Jack has an idea for a religious work based on the opinion of some of the Fathers that while punishment for the damned is eternal, it is intermittent: he proposes to do a sort of infernal day excursion to Paradise."[2] This idea allowed him to develop further the themes introduced in these earlier books: Heaven as fulfillment,

Hell as sham and waste, and early choice as pregnant with eternity. Of course, as Lewis himself pointed out, most of his ideas will be found in some fashion in the works of George MacDonald. Lewis thought enough of MacDonald to produce an anthology of 365 readings, mostly from *Unspoken Sermons*. Two small quotes from entries Lewis labeled "Heaven" and "Hell" will suffice to illustrate his indebtedness. On "Heaven": "For the only air of the soul, in which it can breathe and live, is the present God and the spirits of the just: that is our heaven, our home, our all-right place"; and on "Hell": "The one principle of hell is—'I am my own!' "[3] Here are the core ideas of rich fruit so nourishing in *The Great Divorce*. A whole essay could be written on Lewis's literary debts, which would certainly include attention to the Bible, Augustine, Dante, Milton, Thomas Traherne ("golden and genial"), and large swaths of MacDonald. All urge the reader to choose completion in our Creator.

In *The Great Divorce*, all who are in Hell can take a bus to Heaven, if they wish, though few even wish it. The idea for this "holiday from hell" came from Lewis's reading of Jeremy Taylor, a seventeenth-century divine, shortly after Lewis's own conversion. Taylor mentions reading the obscure idea of a "refrigerium" or respite from suffering in a Parisian missal.[4] Does Lewis believe that souls in Hell actually have a "second chance" or even an occasional rest for the damned? Absolutely not. He says in the Preface that he chose *The Great Divorce* as the title to deliberately contradict William Blake's notion—expressed in his title "The Marriage of Heaven and Hell," a satiric reworking of Milton—that "the road of excess leads to the palace of wisdom" and that opposites must marry before progress is possible.[5] But, Lewis insists, reality presents us with an "'either-or.' If we insist on keeping Hell (or even earth) we shall not see Heaven: if we accept Heaven we shall not be able to retain even the smallest and most intimate souvenirs of Hell."[6] Lewis puts it this way in *The Problem of Pain*: "We can understand Hell in its aspect of privation. All your life an unattainable ecstasy has hovered just beyond the grasp of your consciousness. The day is coming when you will wake to find, beyond all hope, that you have attained it, or else, that it was within your reach and you have lost it forever."[7] Lewis deliberately casts the whole story as a dream vision (as we learn from the subtitle and are reminded at the end) to emphasize the fictional nature of the story—and anything can happen in dreams.

Why, then, does Lewis allow the "hellians" to journey to Heaven and stay if they want?[8] Simply to stress (1) that we choose our eternal destinies, and (2) that by our life choices we turn ourselves into beings suited for one or the other. By presenting his characters at the entrance to Heaven, Lewis can show at once both the process that damns and the result. We hear the hellians' reasons for rejecting Heaven, and as they leave for the "gray town" (Hell), we instantly see the consequence. Tellingly, those from Hell usually fail to even see the beauties of Heaven and most hasten back to Hell. The very first Ghost from the gray town to be mentioned (besides the narrator) doesn't last even a minute in Heaven. "'I don't like it! I don't like it,' screamed a voice, 'It gives me the pip!'"[9] With that she ran to the bus and never returned.

What follows upon their arrival in Heaven is a series of loosely organized encounters between the Ghosts and an appropriate heavenly counterpart. Like its cousin, *The Screwtape Letters,* the design is episodic: there isn't much plot. Although we come to identify with the narrator and his final fate, the interest is not mainly in the resolution of a central conflict or the development of a single character. Rather, our interest is in what sort of persons will take the stage next, what has kept them from Heaven, and what their response will be to the invitation to enter all joy. In the process, we get a short course on human nature and the psychology of sin.

Also like *The Screwtape Letters*, in *The Great Divorce* Lewis blends elements of earth with his vision of Hell. In the latter book, he blends elements of earth with Heaven, too. This not only makes Hell and Heaven more understandable because of the familiar earthly elements, but it makes us grasp the truth that "there is no neutral ground in the universe."[10] It points up the further truth that we bring into our earthly experience intimations of either Heaven or Hell by our choices. We are becoming every moment souls suited for one or the other.

You will have met people who are so full of the spirit of Christ that any destiny other than Heaven is unthinkable. These people also have many of the joys that will characterize Heaven, even in the midst of earthly pain. You will also have met people who hate goodness: who prefer evil companions and evil acts though it makes them wretched and miserable. When they do encounter good persons, they condemn them, perverting their sense of reason by rationalizing evil, even finding ways to blame the good, or God, or religion for their problems and those of the world. They already hate goodness because it implicitly condemns the evil they have chosen. They wouldn't like Heaven if they could have it. They are, in a sense, already in Hell, preferring darkness to light. This we see in each of the Ghosts that returns to Hell.

On the book's design, Evan Gibson notes, the Ghosts and the people from Heaven who meet them are presented in three divisions: five in the first half, five in the last half, and a group in the middle getting short treatment, all having in common a foolish desire to criticize Heaven. Some come all the way from Hell just to spit at Heaven in spite.[11] The first five Ghosts are all inwardly focused. Their besetting sins are: "their inflated inner-image, their intellectual dishonesty, their materialism, their cynicism, their false shame."[12] The five in the second half are also selfish, but their sin involves the desire to control others. Except for the first one, an artist, all in this last group exhibit some kind of perverted family relationship.

As with *The Screwtape Letters*, we learn by negative example how not to behave and by inference how we should behave. It is a series of lessons in Kingdom values, like the parables of Jesus. From the Theological Ghost, we learn that we can slip from a desire to know God and a love of God to a desire to know about God and a love of mere academic, theological pursuit. The Theological Ghost would rather return to Hell where he can dispute about Christ than enter Heaven and know Him. Similarly, the Painter Ghost has slipped successively from loving light and truth, to loving the medium, to loving his own opinions of truth, to loving his reputation. He learns from a heavenly counterpart that no one is much interested in his work, now that he has been dead a while. He instantly abandons Heaven in a vain attempt to restore his now discredited reputation and resurrect his school of painting. Journals, lectures, manifestos, and publicity—these fill his mind as he abandons Truth and ultimately his true self for pretensions.

We also meet a mother who is possessive of her son, and a wife whose earthly life was devoted to remaking her husband in her own image. Both would rather see their family members in Hell for the chance of controlling them than find true love in Heaven, love that cares about the real good of another. In the process of grasping, like all the hellians, they pervert their own personalities and become the sin they choose. Though on the brink of Heaven, all the Ghosts from Hell could say with Milton's Satan:

The mind is its own place, and in itself
Can make a Heaven of Hell, a Hell of Heaven.[13]

Which way I fly is Hell; myself am Hell.[14]

The Great Divorce shows us a parallel truth, one preeminently displayed in Dante's vision: that neither the punishment of Hell nor the reward of Heaven is arbitrary. Lewis's heavenly guide, MacDonald, explains this in the case of the Grumbling Ghost:

The whole difficulty of understanding Hell is that the thing to be understood is so nearly Nothing. But ye'll have had experiences . . . it begins with a grumbling mood, and yourself still distinct from it: perhaps criticising it. And yourself, in a dark hour, may will that mood, embrace it. Ye can repent and come out of it again. But there may come a day when you can do that no longer. Then there will be no *you* left to criticise the mood, nor even to enjoy it, but just the grumble itself going on forever like a machine."[15]

One of the central truths the book teaches is that Heaven is the fulfillment of human potential, Hell the drying up of human potential. "To enter heaven is to become more human than you ever succeeded in being on earth; to enter hell, is to be banished from humanity. What is cast (or casts itself) into hell is not a man: it is 'remains.'"[16] Hell strips away distinctions, and unrelieved sin is shown to be boring. On the other hand, in Heaven we blossom into fully differentiated personalities.

DESIRE AND CHOICE

In discussing this book, we'll have to spend a little time in Lewis's imaginary Hell, but we'll leave that mildewed place for the fresh outdoor world of Heaven before long to look at some of the positive truths that make it so desirable. First, a disclaimer: Lewis's own. He says in the Preface that he is not attempting to describe either Hell or Heaven as he thinks it literally appears as landscape. His real concerns are to show that Heaven is more real than any present physical reality and is the fulfillment of God's desires for us, and that Hell is by comparison "so nearly nothing." He is also concerned to show that everyone chooses his own eternal destiny by turning himself—with the Devil's help or Christ's—into a soul fit for Hell or a soul fit for Heaven.

Throughout his works, Lewis's most persistent theme is our desire for Heaven. Lacking a word to adequately describe this inmost hunger, he borrows one from Wordsworth and Coleridge: the word is "Joy." It is a problematical term in that its usual meaning is happiness, satisfaction, and fulfillment, whereas Lewis's special use is nearly the opposite: It is the absence of satisfaction and fulfillment. He defines Joy as a "stab of desire" for something never satisfied on earth. But this longing is more desirable than any earthly possession or happiness and "to have it again" was the driving force behind much of his youth and early adulthood. When all of our natural desires have been fulfilled, "we remain conscious of a desire which no natural happiness will satisfy."[17] For this reason, it is a major pointer to Heaven and was key in Lewis's own conversion.[18]

Lewis believes that every desire is at its root a desire for Heaven and would agree with Solomon that God has put eternity in our hearts.[19] Augustine put it this way: "our heart is restless, until it repose in thee." Therefore, we are all pilgrims in search of the Celestial City: some lost and looking for joy in all the wrong places, some saved with eyes fixed on the heavenly prize, and some sidetracked on dead-end streets and byways—but all longing for Heaven, whether we know it or not. Nearly all of Lewis's works have the aim of arousing this desire for Heaven or showing us how to live in proper anticipation of our true home.

Heaven is more sharply defined and more keenly desired when contrasted with Hell. So Lewis's story, like Dante's, opens in Hell. And as Dante has his mentor Virgil for a guide, so Lewis's narrator has his mentor George MacDonald as guide. Though stabs of Joy date from his early childhood, Lewis had his desires for Heaven aroused in a special, life-altering way at the age of sixteen when he read George MacDonald's *Phantastes*, so half way through *The Great Divorce*, on the outskirts of Heaven, the narrator (whose biographical details fit Lewis's exactly) meets George MacDonald, who becomes his teacher.

When the narrator asks his teacher if everyone has a chance to get on the bus, MacDonald replies with these soaring words:

Everyone who wishes it does. Never fear. There are only two kinds of people in the end: those who say to God, "Thy will be done," and those to whom God says, in the end, "*Thy* will be done." All that are in Hell, choose it. Without that self-choice there could be no Hell. No soul that seriously and constantly desires joy will ever miss it. Those who seek find. To those who knock it is opened.[20]

The theme of choice and our responsibility to choose not only permeates *The Great Divorce* but is also found throughout Lewis's works. Here's another example from *The Problem of Pain*:

In the long run the answer to all those who object to the doctrine of hell is itself a question: "What are you asking God to do?" To wipe out their past sins and, at all costs, to give them a fresh start, smoothing every difficulty and offering every miraculous help? But He has done so, on Calvary. To forgive them? They will not be forgiven. To leave them alone? Alas, I am afraid that is what He does.[21]

Each of the characters we meet fears that by accepting the invitation to Heaven they will have to give up something that has come to define them. True, they will be called upon to give up sin, but here we must remember Lewis's biblical belief that all was created good and that sin involves choosing something good at the wrong time or in the wrong way. We come to see that each sin veils a common human longing that has its legitimate fulfillment. As these fears are exposed to the good light of Heaven, we learn that behind each is the one big fear: that some desire would be unfulfilled. If I went God's way, I might lose out on something. What Lewis helps us discover is that all desires are, at rock-bottom, for Heaven. All of them. "There have been times," says Lewis, "when I think we do not desire heaven but more often I find myself wondering whether, in our heart of hearts, we have ever desired anything else."[22] Even the earthly pleasures are but temporary signposts to the "solid joys" of Heaven. In examining the hellians' fears and choices in contrast to those of the Solid people form Heaven, we will find something authentic and exhilarating to put in the place of the constriction that is sin.

DESCENT INTO HELL

The technique of using contrasts is central to Lewis's success in portraying Heaven as desirable and Hell as repulsive. From the beginning, even before we learn that the story has opened in Hell, we find the place to be dreary, drab, and literally hollow, since it is a largely unoccupied shell. The people we encounter are peevish, self-centered, grasping, and unpleasant. In *The Great Divorce*, we never enter deep Hell or deep Heaven: We are only on the outskirts of each. Lewis's opening vision of Hell is people standing in line, waiting for a bus that will take them to Heaven. None of the stereotypic flames in this portrayal of Hell. If we think of a foggy, drippy, London winter after the shops have all closed, we wouldn't be far off.

To the narrator's surprise Hell is deserted. It is deserted because in Hell you can have anything you want by just wishing for it. Of course, the whole point of Hell is that you don't wish for the right things. People there are always getting into arguments with the folks next door and wishing new houses into existence farther away from their nettlesome neighbors so that Hell is everexpanding. Napoleon is the nearest of the old rouges of history, and it took a visiting party 15,000 years to get to his place, only to discover him pacing back and forth. They watched him for a year, and all he ever did was pace and mutter, "It was Soult's fault. It was Ney's fault. It was Josephine's fault," and so on, endlessly.[23]

We may be tempted to think that Hell will be an entertaining place because it will have so many colorful people—a bully social club. From George Bernard Shaw, Oscar Wilde, and Groucho Marx to more contemporary comedians, we have heard the rationalizing quip that Hell is where fun is, with all the really interesting people. This has some of the zip of stolen pleasure in it, but we know that this sort of pleasure is a barbed hook and a cheat. So it is with the imagined social life of the "liberated" in Hell, where righteousness quells no libido. Even a moment's thought unveils the greed and self-centeredness behind lust, for example. In the gray town characters, we see Hell imagined in its true colors. Clarence Dye explains Lewis's notion aptly: "His concept of hell is the total alienation of man from God, nature and his fellow man. And this is dramatically portrayed by this image of hell, ... as individuals frantically trying not to be neighbors."[24]

Since Hell is the place where human potential is dried up—a place filled with remains of what were once humans but are now mere shells or ghosts, if you like—it is the last place to seek companionship. Sprinkled throughout Lewis's work, we find characters that typify the constriction into self and sin that is Hell. In *Perelandra* the possessed Weston, so unlike a human that he is called the Unman, descends to unspeakably childish banality, endlessly calling Ransom's name, responding to each reply with "Nothing." From *That Hideous Strength*, the very names of Wither and Frost belie their lost humanity. When there is intelligence, it is always warped and in the service of evil, doing someone in. For these early deconstructionists, even language becomes a tool for confusing and manipulating, not communication and truth. It is all politics and savage abuses of power with this lot. To end up in Hell with these and with Screwtape, Jadis the White Witch, Rishda, and Shift would be to enter a nightmare without the hope of waking. Jean-Paul Sartre in his play *Huis Clos* is closer to the truth than G. B. Shaw when he says, "Hell is other people."[25] But actually Hell is much worse than even the company of the damned suggests. It is having no company at all. It is, as Harry Blamires suggests, "the self, the confined, invulnerable, incommunicable, inescapable self."[26]

Satan gives us the supreme example of created potential shriveling into boredom. He was the archangel Lucifer, second only to God before his own fall. Lewis analyzes his constriction in his study of Milton's *Paradise Lost* and contrasts him with the newly created Adam:

Adam, though locally confined to a small park on a small planet, has interests that embrace "all the choir of heaven and all the furniture of earth." Satan has been in the Heaven of Heavens and in the abyss of Hell, and surveyed all that lies between them, and in that whole immensity has found only one thing that interests Satan. It may be said that Adam's situation made it easier for him, than for Satan, to let his mind roam. But that is just the point. Satan's monomaniac concern with himself and his supposed rights and wrongs is a necessity of the Satanic predicament. Certainly, he has no choice. He has chosen to have no choice. He has wished to "be himself," and to be in himself and for himself, and his wish has been granted. The Hell he carries with him is, in one sense, a Hell of infinite boredom. . . . Satan *wants* to go on being Satan. That is the real meaning of his choice "Better to reign in Hell, than serve in Heav'n."[27]

God could not be just or good without punishing evil, if we take punishment to mean in any way exclusion from Heaven. If he allowed people with evil bents to run free in his kingdom, then Heaven itself would cease to be good.[28] Because evil descends to the banal and self-centered, Hell is monotonous. In Heaven, where each person forever grows into the distinct personality God designed for unique and everexpanding roles, Heaven is the place with all the interesting personalities. To explore the mind of our creator, who knows the history and future path of the electrons at the furthest reach of the cosmos and numbers the particles of plankton strained through the baleens of every whale, and guides the flight of every comet—*that* will be interesting company.

But the damned repeatedly refuse the invitation to Reality and to meet face to face the One the Solid People call "Eternal Fact" and "Love Himself."

To think Hell and its occupants interesting requires the same absurd logic that sees sin as satisfying. It's the glimmer of fool's gold. Like Napoleon, all in Hell have become the sin they have chosen, unillumined by the common grace of God liberally dispensed on the earth, but absent in Hell. Nothing is more boring than the tawdry and unrelieved self. What a deception we are under when we fear that Heaven will be boring, when all along it is Hell we should fear. In Lewis's *Great Divorce*, we see that Hell is a boring place peopled with bores. It should not surprise us that there are no pleasures in Hell. Remember Screwtape's lament that the research and development arm of Hell never succeeded in inventing a pleasure. Besides, Hell only uses pleasure to entrap, then steadily reduces the enjoyment while increasing the desire. We call such ill-gotten pleasures vices. But when pleasure is taken God's way, the enjoyment sweetens the memory and brings us closer to him. Hell is the absence of God, and God is the author of all the pleasures, as the Bible claims and as Augustine, Dante, Milton, and Lewis illustrate at length.

As we will see in the "Ascent into Heaven" section, the signal contribution of this book is to make us feel as well as think that Heaven is the one real place in the universe and, by comparison, earth a Shadowland. What, then, is Hell? It is the ultimate unreality of being "so nearly nothing."[29] Hell exists, but everything there is the debris from what was human (or spirit in the angels' case) with the potential for true reality and fulfillment in Heaven squandered. The problem in depicting Heaven and Hell is one we have already considered: creating something believable when their glories or horrors are so beyond our human experience. What happens when we die? The spirit leaves the body. We think in our one-dimensional, time-bound existence of the resurrection as some time in the future. So when we think of this departed spirit, we imagine ghosts rising like steam. It's just the way our imaginations work, devoid as they are of a sense of category for spirit.

What Lewis does to make our imaginations better fit reality is turn the widespread but mistaken idea about spirit around: in *The Great Divorce* the people from Hell are ghosts; the people from Heaven are solid. Lewis's friend Owen Barfield observed that, paradoxically, "Lewis employs not only material shapes but *materiality itself* to symbolize immateriality."[30] The hellians appear in Heaven as greasy smoke and smudgy stains on the air. The narrator remarks: "One could attend to them or ignore them at will as you do with the dirt on a window pane."[31] As mentioned earlier, when the folk from Hell step on the grass in even the hinterlands of Heaven, it pierces their feet like spikes. Even the grass is more real than they. By contrast, the grass bends normally beneath the feet of the solid people from Heaven. When the narrator, freshly from Hell himself, gets the bright idea that the water will be solid to him like the unbending grass and that he could therefore walk on it, he gets swept off his feet and bumps along on top of the swiftly moving stream, badly bruising his ghostly body. And the spray from a waterfall goes through him like a bullet.

When the narrator asks his heavenly guide, MacDonald, why the people in Heaven don't go down to Hell to try to salvage the hellians, he learns that they can't because those in Heaven are so large and substantial. The bus from Hell had entered Heaven through some tiny crack in the soil. He is told that if a butterfly from Heaven were to swallow all of Hell, it would make no more difference to the butterfly than swallowing a single atom. The hellians are ghosts because they are blown up from their nothingness to the size of the solid people in Heaven. From Hell's perspective, Hell looked vast, though empty. By contrast, Heaven is so spacious that it seems to exist in a different dimension. The narrator remarks, it "made the Solar System itself seem an indoor affair."[32]

If we stop to think a minute, we can see why the spirit must be *more* real. God is spirit. God created the cosmos, the whole physical universe. God is not trapped in His own creation. He is bigger than what He made. Like the heavenly butterfly in *The Great Divorce*, if God were to swallow the whole universe, the effect would be no more than our swallowing an atom. Or if the whole thing were to suddenly collapse upon itself and evaporate into nothing, God would be no less than He is now, and He could make it all over again, if He wished. That is, in fact, what will happen at the resurrection: the present Heaven and earth will pass away, and He will make a new Heaven and a new earth. Spirit is more real and more powerful than flesh. Even in the case of our own persons, we see that it is our spirits that animate our bodies. When the spirit leaves, the flesh rots. The spirit will remain to reanimate our imperishable, heavenly bodies.

As the characters from Hell exit the bus on the outskirts of Heaven they are met by someone they knew on earth who has come out of Deep Heaven to invite them in. All but one returns to Hell for the very reason they went in the first place. It will be instructive to look at a few cases. Lewis's journey motif with its setting in Hell and Heaven makes possible some very effective puns that throw common phrases into a new light. The first Ghost into Heaven to get extended treatment is simply called "The Big Man" in Hell and "The Big Ghost" in Heaven. He is met from Heaven by Len, a man who had worked for him and who had murdered a mutual acquaintance named Jack. Upon seeing that Len is a Solid Person and robed in heavenly splendor, the first words out of the Big Ghost's mouth are, "Well, I'm damned."[33] He spoke as he always had on earth, blaspheming to show his surprise, but now it is literally true, which one look at the solid Len confirms by contrast with his ghostly self.

Len explains that the burden of seeing himself as a murderer had driven him to Christ. The Big Ghost merely persists in claiming the unfairness of it all; considering himself a decent chap, he keeps demanding his "rights." Ironically, the Big Ghost and all in Hell have precisely that: their rights. All have sinned; all deserve Hell. As Len urges him to forget about himself and his rights, the Ghost, saying more than he knows, insists, "'I'm not asking for anybody's bleeding charity.'"[34] In Britain, "bleeding" in this usage is a profane oath referring to Christ's blood spilled on the cross, which is literally the Big Ghost's only hope of Heaven. Len replies, "'Then do. At once. Ask for the Bleeding Charity. Everything is here for the asking and nothing can be bought.'"[35]

Language usage has come full circle from concrete heavenly truth to profane abstraction back to literal heavenly truth. We laugh, we see with new insight, we blush, and we hopefully repent. Meanwhile, The Big Ghost, stubborn as a mule about accepting any Heaven that admits murderers like Len, concludes, "'I'd rather be damned than go along with you. I came here to get my rights, see? Not to go sniveling along on charity tied onto your apron strings. If they're too fine to have me without you, I'll go home.'"[36] So he goes "home" to Hell.

Another character who prefers Hell is the Episcopal priest who is met by a former colleague. And let us not smugly think that Lewis's target in this satirical portrait is the clergy only. What he says applies to anyone who tries to substitute mere religion for the reality of a personal and vital relationship with the living God. The priest is greatly interested in religion and religious questions. To his chagrin, he discovers that no one in Heaven is the least bit interested in his speculations. They don't need his theology because they all have God Himself. The Episcopal ghost prefers questions to answers, questing to arriving, talking about God, and to meeting Him face to face. He has made his choice. In the end, learning that his kind of theology isn't needed in Heaven, he hurries back to Hell and a little Theological Society there to give a paper on "growing up to the measure of the stature of Christ."

The theme that runs through each of the meetings between the solid people of Heaven and the ghosts of Hell is choice. As we have seen in so many instances, sin is ultimately the choosing of self over God. Damnation and Hell are receiving that choice of self over God forever. The priest's interests were not really in theology, but in the fact that the views were his. Later on MacDonald, quoting Milton, explains: "The choice of every lost soul can be expressed in the words 'Better to reign in Hell than serve in Heaven.' There is always something they insist on keeping, even at the price of misery. There is always something they prefer to joy—that is, to reality. Ye see it easily enough in a spoiled child that would sooner miss its play and its supper than say it was sorry and be friends."[37]

ASCENT INTO HEAVEN

Lewis has another good reason for allowing the trip from Hell to Heaven: to provide multiple contrasts as a way of highlighting both hellish and heavenly qualities, contrasts between physical things like landscapes and bodies, and contrasts in the character of the people. Upon arriving at Heaven, the first thing the narrator notices is its expansiveness. Though Hell seemed vast from within, by contrast to Heaven, it is claustrophobic. Heaven "made the Solar System itself an indoor affair."[38] We later learn that the hellians, though it seemed to them a long journey up the side of a cliff, emerged in Heaven from a miniscule crack in the soil between two blades of grass. If a butterfly of Heaven were to swallow all of Hell, the teacher MacDonald tells the narrator, it would make no more difference than swallowing a single atom.[39] How real is Heaven, how much more substantial? Hell could not contain the minutest part of it.

After the landscape, the next thing the narrator notices is the bodies of the hellians. They appear as ghosts, as dirty stains on the air. Because people in Hell are really remains of their human selves with the potential shriveled by sin, when they are expanded to the size of a normal person in Heaven, they are so thin and unsubstantial that they look like ghosts. This is a very effective technique for showing that Heaven is ultimate reality and Hell so nearly nothing.

But the most telling contrast comes in the character of the people. The diabolical and warped are met by the holy and whole. Those from Heaven are fulfilled, content, overflowing with love and the reflected glory of Christ, which makes them luminous. The Ghosts have all come to Heaven for some bogus and selfish reason. The Solid People, as those from Heaven are called, have all made great sacrifices to come long distances from Deep Heaven to the outskirts in hopes of winning some of the Ghosts to Heaven.

The longest journey, however, is made by Christ Himself. We know from some key, though subtle, clues that the bus driver who brings the Ghosts to Heaven is a representative of Christ. First, the narrator's teacher, MacDonald, says that only the greatest can become small enough to fit into Hell. Second, the driver is described as being "full of light." Third, He is rejected by those He came to save: "God! I'd like to give him one in the ear-'ole," snarls one of the Ghosts. The narrator responds: "I could see nothing in the countenance of the Driver to justify all this, unless it were that he had a look of authority and seemed intent on carrying out his job."[40] This episode is a literal enactment of the Apostles' Creed: "He descended into Hell."

Having seen the long parade of Ghosts who come to the outskirts of Heaven only to return to Hell for the same reason they went there in the first place, the narrator naturally inquires of his guide whether any actually accept the invitation to enter Heaven. There are allusions by MacDonald to many who make it in, but we only see one actually making the passage. This is the case of a man whose besetting sin is lust, symbolized by a red lizard who sits on his shoulder, reminding him that his very identity is wrapped up in his lust and that life would be insipid without the flame of desire. An angel meets the Lustful Ghost and implores him for permission to kill the lizard. Through many struggles and though fearful that it may mean his death, he gives permission. Wondrously, the lizard is transformed into a white stallion, which the now Solid man rides joyously into Heaven.

The point is not that people once in Hell can go to Heaven or that sin can progress to goodness: Lewis explicitly denies both, as we have seen. The point is (1) that we must die to self in order to truly live, and (2) that all desires, however masked, are ultimately intended for Heaven. When we give our desires to God, the Author of all the pleasures, He fulfills the desires. The very thing that when grasped would drag us to Hell and pervert our personalities, when given to God is not only fulfilled but becomes a means of grace. God created all things good. Sin is not self-existent; it is a perversion of good.

A word on the Solid People: none in the book who come from Heaven are "great" in an earthly sense. The only one besides Lewis with a popular earthly reputation is his guide MacDonald. The others are all ordinary people with sins running the gambit from pride in one's own talent, to apostasy, and to murder. The main difference is that the Solid people all recognized their need of God and repented; they turned from their sin and received the gift of a new heart (new motives) and eternal life. None suffers the illusion that he or she deserves Heaven. It is a completely undeserved gift. The Solid people urge each of the Ghosts to receive the gift and "enter into joy." Pride keeps them out. All try to justify their sin. One of the impressions we are left with is how easy Heaven is to gain, and how easy it is to lose.

The last paired Ghost and Solid person are treated at the greatest length and deserve special attention. Here, using the technique of analogy (using the earthly to describe the heavenly), we have Lewis's fullest description of a Solid Person. Throughout the book, Lewis has used the technique of distancing. Scripture says, "no eye has seen, nor ear heard, nor the heart of man imagined, what God has prepared for those who love him."[41] Since Heaven is beyond our experience or even our imagining, Lewis avoids error and enhances our anticipation of it by never giving us a glimpse of "Deep Heaven" or even

"Deep Hell." Throughout the narrative, we are always in the in-between time before night falls in Hell or the day dawns in Heaven. Geographically, we are also never allowed into Hell or Heaven proper; we are always on the outskirts. Yet what we see of the fringes is both unspeakably horrific and unspeakably enchanting by comparison to earth. Even here on the outskirts, we see enough to make our blood run fast.

In the last pairing, a self-pitying Ghost named Frank appears as a Dwarf leading by a chain a projection of himself called a Tragedian. He is met by Sarah Smith of Golders Green, who was his wife on earth. Frank's interest in making the pilgrimage from Hell is not in gaining Heaven; it is for gaining pity for his condition, thereby holding the joy of Heaven hostage. In this Lewis answers the age-old question of how there could be joy in Heaven when even one soul suffers the torments of everlasting Hell. Pity cannot hold love hostage. MacDonald, the narrator's guide, explains to him that Heaven will not make a dunghill of "the world's garden for the sake of some who cannot abide the smell of roses."[42] In the end, the Dwarf Frank chooses his self-pity over Heaven and shrinks until nothing is left but the projection of his sin, the Tragedian, which vanishes back to the constriction that is Hell.

Sarah is not brokenhearted; it is not possible in the presence of Him who is true love and joy. She is joined by angels who sing a psalm of her overcoming joy and protection by God. She appears by earthly standards to be a goddess. Indeed, she is a "Great One" in Heaven, though on earth she was the lady next door. She is reaping the rewards of nameless acts of love that characterized every contact with every person and all creation. This love extended even to the animals. Now, in Heaven, these very animals make up a part of her sizable entourage, which also included gigantic emerald angels scattering flowers, followed by numerous boys and girls, and musicians. Of the indescribably beautiful music, the narrator can only say that no one who "read that score would ever grow sick or old."[43] "Dancing light" shined from the entourage. All was in honor of Sarah Smith, who was so gloriously ordinary on earth. And to this the Self-Pitying ghost and all from Hell were invited. We wonder at the depth of pride and perversion that would embolden so many, both in the book and in our own experience, to thumb their noses at the sublime largesse of God.

The Great Divorce ends with dizzying reflections on Time and Eternity, Predestination, and Free Will. Lewis deftly shows that all attempts to solve this ancient paradox fail if they are posed from within time. God being outside of time, sees all in an everpresent now, so from His point of view, all is known and done, even what is yet in the future for us. But from our point of view within time, choices are still before us. Even now, in what may be my twentieth reading of *The Great Divorce*, the concluding pages move me to tears for people without the hope of the Heaven and my own destiny were it not for "Bleeding Charity." Throughout the book, it has been perpetual evening twilight in the Grey Town of Hell and perpetual presunrise dawn in the hinterlands of Heaven where the meetings take place.

Now at the end, as the pilgrim narrator looks into the face of his teacher, George MacDonald, and with the east at his back, the promised sunrise breaks. It will mean eternal day for Heaven and a darkening to eternal night for Hell. The sunlight falls in solid blocks upon the narrator's insubstantial body, and he is stricken with terror, for he has come to these precincts of Heaven as a ghost from Hell: "'The morning! The morning!' I cried, 'I am caught by the morning and I am a ghost.'"[44] In the moment he is seized by the terror of damnation, the narrator awakens from his dream, clutching at a tablecloth and pulling down on his head, not blocks of light, but books. With sweet relief, we realize that he and we are still pilgrims and Heaven still before us. There is yet time to choose and to guide the choice of others.

INFLUENCE AND RECEPTION

While anything approaching precision about a great book's influence is difficult at best, some observations rooted in fact may at least be suggestive. In surveying some the popular books on faith and Heaven from my own shelves, I find that the following books (all published between 1995 and 2006) explicitly cite *The Great Divorce*: Randy Alcorn's *Heaven*, Anthony DeStefano's, *A Travel Guide to Heaven*, John Eldredge's *The Scared Romance*, Hank Hanegraaff's *Resurrection*, Max Lucado's *When Christ Comes*, Lee Strobel's *The Case for Faith*, and Joni Eareckson Tada's *Heaven*. In addition, Harry Blamires, a prolific critic and former pupil of C. S. Lewis at Oxford, has written *New Town* (2005), a book clearly modeled on *The Great Divorce*.[45]

My search of the MLA (Modern Language Association) online bibliography yielded twenty listings, thirteen of them from 1990 to the present: Ten periodicals devoted to Lewis studies five in *Mythlore*, one in a scholarly Christian journal, and four in mainstream literary journals. One indication of the respect accorded *The Great Divorce* is the list of classic writers discussed in these publications, including: Dante, Augustine, Blake, Eliot, and Baudelaire. The themes include: epic, redemption, free will, feminism, time and consciousness, medieval dream vision, law, and immortality. Religion indexes list fewer works, but include articles from *The Harvard Theological Review* and the *Journal of Bible and Religion*.

The online bookseller Amazon provides a popular and easily accessible indicator of sales. On March 29, 2006, out of all the books sold on Amazon, *The Great Divorce* ranked an impressive 926, with a cumulative ranking of 1783. Lewis's most popular book, *Mere Christianity*, ranked 304 for the day and 414 cumulatively—*The Screwtape Letters* is close behind *Mere Christianity*, and all three are ahead of *The Lion, the Witch and the Wardrobe*, no doubt because so many are already in circulation. By comparison, the most popular edition of the classic *The Pilgrim's Progress* ranks 6,389 for the day and 7,505 cumulatively, and Milton's *Paradise Lost* 5,032 and 8,888. These are impressive numbers and show that Lewis's books as a whole have wide appeal, with *The Great Divorce* toward the top of that list.

Perhaps one of the best indicators of influence is foreign translations, since these represent considerable work and investment, while showing something of both the staying power and worldwide reach a book commands. The Lewis collection at Wheaton College's Wade Center has translations of *The Great Divorce* in the following ten languages: Spanish, French, German, Bulgarian, Russian, Japanese, Norwegian, Portuguese, Finnish, and Czech.

The influence of *The Great Divorce* is steady and growing, as Lewis's reputation and value is becoming increasingly established in general. It will likely remain in print and well read, but will also not likely supplant those Lewis titles that have become almost household items. Some suggest that its appeal is hampered by the want of a plot and character development, which may indeed give us a clue to the book's limitations. From somewhere in the back of my mind, however, I hear a voice saying, "but it didn't keep *The Screwtape Letters* from becoming and remaining enormously popular." On the other hand, this narrator is not as colorful a character as Screwtape, whose words are laced with trenchant irony and whose mask both we and Wormwood begin to penetrate from the very beginning. In the case of the unnamed narrator of *The Great Divorce*, we identify with him, but neither love nor hate him—or, as with Screwtape, love to hate him. But in place of a colorful narrator, we get a succession of deftly drawn and varied pairings of people from Heaven and Hell. And while *The Great Divorce* may not have quite the humor of *The Screwtape Letters*, what both books do have in common is a satirical touch, an episodic structure, brevity, psychological penetration, theological range, and an imaginative reach. In the case of the last item, I would even give *The Great Divorce* the edge. It deals with a subject few have contributed to meaningfully. Lewis adds to our knowledge by breaking stereotypes, dramatizing the urgency of choice, and making our eternal destinies imaginable. Because these achievements are so rare, I believe that Lewis's slim volume will continue to wear well through the waxing and waning of theological and literary fashion.

NOTES

1. Though expanded here, the core of this essay appears in my book *Beyond the Shadowlands: C. S. Lewis on Heaven and Hell* (Wheaton, IL: Crossway, 2005) and is used with the permission of the publisher.

2. Roger Lancelyn Green and Walter Hopper, *C. S. Lewis: A Biography*, revised edn. (London: HarperCollins, 2002), 281.

3. George MacDonald, *George MacDonald: 365 Readings*, ed. C. S. Lewis (New York: Collier, 1947), 35, 88.

4. Green and Hooper, *C. S. Lewis: A Biography*, 280. Cf. 1 Peter 2:11 and Philippians 3:20.

5. William Blake, *The Marriage of Heaven and Hell*, ed. Geoffrey Keynes (New York: Oxford University Press, 1975), xviii. For an excellent but brief scholarly treatment of linkage between *The Great Divorce* and Blake and Dante, see Dominic Manganiello, "*The Great Divorce*: C. S. Lewis's Reply to Blake's Dante," *Christian Scholar's Review* 17(4) (Summer 1998), 475–489.

6. Lewis, *The Great Divorce*, Preface, 6.

7. C. S. Lewis, *The Problem of Pain* (New York: Macmillan, 1962), 145.

8. I have coined the term "hellian" as a convenient way of referring to someone from Hell, avoiding the common spelling "hellion" because it connotes an outward rowdiness.

9. Lewis, *The Great Divorce*, 28.

10. C. S. Lewis, "Christianity and Culture." In *Christian Reflections* (Grand Rapids, MI: Eerdmans, 1967), 33.

11. Evan K. Gibson, *C. S. Lewis, Spinner of Tales: A Guide to His Fiction* (Grand Rapids, MI: Eerdmans, 1980), 116.

12. Ibid., 112.

13. Milton, *Paradise Lost* I, 254–255.

14. Milton, *Paradise Lost* IV, 75.

15. Lewis, *The Great Divorce*, 9:75.

16. Lewis, *The Problem of Pain*, 125.

17. C. S. Lewis, "The Weight of Glory," *The Weight of Glory and Other Addresses*. Edited by Walter Hooper (New York: Simon & Schuster, 1996), 8.

18. See Lewis's spiritual autobiography, *Surprised by Joy*. (New York: Harcourt, Brace & World, 1955)

19. Ecclesiastes 3:11.

20. Ibid., 9:72–73.

21. Lewis, *The Problem of Pain*, 128.

22. Ibid., 10, 145.

23. Lewis, *The Great Divorce*, 2, 20.

24. Clarence F. Dye, "The Evolving Eschaton in C. S. Lewis" (Ph.D. Dissertation, Fordham University, New York, 1973), 219.

25. Harry Blamires, *Knowing the Truth about Heaven and Hell: Our Choices and Where They Lead Us* (Ann Arbor, MI: Servant Books, 1988), 149–150.

26. Ibid., 150.

27. C. S. Lewis, *Preface to "Paradise Lost,"* (New York: Oxford University Press, 1961), 13, 102–103.

28. Kenneth Kantzer, "Afraid of Heaven," *Christianity Today* 35(6) (27 May, 1991), 38.

29. Lewis, *The Great Divorce*, 75.
30. Owen Barfield, *Owen Barfield on C. S. Lewis*, ed. G. B. Tennyson (Middletown, CT: Wesleyan University Press, 1989), 88.
31. Ibid., 3, 27.
32. Ibid., 3, 27.
33. Lewis, *The Great Divorce*, 4, 32.
34. Ibid., 4, 34.
35. Ibid. There is some controversy over the etymology "bloody" as a slang term.
36. Ibid., 4, 36.
37. Lewis, *The Great Divorce*, 9, 69–70.
38. Lewis, *The Great Divorce*, 3, 27.
39. Ibid., 122–123.
40. Ibid., 14.
41. I Corinthians 2:9
42. Lewis, *The Great Divorce*, 13, 121.
43. Lewis, *The Great Divorce*, 12, 107.
44. Ibid., 14, 128.
45. Harry Blamires, *New Town* (Grand Rapids, MI: Revell, 2005).

BIBLIOGRAPHY

Barfield, Owen. *Owen Barfield on C. S. Lewis*. Edited by G. B. Tennyson. Middletown, CT: Wesleyan University Press, 1989.
Blake, William. *The Marriage of Heaven and Hell*. Edited by Geoffrey Keynes. New York: Oxford University Press, 1975.
Blamires, Harry. *Knowing the Truth About Heaven and Hell: Our Choices and Where They Lead Us*. Ann Arbor, MI: Servant Books, 1988.
———. *New Town*. Grand Rapids, MI: Revell, 2005.
Dye, Clarence F. "The Evolving Eschaton in C. S. Lewis." Ph.D. Dissertation, Fordham University, New York, 1973.
Gibson, Evan K. *C. S. Lewis, Spinner of Tales: A Guide to His Fiction*. Grand Rapids, MI: Eerdmans, 1980.
Green, Roger Lancelyn and Walter Hooper. *C. S. Lewis: A Biography*. Revised edition. London: HarperCollins, 2002.
Hooper, Walter. *C. S. Lewis Companion & Guide*. San Francisco, CA: HarperCollins, 1996.
Lewis, C. S. *"Preface to "Paradise Lost."* New York: Oxford University Press, 1961.
———. *The Problem of Pain*. New York: Macmillan, 1962.
———. *Surprised by Joy*. New York: Harcourt, Brace, & World, 1955.
———. "The Weight of Glory." In *The Weight of Glory and Other Addresses*. Edited with Introduction by Walter Hooper. New York: Simon & Schuster, 1996, 25–42.
———. *The Weight of Glory and Other Addresses*. Edited with Introduction by Walter Hooper. New York: Simon & Schuster, 1996.

MacDonald, George. *George MacDonald: 365 Readings*. Edited by C. S. Lewis. New York: Collier, 1947.

Manganiello, Dominic. "*The Great Divorce*: C. S. Lewis's Reply to Blake's Dante." *Christian Scholar's Review* 27(4) (Summer 1998): 475–489.

Milton, John. *The Complete Poems and Major Prose*. Edited by Merritt Hughes. New York: Odyssey Press, 1957.

BIBLIOGRAPHY OF SELECTED BOOKS WITH CHAPTERS, SECTIONS, OR ARTICLES ON *THE GREAT DIVORCE*

Adey, Lionel. *C. S. Lewis: Writer, Dreamer, and Mentor*. Grand Rapids, MI: Eerdmans, 1998.

Duriez, Colin. *The C. S. Lewis Encyclopedia*. Wheaton, IL: Crossway Books, 2000.

Gibson, Evan K. *C. S. Lewis, Spinner of Tales: A Guide to His Fiction*. Grand Rapids, MI: Eerdmans, 1980.

Glover, Donald E. *C. S. Lewis: The Art of Enchantment*. Athens, OH: Ohio University Press, 1981.

Hannay, Margaret Patterson. *C. S. Lewis*. New York: Ungar, 1981.

Hein, Rolland. *Christian Mythmakers*. Chicago, IL: Cornerstone, 1998.

Honda, Mineko. *The Imaginative World of C. S. Lewis*. New York: University Press of America, 2000.

Hooper, Walter. *C. S. Lewis Companion & Guide*. San Francisco, CA: HarperCollins, 1996.

Kilby, Clyde. *The Christian World of C. S. Lewis*. Grand Rapids, MI: Eerdmans, 1964.
———. *Images of Salvation in the Fiction of C. S. Lewis*. Wheaton, IL: Harold Shaw Publishers, 1978.

Knowles, Sebastian D. C. *A Purgatorial Flame: Seven British Writers in the Second World War*. Philadelphia, PA: University of Pennsylvania Press, 1990.

Manlove, Colin. *The Chronicles of Narnia: The Patterning of a Fantastic World*. New York: Twayne, 1993.

Martindale, Wayne. *Beyond the Shadowlands: C. S. Lewis on Heaven and Hell*. Wheaton, IL: Crossway, 2005.

Payne, Leanne. *Real Presence*. Grand Rapids, MI: Baker Book Houses, 1995.

Peters, Thomas C. *Simply C. S. Lewis*. Wheaton, IL: Crossway Books, 1997.

Schultz, Jeffrey D. and John G. West, Jr. Editors. *The C. S. Lewis Readers' Encyclopedia*. Grand Rapids, MI: Zondervan, 1998.

Walsh, Chad. *The Literary Legacy of C. S. Lewis*. New York: Harcourt Brace Jovanovich, 1979.

7

Miracles: C. S. Lewis's Critique of Naturalism

Victor Reppert

After the famous Liar, Lunatic, or Lord trilemma, the second most-discussed apologetic argument advanced by C. S. Lewis must be the argument against naturalism found in the third chapter of his book *Miracles: A Preliminary Study*, commonly known as the argument from reason. This is, I suppose, largely my fault, since I wrote a book, *C. S. Lewis's Dangerous Idea: In Defense of the Argument from Reason*,[1] dedicated to the discussion and defense of that argument. The argument was the subject of Lewis's famous exchange with Elizabeth Anscombe,[2] which resulted in Lewis developing a revised version of the argument. Besides my own efforts, the argument has been defended by more recent philosophers such as William Hasker,[3] Richard Purtill,[4] and Angus Menuge.[5] What is more, perhaps the best-known Anglo-American philosopher of religion, Alvin Plantinga,[6] has developed a line of argument that bears a family resemblance to the argument Lewis defended. The argument has, however, had its critics. Not only Anscombe, but also Antony Flew[7] and John Beversluis[8] have criticized Lewis's version of it; Jim Lippard,[9] Keith Parsons,[10] Theodore Drange,[11] and Richard Carrier[12] have criticized my efforts; and Plantinga's argument has attracted a whole host of philosophical opponents.[13]

In this essay, I will begin by discussing the role Lewis's argument plays in the context of his book on miracles. I will then proceed to discuss the argument's antecedents, particularly its place in the apologetic writings of the

British prime minister and philosopher Arthur Balfour.[14] I will then present the argument of Lewis's first edition, explain Anscombe's criticisms, and then present the argument as it appears in the revised edition of *Miracles*. I will attempt to show that it is not the case, as Beversluis maintains, that Anscombe's objections can be pressed further, and that Lewis's revised argument does nothing to meet them.[15] Rather, the argument, in my judgment does successfully survive Anscombe's objections. After that I will discuss some recent versions of the argument, both mine and those of others, and will then also discuss some objections that have been put to it by recent writers.

THE ARGUMENT FROM REASON AND ITS PLACE IN LEWIS'S *MIRACLES*

Lewis was first and foremost a Christian apologist, and not merely a theistic apologist. What this means is that Lewis does not typically follow the "classical" model of apologetics in which it is deemed necessary first to prove the existence of God and then to prove the truth of various Christian doctrines. Lewis's *Miracles* was written in response to a request by Dorothy Sayers, who wrote and told him that there were no good books on the subject. Lewis called the book *Miracles: A Preliminary Study*, and this immediately raises the question "preliminary to what?" That answer is, preliminary to the study of biblical scholarship. An innocent Christian (or non-Christian) might pick up a book on biblical scholarship and assume that the scholarship there presented reflects the state of the evidence for and against a particular miracle claim found in Scripture. What he or she may not be aware of, however, is that the evidence for or against a miracle claim is typically assessed against the backdrop of some presuppositions on the part of the scholar concerning the antecedent likelihood of the miraculous. Some scholars and historians begin their investigations of Scripture with presuppositions that rule out accepting any miracle story as literally true. Rudolph Bultmann, an enormously influential German biblical scholar with whose works Lewis was familiar, wrote:

It is impossible to use electric light and the wireless and to avail ourselves of modern medical and surgical discoveries, and at the same time to believe in the New Testament world of spirits and miracles. We may think we can manage it in our own lives, but to expect others to do so is to make the Christian faith unintelligible and unacceptable to the modern world.[16]

Similarly, earlier this year, in a debate about the Resurrection of Jesus with William Lane Craig, the eminent biblical scholar Bart Ehrman maintained:

What are miracles? Miracles are not impossible. I won't say they're impossible. You might think they are impossible and, if you do think so, then you're going to agree with my argument even more than I'm going to agree with my argument. I'm just going to say that miracles are so highly improbable that they're the least possible occurrence in any given instance. They violate the way nature naturally works. They are so highly improbable, their probability is infinitesimally remote, that we call them miracles. No one on the face of this Earth can walk on lukewarm water. What are the chances that one of us could do it? Well, none of us can, so let's say the chances are one in ten billion. Well, suppose somebody can. Well, given the chances are one in ten billion, but, in fact, none of us can. What about the resurrection of Jesus? I'm not saying it didn't happen; but if it did happen, it would be a miracle. The resurrection claims are claims that not only that Jesus' body came back alive; it came back alive never to die again. That's a violation of what naturally happens, every day, time after time, millions of times a year. What are the chances of that happening? Well, it'd be a miracle. In other words, it'd be so highly improbable that we can't account for it by natural means. A theologian may claim that it's true, and to argue with the theologian we'd have to argue on theological grounds because there are no historical grounds to argue on.[17]

Biblical scholars who follow the lead of Bultmann or Ehrman begin their investigations with the presupposition that any story about what happened in biblical times that contains no miracle is better than a story about those same events that involves God's miraculous intervention. This view was given its classic expression in David Hume's famous "Of Miracles," section X of his *Enquiry Concerning Human Understanding*.[18] The casual reader might think a scholar such as Bultmann or Ehrman has discovered that a nonmiraculous account of, say, the events surrounding the first Easter, is preferable to a miraculous account, when in fact these scholars feel obligated to presuppose, going into their investigations, that miraculous explanations must be avoided.

Bringing such presuppositions to the study of Scripture, in Lewis's view, threatened the very essence of Christianity. The Apostle Paul said "If Christ has not been raised, then our preaching is in vain and your faith is in vain" and "we are of all men most to be pitied" (1 Corinthians 15:14, 19). Thinking clearly and consistently about miracles is critical to understanding the issues surrounding Christianity. Lewis maintained that unlike religions like Hinduism and Buddhism, the miraculous element in Christianity is absolutely critical. "Demythologized" understandings of Christianity, for Lewis, drained Christianity of its content.

People like Bultmann and Ehrman, who study the founding events of Christianity with a deliberate disregard for the miraculous element, use a principle of *methodological naturalism* when investigating biblical texts; that is, in the investigation of those texts only natural processes should be considered, and nothing that would involve the supernatural. What they maintain, essentially, is that, at least for the purpose of investigating historical events, they are obligated to view the physical world as if it were causally closed.

Lewis begins his book on miracles by pointing out that one cannot simply look at the evidence to determine whether some miracle or other has occurred; one must consider the antecedent probability of the miraculous before deciding this. One decision that a person has to make is whether or not one believes that there is anything other than nature, and if so, whether that undermines the causal closure of the physical world. As he puts it:

Many people think one can decide whether a miracle occurred in the past by examining the evidence "according to the ordinary rules of historical inquiry." But the ordinary rules cannot be worked until we have decided whether miracles are possible, and if so, how probable they are. If they are impossible, then no amount of historical evidence will convince us. If they are possible but immensely improbable, then only mathematically demonstrative evidence will convince us; since history never provides that degree of evidence for any event, history can never convince us that a miracle has occurred. If, on the other hand, miracles are not intrinsically improbable, then the existing evidence will not be sufficient to convince us that quite a number of miracles have occurred. The result of our historical enquiries thus depends on the philosophical views with which we have been holding before we even began to look at the evidence. The philosophical question must come first.[19]

To provide an illustration for Lewis's claim, in a debate entitled "Why I am/am not a Christian" between William Lane Craig and Keith Parsons, atheist Keith Parsons challenged the Resurrection of Jesus by appealing to Carl Sagan's maxim "Extraordinary claims require extraordinary evidence."[20] If Sagan's maxim has to be applied to the Resurrection, then the case for it will be very difficult to defend. If we reject or modify Sagan's maxim, then a case for the Resurrection might very well be defensible.

But Lewis is not merely concerned about biblical scholars who are card-carrying methodological or metaphysical naturalists. He is also concerned about the after effects of naturalism on biblical scholars who are not naturalists of either stripe. He writes:

It comes partly from what we may call a "hangover." We all have naturalism in our bones and even conversion does not at once work the infection out of our system. Its assumptions rush back upon the mind the moment vigilance is relaxed.[21]

The Argument from Reason is significant not merely as an argument for theism, but also as an argument against the causal closure of the physical. If we have reason to reject the causal closure of the physical in the case of rational inference, this will make it easier to reject the requirement that accounts of the founding of Christianity reject the causal closure of the physical.

THE CONCEPT OF NATURALISM

Exactly what does Lewis mean by naturalism? Very often the terms Naturalism and Materialism are used interchangeably, but at other times it is insisted that the two terms have different meanings. Lewis says,

What the naturalist believes is that the ultimate Fact, the thing you can't go behind, is a vast process of time and space which is going on of its own accord. Inside that total system every event (such as your sitting reading this book) happens because some other event has happened; in the long run, because the Total Event is happening. Each particular thing (such as this page) is what it is because other things are what they are; and so, eventually, because the whole system is what it is.[22]

As a presentation of naturalism, however, this might be regarded as inadequate by contemporary naturalists, because it saddles the naturalist with a deterministic position. The mainstream position in contemporary physics involves an indeterminism at the quantum-mechanical level. Lewis himself thought that this kind of indeterminism was really a break with naturalism, admitting the existence of a lawless Subnature as opposed to Nature, but most naturalists today are prepared to accept quantum-mechanical indeterminism as a part of physics and do not see it as a threat to naturalism as they understand it. Some critics of Lewis have suggested that his somewhat deficient understanding of naturalism undermines his argument.[23] Lewis, however, insisted on "making no argument" out of quantum mechanics and expressed a healthy skepticism about making too much of particular developments in science that might be helpful to the cause of apologetics.[24]

However, contemporary defenders of the Argument from Reason such as William Hasker and myself have developed accounts of materialism and naturalism that are neutral as to whether or not physics is deterministic or not. Whatever Lewis might have said about quantum-mechanical indeterminacy, the problems he poses for naturalism arise whether determinism at the quantum-mechanical level is true or not.

Materialism, as we understand it, is committed to three fundamental theses:

1) The basic elements of the material or physical universe function blindly, without purpose. Man is the product, says Bertrand Russell, of forces that had no prevision of the end they were achieving. Richard Dawkins's exposition and defense of the naturalistic worldview is called *The Blind Watchmaker: Why the Evidence of Evolution Reveals a World Without Design*[25] not because no one ever designs anything in a naturalistic world, but because, explanations in terms of design must be reduced out in the final analysis. Explanation always proceeds bottom-up, not top-down.

2) The physical order is causally closed. There is nothing transcendent to the physical universe that exercises any causal influence on it.

3) Whatever does not occur on the physical level supervenes on the physical. Given the state of the physical, there is only one way the other levels can be.[26]

The argument from reason is concerned with what philosophers today call prepositional attitudes, states such as believing that proposition p is true, desiring that proposition p be true, doubting that proposition p be true, etc, and how these prepositional attitudes come to be caused. There are three types of materialism, at least so far as propositional states are concerned. One type is called eliminative materialism, which argues that propositional attitudes like belief and desire do not exist. Another kind is called reductive materialism, according to which mental states can be analyzed or reduced in physical terms. A third kind is nonreductive materialism, according to which mental states are not to be analyzed in physical terms, but given the state of the physical, there is only one way the mental can be. All of these positions are consistent with the definition of materialism given above.

As for naturalism, it is hard to see how a worldview could be naturalistic without satisfying the above definition. Perhaps a world could be naturalistic if there was no matter or if the science describing the most basic level of analysis is not physics. However, whatever objections there might be to materialism based on the argument from reason would also be objections to these forms of naturalism. So although the argument is primarily directed at materialism, so far as I can tell, there is no form of naturalism that fares any better against the argument from reason than materialism.

ANTECEDENTS OF LEWIS'S ARGUMENT FROM REASON

Although Lewis seemed never to address his apologetical books primarily to atheists (as opposed to others who might reject Christianity), he did present an argument against the atheistic naturalism, and it is an argument designed to show that the physical is not causally closed. He describes coming to reject a naturalistic worldview in his book *Surprised by Joy*, under the influence of his Anthroposophist friend Owen Barfield. He wrote:

[He] convinced me that the positions we had hitherto held left no room for any satisfactory theory of knowledge. We had been, in the technical sense of the term, "realists"; that is, we accepted as rock-bottom reality the universe revealed to the senses. But at the same time, we continued to make for certain phenomena claims that went with a theistic or idealistic view. We maintained that abstract thought (if obedient to logical rules) gave indisputable truth, that our moral judgment was "valid" and our aesthetic experience was not just pleasing but "valuable." The view was, I think, common at the time; it runs though Bridges' *Testament of Beauty* and Lord Russell's "Worship of a Free Man." Barfield convinced me that it was inconsistent.

If thought were merely a subjective event, these claims for it would have to be abandoned. If we kept (as rock-bottom reality) the universe of the sense, aided by instruments co-ordinated to form "science" then one would have to go further and accept a Behaviorist view of logic, ethics and aesthetics. But such a view was, and is, unbelievable to me.[27]

Now Lewis, when he accepted this argument, did not become a traditional theist but rather an Absolute Idealist, a worldview that does not leave room for the miraculous. In *Surprised by Joy* Lewis gives independent reasons for rejecting Absolute Idealism, and in *Miracles* Lewis also devotes chapter 11, "Christianity and 'Religion'," to criticizing pantheistic worldviews, including Absolute Idealism.

The Argument from Reason did not originate with Lewis. Something like it can be traced all the way back to Plato, and Augustine had an argument connected reason with our appropriation of the knowledge of eternal and necessary truths. Descartes maintained that the higher rational processes of human beings could not be accounted for in materialistic terms, and while Kant denied that these considerations did not provide adequate proof of the immortality of the soul, he did think they were sufficient to rule out any materialist account of the mind. However, naturalism or materialism as a force in Western thought did not become really viable until 1859, when Charles Darwin published the *Origin of Species*.

The earliest post-Darwinian presentation of the Argument from Reason that I am familiar with, and one that bears a lot of similarities to Lewis's argument, is found in Prime Minister Arthur Balfour's *The Foundations of Belief*. Lewis never mentions *The Foundations of Belief* in his writings, but he does say in one place that Balfour's subsequent book *Theism and Humanism* is "a book too little read." According to Balfour the following claims follow from the "naturalistic creed."

1. My beliefs, in so far as they are the result of reasoning at all, are founded on premises produced in the last resort by the "collision of atoms."

2. Atoms, having no prejudices in favour of the truth, are as likely to turn out wrong premises as right ones; nay, more likely, inasmuch as truth is single and error manifold.

3. My premises, therefore, in the first place, and my conclusions in the second, are certainly untrustworthy, and probably false. Their falsity, moreover, is a kind which cannot be remedied; since any attempt to correct it must start from premises not suffering under the same defect. But no such premises exist.

4. Therefore, my opinion about the original causes which produced my premises, as it is an inference from them, partakes of their weakness; so that I cannot either securely doubt my own certainties or be certain about my own doubts.[28]

Balfour then considers a "Darwinian rebuttal," which claims that natural selection acting as a "kind of cosmic Inquisition," will repress any lapses from the standard of naturalistic orthodoxy. The point was made years later by Antony Flew as follows:

[A]ll other things being equal and in the long run and with many dramatic exceptions, true beliefs about our environment tend to have some survival value. So it looks as if evolutionary biology and human history could provide some reasons for saying that it need not be a mere coincidence if a significant proportion of men's beliefs about their environment are in fact true. Simply because if that were not so they could not have survived long in that environment. As an analysis of the meaning of "truth" the pragmatist idea that a true belief is one which is somehow advantageous to have will not do at all. Yet there is at least some contingent and non-coincidental connection between true beliefs, on the one hand, and the advantage, if it be an advantage, of survival, on the other.[29]

However, Balfour offers this reply to the evolutionary argument:

But what an utterly inadequate basis for speculation we have here! We are to suppose that powers which were evolved in primitive man and his animal progenitors in order that they might kill with success and marry in security, are on that account fitted to explore the secrets of the universe. We are to suppose that the fundamental beliefs on which these powers of reasoning are to be exercised reflect with sufficient precision remote aspects of reality, though they were produced in the main by physiological processes which date from a stage of development when the only curiosities which had to be satisfied were those of fear and those of hunger.[30]

Interestingly, Balfour's argument here finds surprising support from Darwin himself. In a letter to William Graham Down, Darwin wrote:

the horrid doubt always arises whether the convictions of man's mind, which has been developed from the mind of the lower animals, are of any value or at all trustworthy. Would any one trust in the convictions of a monkey's mind, if there are any convictions in such a mind?[31]

As can be seen, Balfour's presentation of the argument, and his consideration of counterarguments, anticipated much of the debate on this issue that is still going on a century after his book was written.

THE ARGUMENT OF THE FIRST EDITION

In the first edition of *Miracles*, Lewis presents the version of the argument from reason that Anscombe criticized. We can formalize it as follows:

1. No thought is valid if it can be fully explained as the result of irrational causes.
2. If naturalism is true then all beliefs can be explained in terms of irrational causes.

3. Therefore, if naturalism is true, then no thought is valid.

4. If no thought is valid, then the thought, "materialism is true," is not valid.

5. Therefore, if materialism is true, then the belief "materialism is true" is not valid.

6. A thesis whose truth entails the invalidity of the belief that it is true ought to be rejected, and its denial ought to be accepted.

7. Therefore, naturalism ought to be rejected, and its denial accepted.

This is the argument that drew the criticisms of Roman Catholic philosopher and Wittgenstein student, Elizabeth Anscombe. This critique is significant because of the way in which it forced Lewis to develop and refine his arguments. Too much attention has been paid to the putative psychological effects of this controversy, and conclusions concerning Lewis's success as a Christian apologist have been drawn on the basis of his supposed *emotional* reaction to Anscombe's challenge. Very often this is done without regard to the content of this exchange, and often this is done by people who show by their discussion to have no real understanding of the relevant philosophical issues. Such a procedure, as Bertrand Russell once said of a thesis in the philosophy of mathematics, has all the advantages of theft over honest toil.

ANSCOMBE'S FIRST OBJECTION: IRRATIONAL VERSUS NONRATIONAL

Is it correct for Lewis to talk about physically caused events as having irrational causes? Irrational beliefs, one would think, are beliefs that are formed in ways that conflict with reason: wishful thinking, for example, or through the use of fallacious arguments. On the other hand, when we speak of a thought having a nonrational cause, we need not be thinking that there is any conflict with reason.[32]

While this claim seems correct, it hardly puts an end to the argument from Reason. The problem arises when we consider what a naturalist typically believes. Let's take the theory of evolution as an example. Naturalists are always big on evolution, since invariably they must assign to the evolution process the task of producing the incredibly complex features, say, of the human eye. Traditionally, the existence of the human eye was thought to be so efficient and complex that it had to be the handiwork of God. After all, the artificial replacement of vision by modern medicine is still the stuff of science fiction. Nevertheless, the naturalist is undaunted; she is persuaded that it is all the result of natural selection. However, a naturalist does not merely need to believe that we are the product of evolution through random variation and natural selection, she also has to believe that there was a process of scientific inference that led Charles Darwin to reach his conclusions about natural selection and how it works. Naturalism really does require the existence of rational inferences in order to be legitimate. Now a rational inference is a rational process. A valid or sound argument is an argument on paper in which the premises are true and the conclusion follows logically and inevitably from the premises and therefore must also be true. A rational inference, however, is not just a paper argument; it is an act of knowing on the part of a person that recognizes the content of the premises, accepts the premises as true, perceives the logical relationship between the premises, and concludes that the conclusion must be true as well. In short, naturalists must believe not merely that their own beliefs were not produced by irrational causes, they must maintain that the conclusion that evolution is true was produced, in the mind of Charles Darwin and in their own mind, as the result of a rational process. Otherwise there would be no reason to prefer the deliverances of the natural sciences to a blind acceptance of the Book of Genesis as a way of forming one's beliefs concerning the origin of species.

For that reason, it is possible to restate Lewis's argument in such a way that it does not make reference to irrational causes, and indeed in Lewis's revised chapter the phrase "irrational causes" does not appear.

1. No belief is rationally inferred if it can be fully explained in terms of nonrational causes.
2. If naturalism is true, then all beliefs can be fully explained in terms of nonrational causes.
3. Therefore, if naturalism is true, then no belief is rationally inferred.
4. If any thesis entails the conclusion that no belief is rationally inferred, then it should be accepted and its denial accepted.
5. Therefore, naturalism should be rejected and its denial accepted.

ANSCOMBE'S SECOND OBJECTION: PARADIGM CASES AND SKEPTICAL THREATS

Anscombe also objected to the idea Lewis argued that, were naturalism true, then reasoning would not be valid. She asks, "What can you mean by valid beyond what would be indicated by the explanation you give for distinguishing between valid and invalid reasoning, and what in the naturalistic hypothesis prevents the explanation from being given or meaning what it does."[33] This is a Paradigm Case argument, and the point is this: We can ask whether this particular argument is a good one, but does it really make sense to argue that reasoning might itself be invalid? Anscombe maintains that since the argument that some particular piece of reasoning is invalid involves contrasting it with some other kinds of reasoning that are valid, the question "Could reasoning really be valid?" is really a nonsense question.

One way of using the argument from reason would be to use it as a skeptical threat argument. The idea is that if naturalism is true we will be unable to refute skeptical arguments against reasoning in general. The problem here is that it is far from clear that anyone, naturalist or not, can refute skepticism about reasoning, nor is it considered any great merit for any metaphysical theory that it would be possible to refute this kind of thoroughgoing skepticism. And, if we need to refute skepticism in order to accept some worldview, then it is not at all clear that theism will do that either. If we use our theistic beliefs to defend the basic principles of reasoning, then we would have to formulate that into an argument and then *presuppose* our ordinary canons of logical evaluation in the presentation of that very argument, thereby begging the question.

Rather, one can, it seems to me, present the argument from reason as a best explanation argument. One should assume, at least to begin with, that human beings do reach true conclusions by reasoning, and then try to show, given the fact that people do reach true conclusions by reasoning, that this is best explained in terms of a theistic metaphysics as opposed to a naturalistic metaphysics. Now if we present the argument in this way, and then an opponent comes along and says "I see that your argument presupposes that we have beliefs. I don't think we do, so your argument fails," then we can reply to him by saying that if there are no beliefs then you don't believe what you're saying. Consequently the status of your own remarks as *assertions* is called into question by your own thesis that there are no beliefs, and that this is going to end up having a devastating effect on the very sciences on which you base your arguments. Presenting the argument in this way, it seems to me, gets around the problems based on the Paradigm Case argument.

ANSCOMBE'S THIRD OBJECTION: THE AMBIGUITY OF "WHY," "BECAUSE," AND "EXPLANATION"

The third and main Anscombe objection to Lewis's argument is that he fails to distinguish between different senses of the terms "why," "because," and "explanation." There are, she suggests, four explanation types that have to be distinguished:

1. Naturalistic causal explanations, typically subsuming the event in question under some physical law.

2. Logical explanation, showing the logical relationship between the premises and the conclusion.

3. Psychological explanations, explaining why a person believes as he/she does.

4. Personal history explanations, explaining how, as a matter of someone's personal history, they came to hold a belief.

She suggests that arguments of different types can be compatible with one another. Thus a naturalistic causal explanation might be a complete answer to one type of question with respect to how someone's belief came to be what it was, but that explanation might be compatible with an explanation of a different type.[34]

Now what is interesting is that Lewis, in reformulating his own argument, not only draws the distinctions on which Anscombe had insisted—he actually makes these distinctions the centerpiece of his revised argument. He makes a distinction between Cause and Effect relations on the one hand, and Ground-and-Consequent relations on the other. Cause and effect relations say how a thought was produced, but ground-and-consequent relations indicate how thoughts are related to one another logically. However, in order to allow for rational inference, there must be a combination of ground-consequent and cause-effect relationships that, Lewis says, can't exist if the world is as the naturalist says that it is.

Claiming that a thought has been rationally inferred is a claim about how that thought was caused. Any face-saving account of how we come to hold beliefs by rational inference must maintain that "One thought can cause another thought not by being, but by being, a ground for it."[35]

However, there are a number of features of thoughts as they occur in rational inference that set them apart from other beliefs.

Acts of thinking are no doubt events, but they are special sorts of events. They are "about" other things and can be true or false. Events in general are not "about" anything and cannot be true or false... Hence acts of inference can, and must be considered in two different lights. On the one hand they are subjective events in somebody's psychological history. On the other hand, they are insights into, or knowings of, something other than themselves.[36]

So here we already have three features of acts of thinking as they occur in rational inference. First, these thoughts have to be about something else, and second, they can be true or false. Second, their propositional contents must cause other thoughts to take place. But there is more:

What from the first point of view is a psychological transition from thought A to thought B, at some particular moment in some particular mind is, from the thinker's point of view a perception of an implication (if A, then B). When we are adopting the psychological point of view we may use the past tense, "B followed A in my thoughts." But when we assert the implication we always use the present—"B *follows from* A." If it ever "follows from" in the logical sense it does so always. And we cannot reject the second point of view as a subjective illusion without discrediting human knowledge.[37]

So now, in addition to the three features of thoughts as they occur in rational inference, we can add a fourth, that is, that the act of inference must be subsumed under a logical law. And the logical law according to which one thought follows another thought is true always. It is not local to any particular place or time; indeed laws of logic obtain in all possible worlds.

Lewis then argues that an act of knowing "is determined, in a sense, by what is known; we must know it to be thus because it is thus."[38] P's being true somehow brings it about that we hold the belief that p is true. Ringing in my ears is a basis for knowing if it is caused by a ringing object; it is not knowledge if it is caused by a tinnitus.

Anything that professes to explain our reasoning fully without introducing an act of knowing thus solely determined by what it knows, is really a theory that there is no reasoning. But this, as it seems, is what Naturalism is bound to do. It offers what professes to be a full account of our mental behaviour, but this account, on inspection, leaves no room for the acts of knowing or insight on which the whole value of our thinking, as a means to truth, depends.[39]

UNLIMITED EXPLANATORY COMPATIBILITY AND THE NONCAUSAL VIEW OF REASON

This is a point at which Anscombe, in her brief response to Lewis's revised argument objects, claimed that Lewis did not examine the concept of "full explanation" that he was using. Anscombe had expounded a "question relative" conception of what a "full explanation" is; a full explanation gives a person everything they want to know about something. John Beversluis explicates this idea as follows, using the string quartets of Beethoven as his example:

Fully means "exhaustively" only from a particular point of view. Hence the psychologist who claims to have fully explicated the quartets from a psychological point of view is not open to the charge of self-contradiction if he announces his plans to attend a musicologist's lecture on them. In music, as in psychology, the presence of non-rational causes does not preclude reasons. In fact, there is no limit to the number of explanations, both rational and non-rational, that can be given why Beethoven composed his string quartets . . . All of these "fully explicate" the composition of his string quartets. But they are not mutually exclusive. They are not even in competition.[40]

This is an explication of the idea of an unlimited explanatory compatibilism. It is further supported if one accepts, as Anscombe did when she wrote her original response to Lewis, the Wittgensteinian doctrine that reasons-explanations are not causal explanations at all. They are rather what sincere responses that are elicited from a person when he is asked what his reasons are. As Anscombe puts it:

It appears to me that if a man has reasons, and they are good reasons, and they genuinely are his reasons, for thinking something—then his thought is rational, whatever causal statements can be made about him.[41]

Keith Parsons adopted essentially the same position in response to my version of the argument from reason when he wrote:

My own (internalist) view is that if I can adduce reasons sufficient for the conclusion Q, then my belief that Q is rational. The causal history of the mental states of being aware of Q and the justifying grounds strike me was quite irrelevant. Whether those mental states are caused by other mental states, or caused by other physical states, or just pop into existence uncaused, the grounds still justify the claim.[42]

But the claim that reasons-explanations are not causal explanations at all seems to me to be completely implausible. As Lewis puts it,

Even if grounds do exist, what have they got to do with the actual occurrence of belief as a psychological event? If it is an event it must be caused. It must in fact be simply one link in a causal chain which stretched back to the beginning and forward to the end of time. How could such a trifle as lack of logical grounds prevent the belief's occurrence and how could the existence of grounds promote it?[43]

If you were to meet a person, call him Steve, who could argue with great cogency for every position he held, you might on that account be inclined to consider him a very rational person. But suppose that on all disputed questions Steve rolled dice to fix his positions permanently and then used his reasoning abilities only to generate the best available arguments for those beliefs selected in the above-mentioned random method. I think that such a discovery would prompt you to withdraw from him the honorific title "rational." Clearly the question of whether a person is rational cannot be answered in a manner that leaves entirely out of account the question of how his or her beliefs are produced and sustained.

As for the question of explanatory compatibility, the issues related to the question of whether one causal explanation can exclude one another or whether they can be compatible is rather complex. But in the case of the string quartets of Beethoven, surely the example is a flawed one, because what is being discussed here is different aspects of the composition. The urge to compose them requires a different explanation from the decisions Beethoven made about what melody to compose, how to put the harmony together, and so on. If Beethoven was obsessed with writing for string instruments, we still do not know why he chose quartets as opposed to, say, cello solos.

Second, it seems clear that there have to be some limits on explanatory compatibility. Consider how we explain how presents appear under the Christmas tree. If we accept the explanation that, in spite of the tags on the presents that say Santa Claus, the presents were in fact put there by Mom and Dad, this would of course conflict with the explanation in terms of the activity of Santa Claus. An explanation of disease in terms of microorganisms is incompatible with an explanation in terms of a voodoo curse. In fact, naturalists are the first to say, "We have no need of that hypothesis" if a naturalistic explanation can be given where a supernatural explanation had previously been accepted.

Further, explanations, causal or noncausal, involve ontological commitments. What plays an explanatory role is supposed to exist. So if we explain the existence of the presents under the Christmas tree in terms of Santa Claus I take it that means that Santa Claus exists in more than just a nonrealist "Yes, Virginia," sense.

Even the most nonreductivist forms of materialism maintain that there can be only one kind of causation in a physical world, and that is physical causation. It is not enough simply to point out that we can give different "full" explanations for the same event. Of course they can. But given the causal closure thesis of naturalism there cannot be causal explanations that require nonmaterialist ontological commitments. The question that is still open is whether the kinds of mental explanations required for rational inference are compatible with the limitations placed on causal explanations by naturalism. If not, then we are forced to choose between saying that there are no rational inferences and accepting naturalism. But naturalism is invariably presented as the logical conclusion of a rational argument. Therefore the choice will have to be to reject naturalism.

Lewis maintains that if we acquired the capability for rational inference in a naturalistic world it would have to have arisen either through the process of evolution or as a result of experience. However, he says that evolution will always select for improved responses to the environment, and evolution could do this without actually providing us with inferential knowledge. In addition, while experience might cause us to expect one event to follow another, to logically deduce that we should expect one effect to follow another is not something that could be given in experience.

THREE ARGUMENTS FROM REASON

In my book, *C. S. Lewis's Dangerous Idea: In Defense of the Argument from Reason*, I distinguished necessary conditions of rational inference, which I maintained cause problems for naturalism, and which I maintain are better handled on theistic assumptions as opposed to naturalistic assumptions. These include intentionality or aboutness, truth, mental causation in virtue of propositional content, the psychological relevance of logical laws, the existence of an enduring person throughout the process of rational inference, and the reliability of our rational faculties. So instead of one Argument from Reason, I concluded that there are really six. The first four I have argued have been alluded to in the course of my discussion of Lewis's *Miracles*. The last one has been developed by Plantinga and is the centerpiece of his argument against naturalism, but was also prefigured in his predecessor Balfour. I want to discuss three of the arguments here: the argument from intentionality, the argument from mental causation in virtue of content, and the argument from the psychological relevance of logical laws. In doing so I will consider and respond to the objections of Richard Carrier.[44]

THE ARGUMENT FROM INTENTIONALITY

One of them is the claim that our thoughts are about other things. Philosophers today refer to this "aboutness" as intentionality. In my book I develop an "argument from intentionality," according to which we have good reason to reject a naturalistic worldview because naturalism cannot account for the fact that our thoughts are about other things.

Physical states have physical characteristics, but how can it be a characteristic of, say, some physical state of my brain, that it is about dogs Boots and Frisky, or about my late Uncle Stanley, or even about the number 2. Can't we describe my brain, and its activities, without having any clue as to what my thoughts are about?

To consider this question, let us give a more detailed account of what intentionality is. Angus Menuge offers the following definition:

1. The representations are about something.
2. They characterize the thing in a certain way.
3. What they are about need not exist.
4. Where reference succeeds, the content may be false.
5. The content defines an intensional context in which the substitution of equivalents typically fails.[45]

So, if I believe that Boots and Frisky are in the backyard, this belief has to be about those dogs; I must have some characterization of those dogs in mind that identifies them for me; my thoughts can be about them even if, unbeknownst to me, they have just died; my reference to those two dogs can succeed even if they have found their way into the house; and someone can believe that Boots and Frisky are in the backyard without believing that "the Repperts' 13-year-old beagle" and "the Repperts' 8-year-old mutt" are in the back yard.

It is important to draw a further distinction, a distinction between original intentionality, which is intrinsic to the person possessing the intentional state, and derived or borrowed intentionality, which is found in maps, words, or computers. Maps, for example, have the meaning that they have, not in themselves, but in relation to other things that possess original intentionality, such as human persons. There can be no question that physical systems possess derived intentionality. But if they possess derived intentionality in virtue of other things that may or may not be physical systems, this does not really solve the materialist's problem.

The problem facing a physicalist account of intentionality is presented very forcefully by John Searle:

Any attempt to reduce intentionality to something nonmental will always fail because it leaves out intentionality. Suppose for example that you had a perfect causal account of the belief that water is wet. This account is given by stating the set of causal relations in which a system stands to water and to wetness and these relations are entirely specified without any mental component. The problem is obvious: a system could have all those relations and still not believe that water is wet. This is just an extension of the Chinese Room argument, but the moral it points to is general: You cannot reduce intentional content (or pains, or "qualia") to something else, because if you did they would be something else, and it is not something else.[46]

Admittedly, this is merely an assertion of something that needs to be brought out with further analysis. It seems to me that intentionality, as I understand it, requires consciousness. There are systems that behave in ways such that, in order to predict their behavior, it behooves us to act as if they were intentional systems. If I am playing chess against a computer, and I am trying to figure out what to expect it to play, then I am probably going to look for the moves I think are good and expect the computer to play those. I act as if the computer were conscious, even though I know that it has no more consciousness than a tin can. Similarly, we can look at bee dances and describe them in intentional terms; the motions the bees engage in enable the other bees to go where the pollen is, but it does not seem plausible to attribute a conscious awareness of what information is being sent in the course of the bee dance. We can look at the bees as if they were consciously giving one another information, but the intentionality is as-if intentionality, not the kind of original intentionality we find in conscious agents. As Colin McGinn writes:

I doubt that the self-same kind of content possessed by a conscious perceptual experience, say, could be possessed independently of consciousness; such content seems essentially conscious, shot through with subjectivity. This is because of the Janus-faced character of conscious content: it involves presence to the subject, and hence a subjective point of view. Remove the inward-looking face and you remove something integral—what the world seems like to the subject.[47]

If we ask what the content of a word is, the content of that word must be the content for some conscious agent; how that conscious agent understands the word. There may be other concepts of content, but those concepts, it seems to me, are parasitical on the concept of content that I use in referring to states of mind found in a conscious agent. Put another way, my paradigm for understanding these concepts is my life as a conscious agent. If we make these words refer to something that occurs without consciousness, it seems that we are using the byway of analogy with their use in connection with our conscious life.

The intentionality that I am immediately familiar with is my own intentional states. That's the only template, the only paradigm I have. I wouldn't say that animals are not conscious, and if I found good evidence that animals could reason it would not undermine my argument, since I've never been a materialist about animals to begin with. Creatures other than myself could have intentional states, and no doubt do have them, if the evidence suggests that what it is like to be in the intentional state they are in is similar to what it is like to be in the intentional state that I am in.

Richard Carrier wrote a rather lengthy critique of my book. But in his response to the argument from intentionality, we find him repeatedly using terms that make sense to me from the point of view of my life as a conscious subject. However, I am not at all sure what to make of them when we start thinking of them as elements in the life of something that is not conscious. His main definition of "aboutness" is this:

Cognitive science has established that the brain is a computer that constructs and runs virtual models. All conscious states of mind consist of or connect with one or more virtual models. The relation these virtual models have to the world is that of corresponding or not corresponding to actual systems in the world. Intentionality is an assignment (verbal or attentional) of a relation between the virtual models and the (hypothesized) real systems. Assignment of relation is a decision (conscious or not), and such decisions, as well as virtual models and actual systems, and patterns of correspondence between them, all can and do exist on naturalism, yet these four things are all that are needed for Proposition 1 to be true.[48]

Or consider the following:

Returning to my earlier definition of aboutness, as long as we can know that "element A of model B is hypothesized to correspond to real item C in the universe" we have intentionality, we have a thought that is about a thing.[49]

Or:

Because the verbal link that alone completely establishes aboutness—the fact of being "hypothesized"—is something that many purely mechanical computers do.[50]

Or again:

Language is a tool—it is a convention invented by humans. Reality does not tell us what a word means. We decide what aspects of reality a word will refer to. Emphasis here: we decide. We create the meaning for words however we want. The universe has nothing to do with it—except in the trivial sense that we (as computational machines) are a part of the universe.[51]

Now simply consider the words, *hypothesize* and *decide* that he uses in these passages. I think I know what it means to decide something as a conscious agent. I am aware of choice 1 and choice 2, I deliberate about it, and then consciously choose 1 as opposed to 2, or vice versa. All of this requires that I be a conscious agent who knows what my thoughts are about. That is why I have been rather puzzled by Carrier's explaining intentionality in terms like these; such terms mean something to me only if we know what our thoughts are about. The same thing goes for hypothesizing. I can form a hypothesis (such as, all the houses in this subdivision were built by the same builder) just in case I know what the terms of the hypothesis mean, in other words, only if I already possess intentionality. That is what these terms mean to me, and unless I'm really confused, this is what those terms mean to most people.

Again, we have to take a look at the idea of a model. What is a model? A model is something that is supposed to resemble something else. But if we explain "X is about Y" at least partially in terms of "X is a model for Y," I really don't think we've gotten anywhere. How can X be a model for Y if it isn't about Y in the first place.

Nevertheless we may be able to work though the critique and find how he proposes to naturalize the concepts.

Material state A is about material state B just in case "this system contains a pattern corresponding to a pattern in that system, in such a way that computations performed on this system are believed to match and predict behavior in that system."[52]

In correspondence with me Carrier said this:

As I explain in my critique, science already has a good explanation on hand for attentionality (how our brain focuses attention on one object over others). Combine that with a belief (a sensation of motivational confidence) that the object B that we have our attention on will behave as our model A predicts it will, and we have every element of intentionality.[53]

But I am afraid I don't see that this naturalization works. My objection to this is that in order for confidence to play the role it needs to play in Carrier's account of intentionality that confidence has to be a confidence that I have an accurate map, but confidence that P is true is a propositional attitude, which presupposes intentionality. In other words, Carrier is trying to bake an intentional cake with physical yeast and flour. But when the ingredients are examined closely, we find that some intentional ingredients have been smuggled in through the back door.

Here is another illustration:

The fact that one thought is about another thought (or thing) reduces to this (summarizing what I have argued several times above already): (a) there is a physical pattern in our brain of synaptic connections physically binding together every datum about the object of thought (let's say, Madell's "Uncle George"), (b) including a whole array of sensory memories, desires, emotions, other thoughts, and so on, (c) which our brain has calculated (by various computational strategies) are relevant to (they describe or relate to) that object (Uncle George), (d) which of course means a hypothesized object (we will never really know directly that there even is an Uncle George: we only hypothesize his existence based on an analysis, conscious and subconscious, of a large array of data), and (e) when our cerebral cortex detects this physical pattern as obtaining between two pieces of data (like the synaptic region that identifies Uncle George's face and that which generates our evidentially based hypothesis that the entity with that face lives down the street), we "feel" the connection as an "aboutness" (just as when certain photons hit our eyes and electrical signals are sent to our brain we "feel" the impact as a "greenness").[54]

Now did you notice the word "about" in step A of Carrier's account of intentionality? If there is something in the brain that binds together everything about Uncle George, and that is supposed to explain how my thought can be about Uncle George, then it seems pretty clear to me that we are explaining intentionality in terms of intentionality.

What I think the deepest problem is in assigning intentionality to physical systems is that when we do that norms of rationality are applied when we determine what intentional states exist, but normative truths are not entailed by physical facts. In the realm of ethics, add up all the physical, chemical, biological, psychological, and sociological facts about a murder for hire, and nothing in that description will entail that it was a wrongful act. Similarly, scientific information about what is will not tell you what an agent ought to believe, but we need to know what an agent ought to believe in order to figure out what he or she does believe.

According to John Searle:

> So far no attempt at naturalizing content has produced an explanation (analysis, reduction) of intentional content that is even remotely plausible. . . . A symptom that something is radically wrong with the project is that intentional notions are inherently normative. They set standards of truth, rationality, consistency, etc., and there is no way that these standards can be intrinsic to a system consisting entirely of brute, blind, nonintentional causal relations. There is no mean component to billiard ball causation. Darwinian biological attempts at naturalizing content try to avoid this problem by appealing to what they suppose is the inherently teleological [i.e., purposeful], normative character of biological evolution. But this is a very deep mistake. There is nothing normative or teleological about Darwinian evolution. Indeed, Darwin's major contribution was precisely to remove purpose, and teleology from evolution, and substitute for it purely natural forms of selection.[55]

So any attempt to naturalize intentionality will end up bringing intentionality in through the back door, just as Carrier's account does. When you encounter a new or unfamiliar attempt to account for intentionality naturalistically, look it over very carefully, and you should be able to find out where the bodies are buried.

Other naturalists have been more modest in the way in which they reconcile intentionality and naturalism. They maintain that intentional states may not be reducible to physical states, as Carrier appears to be arguing, but they do think that these states are supervenient upon physical states. They very often agree that there is a mystery as to how intentional states can exist in a physicalistic universe. This is certainly a possibility for the naturalist, but it runs the risk, as we shall see, of making propositional states epiphenomenal, that is, causally irrelevant. This will be a serious problem for the naturalist, since a naturalist presupposes the existence of mental causation when they argue on behalf of naturalism.

THE PROBLEM OF MENTAL CAUSATION

My next argument is the Argument from Mental Causation. If naturalism is true, even if there are propositional states like beliefs, then these states have to be epiphenomenal, without a causal role. Now careful reflection on rational inference, if we think about it, commits us to the idea that one mental event causes another mental event in virtue of its propositional content.

Now if events are caused in accordance with physical law, they cause one another in virtue of being a particular type of event. A ball breaks a window in virtue of being the weight, density, and shape that it is in relation to the physical structure of the window. Even if it is the baseball that Luis Gonzalez hit against Mariano Rivera that won the 2001 World Series, its being that ball has nothing to do with whether or not it can break the window now.

So let us suppose that brain state A, which is token identical to the thought that all men are mortal, and brain state B, which is token identical to the thought that Socrates is a man, causes the belief that Socrates is mortal. It isn't enough for rational inference that these events be those beliefs, it is also necessary that the causal transaction be in virtue of the content of those thoughts. If anything not in space and time makes these thoughts the thoughts that they are, and if naturalism is true, then the propositional content is irrelevant to the causal transaction that produces the conclusion, and we do not have a case of rational inference. In rational inference, as Lewis puts it, one thought causes another thought not by being, but by being seen to be the ground for it. But causal transactions in the brain occur by virtue of the brain's being in a particular type of state that is relevant to physical causal transactions. Only that property of the brain can be relevant to what the brain does, according to a naturalistic account of causation.

What this means is that those forms of substance materialism that accept property dualism invariably render the "mental" properties epiphenomenal. If the physical properties are sufficient to produce the physical effect, then the mental properties are irrelevant unless they are really physical properties "writ large," so to speak. And mental states that are epiphenomenal cannot really participate in rational inference.

Carrier's account of mental causation clearly presupposes a reductive, rather than a nonreductive materialism. He writes:

Every meaningful proposition is the content or output of a virtual model (or rather: actual propositions, of actual models; potential propositions, of potential models). Propositions are formulated in a language as an aid to computation, but when they are not formulated, they merely define the content of a nonlinguistic computation of a virtual model. In either case, a brain computes degrees of confidence in any given proposition, by running its corresponding virtual model and comparing it and its output with observational data, or the output of other computations. Thus, when I say I "accept" Proposition A this means that my brain computes a high level of confidence that Virtual Model A corresponds to a system in the real world (or another system in our own or another's brain, as the case may be); while if I "reject" A, then I have a high level of confidence that A does not so correspond; but if I "suspend judgment," then I have a low level of confidence either way. By simply defining "proposition" as

I have here, Proposition 3 follows necessarily from Propositions 1 and 2. Therefore naturalism can account for this as well.[56]

But I see a serious problem with this whole concept. In order for the content of the mental state to be relevant to the production of a rational inference, it seems to me that everyone who believes that Socrates is mortal would have to be in the same type of brain state as everyone else who believes that Socrates is mortal. Is this plausible?

But more than that, here again we find Carrier explaining one kind of mental activity in terms of another mental activity and then explaining it "naturalistically" by saying "the brain" does it. My argument is, first and foremost that something exists whose activities are to be fundamentally explained in intentional and teleological terms. Whether we call it a brain, a part of the brain, a soul, a banana, or a bowling ball is not essential to my argument; if the fundamental explanations are intentional, then I have established all that I am trying to establish.

THE ARGUMENT FROM THE PSYCHOLOGICAL RELEVANCE OF LOGICAL LAWS

My next argument concerns the role of logical laws in mental causation. In order for mental causation to be what we ordinarily suppose it to be, it is not only necessary that mental states be causally efficacious by virtue of their content, it is also necessary that the laws of logic be relevant to the production of the conclusion. That is, if we conclude "Socrates is mortal" from "All men are mortal" and "Socrates is a man," then not only must we understand the meanings of those expressions, and these meanings must play a central role in the performance of these inferences, but what Lewis called the ground-and-consequent relationship between the propositions must also play a central role in these rational inferences. We must know that the argument is structured in such a way that in arguments of that form the conclusion always follows from the premises. We do not simply know something that is the case at one moment in time, but we know something that must be true in all moments of time, in every possible world. But how could a physical brain, which stands in physical relations to other objects and whose activities are determined, insofar as they are determined at all, by the laws of physics and not the laws of logic, come to know, not merely that something was true, but could not fail to be true regardless of whatever else is true in the world.

We can certainly imagine, for example, a possible world in which the laws of physics are different from the way they are in the actual world. We can imagine, for example, that instead of living in a universe in which dead people tend to stay dead, we find them rising out of their graves on a regular basis on the third day after they are buried. But we cannot imagine a world in which, once we know which cat and which mat, it can possibly be the case that the cat is both on the mat and not on the mat. Now can we imagine there being a world in which $2 + 2$ is really 5 and not 4? I think not.

It is one thing to suggest that brains might be able to "track" states of affairs in the physical world. It is another thing to suggest that a physical system can be aware, not only that something is the case, but that it must be the case; and that not only it is the case but that it could not fail to be the case. Brain states stand in physical relations to the rest of the world, and are related to that world through cause and effect, responding to changes in the world around us. How can these brain states be knowings of what must be true in all possible worlds?

Consider again the difficulty of going from what is to what ought to be in ethics. Many philosophers have agreed that you can pile up the physical truths, and all other descriptive truths from chemistry, biology, psychology, and sociology, as high as you like about, say, the killings of Nicole Brown Simpson and Ronald Goldman, and you could never, by any examination of these, come to the conclusion that these acts were really morally wrong (as opposed to being merely widely disapproved of and criminalized by the legal system). Even the atheist philosopher J. L. Mackie argued that if there were truths of moral necessity, these truths, and our ability to know those truths, do not fit well into the naturalistic worldview, and if they existed, they would support a theistic worldview.[57] Mackie could and did, of course, deny moral objectivity, but my claim is that objective logical truths present an even more serious problem for naturalism, because the naturalist cannot simply say they don't exist on pain of undermining the very natural science on which his worldview rests.

Arguing that such knowledge is trivial because it merely constitutes the "relations of ideas" and does not tell anything about the world outside our minds seems to me to be an inadequate response. If, for example, the laws of logic are about the relations of ideas, then not only are they about ideas that I have thought already, but also they are true of thoughts I haven't even had yet. If contradictions can't be true because this is how my ideas relate to one another, and it is a contingent fact that my ideas relate to one another in this way, then it is impossible to say that they won't relate differently tomorrow.

Carrier responds somewhat differently. He says:

For logical laws are just like physical laws, because physical laws describe the way the universe works, and logical laws describe the way reason works—or, to avoid begging the question, logical laws describe the way a truth-finding machine works, in the very same way that the laws of aerodynamics describe the way a flying-machine works, or the laws of ballistics describe the way guns shoot their targets. The only difference between logical laws and physical laws is that the fact that physical laws describe physics and logical laws describe logic. But that is a difference both trivial and obvious.[58]

What this amounts to, it seems to me, is a denial of the absolute necessity of logic. If the laws of logic just tell us how truth-finding machines work, then if the world were different a truth-finding machine would work differently. I would insist on a critical distinction between the truths of mathematics, which are true regardless of whether anybody thinks them or not, and laws governing how either a person or a computer ought to perform computations. I would ask "What is it about reality that makes one set of computations correct and another set of computations incorrect?"

William Vallicella provides an argument against the claim that the laws of logic are empirical generalizations:

1. The laws of logic are empirical generalizations. (Assumption for reduction).

2. Empirical generalizations, if true, are merely contingently true. (By definition of "empirical generalization": empirical generalizations record what happens to be the case, but might have not been the case.)

3. The laws of logic, if true, are merely contingently true. (From 1 and 2).

4. If proposition p is contingently true, then it is possible that p be false. (True by definition)

5. The laws of logic, if true, are possibly false. (From 3 and 4).

6. LNC is possibly false: there are logically possible worlds in which p & ~p is true.

7. But (6) is absurd (self-contradictory): it amounts to saying that it is logically possible that the very criterion of logical possibility, namely LNC, be false. Therefore 1 is false, and its contradictory, the clam that the laws of logic are not empirical generalizations, is true.[59]

Logic, I maintain, picks out features of reality that must exist in any possible world. We know, and have insight into these realities, and this is what permits us to think. A naturalistic view of the universe, according to which there is nothing in existence that is not in a particular time and a particular place, is hard-pressed to reconcile their theory of the world with the idea that we as humans can access not only what is, but also what must be.

I conclude, therefore, that there is something deeply mysterious about a world that is at bottom material rather than mental producing beings that have intentional/prepositional mental states, in which we find mental causation in virtue of the content of the mental state, and who are aware of and employ the laws of logic in rational inference. However, if the Maker of the universe is a rational being, as God is supposed to be, then this becomes a good deal less mysterious. I conclude, therefore, that the argument from reason is unrefuted and constitutes a substantial reason for preferring a theistic understanding of the universe to a naturalistic one.

NOTES

1. Victor Reppert, *C. S. Lewis's Dangerous Idea: In Defense of the Argument from Reason* (Downer's Grove, IL: Inter-Varsity Press, 2003). Other essays of mine on the subject include "The Lewis-Anscombe Controversy: A Discussion of the Issues," *Christian Scholar's Review* 19(3) (1989); "The Argument from Reason," *Philo* 2 (1999), 33–45; "Reply to Parsons and Lippard," *Philo* 3 (2000), 76–89; "Causal Closure, Mechanism, and Rational Inference, *Philosophia Christi*, 2nd. Ser., 3 (2) (2001); "Several Formulations of the Argument from Reason," *Philosophia Christi*, 2nd ser., 5(1) (2003), 9–34; "Some Supernatural Reasons Why My Critics are Wrong," *Philosophia Christi,* 2nd ser., 5(1) (2003); "The Argument from Reason and Hume's Legacy," in James Sennett and Douglas Groothuis' *In Defense of Natural Theology: A Post-Human Assessment* (Downers Grove, IL: InterVarsity Press, 2005), 253–270.

2. Anscombe's rebuttal to Lewis is found in G. E. M Anscombe, *The Collected Papers of G. E. M. Anscombe, 3 vols.* (Minneapolis, MN: University of Minnesota Press, 1981), 224–231. A brief response to Lewis's revision is found on pp. x–xi of the same volume.

3. William Hasker, "The Transcendental Refutation of Determinism" *Southern Journal of Philosophy* 11 (1973): 175–183; and "Why the Physical Isn't Closed," chapter 3 of *The Emergent Self* (Ithaca, NY: Cornell University Press, 1999), 58–80; compare as well the chapter in this volume, "What About a Sensible Naturalism," 53–62.

4. Richard Purtill, *Reason to Believe* (Grand Rapids, MI: Eerdmans, 1974), 44–46.

5. Angus Menuge, "Beyond Skinnerian Creatures: A Defense of the Lewis-Plantinga Argument against Evolutionary Naturalism," chapter 6 of *Agents Under Fire* (New York: Rowman and Littlefield Publishers, 2004), 149–174.

6. Alvin Plantinga, "Is Naturalism Irrational?" chapter 12 of *Warrant and Proper Function* (New York: Oxford University Press, 1993); *Warranted Christian Belief* (New York, Oxford University Press, 2000), 227–240, 281–284, 350–351; and "Reply to Beilby's Cohorts" in *Naturalism Defeated: Essays on Plantinga's Evolutionary Argument against Naturalism*, ed. James Beilby (Ithaca, NY: Cornell University Press, 2002).

7. Antony Flew, "The Third Maxim," *The Rationalist Annual* (1957), 63–66; and "Determinism and Validity Again," *The Rationalist Annual* (1958), 39–51.

8. John Beversluis, "Reason," chapter 4 of *C. S. Lewis and the Search for Rational Religion* (Grand Rapids, MI: Eerdmans, 1985), 58–83.

9. Jim Lippard, "Historical but Indistinguishable Differences: Some Notes on Victor Reppert's Paper," *Philo* 2(1) (1999).

10. Keith Parsons, "Further Reflections on the Argument from Reason," *Philo* 3(1) (2000), and "Need Reasons be Causes? A Further Reply to Lewis's Argument from Reason, *Philosophia Christi*, 2nd ser. (5), 63–75.

11. Theodore Drange, "Several Unsuccessful Formulations of the Argument from Reason," *Philosophia Christi,* 2nd ser. (5), 35–52.

12. Richard Carrier, "Critical Review of Victor Reppert's Defense of the Argument from Reason," http://www.infidels.org/library/modern/richard_carrier/reppert.html (accessed July 30, 2006).

13. Most of these responses are found in *Naturalism Defeated: Essays on Plantinga's Evolutionary Argument Against Naturalism*, ed. James Beilby (Ithaca, NY: Cornell University Press, 2002).

14. Arthur Balfour, *The Foundations of Belief: Notes Introductory to the Study of Theology.* 8th ed., revised with a new introduction and summary (New York: Longmans, 1906), 279–285.

15. Beversluis, *C. S. Lewis and the Search for Rational Religion*, 73.

16. Rudolph Bultmann, "New Testament and Mythology," *in Kerygma and Myth: A Theological Debate*, ed. H. W. Bartsch, trans. R. H. Fuller (New York: Harper & Row, 1961), 5.

17. Ehrman's response can be found in his opening statement of the debate, found at this site: http://www.holycross.edu/departments/crec/website/resurrection-debate-transcript.pdf, 12 (accessed July 30, 2006).

18. David Hume, *Enquiries Concerning Human Understanding and Concerning the Principles of Morals*, ed. L. A. Selby-Bigge, 2nd. ed. (Oxford: Oxford University Press, 1972 [1902]), 109–131.

19. C. S. Lewis, *Miracles: A Preliminary Study* (New York: Macmillan, 1960), 3–4.

20. William Lane Craig and Keith Parsons, "Why I am/am not a Christian," video recording of a debate held at a Prestonwood Baptist Church in Dallas, Texas, on June 15, 1998.

21. Lewis, *Miracles: A Preliminary Study*, 164.

22. Ibid. 12.

23. This is emphasized in Nicholas Tattersall, "A Critique of *Miracles* by C. S. Lewis," http://www.infidels.org/library/modern/nicholas_tattersall/miracles.html (accessed July 30, 2006). Austin Cline, "C. S. Lewis and Naturalism: Can Naturalism Explain Reason, Nature, and Morality" http://atheism.about.com/od/cslewisnarnia/a/naturalism.htm (accessed July 30, 2006); and Ed Babinski, http://www.edwardtbabinski.us/creationism/lewis_naturalism.html (accessed July 30, 2006).

24. Lewis, *Miracles: A Preliminary Study*, 13–14.

25. Richard Dawkins, *The Blind Watchmaker: Why the Evidence of Evolution Reveals a Universe without Design* (New York: W. W. Norton, reprinted edition, 1996).

26. Hasker, *The Emergent Self*, 60–64; Reppert, *C. S. Lewis's Dangerous Idea*, 50–54.

27. C. S. Lewis, *Surprised by Joy* (San Diego, CA: Harcourt Brace, 1955), 208.

28. Balfour, *The Foundations of Belief: Notes Introductory to the Study of Theology*, 285–286.

29. Antony Flew, "Determinism and Validity Again," 46–47.

30. Balfour, *The Foundations of Belief: Notes Introductory to the Study of Theology*, 287–288.

31. Anscombe, *Metaphysics and the Philosophy of Mind*, 226–267.

32. Ibid.

33. Ibid.

34. Ibid.

35. Lewis, *Miracles: A Preliminary Study*, 17.

36. Ibid.

37. Ibid.

38. Ibid., 18

39. Ibid.

40. Beversluis, *C. S. Lewis and the Search for Rational Religion*, 73–74.

41. Anscombe, *Metaphysics and the Philosophy of Mind*, 229.

42. Parsons, "Further Reflections on the Argument from Reason," 101.

43. Lewis, *Miracles: A Preliminary Study*, 16.

44. Carrier, "Critical Review of Victor Reppert's Defense of the Argument from Reason."

45. Menuge, *Agents Under Fire*, 12

46. John Searle, *The Re-Discovery of the Mind* (Cambridge, MIT Press, 1992), 51.

47. Colin McGinn, *The Problem of Consciousness* (Oxford: Blackwell Publishers, 1991), 34.

48. Carrier, "Critical Review of Victor Reppert's Defense of the Argument from Reason," op. cit.

49. Ibid.

50. Ibid.

51. Ibid.

52. Ibid.

53. E-mail correspondence with Richard Carrier.

54. Carrier, "Critical Review of Victor Reppert's Defense of the Argument from Reason," op. cit.

55. Searle, John, *The Re-Discovery of the Mind*, 50–51.

56. Carrier, "Critical Review of Victor Reppert's Defense of the Argument from Reason," op. cit.

57. J. L. Mackie, *The Miracle of Theism* (Oxford: Clarendon Press, 1982), 115–118.

58. Carrier, "Critical Review of Victor Reppert's Defense of the Argument from Reason," op. cit.

59. William Vallicella, "Are the Laws of Logic Empirical Generalizations?" http://maverickphilosopher.blogspot.com/2004/08/are-laws-of-logic-empirical.html (accessed July 30, 2006).

BIBLIOGRAPHY

Anscombe, G. E. M. *Metaphysics and the Philosophy of Mind. Vol. 2 of The Collected Papers of G. E. M. Anscombe*, 3 vols. Minneapolis, MN: University of Minnesota Press, 1981.

Balfour, Arthur. *The Foundations of Belief Notes Introductory to the Study of Theology*, 8th edn. New York: Longmans, 1906.

Beversluis, John. *C. S. Lewis and the Search for Rational Religion*. Grand Rapids, MI: Eerdmans, 1985.

Hasker, William. *The Emergent Self*. Ithaca, NY: Cornell University Press, 1999.

Menuge, Angus. *Agents Under Fire*. New York: Rowman and Littlefield, 2004.

Plantinga, Alvin. *Warrant and Proper Function*. New York: Oxford University Press, 1993.

———. *Warranted Christian Belief*. New York: Oxford University Press, 2000.

Reppert, Victor. *C. S. Lewis's Dangerous Idea: In Defense of the Argument from Reason*. Downer's Grove, IL: Inter-Varsity Press, 2003.

Stealing Past the Watchful Dragons: C. S. Lewis's Incarnational Aesthetics and Today's Emerging Imagination

Philip Harrold

Resonances of the apologetical insights of C. S. Lewis speaking to a post-Christian era emerge in the most unlikely of places.[1] To wit, not long ago, at a gathering in Lambeth Palace, London, an "alternative worship" service was vividly described as follows:

On the first visit to a service, the main impression is visual. Screens and hanging fabrics, containing a multiplicity of colours, moving and static images continuously dominate the perceptions. There are other things: the type of music, often electronic, whose textures and range seem curiously attuned to the context of worship, smells, the postures adopted by the other worshippers, . . . As the mental picture begins to fill up with details, there is a growing appreciation that considerable technological complexity is sitting alongside simplicity and directness. The rituals—perhaps walking though patterns, tieing [sic] a knot, or having one's hands or feet anointed—are introduced with simple, non-fussy directions. The emphasis is on allowing people to do what will help, liberate, and encourage their worship rather than on the orchestration of a great event. . . . Where something is rather obscure, its purpose is to invite further reflection, perhaps teasing the worshippers to look deeper beyond the surface meaning. . . . For many of those who stay, they have never before had an experience of Christian worship like it. It is as though they have come to a new place which they instantly recognize as home."

Then, as now, the Reverend Dr. Paul Roberts pleaded for a renewed appreciation of the artistic sensibility in worship, not for art's sake alone, but as part of a "vibrant missionary engagement" with postmodern aesthetics—embracing its "richer, multi-layered, and more fluid textuality—envisioning meanings and appreciating multivalence through a variety of media."[2]

Roberts presently serves Anglican parishes in Bristol, England, while co-hosting "alternativeworship.org," a self-described "gateway for anyone researching Alternative Worship and new forms of church." A similar Web-based service is provided at Vintagechurch.org by a counterpart to Roberts on my side of the pond, Dan Kimball, pastor at Santa Cruz Bible Church in California. Accordingly, Kimball wants the aesthetics at his church "to scream out who we are and what we are about the moment people walk in the doors."[3] Neither enterprise sees itself as trendy, seeker-sensitive, or mere window-dressing. Rather, the basic conviction is that arts speak to more fundamental concerns regarding the transcendent realities of truth, goodness, and beauty. Assuming that "people who value beauty might eventually look for truth," the arts become a tool of evangelism, a pathway to God.[4] Indeed, Brian McLaren, a leading spokesperson for the Emergent Church/Conversation [EC] in the United States, believes that "image (the language of imagination) and emotion (including the emotion of wonder) are essential elements of fully human knowing, and thus we seek to integrate them in our search for this precious, wonderful, sacred gift called truth . . ."[5] Otherwise, the gospel remains "flattened, trivialized, and rendered inane," observes McLaren—with a message stuck in the small world of "Sunday School Christianity," unable to connect with a postmodern culture that is visually inclined, aesthetically charged, and open to—if not in outright pursuit of—mystery.[6]

Seasoned insiders to the EC like Alan Roxburgh, a writer and theological educator in Vancouver, BC, admire such "wonderfully creative movements of bright young leaders," while, at the same time worrying that they might cater to self-actualization, becoming "purveyors of more experiential, artsy, aesthetic forms of religious goods and services."[7] The aesthetic media may very well morph into the message, confusing style and substance—"undeniably cool," yes, but never actually answering the question, "What is the Gospel?" Scott Bader-Sayre and Andy Crouch, authors of two important cover-page articles on the EC in *The Christian Century* and *Christianity Today* (respectively), heartily endorse the recovery of a sense of mystery and transcendence through the arts—especially for those who have given up on the "small life" and superficiality of contemporary evangelicalism. Perhaps the emerging experience—in worship gatherings as well any artistic engagement with the wider world—will also nudge today's alienated youth to see beyond their angst, into the numinous, finding a spiritual place they can call home. But all this relevance, according to Bader-Sayre, will have to be "modulated" by resistance—by the counter-cultural move to "[interpret] the culture to itself" in light of the hope conveyed in the story of Jesus Christ.[8] Lauren Winner expresses the tension well when she asks, "How do you simultaneously attend to the culture *and* be a pocket of resistance?"[9]

If any of this sounds familiar, it is likely because the contemporary EC interest in artistic expression is reminiscent of the challenges and opportunities C. S. Lewis encountered as he *smuggled* theology into his own post-Christian world through the literary media of fantasy and myth. I see two significant areas of correspondence here.

First, regarding context, Lewis was just as persuaded then as the EC is now that the church was in a "missionary situation." Writing in 1945, he observed: "A century ago our task was to edify those who had been brought up in the Faith: our present task is chiefly to convert and instruct infidels."[10] Given the pervasive spiritual alienation of his day and, indeed, of his own early life, Lewis advised an indirect or "latent" approach to evangelism that nurtured, through the poetic and mythic imaginations, a disposition to *hear* (preevangelism) then *believe* (preapologetics) the Gospel.[11] Just as Paul Roberts hopes that today's "alternative" worship services will "tease" their participants to "look deeper" at life and its ultimate destination, Lewis hoped his fantasy writing would, at the least, awaken deep longings for transcendence. Both see reenchantment and its attendant aesthetic practices as evangelistic endeavors in a world filled with competing ideologies and narratives, or perhaps a world that has no story to tell at all.[12]

Secondly, there is an apparent correspondence between the missional aesthetics of Lewis and the EC in the way both understand the stealthy relationship between artistic or literary expression and apologetics. Lewis actually used the term *smuggle* in reference to his fictional works much the same way that EC proponents speak today of the subversive ways they are communicating the Gospel in the eclectic vernacular of postmodern culture. In a letter to Anglican nun Sister Penelope (CSMV), written in the summer of 1939, Lewis observed how "any amount of theology can now be smuggled into people's minds under cover of romance without their knowing it." He recalled his early experience of "*almost* believing in the gods"—indeed, feeling something akin to "holiness"—through George MacDonald's "fantasies for grown-ups."[13] Later in life, in a more familiar passage from his essay, "Sometimes Fairy Stories May Say Best What's to Be Said," Lewis observed:

I thought I saw how stories of this kind could steal past a certain inhibition which had paralysed much of my own religion in childhood. . . . But supposing that by casting all these things [Christian teachings] into an imaginary world, stripping them of their stained-glass and Sunday school associations, one could make them for the first time appear in their real potency? Could one not thus steal past those watchful dragons? I thought one could.[14]

Indeed, Lewis knew those "watchful dragons" quite well because he had moved in fits and starts beyond the smallness of his Sunday School Christianity into a "region of awe"—a spiritual journey of deconversion and reconversion that anticipated much of the religious autobiography we see among today's self-described postmoderns.[15] Smuggling was, in effect, an act of "redemptive deconstruction," according to Louis Markos: "Lewis dissociated the signifieds of Christian theology from their typical, uninspiring signifiers (their Sunday school associations) and attached them instead to a new set of signifiers with the power to reinvigorate and inspire young and old alike."[16] He accomplished this through bold use of allegory, myth, and symbol—genres and literary devices that are most amenable to an incarnational aesthetic, the "transposing" of divine presence or, at least, transcendent meaning into a "lower" medium of communication.[17] Little wonder that emergent writers like Charlie Peacock, Brian McLaren, and the late Mike Yaconelli admire Lewis for his "imaginative and mystical sensitivities," especially his literary "portals," which lead the reader beyond the confines of the self and the stifling pragmatism of contemporary evangelicalism into a world of "dangerous wonder."[18]

There remains, however, a crucial, yet often overlooked, *social* aspect in Lewis's incarnational aesthetic—an aspect I term the *sympathetic imagination*. Because this horizontal dimension directly challenges the persistent individualism of late-modernity it seems particularly relevant to the EC's aesthetic engagement with contemporary culture. We begin with Lewis's most explicit statement concerning the role of sympathy in the exercise of the imagination, as found in *Miracles* (1947). In his chapter on the Incarnation—"the Grand Miracle"—he explains how God becoming man is replicated "in a very minor key" throughout all of nature by the sympathetic relations humans enjoy with each other and even with animals:

What we can understand, if the Christian doctrine [Incarnation] is true, is that our own composite existence is not the sheer anomaly it might seem to be, but a faint image of the Divine Incarnation itself—the same theme in a very minor key. We can understand that if God so descends into a human spirit, and human spirit so descends into Nature, and our thoughts into our senses and passions, and if adult minds (but only the best of them) can descend into sympathy with children, and men into sympathy with beasts, then everything hangs together and the total reality, both Natural and Supernatural, in which we are living is more multifariously and subtly harmonious than we had suspected. We catch sight of a new key principle—the power of the Higher, just in so far as it is truly Higher, to come down, the power of the greater to include the less.[19]

An awareness of these "transpositions"—especially through an exercise of the poetic imagination—means that we must not "overlook the rich sources of relevant imagery and association" available through our deepest apprehensions.[20]

At this point, Lewis is most interested in developing the incarnational principles of recapitulation and vicariousness as they intimate the Grand Miracle, but he also acknowledges their profound social and moral implications. In marked contrast with the natural human tendency of self-sufficiency, he emphasizes how identification with and sacrificing for others, and receiving their selfless offerings in return, is a way of disclosing, albeit imperfectly (or "faintly"), a fundamental attribute and activity of the Divine Life in the world. "Self-sufficiency, living on one's own resources, is a thing impossible" here, because "[e]verything is indebted to everything else, sacrificed to everything else, dependent on everything else."[21] In this way, our everyday world begins to take on new meaning and significance:

Thus, as we accept this doctrine of the higher world we make new discoveries about the lower world. It is from that hill that we first really understand the landscape of this valley. Here, at last, we find (as we do not find either in the Nature-religions or in the religions that deny Nature) a real illumination: Nature is being lit up by a light from beyond Nature. Someone is speaking who knows more about her than can be known from inside her.[22]

Lewis had long been interested in what Thomas L. Martin calls "possible-worlds semantics." The artistic imagination was never just about the way things were, but the way things might be, or even should be. When the reader, for instance, encounters a literary world that seems strangely beyond her own time or place, she finds in the language—in the combination of words, especially metaphors—as well as the stories and their interactions an alternative reality. The text has an ontology all its own that not only enables her to move beyond the this-worldly limitations of language and literary form, but the provincialisms of the self as well. To read on is to accept the other world on its own terms.[23] J. R. R. Tolkien's appeal to the power of myth and the subcreating role of the writer are well-known sources of inspiration for this literary quality in Lewis, but we should also credit his close friend, Owen Barfield, with a deep appreciation of "imaginative vision" and its moral dimensions. In the unpublished letters exchanged during their so-called "Great War" debate, Barfield had encouraged Lewis's growing appreciation of the "felt change of consciousness" brought about by poetic imagination.[24]

While never able to embrace Barfield's subjective idealism outright, Lewis did recognize the imagination's capacity to awaken a sense of "universal empathy" and a "growing wholeness" marked by sympathetic and reciprocal relations between living things—a vision that combined the aesthetic and mystical, as well as cognitive and moral dimensions of consciousness. During his (re-) conversion to theism, Lewis speculated that the most significant outcome of this poetic insight was "an enriched and corrected will" guided by the "universal good" as manifested in moral intuition.[25]

Lewis's restrained acceptance of this amalgam of thought-feeling-awareness was based in part on an important distinction made by idealist philosopher, Samuel Alexander, between enjoyment (or desire) and contemplation. In *Surprised by Joy*, Lewis noted how incompatible the emotions of love, hate, fear, hope, or desire associated with an object were with the contemplation of these "inner activities" themselves. For example, "You cannot hope and also think about hoping at the same moment; for in hope we look to hope's object and we interrupt this by (so to speak) turning round to look at the hope itself." In this way, Lewis observed, "All introspection is in one respect misleading" because it actually shuts down the passage of hope, longing, desire, etc. by deflecting our attention away from the object.[26] With regard to Joy, in particular, he learned not to long for it as an "aesthetic experience," but instead to hear Joy proclaim, "You want—I myself am your want of— something other, outside, not your nor any state of you." As we read on in Lewis's autobiography, we see how Joy became the "Who" that he desired— the God with whom he could find "personal relation." Even at this critical stage, however, Lewis recognized the wider reunifying implications of this spiritual longing:

In so far as we really are at all (which isn't saying much) we have, so to speak, a root in the Absolute, which is the utter reality. And that is why we experience Joy: we yearn, rightly, for that unity which we can never reach except by ceasing to be the separate phenomenal beings called "we."

Realizing that the object of this yearning was a Who and not a What brought Lewis into "the region of awe"—with its "road right out of the self," its "commerce" with, and submission to, the numinous, its disturbing ability to remind us of our "fragmentary and phantasmal nature."[27] Eventually, as we shall see, this region became an intersubjective arena as well—one conspicuously marked by sympathetic relations.

In the midst of his intense philosophical exchange with Barfield, Lewis's Oxford brand of idealism—combining Kant's moral imperative with classical moral philosophy and an emerging theism—was also modulated by

Coleridge's theory of the creative imagination. This was an important development for Lewis because it was his growing interest in the imagination that enabled him to eventually see Christianity as a solution to some nagging concerns: the relationship between desire and the metaphysical reality of natural law, and, more generally, between the perceiving subject and the perceived object.[28] Instead of an unreachable and unknowable Absolute, Lewis saw how natural law reflected the Divine will and grounded the moral life of humanity. Lewis felt he could actually participate in this life with a degree of concreteness and resolve that had heretofore evaded him. But it was through an imagination attuned to sympathetic relations that he most acutely perceived its goodness, truth, and beauty.[29]

Barfield's understanding of Coleridge and the poetic imagination was critical to this realization. It was as if language was able to restore to humanity the intuitive sense of "conscious participation in the world-process," or, as Lewis came to prefer, the heavenlies.[30] From a literary standpoint, this intuition operated chiefly through metaphor: "Reality, once self-evident, and therefore not conceptually experienced, but which can *now* only be reached by an effort of the individual mind—that is what is contained in a true poetic metaphor."[31] Based on Coleridge's notion of the "secondary" or "esemplastic" imagination, Barfield highlighted the mind's *participation* in the phenomena, enabling it to construct something that is both meaningful and felt, eliciting the reader's sympathy toward the immanental truth conveyed in and through the literary medium. While initially reluctant to embrace the truth-bearing aspects of this romantic theory of imagination, Lewis grew to appreciate how it helped him perceive, albeit in a limited way, what the Spirit perceived, especially in terms of an "absolute relevance" that saw each object in its proper relation and context. Through poetic language, a moral sense arose in which one saw particulars in relation to wholes, disclosing truth not in themselves, but in their relations to what was outside them. This exercise of the imagination possessed moral value, elicited a moral response, and enriched, even corrected, the will. In doing so, metaphors and other tools of the imagination restored the "connective tissue," the relationality or mutuality of things. This is what it meant to see the world that was "actually out there" more spiritually—"more really."[32]

Later, in a brief, but highly suggestive discussion in the Epilogue to *An Experiment in Criticism* (1961), Lewis correlated this sympathetic disposition with the benefits of literary practice and experience. Chiefly among them was the capacity of the imagination to enter into the perspectives and experiences of others:

Good reading, therefore, though it is not essentially an affectional or moral or intellectual activity, has something in common with all three. In love we escape from our self into one other. In the moral sphere, every act of justice or charity involves putting ourselves in the other person's place and thus transcending our own competitive particularity. In coming to understand anything we are rejecting the facts as they are for us in favor of the facts as they are. The primary impulse of each is to maintain and aggrandize himself. The secondary impulse is to go out of the self, to correct its provincialism and heal its loneliness. In love, in virtue, in the pursuit of knowledge, and in the reception of the arts, we are doing this.

For Lewis, the immediate "good of literature" was that it "admits us to experiences other than our own," and, in so doing, "heals the wound, without undermining the privilege, of individuality."[33] Of course, this required a "baptized imagination"—one that permitted any artistic or literary endeavor, even the "sub-Christian" variety, to point upwards to God.[34] But, again, note that for Lewis, this imagination had a profound horizontal dimension as well—one that began and ended in a phenomenology of sympathetic relations with others.[35]

Here, we find the sort of concreteness that Lewis appreciated in the "spontaneous tendency of religion" to resort to poetic expression. After all, for Lewis, it was poetic, not "ordinary" language that conveyed the *presence* of the object, or the other, as much as its meaning. This is what I think Lewis had in mind when he extolled the remarkable powers of great literature—the way it used "factors within our experience so that they become pointers to something outside our experience." To what can he be referring except the arena of intersubjectivity, where love, transgression, alienation, and forgiveness all provide opportunities to "verify" fundamental Christian ideas? Forgiveness, for one, resists precise definition, but it can be communicated with uncanny specificity and emotional impact in poetic language and a wide array of other artistic forms. Ultimately, Lewis despaired that while this storehouse of "hints, similes, [and] metaphors" was crucial to late-modern apologetics, it was underappreciated, and, consequently, underutilized.[36]

This may not be the case today, especially considering the EC's enthusiastic and, at times, exotic attempts at new forms of Christian worship and community. The EC, in fact, describes itself as both aesthetically driven *and* intensely relational.[37] Writing for Emergentvillage.com, Troy Bronsink insists that "[t]he church must find a way, like Ezekiel, to imaginatively indwell the story of God's mission through the performative nature of the arts."[38] The problem, as Paul Roberts and others inside the movement observe, is that EC aesthetics and ecclesiology are "still unformed and provisional;" they are only just beginning to recover something comparable to Lewis's imaginative breadth and substance.[39] It would be much too modern, of course, to build anything on a blueprint, let alone *one* blueprint (!), but the distinctive *poesis* offered by Lewis is remarkably fluid, adaptive, and missional. More importantly, it modulates the EC's passion for relevance with a relational phenomenology of sympathetic imagination that strongly resists, as St. Anne's did in *That Hideous Strength*, potent cultural pressures of competitive individuality, on the one hand, and reductive homogenization (the proverbial "lowest common denominator"), on the other.

So what sort of connections, albeit tentative, exist between Lewis's incarnational aesthetic and the recovery of the poetic imagination in today's emergent Christian communities? Who is translating the modern Lewis into a postmodern "missionary situation," and what, in particular, draws them, consciously or otherwise, to his peculiar mode of "redemptive deconstruction"? The emerging "conversation" is often organized into collaborative endeavors between popular practitioners, on the one hand, and theologians or, dare we say, "theorists," on the other.[40] Among the popularizers, Brian McLaren, Charlie Peacock, and Lauren Winner are particularly attentive to the "re-imagining" project. McLaren marvels at how Lewis's fantasy literature "depends on something beyond mere rationality," requiring imagination and vision as venues of "the mystical, where 'consciousness is engulfed' by something beyond itself." Lewis represents that venerable Christian tradition of rebuking, "arrogant intellectualizing," and its "conceptual cathedrals of proposition and argument." His appreciation of poetic language, especially the evocative power of metaphors, was balanced by a hermeneutical suspicion of its idolatrous potential. Anticipating the postmodern debate regarding the efficacy of language, Lewis likened such language to a "window through which one glimpses God, but never a box in which God can be contained." Citing Lewis's poem, "A Footnote to All Prayers," McLaren recalls how Lewis warned people against self-deception in prayer, "thinking that their images or thoughts of God *are* actually God." He then affirms Lewis's concluding petition that God "take not ... our literal sense" but translate, instead, "our limping metaphors into God's 'great, /unbroken speech.'"[41]

McLaren is joined by Leonard Sweet and Jerry Haselmayer in a coedited book suggestively titled, *A is for Abductive: The Language of the Emerging Church*. Under "N is for Narrative," the authors credit Lewis and the Inklings with reminding us of how easily we are "dulled and desensitized to the splendor of the Christian story," alluding to Lewis's recollection of the visionary paralysis caused by "Sunday school associations" and their "watchful dragons." Indeed, for emergents the time has come to follow Lewis's literary strategy: "We need to go out and come in again" via the "priceless galleria of images, stories, metaphors, rituals, and hymns as well as historians, philosophers, dramatists, novelists, poets, scientists, and prophets."[42] Here are echoes of his Epilogue to *An Experiment in Criticism*: "One of the things we feel after reading a great work is 'I have got out.' Or from another point of view, 'I have got in'; pierced the shell of some other monad and discovered what it is like inside."[43]

The imagination, for Charlie Peacock, is "necessary to moral and ethical reflection and often inspires the actions that come out of such reflection." It can be a "perfectly tuned engine of a truly good, creative life." It is a mode of spiritual vision, but it has epistemological significance as well. Citing Lewis's description of the imagination as an "organ of meaning," Peacock marvels at its capacity to show God's brilliance *and* serve as a "way of knowing that leads to ways of being and doing congruent with the will of God."[44] Similarly, it is the imagination that enables us to see in the shadows of the present life a glorious future with God—a vision Lauren F. Winner sees beautifully portrayed in the final volume of the Narnia Chronicles, *The Last Battle*. In the concluding scene, which depicts the end of time, she quotes from Lewis:

... the things that began to happen ... were so great and beautiful that I cannot write them. And for us this is the end of all the stories, and we can most truly say that they all lived happily ever after. But for them it was only the beginning of the real story. All their life in this world and all their adventures in Narnia had only been the cover and the title page: now at last they were beginning Chapter One of the Great Story, which no one on earth has read: which goes on forever: in which every chapter is better than the one before."[45]

This eschatological vision evokes powerful human responses in the here-and-now—promptings of longing for, and praise to, God. It is, of course, triggered by Lewis's "baptized imagination" and its gaze through or beyond the "appearances" and "successive moments" of this life into the region of awe—a region that is ultimate ... no longer successive. It is a vision that is shaped and colored by a literary imagination, with its grand narratives and potent metaphors of "homecoming" and "reunion with a beloved."[46]

Winner, Peacock, and McLaren share with Lewis an "Enlightenment cynicism" and a journey of deconversion out of the epistemological confines of modernity. At the very least, for Winner, "the sum of the parts will never capture the whole" because there is such a thing as "the real story" and its "eternal reality"—a reality that beckons even now through the workings of the imagination. In this respect, Lewis was remarkably prescient, as Donald E. Glover observes:

One of the most fascinating aspects of Lewis's conversion is often lost in the critic's hurry to get on to what Lewis became, forgetting what he was before. Up to this point, Lewis had been the typical intellectual student and then tutor of his day.... Yet [his] letters show a gradual shift toward the thoughtful analysis of the role played by emotion and sensuous response in an otherwise rational man's life.... The result of his quite rational consideration of the meaning and role of the imagination as it created images of beauty in the reader's mind was the realization that he had stopped short of understanding the aim of this delight, mistaking it for an end in itself.[47]

Lewis, as we have seen, gradually overcame this limitation in much the same way that a new generation of postmoderns has deconstructed the boundaries of the modern imagination. For this reason, they are drawn to the spatial metaphors of Lewis's "region of awe" as well as his mythic forms and their powerful ability to fuse horizons between author, text, and reader. In short, the Emerging Church/Conversation finds in Lewis inspiration and, in some sense, legitimation for its own imaginative improvisations.

When we turn to the EC-friendly theologians and theorists, we encounter an equally varied range of links to Lewis's incarnational aesthetics. David C. Downing has noted how effectively Lewis speaks to our present era of postmodern deconstruction "because of his intellectual agility, his willingness to adopt de-centering strategies at the operational level, while rejecting self-canceling denials about the possibility of 'a still point in the turning world.' "[48] Lewis was certainly aware of the social construction of knowledge, the inaccessibility of pure objectivity, and the historical relativity of models. In the Epilogue to *The Discarded Image*, he observed:

No Model is a catalogue of ultimate realities, and none is a mere fantasy. Each is a serious attempt to get in all the phenomena known at a given period, and each succeeds in getting in a great many. But also, no less surely, each reflects the prevalent psychology of an age almost as much as it reflects the state of that age's knowledge. . . . It is not impossible that our own Model will die a violent death, ruthlessly smashed by an unprovoked assault of new facts. . . . But nature gives most of her evidence in answer to the quests we ask her. Here, as in the courts, the character of the evidence depends on the shape of the examination, and a good cross-examiner can do wonders. He will not indeed elicit falsehoods from an honest witness. But, in relation to the total truth in the witness's mind, the structure of the examination is like a stencil. It determines how much of that total truth will appear and what pattern it will suggest.[49]

Of particular concern, then, is the relationship between truth and imagination, especially the literary imagination—a concern that preoccupied Lewis and those who find in him a unique capacity to hold together a "metaphysical affirmation and epistemological humility."[50]

Along these lines, the Lewis-inspired phenomenology of philosopher Dallas Willard and theologian Kevin Vanhoozer has proven especially relevant in EC circles. Willard is best known for his books on spiritual formation, including *The Spirit of the Disciplines* (1991) and *The Divine Conspiracy* (1998), and it is in this arena that he is often viewed as a mentor for the emerging church.[51] But behind the scenes, the more theologically and philosophically inclined emergents also pay attention to his work on the philosophy of Edmund Husserl and the phenomenology of knowledge. It is out of this background of scholarly pursuits that Willard writes with unusual clarity and conviction about the "inner gathering of the self," the benefits of solitude and silence, and, perhaps, most challenging of all, a robust understanding of the correspondence theory of truth.[52] Willard is particularly concerned with an enduring evangelical tension between the personal experience of God and the authority of the Bible, as it is actually believed and practiced. Postevangelicals, especially emergents, are drawn to his provocative redefinition of the spiritual life in light of this tension—a project that is closely connected to his phenomenological epistemology.

Regarding the latter, Willard identifies Lewis with the "classical" theory of correspondence—the idea that "truth is a matter of a belief or idea (representation, statement) *corresponding* to reality." Borrowing from an illustration in Lewis's *Mere Christianity*, Willard explains:

In the course of rejecting the view that moral laws are mere social conventions he [Lewis] insists that they are, to the contrary, "Real truths." "If your moral ideas can be truer, and those of the Nazi less true," he says to his reader, "there must be something— some Real morality—for them to be true about. The reason why your idea of New York can be truer or less true than mine is that New York is a real place, existing quite apart from what either of us thinks. If when each of us said 'New York' each meant merely 'the town I am imagining in my own head,' how could one of us have truer ideas than the other? There would be no question of truth or falsehood at all."[53]

Acknowledging the difficulties that this theory faces in a postmodern climate of "disdain of truth," Willard defends Lewis's epistemology, in part, on phenomenological grounds, stressing how its objective ground for meaning "is a relation of a wholly new kind, as remote, as mysterious, as opaque to empirical study, as soul itself." Lewis understood that "real truth" and its relation to meaning and reason is objective in a "strong" or intuitive sense, "comprehensible even though non-empirical." The reality of this truth is "unyielding in the face of belief, desire, tradition and will," while, at the same time, our beliefs and perceptions are relative. What matters is the means by which we *aim* these beliefs, perceptions, and resulting actions toward truth: "by comparing them to what they are about, or by careful inference, or even by acting on them, *just as* we can check in various ways whether the sighting mechanism on a rifle is 'true'—possibly by firing it and comparing the result with the setting of the sighting mechanism."[54]

This dispositional approach to the "truth question" is paramount throughout Willard's writings, but it is most rigorously developed in his scholarly discussions of intuition in Husserlian phenomenology—an analysis that not only exceeds the scope of this paper, but also remains far beyond the direct purview of most EC readers. What is most important to note, for present purposes, is that this understanding of intuition possesses for both Willard and Lewis a potent mystical quality.[55] By *mystical*, Willard means that our deepest intuitions or insights are constituted by a kind of nonempirical "viewing" of objects and objectivity that actually brings us into relation with them, as part of a greater whole. Consciousness, in fact, bends toward the reality of things even before we rely on language to organize or define the experience.[56] This "inner experience" is also mystical in terms of the classic directness of the "phenomenological imperative"—"seeing for *oneself*" or knowledge "by acquaintance." This is the sort of "essence intuition" that is implied throughout much of Lewis's work as well, especially, as we have seen, after his encounter with Barfield and his embrace of Coleridge's theory of imagination. For Willard, this literary enterprise, with its associated "feelings, memories, images, perceptions, valuations and so forth" is ultimately grounded in "underivative intuitions of the objects" that prompt these varied responses (that is "experience essences") and disclose their meanings.[57] Willard finds Lewis helpful in demystifying some of this phenomenology for a wider audience, but, ultimately, his concern is epistemological. "We are in a world other than ourselves," Willard insists, "and we are equipped to deal with it as it is, correcting our mistakes and misperceptions as we go." [58]

Willard appreciates Lewis's cautious appeal to the imagination for much the same reason that Lewis scholars David C. Downing and Bruce Edwards both admire Lewis as a "discerning critic." "[H]ow is it," Downing asks, "that such an unshrinking foundationalist could also present analysis which parallels the de-centering strategies of several postmodern commentators?"[59] How could Lewis's rich metaphysics and mystical intuition of the "burning and undimensioned depth of the Divine Life" be reconciled with his redemptive deconstruction—as able and willing as Derrida, as Edwards puts it, to "sift the text [and the imagination] for internal incongruity, contradiction, and ambiguity"[60] while, at the same time, expressing an openness to revelatory illumination originating in the "region of awe."[61] This remarkable way of knowing draws those who find the postmodern critique of traditional epistemology compelling even as they struggle to retain some semblance of traditional Christian belief. What attracts them, at the most basic level, is the participatory and relational aspect of the phenomenological imperative, as stated above. As an EC writer at VanguardChurch.blogspot.com observes, "Where Christian apologetics in the modern era sought to explain 'Evidence that Demands a Verdict' (a form of apologetics that served its purpose in the modern era but would have been of reign in the pre-modern era and is increasingly foreign in the postmodern era), Christianity in a postmodern era must instead invite people into *interaction with this Living God*." Lewis anticipated this emerging mandate, and his following, as a result, includes not only philosophers like Willard, but also theologians like Kevin Vanhoozer—one of the most frequently cited thinkers in the EC world today.

The VanguardChurch blog to which we have just referred goes on to credit Vanhoozer with developing a "postpropositional perspective on Scripture." At another EC Web site, he is praised for not beginning his hermeneutical inquiries with distinctively modern concerns like inerrancy and inspiration, but rather the "drama of doctrine" as it is "meant to be played out using the script of God as its text."[62] Yet another EC blogger begins his posting with the following quotation from Vanhoozer to drive home the point that biblical vision is essentially a work of the imagination:

The imagination, together with its linguistic offspring (e.g., metaphor), is another of those repressed themes in modernity. Rationalists held the imagination in low regard, while romantics understood its importance but failed to discipline it. By *imagination* I mean the power of synoptic vision—the ability to synthesize heterogeneous elements into a unity. The imagination is a cognitive faculty by which we see as whole what those without imagination see only as unrelated parts. Stories display the imagination in action, for it is the role of the plot (mythos) to unify various persons and events in a single story with a beginning, middle, and end.

Lewis would have agreed wholeheartedly with each of these observations, so it is not surprising that he is appreciatively invoked by Vanhoozer in the next quotation:

C. S. Lewis insists that the imagination is a truth-bearing faculty whose bearers of truth are not propositions but *myths*. Myths enable us both to "taste" and to "see": to experience 'as a concrete what can otherwise be understood only as an abstraction." What gets conveyed, therefore, is not simply the proposition but something of the reality itself: not simply information about God, but God's triune identity itself as this is displayed in and through his creative and redemptive work. Further, the words of Scripture do not simply inform us about God but act as the medium of divine discourse. It is these words—the stories, the promises, the warnings, etc.—that ought to orient Christians vis-à-vis reality.[63]

Vanhoozer and Lewis are very much on the same page, at least as far as the bloggers at NextReformation.com are concerned. What they most appreciate about Vanhoozer is what they appreciate about Lewis—a way to think, or, perhaps we should say, *imagine* as Christians about the "post/modern way."

Whereas Willard generally emphasizes the "flow of consciousness," its inseparability from the world, and, following Husserl, its prelinguistic cognition, Vanhoozer more sharply focuses the consciousness on texts, especially their authorial intent as ontological grounding. In other words, Willard's phenomenology requires that we rightly *act* on the text, presupposing the Holy Spirit's presence. Vanhoozer's hermeneutical method requires that we must rightly *interpret* the text first. Both agree that "it is by action that we enter the reality of the world which the Bible is about." As Willard suggests, "It is residing in Jesus' word that permits us to enter the reality of God's rule and become free from domination by other realities."[64] In effect, an "intention relation" is necessary, especially in the case of texts, for the disclosure of meaning. This intention is fundamentally moral in nature, as we have seen, requiring submission to the text or "active obedience" such that the text retains its objective status—its *otherness*.[65]

In an essay inspired by Lewis's depiction of modernity in *Pilgrim's Regress*, Vanhoozer expresses this intentionality in terms of a well-trained imagination:

Theological wisdom is a matter of learning how to read and relate to reality rightly. The wise person is the one who understands and participates fittingly in the created order. We get wisdom by letting the biblical texts train our imaginations to see how things fit together theodramatically as Scripture depicts the world as created and redeemed; this picture generates a certain ethos that in turn shapes our moral character. Scripture also depicts the love of God—which is the summation of the law and hence the essence of Christian ethics—in the face of Jesus Christ. Ethics is about how to participate fittingly in the form of the good personified in Jesus Christ. Christianity thus represents an alternative way of doing justice to the other. Thanks to the theodramatic imagination, we see the other not as an unknowable, and hence unlovable, cipher, but as Jesus sees the other, as *neighbor*. In sum, the Bible *situates* both me and the other in a larger theodrama that orients right action by calling us to love others as God has loved us.

Vanhoozer echoes Lewis's call for reenchantment in late modernity through a recovery of this *mythos*. Such a move restores, in a more general sense, our "capacity to see what is there," which is, simultaneously, the capacity to see beyond the confines of the self. Simone Weil called this "attention," which Vanhoozer recalls is "the ability to transcend oneself in order to see things as they are." Just as Lewis was alert to the visionary solipsism of the Victorian romantics, Vanhoozer warns against postmodern varieties of narcissism that deflect attention away from the object of our attention toward the feelings associated therewith. Consequently, he finds Lewis's "map" in *Pilgrim's Regress* helpful in representing the postmodern turn.[66]

Vanhoozer also finds Lewis's short essay, "Meditation in a Toolshed" particularly useful in illuminating the contours of our deconstructed world. It was originally intended to illustrate the difference between looking at and looking along. It begins with a brief story:

I was standing today in the dark toolshed. The sun was shining outside and through the crack at the top of the door there came a sunbeam. From where I stood that beam of light, with the specks of dust floating in it, was the most striking thing in the place. Everything else was almost pitch-black. I was seeing the beam, not seeing things by it.

Then I moved, so that the beam fell on my eyes. Instantly the whole previous picture vanished. I saw no toolshed, and (above all) no beam. Instead I saw, framed in the irregular cranny at the top of the door, green leaves moving on the branches of a tree outside and beyond that, 90 odd million miles away, the sun. Looking along the beam, and looking at the beam are very different experiences.[67]

For Vanhoozer, the story is about the nature of knowledge. In Lewis's modern world, the primary goal was to look *at* things—"those who are a step removed from the experience on which they bring their analytic-critical technique to bear." This required distance and disinterestedness—an attitude that prevailed in every arena of inquiry, including the study of the Bible. "By and large," Vanhoozer notes, "biblical scholars look *at* the Bible—at questions of its authorship, at questions of its composition, at questions of its historical reliability—instead of *along* it."[68]

This brings Vanhoozer to Lewis's question: "is knowing God more like *seeing* or *tasting*?" Postmoderns have offered deconstructed language, ethics, and aesthetics as possible venues for answering this question, but it is the biblical-poetic imagination that ultimately plays the leading role in our engagement with the communicative agency of God. Vanhoozer concludes by listing the essential ingredients in this renewed encounter with the Bible. First, God has designed the imagination in such a way that we can actually see what is there, "particularly when the senses alone are unable to observe it." The imagination bears this truth, though primarily in mythic form and in accordance with the constraints of the Scriptures themselves. Secondly, in this age of "image anemia," we cannot only see what is there—in the world of the text—but participate in it by looking along its grain. There are, of course, different ways of seeing and "experiencing thinking" that allow us to enter this world, but the Scriptures remain our common "port of entry." Thirdly, in the world of the text we see God, the world, and ourselves differently—in accordance with the divine communicative action—and we respond in faith. As a result, we become "wiser for our travels" and we "become right with God."[69]

Through, in part, the Lewis-inspired phenomenology and hermeneutics of Willard, Vanhoozer, and their popularizers, the EC has debunked the modern notion that "looking *at* is, by its own nature, intrinsically truer or better than looking *along*."[70] In whatever way Lewis's insight is applied—in the creation of new forms of worship, new channels of literary endeavor (especially on the

Internet), or new venues in the performing arts—there will remain an abiding reference to the "The Grand Miracle." Through its "knowledge by acquaintance," we find grounding for the sympathetic imagination. Its harmonies, associations, and transpositions subvert our self-sufficiencies, provincialisms, and pragmatic reductions. In its amalgam of thought-feeling-awareness we reunite, at least provisionally, the perceiving subject with the perceived object. Knowledge by acquaintance becomes knowledge through participation, with a "baptized vision" of particulars in relation to wholes that elicits a potent moral response.

Through the "hints, similes, and metaphors" of the sympathetic imagination, Brian McLaren encounters the mystical, Charlie Peacock finds a deeper sense of congruence with the divine will, and Lauren Winner sees beyond appearances to a much anticipated "homecoming." No wonder that Lewis declares the Incarnation to be "the central miracle asserted by Christians." It was his chief source of inspiration, and he devoted most of his life to letting it work its peculiar magic in his mind and craft. "It digs beneath the surface, works through the rest of our knowledge by unexpected channels, harmonises best with our deepest apprehensions and our 'second thoughts,'" he observed, "and in union with these undermines our superficial opinions."[71] For Lewis, that's what incarnational aesthetics was all about. And, perhaps, that is ultimately what the emerging imagination is about today.

NOTES

1. Shorter versions of this paper have been delivered at the C. S. Lewis Summer Institute, Cambridge University, Cambridge, England (July 24–August 6, 2005) and the C. S. Lewis & Friends Colloquium, Taylor University, Upland, Indiana (June 1–4, 2006).

2. Paul Roberts, "Liturgy and Mission in Postmodern Culture: Some Reflections Arising from 'Alternative' Services and Communities," http://seaspray.trinity-bris.ac.uk (accessed September 5, 2003). The author is an ordained priest in the Church of England, serving parishes in Bristol. This online paper was presented at the "Alternative Worship Day" gathering at Lambeth Palace in 1995.

3. Dan Kimball, *The Emerging Church: Vintage Christianity for New Generations* (Grand Rapids, MI: Zondervan-Emergent-YS, 2003), 135. Kimball's church site can be visited online at http://vintagechurch.org.

4. Andy Crouch, "Visualcy: Literacy Is Not the Only Necessity in a Visual Culture," *Christianity Today* (June 2005), 62.

5. Brian McLaren, "An Open Letter to Chuck Colson," *A New Kind of Christian*, http://www.anewkindofchristian.com/archives/000018.html (accessed December 2003).

6. McLaren, *A Generous Orthodoxy* (Grand Rapids, MI: Zondervan, 2004), 145; also quoted in an interview with Jason Byassee, "New Kind of Christian: An Emergent Voice," *Christian Century* (November 30, 2004), 29.

7. These concerns are raised by Alan Roxburgh, "Emergent Church: Filled with Creativity, Energetic Potential," *Allelon Ministries* (June 15, 2005), http://www.allelon.org/articles/article.cfm?id=194&page=1 (accessed July 19, 2006).

8. Scott Bader-Sayre, "The Emergent Matrix: A New Kind of Church?" *The Christian Century* (November 30, 2004), 20–27; and Andy Crouch, "The Emergent Mystique," *Christianity Today* (November 2004), 36–41.

9. Winner, quoted in Bader-Sayre, 26. Winner is author of the popular spiritual autobiography *Girl Meets God: A Memoir* (New York: Random House, 2002).

10. C. S. Lewis, "Christian Apologetics," in *God in the Dock: Essays on Theology and Ethics*, ed. Walter Hooper (Grand Rapids, MI: Eerdmans, 1970), 93–94.

11. Stephen M. Smith, "Awakening from the Enchantment of Worldliness: The Chronicles of Narnia as Pre-Apologetics," in *The Pilgrim's Guide: C. S. Lewis and the Art of Witness*, ed. David Mills (Grand Rapids, MI: Eerdmans, 1998), 168–181.

12. Regarding Lewis's explicit evangelistic agenda, see especially his essay "Christianity and Culture," in *Christian Reflections*, ed. Walter Hooper (Grand Rapids, MI: Eerdmans, 1967), 12–36.

13. Lewis, Magdalen College, Oxford, to Sister Penelope CSMV, July 9 (August) 1939, in *The Collected Letters of C. S. Lewis*, ed. Walter Hooper, vol. 2, *Books, Broadcasts, and the War, 1931–1949* (San Francisco, CA: Harper, 2004), 262–263.

14. Lewis, "Sometimes Fairy Stories May Say Best What's To Be Said," in *Of Other Worlds: Essays and Stories*, compiled and with Preface by Walter Hooper (New York: Harvest Book, Harcourt, 1996), 37.

15. Lewis, *Surprised by Joy: The Shape of My Early Life* (New York: Harcourt, Brace and Co., 1955), 221. Some prominent examples of deconversion and reconversion from EC circles include: Gordon Lynch's *Losing My Religion? Moving on from Evangelical Faith* (London: DLT, 2003); Dave Tomlinson's *The Post-Evangelical* (El Cajon, CA: Emergent YS-Zondervan, 2003); Donald Miller, *Blue Like Jazz* (Nashville, TN: Thomas Nelson, 2003); and Brian McLaren, *Generous Orthodoxy* (Zondervan, 2004), especially, chapter 9. For a helpful critical assessment of the deconversion phenomenon in contemporary evangelicalism, see Kurt A. Richardson, "Disorientations in Christian Belief: The Problem of De-traditionalization in the Postmodern Context," in *The Challenge of Postmodernism: An Evangelical Engagement*, ed. David S. Dockery (Grand Rapids, MI: Baker Books, 1995), 53–56.

16. Louis Markos, *Lewis Agonistes: How C. S. Lewis Can Train Us to Wrestle with the Modern and Postmodern World* (Nashville, TN: Broadman & Holman, 2003), 139.

17. Lewis, "Transposition," in *The Weight of Glory* (San Francisco, CA: Harper, 1949/1976, rev. 1980), 98–99. Transposition, for Lewis, is not strictly a literary strategy, but rather a broad statement of principle regarding the analogous relations between the spiritual and natural or the higher and the lower realms. Later in this

passage, Lewis referred to the sacramental as a more advanced instance of transposition in Christian theology (p. 102).

18. Charlie Peacock, *New Way to Be Human* (Colorado Springs, CO: Shaw Books, 2004), 176; McLaren, *Generous Orthodoxy*, 150–151; Yaconelli, quoted by McLaren, 77.

19. Lewis, *Miracles: A Preliminary Study* (New York: Macmillan, 1947), 111.

20. Ibid., 113.

21. Ibid., 118.

22. Ibid., 120.

23. Thomas L. Martin, "Lewis: A Critical Prospective," in *Reading the Classics with C. S. Lewis*, ed. Thomas L. Martin (Grand Rapids, MI: Baker Academic, 2000), 382–384.

24. For a detailed summary and analysis of these letters, see Lionel Adey, *C. S. Lewis' "Great War" with Owen Barfield* (Cumbria, UK: Ink Books, 1978).

25. Lewis to Barfield, n.d., "*The Great War*," vol. 1, 13, Barfield-Lewis Letters, The Marion E. Wade Center, Wheaton College, Wheaton, Illinois; see also Lewis, 1929/1930 (?) "*De Bono et Malo,*" Ms. [photocopy], 8, Edwin W. Brown Collection Center, Taylor University, Upland, Indiana. The latter manuscript was Lewis's final installment in the exchange of treatises during the "War." Regarding the importance of Barfield in this thought, Lewis recalled: "But I think he changed me a good deal more than I him. Much of the thought which he afterward put into *Poetic Diction* had already become mine before that important little book appeared. It would be strange if it had not. He was of course not so learned then as he has since become; but the genius was already there." See *Surprised by Joy*, 200; also Alan Jacobs, *The Narnian: The Life and Imagination of C. S. Lewis* (San Francisco, CA: Harper, 2005), 90–91.

26. Lewis, *Surprised by Joy*, 217–218.

27. Ibid., 221–223.

28. For more on this transition, see James Patrick, "The Heart's Desire and the Landlord's Rules: C. S. Lewis as a Moral Philosopher," in *The Pilgrim's Guide: C. S. Lewis and the Art of Witness*, ed. David Mills (Grand Rapids, MI: Eerdmans, 1998), 70–85; and David Downing, *The Most Reluctant Convert: C. S. Lewis's Journey to Faith* (Downers Grove, IL: InterVarsity Press, 2002), 123–137.

29. Lewis to Barfield, 1928, "Clivi Hamiltonis Summae Metaphysices Contra Anthroposophos Libri II," Part II ("Value"), Section XIV, Ms. [photocopy], Edwin W. Brown Collection. See also Adey, "*Great War*," 69–78.

30. Lewis, *Surprised by Joy*, 210: "The Absolute there 'there,' and that 'there' contained the reconciliation of all contraries, the transcendence of all finitude, the hidden glory which was the only perfectly real thing there is. In fact, it had much of the quality of Heaven."

31. Barfield, *Poetic Diction: A Study in Meaning* (Middletown, CT: Wesleyan University Press, 1973 [original date of publication, 1928]), 88.

32. Lewis, "Summae," Part II ("Value"), Section XX, Edwin W. Brown Collection. For a more detailed analysis of this passage, see Adey, "*Great War*," 84–87.

33. Lewis, "Epilogue," in *An Experiment in Criticism* (Cambridge University Press, 1961), 130, 139, 140.

34. Lewis spoke of his own baptized imagination in his preface to *George Mac-Donald: An Anthology* (San Francisco, CA: Harper, 1946), xxxviii; see also *Surprised by Joy*, 179–180.

35. The term "phenomenology" is often used in the sense of Rudolf Otto's notion of the *numinous*—the experience of "the holy" aside from its moral or rational aspects. Lewis appreciated Otto's phenomenological description of the universal or essential aspects of religious experience, but he also acquired a taste for philosophical phenomenology from the lingering neo-Hegelianism at Oxford University—especially that of T. H. Green (d. 1882), F. H. Bradley (d. 1924), and Bernard Bosanquet (d. 1923), all of whom were "mighty names" in Lewis's intellectual formation. Their cumulative effect on Lewis was to provide a door *into* Christianity; this according a letter he wrote to Paul Elmer More, October 25, 1934, in *The Collected Letters of C. S. Lewis*, p. 145. Green and Bradley, in particular, appropriated the venerable notion of sympathy into their modified Hegelianism as a mode of moral reasoning. It was also a more popular expression of ethical sentimentalism that influenced evangelical piety throughout the late eighteenth and nineteenth centuries. John MacCunn provides an introduction to Green's version of sympathy in a standard work that was contemporary with Lewis's philosophical studies; see *Six Radical Thinkers* (New York: Russell & Russell, 1910/1964), 215–266. For a recent overview of Lewis's idealist phase, see David C. Downing, *The Most Reluctant Convert: C. S. Lewis's Journey to Faith* (Downers Grove, IL: InterVarsity Press, 2002), 123–137.

36. Lewis, "The Language of Religion," in *Christian Reflections*, 137–138. For a helpful survey of how Lewis accomplished this in his fictional works, see Kath Filmer-Davies, "Fantasy," in *Reading the Classics with C. S. Lewis*, ed. Thomas L. Martin (Grand Rapids, MI: Baker Academic, 2000), 285–296. Thus, in *The Narnia Chronicles*, we see how community forms through the mutuality and cooperation of siblings, each with their own distinctive roles and individualities, but also varying capacities of affection and friendship. We also see how the wicked witch, Jadis, seeks to destroy these sympathetic relations and, in the telling of the story, we find ourselves identifying with the struggle to resist and, sometimes, redeem the resulting brokenness. The Space Trilogy takes us further into the realm of human and social psychology, but, as Kath Filmer-Davies has observed, as much through an exploration of *inner* space, as outer. In *The Great Divorce*, we plunge into the dark world of human selfishness while, in Lewis's last novel, *Till We Have Faces*, we encounter the fundamental human tension between submission and control. In all of these works of fantasy, the immediate concern with interpersonal dynamics remains accessible to our (the reader's) sympathetic imagination. Accordingly, by the very act of "good reading"

we are moving about in a world that is creatively designed to nudge us beyond the tiny sphere, if not prison, of our own self-interest.

37. See, for example, Dan Devadatta, Strangers but Not Strange: A New Mission Situation for the Church (I Peter 1:1–2 and 17–25), in Craig Van Gelder, ed., *Confident Witness—Changing World: Rediscovering the Gospel in North America* (Grand Rapids, MI: Eerdmans, 1999), 110–124; James Wm. McClendon, Jr., "The Practice of Community Formation," in Nancey Murphy et al., *Virtues & Practices in the Christian Tradition: Christian Ethics After MacIntyre* (Harrisburg, PA: Trinity Press, 1997), 85–110; and The Rutba House, ed., *School(s) for Conversion: 12 Marks of a New Monasticism* (Eugene, OR: Cascade Books, 2005).

38. Bronsink, "Arts: Imaginatively Indwelling God's Word in Postmodernity," 10, http://www.emergentvillage.com/downloads/resources/other/ARTS_Imaginatively Dwelling.pdf (accessed July 1, 2006).

39. Paul Roberts, "Considering Emerging Church," *Thinking Anglicans* (August 28, 2003) http://www.thinkinganglicans.org.uk/archives/000129.html (accessed July 6, 2006).

40. An example of such collaboration has been the recent series of annual Emergent-YS Conventions, each designed to break-down the modern rupture between theory and practice, especially regarding "critical concerns" like "Creating a Climate for Creativity and Innovation in Ministry" or "Reimagining Spiritual Formation: The Role of Missional Communities," Emergent-YS Convention, Nashville, Tennessee (May 18–21, 2005).

41. McLaren, *Generous Orthodoxy*, 151, 154, 155.

42. Leonard Sweet, Brian D. McLaren, and Jerry Haselmayer, *A is for Abductive: The Language of the Emerging Church* (Grand Rapids, MI: Zondervan, 2003), 206.

43. Lewis, *An Experiment in Criticism*, 138.

44. Peacock, *New Way to Be Human*, 176.

45. Lauren F. Winner, *Girl Meets God*, 193–194.

46. See, especially, Lewis's essay "On Stories," in *Of Other Worlds: Essays and Stories* (San Diego, CA: Harcourt, Inc., 1966), 3–21; and *Surprised by Joy*, 220–222.

47. Donald E. Glover, *C. S. Lewis: The Art of Enchantment* (Athens, OH: Ohio University Press, 1981), 18–19.

48. David. C. Downing, "From Pillar to Postmodernism: C. S. Lewis and Current Critical Discourse," *Christianity and Literature* 46 (Winter 1997): 169–178.

49. Lewis, *The Discarded Image: An Introduction to Medieval and Renaissance Literature* (Cambridge University Press, 1964), 222–223. I am indebted to David Downing for drawing my attention to this passage.

50. Downing, "From Pillar to Postmodernism," 176.

51. Willard's popularity is noted in Andy Crouch, "The Emergent Mystique," 40. Eric Hurtgen, "Stepping into Community," http://www.relevantmagazine. com/god_article.php?id=6964 (accessed July 6, 2006).

52. For a sampling of Emergent interest in such Willard-related topics, see, for example, Eric Hurtgen, "Stepping into Community"; and Tomlinson, *The Post-Evangelical*, 11–13.

53. Willard, "Truth in the Fire: C. S. Lewis and Pursuit of Truth Today," http://www.dwillard.org/articles/artview.asp?artID=68 (accessed July 6, 2006). Willard quotes from Lewis, *Mere Christianity* (New York: Macmillan, 1943), 11.

54. Willard, "Truth in the Fire," 5–10.

55. Indeed, this has become a cause of nagging controversy for Willard in many of his popular writings on spiritual formation. See, for example, a blogsphere "rant" on Willard's "inner light" mysticism, http://emergentno.blogspot.com (accessed July 6, 2006).

56 . Willard, "Degradation of Logical Form," http://www.dwillard.org/articles/artview.asp?artID=24 (accessed July 6, 2006) (originally in *Axiomathes* [1997]: 42–43).

57. Willard, "Historical and Philosophical Foundations of Phenemenology," 3, 6, http://www.dwillard.org/articles/artview.asp?artID=32 (accessed July 6, 2006).

58. Willard, "Truth in the Fire," 14.

59. Downing, "From Pillar to Postmodernism," 176.

60. Bruce L. Edwards, "Rehabilitating Reading: C. S. Lewis and Contemporary Critical Theory," in *The Taste of the Pineapple: Essays on C. S. Lewis as Reader, Critic, and Imaginative Writer*, ed. Bruce Edwards (Bowling Green, OH: Bowling Green State University Popular Press, 1988), 29.

61. Downing, "From Pillar to Postmodernism," 176.

62. Scot McKnight, "Emergent Voices" [cited March 2, 2006] http://www.jesuscreed.org.

63. "Imagination and Biblical Vision" [cited June 14, 2006] http://nextreformation.com, quoting from Vanhoozer's "Pilgrim's Digress: Christian Thinking on and about the Post/Modern Way," in *Christianity and the Postmodern Turn: Six Views*, ed. Myron B. Penner (Grand Rapids, MI: Brazos Press, 2005), 71–103.

64. See Willard's review of Vanhoozer's hermeneutical method in "Hermeneutical Occasionalism," in *Disciplining Hermeneutics: Interpretation in Christian Perspective*, ed. Roger Lundin (Grand Rapids, MI: Eerdmans, 1997), 167–172.

65. Kevin J. Vanhoozer, *Is There a Meaning in This Text? The Bible, the Reader, and the Morality of Literary Knowledge* (Grand Rapids, MI: Zondervan, 1998), 74–80.

66. Vanhoozer, "Pilgrim's Digress," 90.

67. Lewis, "Meditation in a Toolshed," in *God in the Dock: Essays on Theology and Ethics*, ed. Walter Hooper (Grand Rapids, MI: Eerdmans, 1970), 212–215.

68. Kevin J. Vanhoozer, *First Theology: God, Scripture & Hermeneutics* (Downers Grove, IL: InterVarsity Press, 2002), 18.

69. Ibid., 36–39.

70. Lewis, "Meditation in a Toolshed," 215.

71. Lewis, *Miracles*, 131.

BIBLIOGRAPHY

Adey, Lionel. *C. S. Lewis' 'Great War' with Owen Barfield*. Cumbria, UK: Ink Books, 1978.

Bader-Sayre, Scott. "The Emergent Matrix: A New Kind of Church?" *The Christian Century* 30 (November 2004), 20–27.

Barfield, Owen. *Poetic Diction: A Study in Meaning*. Middletown, CT: Wesleyan University Press, 1928/1973.

Bronsink, Troy. "Arts: Imaginatively Indwelling God's Word in Postmodernity" [November 28, 2001]. At http://www.emergentvillage.com/downloads/resources/other/ARTS_ImaginativelyDwelling.pdf (accessed July 19, 2006).

Byassee, Jason. "New Kind of Christian: An Emergent Voice." *Christian Century* 30 (November, 2004), 29.

Crouch, Andy. "The Emergent Mystique." *Christianity Today* (November 2004): 36–41.

———. "Visualcy: Literacy Is Not the Only Necessity in a Visual Culture." *Christianity Today* (June 2005), 62.

Devadatta, Dan. Strangers But Not Strange: A New Mission Situation for the Church (I Peter 1:1–2 and 17–25). In *Confident Witness—Changing World: Rediscovering the Gospel in North America*. Edited by Craig Van Gelder. Grand Rapids, MI: Eerdmans, 1999, 110–124.

Downing, David C. "From Pillar to Postmodernism: C. S. Lewis and Current Critical Discourse." *Christianity and Literature* 46 (Winter 1997), 169–178.

———. *The Most Reluctant Convert: C. S. Lewis's Journey to Faith*. Downers Grove, IL: InterVarsity Press, 2002.

Edwards, Bruce. "Rehabilitating Reading: C. S. Lewis and Contemporary Critical Theory." In *The Taste of the Pineapple: Essays on C. S. Lewis as Reader, Critic, and Imaginative Writer*. Edited by Bruce Edwards. Bowling Green, OH: Popular Press, 1988.

Filmer-Davies, Kath. "Fantasy." In *Reading the Classics with C. S. Lewis*. Edited by Thomas L. Martin. Grand Rapids, MI: Baker Academic, 2000, 285–296.

Glover, Donald E. *C. S. Lewis: The Art of Enchantment*. Athens, OH: Ohio University Press, 1981.

Hurtgen, Eric. "Stepping into Community," http://www.relevantmagazine.com/god_article.php?id=6964. (Accessed July 6, 2006).

Jacobs, Alan. *The Narnian: The Life and Imagination of C. S. Lewis*. San Francisco, CA: Harper, 2005.

Kimball, Dan. *The Emerging Church: Vintage Christianity for New Generations*. Grand Rapids, MI: Zondervan-Emergent-YS, 2003.

Lewis, C. S. "Christian Apologetics." In *God in the Dock: Essays on Theology and Ethics*. Edited by Walter Hooper. Grand Rapids, MI: Eerdmans, 1970, 89–103.

———. "Christianity and Culture." In *Christian Reflections*. Edited by Walter Hooper. Grand Rapids, MI: Eerdmans, 1967, 12–36.

———. "*De Bono et Malo*" [Ms. 1929/1930 (?) photocopy, 8, Barfield-Lewis Letters]. Edwin W. Brown Collection Center, Taylor University, Upland, Indiana.

———. *The Discarded Image: An Introduction to Medieval and Renaissance Literature.* Cambridge: Cambridge University Press, 1964.

———. *An Experiment in Criticism.* Cambridge: Cambridge University Press, 1961.

———. *George MacDonald: An Anthology.* San Francisco, CA: Harper, 1946.

———."The Language of Religion." In *Christian Reflections.* Edited by Walter Hooper. Grand Rapids, MI: Eerdmans, 1967, 129–141.

———. "Meditation in a Toolshed." In *God in the Dock: Essays on Theology and Ethics.* Edited by Walter Hooper. Grand Rapids, MI: Eerdmans, 1970, 212–215.

———. *Mere Christianity.* New York: Macmillan, 1943.

———. *Miracles: A Preliminary Study.* New York: Macmillan, 1947/1960.

———. "On Stories." In *Of Other Worlds: Essays and Stories.* San Diego, CA: Harcourt, Inc., 1966, 3–21.

———. "Sometimes Fairy Stories May Say Best What's To Be Said." In *Of Other Worlds: Essays and Stories.* Compiled by Walter Hooper. New York: Harvest Book, Harcourt, 1996, 35–38.

———. "Summae" [Part II ("Value"), Section XX, photocopy]. Edwin W. Brown Collection, n.d.

———. *Surprised by Joy: The Shape of My Early Life.* New York: Harcourt, Brace and Co., 1955.

———. "Transposition." In *The Weight of Glory.* San Francisco, CA: Harper, 1980, 91–115.

Lewis, C. S. to Owen Barfield, n.d., "The Great War" [Vol. 1, 13, Barfield-Lewis Letters]. At the Marion E. Wade Center, Wheaton College, Wheaton, Illinois.

Lewis, C. S. to Owen Barfield. "Clivi Hamiltonis Summae Metaphysices Contra Anthroposophos Libri II," [1928, Part II ("Value"), Section XIV, Ms. [photocopy]). Edwin W. Brown Collection.

Lewis, C. S. to Paul Elmer More, October 25, 1934. In *The Collected Letters of C. S. Lewis*, vol. 2. *Books, Broadcasts, and the War, 1931–1949.* San Francisco, CA: Harper, 2004.

Lewis, C. S., Magdalen College-Oxford, to Sister Penelope CSMV, July 9 (August) 1939. In *The Collected Letters of C. S. Lewis.* Edited by Walter Hooper. Vol. 2. *Books, Broadcasts, and the War, 1931–1949.* San Francisco, CA: Harper, 2004.

Lynch, Gordon. *Losing My Religion? Moving on From Evangelical Faith.* London: DLT, 2003.

MacCunn, John. *Six Radical Thinkers.* New York: Russell & Russell, 1910/1964.

Markos, Louis. *Lewis Agonistes: How C. S. Lewis Can Train Us to Wrestle with the Modern and Postmodern World.* Nashville, TN: Broadman & Holman, 2003.

Martin, Thomas L. "Lewis: A Critical Prospective." In *Reading the Classics with C. S. Lewis.* Edited by Thomas L. Martin. Grand Rapids, MI: Baker Academic, 2000, 371–392.

McClendon, James Wm. Jr. "The Practice of Community Formation." In *Virtues & Practices in the Christian Tradition: Christian Ethics After MacIntyre*. Edited by Nancey Murphy, Brad J. Kallenberg, and Mark Thiessen. Harrisburg, PA: Trinity Press, 1997, 85–110.

McKnight, Scot. "Emergent Voices" [March 2, 2006], http://www.jesuscreed. org/?cat=2&paged=6 (accessed July 16, 2006).

McLaren, Brian. *A Generous Orthodoxy*. Grand Rapids, MI: Zondervan, 2004.

———. "An Open Letter to Chuck Colson" [December 2003], http:// www.anewkindofchristian.com/archives/000018.html (accessed July 19, 2006).

Miller, Donald Miller. *Blue Like Jazz*. Nashville, TN: Thomas Nelson, 2003.

Patrick, James. "The Heart's Desire and the Landlord's Rules: C. S. Lewis as a Moral Philosopher." In *The Pilgrim's Guide: C. S. Lewis and the Art of Witness*. Edited by David Mills. Grand Rapids, MI: Eerdmans, 1998, 70–85.

Peacock, Charlie. *New Way to Be Human*. Colorado Springs, CO: Shaw Books, 2004.

Richardson, Kurt A. "Disorientations in Christian Belief: The Problem of De-traditionalization in the Postmodern Context." In *The Challenge of Post-modernism: An Evangelical Engagement*. Edited by David S. Dockery. Grand Rapids, MI: Baker Books, 1995, 53–66.

Roberts, Paul. "Considering Emerging Church" [August 28, 2003], http://www. thinkinganglicans.org.uk/archives/000129.html (accessed July 20, 2005).

———. "Liturgy and Mission in Postmodern Culture: Some Reflections Arising from 'Alternative' Services and Communities" [1995], http://seaspray.trinity-bris.ac.uk/~robertsp/papers/lambeth.html (accessed September 5, 2003).

Roxburgh, Alan. "Emergent Church: Filled with Creativity, Energetic Potential" (June 15, 2005), http://www.allelon.org/articles/article.cfm?id=194&page=1 (accessed July 19, 2006).

Rutba House. *School(s) for Conversion: 12 Marks of a New Monasticism*. Eugene, OR: Cascade Books, 2005.

Smith, Stephen M. "Awakening from the Enchantment of Worldliness: The Chronicles of Narnia as Pre-Apologetics." In *The Pilgrim's Guide: C. S. Lewis and the Art of Witness*. Edited by David Mills. Grand Rapids, MI: Eerdmans, 1998, 168–181.

Sweet, Leonard, Brian D. McLaren, and Jerry Haselmayer. *A is for Abductive: The Language of the Emerging Church*. Grand Rapids, MI: Zondervan, 2003.

Tomlinson, Dave. *The Post-Evangelical*. El Cajon, CA: Emergent YS-Zondervan, 2003.

Vanhoozer, Kevin J. *First Theology: God, Scripture & Hermeneutics*. Downers Grove, IL: InterVarsity Press, 2002.

———. *Is There a Meaning in This Text? The Bible, the Reader, and the Morality of Literary Knowledge*. Grand Rapids, MI: Zondervan, 1998.

———. "Pilgrim's Digress: Christian Thinking on and about the Post/Modern Way." In *Christianity and the Postmodern Turn: Six Views*. Edited by Myron B. Penner. Grand Rapids, MI: Brazos Press, 2005, 71–103.

Willard, Dallas. "Degradation of Logical Form," http://www.dwillard.org/articles/artview.asp?artID=24 (accessed July 6, 2006).

———. "Hermeneutical Occasionalism." In *Disciplining Hermeneutics: Interpretation in Christian Perspective*. Edited by Roger Lundin. Grand Rapids, MI: Eerdmans, 1997, 167–172.

———. "Historical and Philosophical Foundations of Phenemenology," http://www.dwillard.org/articles/artview.asp?artID=32 (accessed July 6, 2006).

———. "Truth in the Fire: C. S. Lewis and Pursuit of Truth Today," http://www.dwillard.org/articles/artview.asp?artID=68 (accessed July 6, 2006).

Winner, Lauren. *Girl Meets God: A Memoir.* New York: Random House, 2002.

9

Letters to Malcolm:
C. S. Lewis on Prayer

Marjorie Lamp Mead

Letters to Malcolm: Chiefly on Prayer, which contains the most developed statement of C. S. Lewis's mature faith, is unfortunately one of his least known works of religious thought. A slim volume of only 124 pages in the American first edition, it consists of twenty-two fictional letters addressed by the author to a "friend." The subject matter of this correspondence covers a range of religious topics, but as the title indicates, it primarily revolves around questions and concerns related to prayer.

The fact that many readers assume that Malcolm, the book's imaginary correspondent, is an actual person is a testimony to Lewis's skill at epistolary fabrication—an ability he first demonstrated in *The Screwtape Letters*, some twenty years earlier. By providing Malcolm with a fictional wife, Betty, and a son named George, Lewis created a believable, "real-life" context in which the everyday aspects of prayer could be explored. As a result, this format enabled his consideration of prayer to pass beyond the merely theoretical into the actual and the practical. Or to put it another way, this fictional conversation brought alive what could have become simply an abstract philosophical discussion— and thereby contributed significantly to the impact of this book.

When Lewis first began to write a book-length study on the subject of prayer, he did not envision such an approach. Indeed, his initial attempt followed the more traditional pattern of a carefully reasoned and sustained argument. However, this way of approaching the subject did not proceed smoothly for Lewis, and the work on prayer was never completed in this form. We know something of the abortive history of this original attempt due to a few intriguing mentions in Lewis's correspondence. Most of these references occur in letters that Lewis wrote to Don Giovanni Calabria, an Italian priest and founder of the Congregation of The Poor Servants of Divine Providence in Verona. The two men began corresponding in 1947 after Don Giovanni read *The Screwtape Letters*. Through their exchange of letters, the two men had grown to deeply respect one another, and accordingly, Lewis often shared spiritual concerns with this pen-friend. One of these concerns focused on prayer—and in particular, on a question that Lewis was striving to answer as he began to compose his new book on prayer.

The first mention of this writing project occurs in a letter of January 5, 1953, when Lewis wrote to Don Giovanni asking for his prayers for a book that he was just beginning. Lewis explained that he had in mind a volume written for the laity on the practice of private prayer. His intention was to especially target those who were new to the Christian faith and had not yet developed a regular habit of prayer. Lewis went to say that while he felt there were already many beneficial books on prayer, in his estimation they were aimed at those who were already mature Christians, and perhaps, even members of religious communities. His book, in contrast, was intended primarily to assist the beginner in prayer—for Lewis remembered well the difficulties he, himself, had faced when he first began to pray after he became an adult convert.

But in spite of Lewis's desire to write this type of book, he began to encounter numerous difficulties from the first. Uncertain whether or not he should even continue on, he wrote to his friend, Don Giovanni, to enlist his prayers for the task, fearing that adversity might cause him to withdraw too hastily from what God was calling him to do; but also being concerned that he not forge ahead, if he was not qualified to do so. In addition to marking the preliminary stages of Lewis's effort to write on prayer, the specifics of this prayer request are illustrative of Lewis's Christian character—for it not only demonstrates his desire to be obedient to God's call upon his talents, but it also underscores his genuine humility. At this point in his career, Lewis was already an internationally celebrated success as an author and Christian spokesperson. Yet, in spite of all the outward acclaim, he did not presume that he necessarily possessed the wisdom to write on such a fundamental aspect of his faith.

Just a few days after his letter to Don Giovanni stating that he was beginning the book on prayer, Lewis wrote again to ask for help with an issue that was baffling him: how is it possible to reconcile two seemingly contradictory models of prayer that were present in the New Testament? The first model requires that we submit our request to God and thereby be willing to receive a possible denial. In contrast, the second model taught that we should pray with full confidence that we will receive a positive answer. Lewis's quandary—which he placed before Don Giovanni—was very simply this:

> How is it possible for a man, at one and the same moment of time, *both* to believe most fully that he *will* receive *and* to submit himself to the Will of God—Who is perhaps refusing him? . . . How is it possible to say simultaneously, "I firmly believe that Thou wilt give me this," and, "If Thou shalt deny me it, Thy will be done"? How can one mental act both exclude possible refusal and consider it?[1]

We have no record of how Don Giovanni responded to this question. But we do know that Lewis continued to struggle to find a satisfactory way to reconcile this difficult paradox. In fact, several months after he first posed this query, he writes again to update Don Giovanni. After mentioning that he is still at work on his book on prayer, Lewis then adds: "About this question which I submitted to you, I am asking all theologians: so far in vain."[2]

A further indication of this unresolved matter could be found in an address that Lewis gave at the end of 1953 to the Oxford Clerical Society. At the time of this talk, it had been almost a year since he first wrote to Don Giovanni indicating that he was beginning to write on the topic of prayer. Throughout the subsequent months, Lewis continued to wrestle with this question, but with little apparent success as it formed the basis of his December talk—"Petitionary Prayer: A Problem without An Answer." He began the talk by articulating his confusion over how it might be possible to reconcile Pattern A ("Thy will be done") with Pattern B (confident faith that what is asked will in fact be received). After setting up the initial problem, he goes on to spend the remainder of his time, exploring and eventually rejecting various potential answers to this question as being inadequate. Toward the end of his presentation, he makes the following confession: "I have no answer to my problem, though I have taken it to about every Christian I know, learned or simple, lay or clerical, within my own Communion or without."[3]

Far from despairing over this unresolved problem, however, Lewis goes on to offer that he does not believe that the answer to this question resides in a forced or manufactured sense of certitude. In other words, whatever it does mean to pray with a confident sense of the final outcome, Lewis rejects the notion that the solution is a simple matter of exerting one's willpower. Nor, does he accept the view that God is placing before his followers an unfair expectation (that is, requiring the exercise of a type of faith, which cannot truly be exercised apart from God, himself, bestowing it).

At this point in his Christian life, more than two decades after his conversion, Lewis is not afraid to acknowledge that he faces a problem he cannot solve. But significantly, this ambiguity does not cause him to give up on prayer. As he readily affirms in this talk to the Oxford clerics, the reality of answered prayer in his own life is abundant and filled with many good things, even though he does not yet understand all that the scriptures teach about it. However, just two months after he gave this address, Lewis wrote to his friend, Sister Penelope (a member of the Anglican Convent of the Community of St. Mary the Virgin at Wantage, England) acknowledging he had finally yielded to the obstacles that he could not overcome and stopped writing his book on prayer, as "it was clearly not for me."[4] Lewis's confidence in the act of prayer, itself, remained unabated, but his ability to write about it had clearly reached an impasse.

Even though this early composition of Lewis's on prayer was never completed nor published, we are fortunate that it has survived as a forty-eight-page manuscript fragment.[5] In looking at this early work, it is evident that Lewis was struggling with more than the apparent conflict between the two models of prayer that he wrote about to Don Giovanni. In fact, this draft manuscript reveals various false starts that, for the most part, revolve around his explanation of the prayer of Adoration. What we cannot determine from this manuscript is whether or not these multiple drafts reflect Lewis's normal mode of writing, or whether they are instead a reflection of his difficulties with the topic of prayer. The answer may very well be that both elements are true. It has generally been believed that Lewis was a first-draft writer, who did little revision—and indeed these pages bear remarkably few cross-outs given that it is a handwritten manuscript. But what also becomes noticeable from reviewing this fragment is that Lewis used clean pages to try his multiple variants. Thus, it is possible, though not certain, that he may have used a similar approach in other compositions. In which case, once he had determined his final draft, the other variant pages would have been thrown out and all indications of his *major* revision process would have been lost. However, whether or not this speculation about his writing method is true or not, it is obvious that at this point in time Lewis was not finding it easy to record his thoughts on prayer.

This manuscript fragment is intriguing for other reasons as well. It is significant to note that what Lewis does say in this draft is consistent with what he would later write about prayer in his published volume, *Letters to Malcolm*. Generally speaking, it does not appear that his view of prayer was radically altered during the intervening decade between the two approaches, but only that his understanding was clarified and deepened. Not surprisingly, the style of this fragment is similar in tone and approach to his apologetic works such as *Mere Christianity* and *The Problem of Pain*. As he did in those works, Lewis skillfully utilizes examples from everyday life to shed light on confusing issues, but there are less of these real-life parallels than in his other works. As a result, he spends more time in straightforward and carefully reasoned arguments. Thus, the text tends to require more of the reader—a potential hazard of which Lewis was no doubt well aware.

In one brief section of this draft, Lewis tries an alternative approach by creating two fictional characters (Mr. Drysdale and Mr. Land) and using their differing experiences to aid his discussion of prayer. In both examples, he is attempting to clarify the essential importance of good intentions in our prayers. Given that the results of prayer are solely up to God, Lewis maintains that good intentions are all we can and should contribute to our prayers. The rest remains in God's hands. The use of these imaginary examples to explain this concept underscores the difficulty that Lewis was encountering. Finding satisfactory parallels from everyday life to illuminate prayer was proving unusually challenging, so he resorted to fictional cases. Later, in *Letters to Malcolm*, this same fictional technique would prove to be the crucial element that finally allowed him to break through creative and conceptual barriers to produce a full-length work on prayer.

It is also helpful to notice that sections of this manuscript eventually reappeared in revised form in chapter 9 of Lewis's *Reflections on the Psalms* (which was published in 1958, some four years after Lewis abandoned his first attempt at writing a book on prayer). The overall topic of this chapter is the prayer of adoration—or praise. The common portions between these two texts have to do with the obstacles that the scriptural injunction to praise God usually raises in the minds of modern men and women, who erroneously perceive the commandment for adoration as a demonstration of coerced flattery, which is therefore false. Accordingly, Lewis spends a great deal of effort attempting to overcome this misperception (acknowledging that it was something that he struggled with when he first became a Christian). In the manuscript fragment, he uses a lengthy descriptive account of an immense gathering of creatures coming together to worship their Creator as a way of illustrating that praise, truly understood, is overwhelming delight and not servile duty (a sequence that is reminiscent of the Great Dance passage at the end of his science fiction novel, *Perelandra*). He also tries several times to work out plausible parallels between an earthly monarch and the duty owed to her or his temporal position as a way of demonstrating that we not only owe God our praise, we actually long to praise—because such praise completes, enhances, and perfects our delight and appreciation. Thus, we "enjoy" God when we express our adoration. Ultimately, Lewis concludes that the fundamental difficulty for modern women and men is that they do not know how to "bow" spiritually, and therefore they resist what would truly make them happy beyond all imagining. It should further be noted that because Lewis found his work with the Psalms to be a sufficiently helpful means of illustrating this concept, he did not feel it necessary to cover this topic to any great extent when he later wrote *Letters to Malcolm*.

There are additional places within this manuscript that echo Lewis's other works. For instance, he briefly raises the distinction between "looking at" something and "looking along"[6] —a key Lewisian concept that he had earlier developed more fully in the essay, "Meditation in a Toolshed" (published July 17, 1945 in *The Coventry Evening Telegraph*). This application of an important concept on the difference between enjoyment and contemplation that he gathered from Samuel Alexander's *Space, Time and Deity* (1920) is also touched upon in Letter 1 of *Letters to Malcolm*. A second example of this reiteration of themes is found in the problem of why we need to ask God for anything since he is omniscient;[7] a matter that Lewis had explored in greater detail in a prior essay "Work and Prayer" (published May 28, 1945 in *The Coventry Evening Telegraph*). None of this repetition and elaboration of subject matter is surprising. As with most authors, themes reoccur and are explored from various perspectives over and over again until the writer has exhausted what he desires to say. Prayer, in particular, was a topic that continually cropped up on Lewis's writings.

As with most of Lewis's religious works, there are brief biographical allusions scattered throughout the manuscript. However, one of the most intriguing of these connections is not identified by Lewis, though knowledge of his biography highlights the association. In this instance, a reference to the dangers of introspective prayer, and in particular the destructiveness of overzealousness in prayer,[8] poignantly conjures up Lewis as a young boy lying awake in his drafty, moonlit Wynyard dormitory, attempting to pray, feeling it was a failure, and then miserably repeating his prayers over again in a vain effort to "get it right."[9] Perhaps it was this boyhood experience with an overly sensitive false conscience, more than any other, which taught him the futility of basing prayer upon manufactured emotions (a subject that he discusses with great insight at various points throughout *Letters to Malcolm*; most extensively toward the end of Letter 6).

One final biographical connection of special interest to be found in the manuscript fragment is Lewis's declaration that he was raised outside the Christian tradition.[10] Certainly, by all outward standards, his immediate family and childhood experiences were firmly grounded in the Christian faith: as an infant he was baptized by his grandfather, and throughout his early years, he attended worship services regularly at St. Mark's Church Dundela, where his father served as Sunday School Superintendent. His mother's final gift to him was a leather-bound Bible. And there is no doubt that he was taught the basics of Christianity as a boy. But nonetheless, as this comment makes clear, Lewis, himself, did not feel that he assimilated the Christian faith sufficiently so that it had become a part of his own mindset. As a result, he identified instead with those raised outside the faith. An intriguing comment and an insightful one, it underscores Lewis's innate ability to comprehend the questions and context of his unbelieving readers; a perspective that obviously aided him in his religious writings.

Before leaving our discussion of this manuscript fragment, it is worthwhile to record some of the basic summary statements on prayer that Lewis makes here. He views prayer as a necessary part of the life of every Christian, something that we are instructed to do. And because prayer is ultimately personal intercourse with God, it is of overwhelming importance. It is also an act of endless delight as through the prayer of worship or adoration, we are invited to "to glorify God and enjoy him forever" (here Lewis quotes the answer to the first question of the *Westminster Shorter Catechism* (1647), as he later does in Letter 21 of *Letters to Malcolm*). And finally, he observes three significant aspects of human interaction (enjoyment, request, and confession), and accordingly notes that our conversation or prayer with God reflects the same three elements (adoration, petition, and penitence). In drawing this parallel, Lewis emphasizes the *relational* characteristic of prayer. He also points out that the only prayer that is eternal is the Prayer of Adoration (since in heaven, there will be no need for either request or confession). Thus, in making this observation, he stresses the importance of our learning to worship or adore in our current earthly state, as this will be the sole type of prayer that endures forever.

Even though Lewis never completed this early draft on prayer, it is clear that this unfinished manuscript had continuing value to him. As already indicated, he utilized some of it directly by incorporating portions of what he had earlier written into his subsequent publications such as *Reflections on the Psalms*. In addition, the fact that he kept the manuscript fragment at all is noteworthy. Unlike some authors, who retain manuscript copies permanently in their files, it was not Lewis's usual practice to do so (and as a result, relatively few of his manuscripts that were published in his lifetime have survived). In spite of his failure to complete this manuscript, it is evident that Lewis did not consider that he was finished with the subject matter. And indeed, as we know, he was not.

Ten years after this first draft on prayer was composed, Lewis began to work on a new book that approached the topic in a creatively different manner. Having learned from his first attempt that describing prayer in a theoretical way was challenging, as it did not allow him sufficient scope for unresolved questions, he now approached it by a device that he had used to great effect in *The Screwtape Letters*. In once again employing the technique of a fictional correspondent, Lewis was able to shift from the constraints of a conceptual approach to a more discursive and free-flowing style—in essence, to engage the reader in an informal conversation about prayer, which in turn, gave him great liberty in regard to themes and methodology. As a result, what had required paragraphs, even pages, of setup in the early draft manuscript could now be handled with much less detail in this conversational approach.

As is typical of a casual discussion, rather than a reasoned statement of argumentation, there is no linear organizational pattern to this book. Indeed, as one reads *Letters to Malcolm*, it becomes apparent that any given subject may weave in and out, as threads of thought are first raised and then dropped, only to be picked up again in a later letter. This somewhat random structure adds a note of realism to the volume, as this unsystematic manner reflects the usual pattern of an informal conversation, but it also makes summary statements about the content more difficult.

Letters to Malcolm was published on January 27, 1964, two months after Lewis's death,[11] and was the last manuscript he personally prepared for publication.[12] He began to write it in January 1963 and had completed it by April. In spite of the fact that the composition of this book proceeded much more smoothly than his earlier effort, he was still characteristically modest about the result. As he confided on April 22 to an American correspondent of long standing, Mary Willis Shelburne: "I've finished a book on Prayer. Don't know if it is any good."[13] Such diffidence was misplaced, however, and the work was enthusiastically received by his publisher, Jocelyn Gibb, who declared that this work "has knocked me flat. Not quite; I can just sit up and shout hurrah, and again, hurrah."[14] He further added that it was the best Lewis had penned since *The Problem of Pain*, which was written more than two decades earlier. But in spite of this enthusiastic response, Lewis continued to remain unassuming about what he had written. In replying to Gibb's request for a dust jacket blurb for the book, Lewis cautioned "I'd like you to make the point that the reader is merely being allowed to listen to two ordinary laymen discussing the practical and speculative problems of prayer as these appear to them."[15] He then went on to underscore that he wasn't claiming to *teach* about prayer in this book.

This final comment by Lewis is most revealing of why he chose to write *Letters to Malcolm* in the epistolary format. Only by approaching the subject of prayer in this way could he avoid making the structured authoritative statements that a more formal work of exposition would demand. This does not mean that Lewis does not include forceful statements on the nature of prayer in *Letters to Malcolm*, for he does do so frequently throughout this volume. Yet this conversational approach allows him significant freedom in how he supports such statements; it also enables him to add brief comments here and there, without detailed substantiation. One might almost say that the use of letters as the context permits Lewis to simply offer opinions, instead of being required to develop and defend his arguments. Not that Lewis was ever adverse to the give and take of argumentation. But as he makes manifestly clear in *Letters to Malcolm*, when talking about prayer, one often encounters mysteries that supersede orderly explanation. Lewis maintained that the ultimate answers to such queries reside instead in the character and promises of God. And this, in turn, is a matter for faith; and such faith is not subject to empirical proof.

Even though the organizational structure of *Letters to Malcolm* reflects the random nature of a conversation, there are still broad themes that can be detected. The most significant idea, which overarches the entire volume, is the *relational* nature of prayer—for it is in prayer that God invites us to enter into the most "private and intimate" relationship possible between two creatures.[16] This essential concept was certainly emphasized in Lewis's earlier draft, but in the published book, he has taken it much further. He makes it clear that while the context of prayer is relational (that is, between oneself and God), the focus of our prayer is to be on God—and not on self, or on others, or even on questions of doctrine. Once we give our attention to something other than God, our prayer is diminished. However, given that we are imperfect, how is it possible for us to pray in this way? Lewis offers us this hopeful word: "Meantime, however, we want to know not how we should pray if we were perfect but how we should pray being as we are now."[17] In other words, to begin with, we should simply pray as we can, and not attempt to do what we cannot.

In spite of its essential importance, Lewis recognized that prayer also presents great challenges. As a result, he offers suggestions that he hopes will benefit others as they struggle to learn how to pray. For example, he explains that even as gratitude for pleasures given can lead us to Adoration, and thereby to a right focus on God (Letter 17); so, in contrast, does an inappropriate response to pleasures—a desire for "encore"—lead us astray as we concentrate instead on the object we desire, and thereby look away from God (Letters 5 and 17). Yet even as we struggle with our own failures, Lewis cautions against relying too much on our own emotional state while praying (Letter 15), as well as warning of the dangers of excessive introspection (Letter 6). Whenever the focus of our prayer shifts away from God to ourselves, even when our intention is good, we put ourselves at risk. Thus, Lewis advises: "I sometimes pray not for self-knowledge in general but for just so much self-knowledge at the moment as I can bear . . . the little daily dose."[18]

Even though the ultimate heart of our prayer is to be centered on God, Lewis does not intend to encourage us to strive for a mystical experience (as he feels this is usually given only to those who are spiritually mature and even then, only at certain moments, Letters 2 and 12). Nor does Lewis disparage the prayer of request or petitionary prayer as being of lesser stature (as Jesus, himself, instructed us to pray for our needs, Letter 7). Therefore, as Lewis reminds us in Letter 4, it is not the type or manner of prayer that is most important, but rather the aim of prayer—which is for us to be fully *known* by God. However, we can only enter into this relationship, enter into God's holy presence, because we have been invited to do so. And in doing so, we discover our deepest longing, which Lewis believes is to be noticed or to be known by God. But the act of being made known only occurs when we confess our sins and present our requests, and thereby "unveil" ourselves before God. Prayer, in this way, removes "veils" or barriers between God and us and allows us to enter into *personal* contact between the one praying and God. (Lewis deals imaginatively with the subject of unveiling in his novel, *Till We Have Faces*, and with the related idea of naked spirituality in Letter 4 of *The Screwtape Letters*; both of these concepts have to do with our willingness—or our lack of willingness—to reveal ourselves openly to God in an authentic encounter.)

Because of our human nature, such unveiling, while necessary, is not easy. Consequently, in order to make ourselves known to God, we must acquire a "trained habit" of prayer (Letter 1). We do this in part through worship and adoration. Developing a trained habit of prayer obviously involves disciplined practice, as well as making wise choices in how, and when, and where to pray. Lewis does not neglect these everyday aspects of prayer, and he gives many practical suggestions in this regard (Letter 3). For example, he discusses the merit of using readymade prayers versus praying extemporaneously (Letter 2); and in fact, when he ends up offering his own technique of "festooning" written prayers (Letter 5), he effectively combines the benefits of readymade with the personal advantage of employing one's own words. Lewis also reminds us that as important as our own choices and actions are in the learned discipline of prayer (Letter 21), it is only through the Holy Spirit that we are able to pray at all (Letter 4).

As the subtitle to this work indicates, in *Letters to Malcolm: Chiefly on Prayer*, Lewis also deals with many subjects that are only peripherally related to prayer. In particular, his discussions of worship difficulties (avoidance of the "liturgical fidget") in Letter 1, and his insightful words on the sacramental meaning and import of the Eucharist in Letter 19 are especially rewarding.

In spite of the fact that prayer has an ancient and historic tradition, Lewis firmly believed it was relevant to the contemporary world. Accordingly, in *Letters to Malcolm*, he intentionally engaged with some of the difficult questions raised by modernist theologians. And even though, as he explained in a letter to his editor, Jocelyn Gibb, he did not intend to unnecessarily create controversy in this book, nonetheless, "the wayfaring Christian cannot quite ignore recent Anglican theology when it has been built as a barricade across the high road."[19] We see in this comment, the same impulse that Lewis demonstrates in his correspondence—a desire to share spiritual insights that have helped him grapple with difficulties, and which he believed could help others as well. It is clear that Lewis took seriously the biblical injunction to be of assistance to other believers, as his generous offer to a recent convert demonstrates: "My prayers are answered. . . . Blessings on you and a hundred thousand welcomes. Make use of me in any way you please: and let us pray for each other always."[20] Not only does this letter illustrate Lewis's concern for the spiritual welfare of another, but it also shows his own disciplined practice of prayer. Before his own conversion, Lewis was very much the independent individualist, but once he became a Christian, he obediently accepted that he had a responsibility to assist others in their spiritual journeys.

Some of the contemporary issues that Lewis was attempting to address were those "barriers" raised by Dr. J. A. T. Robinson, the Bishop of Woolwich, in his book, *Honest to God.* This provocative volume was published in March 1963, when Lewis was working on *Letters to Malcolm.* After a summary of *Honest to God* titled, "Our Images of God Must Go," appeared in *The Observer,* Lewis quickly wrote a rebuttal, "Must Our Image of God Go?"[21] In addition to this brief article, Lewis also included a response to Bishop Robinson in Letters 3 and 14 of *Letters to Malcolm.* This was all Lewis was interested in writing on the subject, for when an American journal asked him to contribute another article on *Honest to God,* Lewis declined, explaining that he had already given "implied answers to some of Robinson's nonsense in parts of a book on prayer which I've just finished, and I can 'do my bit' much better that way."[22] In his rejoinders to Robinson, Lewis was attempting to combat the modern tendency to "de-mythologize" traditional Christian doctrines and thereby freely eliminate what the modernists felt was outdated and no longer relevant. Not surprisingly, Lewis disagreed with the validity of this methodology. In a similar vein, Lewis engaged the thought of Cambridge theologian, A. R. Vidler (particularly in Letters 6 and 11). In his essay, "Religion and the National Church," Vidler suggested that we may find it inevitable that "many of the religious elements in historic Christianity . . . may thus be outgrown, or survive chiefly as venerable archaisms or as fairy-stories or children."[23] Firmly rejecting this premise and once again defending the importance of retaining traditional doctrines, Lewis cautioned: "If we are free to delete all inconvenient data we shall certainly have no theological difficulties; but for the same reason no solutions and no progress."[24]

In addition to theological problems related to prayer, there were also practical problems that Lewis confronted in *Letters to Malcolm*. The source for many of these issues is obviously based on Lewis's own life experiences. He indicates as much in the text. But it is interesting to note that even though Malcolm is not an actual person, the letters in the published volume do reflect genuine interactions that Lewis had with others. For just as Lewis turned to friends like Don Giovanni Calabria and Sister Penelope to discuss his personal questions about prayer, so did many of Lewis's own readers turn to him. A comparison of the text of *Letters to Malcolm* with replies that Lewis wrote to various correspondents demonstrates how often the ideas he first postulated in private letters eventually ended up in his published work. To give just one example, writing in response to Reverend R. Morgan Roberts's questions on the devotional life,[25] Lewis replied with a list of practical advice, including the desirability of not leaving one's prayers until the end of the day when one is tired (Letter 3), the importance of avoiding excessive introspection (Letter 6), the dangers of manufactured emotions (Letter 15, 18, and 21), and a caution against praying without words when fatigued (Letter 3). Each one of these suggestions can be found in *Letters to Malcolm* as indicated in parenthesis above, and illustrate the ways in which Lewis's actual correspondence often foreshadowed the content of his fictional letters from his published book.

Not all of Lewis's discussions on prayer took place via letters, however. For example, there were his conversations with Father R. E. Head, his parish priest for more than a decade. Father Head first came to the Church of the Holy Trinity, Headington Quarry, Oxford in 1952 as Curate, and became Vicar in 1956 (where he served until his retirement in 1990). Walter Hooper states that the subject matter of *Letters to Malcolm* "owes much to Father Head"[26] and Father Head, himself, further refined that claim by explaining that Lewis's "conversations with me regarding prayer, which took place on various occasions, are mentioned in *Letters to Malcolm* number twelve."[27] Another Oxford friend, Clifford Morris, also made a modest contribution to this volume. As Lewis's taxi driver for many years, Morris and Lewis shared numerous conversations, some of which very likely dealt with prayer; but it was Morris's recommendation of the works of Alexander Whyte, a well-known Puritan preacher from Edinburgh, which was acknowledged by Lewis in Letter 18.[28]

Within the text of *Letters to Malcolm* there are several autobiographical references that are worthy of particular notice. Poignantly, there are several oblique references to the death of his wife, Joy Davidman Lewis. For example, in Letter 8, Lewis refers to a time when he went through great difficulties, and discusses his reactions during those days to his friend's attempt at comforting him, to the torture of false hopes, and the difficulties of praying while in the midst of such anguish. There are definite echoes of *A Grief Observed* in these words, and undoubtedly, when writing this section, Lewis drew upon memories of his own painful suffering during Joy's illness and death. Thus, Lewis's actual experience with grief and fear adds a heightened sense of authenticity to his words.[29]

Another autobiographical reference can be found in Letter 20, where Lewis opens with the joyful declaration that recently, while at prayer, he was at long last able to forgive an individual that he had been struggling to forgive for over thirty years. There is little doubt that the person forgiven refers to Robert Capron, the tyrannical headmaster of Wynyard School in Watford, England. This is the boarding school where Lewis was sent shortly after his mother's death in 1908, when he was not quite ten years old, and which he describes so vividly in his autobiography, *Surprised by Joy* (chapter II, "Concentration Camp"). Lewis's experience at the school was filled with misery, mostly due to this brutal headmaster. A confirmation of this identification of Capron with the individual forgiven can be found in a letter Lewis wrote in July 1963, just a short while after he had completed his manuscript of *Letters to Malcolm*: " . . . only a few weeks ago I realised that I at last *had* forgiven the cruel schoolmaster who so darkened my childhood. I'd been trying to do so for years; and like you, each time I thought I'd done, I found, after a week or so it all had to be attempted over again. But this time I feel sure it is the real thing."[30] Strong parallels between the wording of the fictional letter and the actual letter of July 1963 corroborate that the statements in *Letters to Malcolm* truly reflect Lewis's real-life experience of forgiveness. Once again in using an example from his own life, Lewis goes beyond merely a theoretical discussion. Instead, he is sharing with his reader, through this fictional format, what he has learned as a result of his own difficult encounters with the pain of everyday life.

Unquestionably, this authenticity greatly enhanced Lewis's ability to communicate truths about the spiritual life in *Letters to Malcolm*. Because he approached the subject of prayer with humility and openly acknowledged that he was a fellow learner, the average reader found Lewis easily approachable in his expression of the Christian faith. It is important to note that even though Lewis offered insights based upon his personal experience, nonetheless he was careful to test this learned truth against the objective teachings of scripture—always relying upon scripture as his final authority. Further, whenever Lewis encountered the mysteries inherent in a life of faith, he was not afraid to admit that he did not always know the answer. In such cases, he offered his reader such help as he could, and then confidently rested for ultimate assurance in the character and promises of God. Lewis realized from his own life just how challenging prayer could be, but given his understanding of prayer as *personal* relationship with God, he also rejoiced in the glorious wonder of it.

In spite of the autobiographical nature of *Letters to Malcolm*, there is not sufficient space in this essay to spend extensive time on Lewis's personal practices of prayer. Some of this can be gleaned naturally from the text, itself, but it is important to underscore that for Lewis prayer was not simply an abstract theological concept; it was an everyday essential of his lived experience. Thus, on a daily basis, Lewis devoted considerable time to prayer. He also unfailingly practiced intercessory prayer, consistently praying for a large number of individuals (many of whom he had never met personally, but only knew through his vast correspondence), and also humbly requesting prayer for his own needs from others. And in so doing, he obediently fulfilled the scriptural command that we should pray for one another.

In the final analysis, it is clear that Lewis firmly believed in the concrete reality of prayer as he wrote about it in *Letters to Malcolm*. Most significantly, he recognized that prayer could not simply be understood by studying theological doctrine, but rather, it could only be fully apprehended through learned experience. As a result, C. S. Lewis's greatest desire for himself and for others was that each one of us should "be busy learning to pray.[31]

APPENDIX A: CONTEMPORARY REVIEWS

In looking at contemporary reviews of *Letters to Malcolm*, it quickly becomes apparent that they are generally positive. As is to be expected, some are more enthusiastic than others, but nearly all are appreciative of the value of this work. Perhaps this is what one would expect given that reviewers were well aware that this is the last work Lewis prepared for publication before his death. As such, many of these reviews become a tribute of sorts to the entire body of Lewis's prior work. It is noteworthy that several reviewers are uncertain as to whether or not Malcolm was a real person or simply a literary device. Following are excerpts from a spectrum of reviews, British and American, both favorable and modestly negative.

Great Britain

"Happy On His Knees." *The Times* (London) (January 30, 1964), 15b.

Unaffected piety, clarity of expression, wit, a streak of theological donnishness were the strands that C. S. Lewis intertwined in his writings, of which this must sadly be one of the last.

"Posthumous Papers." *Church Times* (January 31, 1964).

With the death of C. S. Lewis, a glory departed. But regret must then immediately give place to gratitude for so generous a legacy as this. Here is a book which (in many parts, at least) is as good as anything he ever wrote. And that means very good indeed. . . . It is the grasp of the reality of God, the determination to put truth before passing fashion, the apprehension of the mystery and the glory of grace which help to make this book pure treasure.

Father Illtud, O. P. Evans. *The Tablet* (218) (February 1, 1964), 128.

The return, at the end, to the writing that brought him greatest fame, must still the speculations of those who assumed that the long years of spiritual silence since *Screwtape* and *Mere Christianity* meant some slackening of the strength of an apologetic that had no English parallel.

Francis King. "Hear Us, O Lord." *New Statesman* (67) (February 21, 1964), 302.

Mr Lewis admits these difficulties [of prayer] honestly; whether he can be considered to have answered them effectively will largely depend on the faith of the reader. The unbeliever is likely to enjoy the book most for its shrewd asides. . . . [which] are expressed with the admirable directness and simplicity which characterized the style of this often indirect and highly complex man.

"Final Achievement." *The Times Literary Supplement* (February 27, 1964), 173.

The secret of [Lewis's] power . . . probably lay in the fact that he had himself found the way to Christian belief with great difficulty; he genuinely knew what it was like not to believe; he could never therefore quite see himself in the position of someone who, untroubled by doubts, simply hands out the Faith. He knew that the path was difficult and had to be kept with courage. Thus when he came to write he never under estimated the problems. . . . His power of clear exposition was considerable, and the friendly sincerity of his writings made a ready appeal even to people who do not normally read religious books. Now the astonishingly large output is finished, but this last book may well be one to be more valued than many of the others.

J. D Pearce-Higgins. "C. S. Lewis and Prayer." *The Modern Churchman* (July 1964), 251–252.

Interesting and suggestive as always, this book . . . reveals at once the strength and limitations of the late Professor C.S. Lewis's religious and spiritual outlook. . . . there are many valuable insights in this discursive book on all manner of spiritual topics, in which the independence and originality of this powerful personality are displayed, and . . . I have read the book with great profit and pleasure as well as occasional irritation and disappointment. This book would not teach me HOW to pray if I did not know. . . . "

A. Hamilton. "Strange Bedfellows." *Books and Bookmen*, II (February 1966), 38.

In *Letters to Malcolm*, we are "fortunate to be given a clearer exegesis of the religious man's 'most intimate relationship' than most young men ever hear from any chaplain."

United States

Alan Pryce-Jones. "C. S. Lewis' Last Book." *New York Herald Tribune* (February 13, 1964), 21.

In this final book of his . . . he writes informally about the difficulties of addressing God. . . . It is not possible to be very original in this field of thought: St. François de Sales said it all 350 years ago. But each generation has its own especial aspirations and worries; each needs a reformulation of familiar ideas; and for the present day, Lewis has an important communication to make. It is by no means addressed only to religious, let alone sectarian, readers. Nobody with an inner life, however disheveled and incoherent that life may be, will fail to delight in his cogency. In his modesty, too.

K. T. Willis. *Library Journal* (89) (February 15, 1964), 871.

The reader must expect CSL to have definite opinions on both private prayer and prayers in public. His methods, manners, and subjects have always had his touch that has made him a guide to many and a thorn to some. These letters will be welcomed in libraries—and in homes.

C. J. McNaspy. *America* (110) (February 15, 1964), 231, 234–235.

Few writers of our time, and still fewer spiritual writers, had rung so many interior bells or touched so many hearts as did the late C. S. Lewis. This, a work completed just before his death . . . shows no evidence of a flagging spirit. They will remind readers of *The Screwtape Letters*. . . . Yet these are quite different—direct, warm and personal. . . . Anyone fortunate enough to be at Oxford in the years following the war remembers the spark that Lewis constantly kindled. . . . These were the days when Sartrian breezes blew across the Channel, when logical positivism was virtually unchallenged, when you had to go about quoting Kierkegaard. But there was Lewis to puncture the stateliest balloons, ask embarrassingly simple questions and take the sting out of undergraduate *Angst*. . . . the posthumous *Letters to Malcolm: Chiefly on Prayer* will disappoint none of Lewis's admirers.

Sister Mary William. *Best Sellers* (3) (February 15, 1964), 397.

C. S. Lewis was a thoughtful, good man, a man of spirit. Some of his ideas do not echo the beliefs of Roman Catholics and for this reason, "Letters to Malcolm" had best be read by the mature reader. . . . As one reads one tends to become Malcolm and present arguments and reasons for and against C.S. Lewis's attitudes toward prayer. This is good; there are numerous points to be debated and clarified.

"Prayer: Better without Words." *Time* (83) (February 28, 1964), 63.

. . . Prayer, like good conversation, seems to be one of the lost arts of the 20th century. After mumbling through the Lord's Prayer, modern man wonders what to do next. . . . What kind of words should he use? These are layman's questions, and they provoked a layman's answer from Clive Staples Lewis, the devout, witty Oxford don.

Chad Walsh. "The Keynote is Honesty." *The New York Times* (March 1, 1964), 12, 14.

. . . Here is a book in which Lewis reveals himself at prayer. Appropriately enough, there is less brilliance and verve than in many of his other books. He deals mainly with the day-by-day Christian, himself, trying to pray meaningfully and not finding it either easy or particularly exciting. The keynote to the book is honesty. . . . All through the book he is concerned to vindicate the idea of a personal God with whom each person, one by one, enters into living relationship. . . . "Letters to Malcolm" is a down-to-earth book by a man who was a warm human being, the possessor of a clear mind, and whose commitment to Christianity was as steadfast as his refusal to put on spiritual airs. . . . If this is indeed Lewis's last book there is something fitting about so modest and unpretentious a volume bringing to an end the long and often scintillating series.

Nathan A. Scott, Jr. "Dialogue with Deity." *Saturday Review* (47) (March 7, 1964), 41.

. . . The late C. S. Lewis has given us a beautifully executed and deeply moving little book on the subject of private prayer. . . . [the reader will] feel a kind of spiritual authenticity in this book far surpassing that which was often characteristic of Lewis's theological writing. . . . But unlike some who are today attempting . . . to give us "the secular meaning of the Gospel" . . . , C. S. Lewis was not prepared to dissolve the great realities of the Christian faith into the maxims of moral allegory and ethical abstraction. We may stutter and stammer when we begin to try to conceptualize what is objectively going on in the dialogue between the human soul and God, but, as he reminds us, the great fact surely is that the dialogue persists and is "means of grace and hope of glory". . . . And apart from *The Screwtape Letters*, it may well prove to be the profoundest of C. S. Lewis's many essays in theological apologetic.

Jeffrey Hart. "C. S. Lewis: 1898–1963." *National Review* (16) (March 24, 1964), 242–243.

For at least two generations most of the notable Christian intellectuals in England and America, such men as Eliot, Waugh, and C. S. Lewis, have been converts. . . . The fact that they are converts, however, involves these Christian intellectuals in certain disabilities. For the convert, belief can seldom be the natural thing it was for the older sort of Christian. . . . and C. S. Lewis writes poignantly of it in his last book, a series of superb letters to a friend on the subject of prayer. . . . because Christianity has been for [Lewis and these other intellectual converts] a consciously conceived acquisition, they have a special kind of value as Christian writers. . . . they allow us to see a great system of meaning gradually being recovered, a tradition being re-imagined in all its depth and complexity.

Gilbert Roxburgh. *Critic* (22) (June–July 1964), 59.

Lewis as a writer is . . . clear and wise, and that is why he is the foremost author on religious subjects in our time, Catholic or non-Catholic. I think his best work is *The Four Loves*, but *Letters to Malcolm* is second. . . . [It] is a modern contemporary book of lasting importance.

J. D. Douglas. (Scottish-born theologian). "Keep'em Guessing." *Christianity Today* (July 31, 1964), 36–37.

In this present volume [Lewis] is again the despair of the rigidly orthodox and the scourge of liberalism. . . . This book calls also for discernment in that Lewis curiously takes advantage here and there of his non-professional status theologically to get across views not always either systematic or logical. Yet one is never quiet certain in such places that he is not writing tongue in cheek, and we are left guessing to the end. Knowing Lewis, it seems likely he intended it that way.

APPENDIX B: CRITICAL RESPONSE

As with all books, the response to *Letters to Malcolm* was varied. Lewis's close friend, J. R. R. Tolkien found the work to be immensely troubling. Nearly a year after Lewis's death, Tolkien wrote candidly to David Kolb, S. J.: "I personally found *Letters to Malcolm* a distressing and in parts horrifying work. I began a commentary on it, but if finished it would not be publishable."[32] Tolkien's reaction to Lewis's work, titled "The Ulsterior Motive," was never published in its entirety, but it has survived and is currently a part of the Tolkien manuscript collection at the Bodleian Library, Oxford. However, only a few people have been able to read the essay, and it is not currently available to researchers. Thus, our only glimpses of its content come from a few brief extracts quoted in Humphrey Carpenter's *The Inklings*.[33]

In reading these passages, it is evident that Tolkien's initial critique of Lewis's *Letters to Malcolm* eventually broadened into his recollections of the painful friction that was occasionally present in their friendship. This periodic strain that Tolkien experienced was the direct result of their theological differences. A devout Roman Catholic, Tolkien carried a deep awareness of the fact that Protestant members of his extended family had abandoned his widowed mother, when she was in great financial need, simply because she had converted to Catholicism. On the contrary, Lewis was the product of a prosperous Northern Irish Protestant family where faith was at times closely allied with the politics of Irish Unionism, which sought to retain the link with Great Britain. And even though Lewis's own devotional practices became increasingly Anglo-Catholic as he grew older, to Tolkien's deep disappointment, Lewis remained a lifelong Anglican (Protestant). Accordingly, given Tolkien's foundational disagreement with the very fact of Lewis's religious writings (as he believed that such works should be solely the task of trained theologians, and not of laymen such as Lewis), coupled with Lewis's upbringing in the politically divisive atmosphere of Belfast, it is not unexpected that there were at times strong disagreements, and even tensions, between the two men. Perhaps what is surprising is how solid and genuine their friendship was in spite of their differences.

One other brief quotation completes Tolkien's published commentary on *Letters to Malcolm*. A. N. Wilson provides the following excerpt taken from Tolkien's own copy of *Letters to Malcolm*: "This book is not 'about prayer,' Tolkien writes in the margin, 'but about Lewis praying'. 'But,' he adds on the flyleaf, 'the whole book is always interesting. Why? Because it is about Jack [C. S. Lewis], by Jack, and that is a topic that no one who knew him well could fail to find interesting even when exasperating.'"[34] Tolkien goes on to elaborate that he did not intend to convey that Lewis was egocentric in terms of being a proud man, but rather that when Lewis wrote his words often reflected his own life experiences, and thus, were autobiographical. For some, like Tolkien, this autobiographical element could be exasperating, but for others, the personal element enhanced the text.

It is interesting to note as well that while Tolkien particularly objected to any layman writing on theological topics, in contrast, Lewis saw his "amateur" standing as a strength since as a "beginner," he was more deeply aware of the questions held by others who were also beginners in the faith—and thus, able to address their concerns in ways that professional theologians could not. See for example his opening to *Reflections on the Psalms*, where he confesses "I write for the unlearned about things in which I am unlearned myself. . . . The fellow-pupil can help more than the master because he knows less. The difficulty we want him to explain is one he has recently met."[35] This is not the only place where Lewis acknowledges the benefits of his layman's status.

Critical response apart from the contemporary reviews (Appendix A) has continued to view *Letters to Malcolm* as a significant and valuable work in the overall canon of C. S. Lewis's writings. Many of these critics are widely and deeply read in terms of Lewis's writings, and they bring this knowledge to bear as they interact with this text. For example, Peter Schakel, the author of numerous works on Lewis, offers this insight:

[Letters to Malcolm] is in a sense an expository work, intended to clarify and illuminate ideas; but it is at the same time a creative work, engaging many of the same writing skills as a story or novel. The two sides, rational and imaginative, are fully integrated and reveal the wholeness and ease Lewis achieved in his final years.... the book is meant, like a story or a poem, to be read straight through and to be received primarily through the imagination rather than the intellect.[36]

One of the first Lewis's scholars, Chad Walsh, had this to say about *Letters to Malcolm*: "This book was written after the death of his wife Joy, and this loss seems to color much of what he says. He refers to the event frequently, and there is also a curious gentle, unglittering style.... It lacks the dynamic thrust of many other books that Lewis wrote, but its very modesty gives it an enduring quality."[37]

Another early Lewis scholar, Clyde S. Kilby, offered the following comment: "The rich conception of God as creative artist continues in the posthumous volume.... Lewis called this book more nearly autobiography than theology.... Some years ago he wrote me that he had done a book on prayer but was not satisfied with it. That he still felt the tentative nature of his conclusions may be evident in the fact that he has put the book in the form of off-hand letters to an old college friend."[38]

Other critics such as Lyle W. Dorsett (*Seeking the Secret Place*), David Downing (*Into the Region of Awe*), and Paul Ford (*C. S. Lewis, Ecumenical Spiritual Director*) offer their commentary on *Letters to Malcolm* in the context of fuller discussions on Lewis's devotional life. Perry D. LeFevre has a helpful chapter on Lewis's view of prayer in his book, *Understandings of Prayer*, in which he observes: "*Letters to Malcolm* is written with a dry humor unique in the literature on prayer."

For those who would welcome assistance in deciphering the many allusions scattered throughout *Letters to Malcolm*, there are two helpful Web sites: Peter Schakel, http://hope.edu/academic/english/schakel/Let2malc.htm; and Arend Smilde, http://www.solcon.nl/arendsmilde/cslewis/reflections/e-malcolmquotes.htm. In addition to his clarifying annotations, Peter Schakel includes a brief statement on the subject matter of each individual letter. Walter Hooper has also produced a detailed topical overview of the book, letter by letter, in his *C. S. Lewis: A Companion and Guide*.

Paul Ford has created a very helpful bibliography to the many significant references to prayer scattered throughout C. S. Lewis's writings (with the exception of his correspondence); Ford does include examples from Lewis's fiction: http://www.pford.stjohnsem.edu/ford/cslewis/documents/

bibliographies/CSL%20Prayer%20Bibliography.pdf. Finally, Paul Ford's encyclopedia entry in *Classics of Christian Spirituality* (edited by Frank N. Magill) offers an insightful introduction to *Letters to Malcolm*; this entry also includes an annotated recommended reading list to key works by Lewis that deal with the subject of prayer.

APPENDIX C: ESSAYS ON PRAYER

Those interested in reading more on Lewis's view of prayer should also take note of the following three essays that predate *Letters to Malcolm*. The subject of each one of these essays primarily revolves around the issue of the Prayer of Request. How are such prayers answered? Why are they sometimes not answered? Are such prayers of lesser importance than prayers of adoration? Much of what Lewis discusses in these essays was later incorporated into *Letters to Malcolm*, but reading his earlier grapplings with these questions can be instructive as they illustrate the progression of Lewis's unfolding understanding on the subject of petitionary prayer. A brief abstract of each essay follows, in chronological order.

"Work and Prayer" (essay) first appeared in *The Coventry Evening Telegraph* (May 28, 1945), and later published in *God in the Dock*, edited by Walter Hooper (Grand Rapids, MI: Wm. B. Eerdmans, 1970).

In this essay, Lewis addresses the concerns that the prayer of request is both lesser and ultimately pointless. In response to the first criticism, Lewis declares that the entire historical tradition of petitionary prayer (including the Lord's Prayer) holds too significant a place within the Christian faith to simply be dismissed as a "lesser" form of prayer. Second, he states that the argument against the futility of asking God for things is equally applicable to any human action (that is, if something is good and God wants it accomplished, then it will happen without our asking or doing anything; accordingly, there is no useful purpose in our prayers or our actions). However, our experience with life demonstrates the fallacy of that assumption as our actions are clearly necessary and they do, in fact, produce results. Thus in this regard, actions (or Work) and prayer are similar—in that God has chosen to allow us to contribute to events in both of these ways. But because of the potency of prayer, God has retained a discretionary "veto" in terms of prayer, which differs from the freedom (free will) we are allowed to exercise in terms of our actions.

"Petitionary Prayer: A Problem without an Answer" was originally read to the Oxford Clerical Society on December 8, 1953, and later published in *Christian Reflections*, edited by Walter Hooper (Grand Rapids, MI: Wm. B. Eerdmans, 1967).

Christian teaching on the prayer of request has held two apparently contradictory positions over the years. The first pattern is taught by Jesus himself, and instructs us to pray "Thy will be done"; we thereby present our requests as conditional to God's will. Intellectually this approach is easily understandable (though practically speaking, submitting our requests to God's authority may be difficult). The second pattern is found throughout the New Testament: we are to exercise a standard of unwavering faith, by which we are promised will come mighty works; in other words, a successful result to a prayer's request is promised. Thus, one type of prayer is conditional and the other is a definite result. Lewis asks: how can both be truth at once? He replies to his own question by saying that some answer this quandary by saying that prayers must be made according to the will of Christ—and such prayers made according to Christ's spirit will be granted. But this response does not take into account numerous difficulties (including Christ's prayer in Gethsemane). Ultimately, Lewis feels this is a question with no satisfactory answer. But he emphasizes that faith is not manufactured emotion (that is, it is not an act of strong willpower based upon obedient emotion). Instead, Lewis declares that faith is a gift of God, and not a result of our efforts. Thus, though uncertainty and mystery remain, Lewis trusts ultimately in his knowledge of God.

"The Efficacy of Prayer" first appeared in *The Atlantic Monthly* (January 1959), and was later published in *The World's Last Night* (New York: Harcourt Brace Jovanovich, 1960).

This essay discusses the causal efficacy or effectiveness of petitionary prayer. When we pray to God and make a request, how do we know that our prayer achieved the result? In other words, is answered prayer simply a fortunate coincidence that would have occurred whether or not we had asked for it? In discussing these questions, Lewis underscores that prayer is always request, so it may be denied—and as such, we cannot view it as "magic." Instead, our assurance in prayer is based upon personal knowledge of the divine that is a result of our relationship with God. Further, petitionary prayer is just one aspect of the totality of prayer. But it is crucial to note that prayers of request are both allowed and commanded by scripture.

An interesting side note concerns Lewis's statement in this essay that it would be impossible to prove the efficacy of prayer by use of scientific experiments since the very nature of prayer (that is, asking God to heal someone for their sake and not to "test" God's response) precludes such an action. However, in recent years, experiments of this nature have in fact been done. As a March 31, 2006, article by Benedict Carey in *The New York Times* explains: "At least 10 studies of the effects of prayer have been carried out in the last six years, with mixed results." But at least one professor quoted in the article appears to agree with Lewis's reservations about the experiments: " 'The problem with studying religion scientifically is that you do violence to the phenomenon by reducing it to basic elements that can be quantified, and that makes for bad science and bad religion,' said Dr. Richard Sloan, a professor of behavioral medicine at Columbia and author of a forthcoming book, *Blind Faith: The Unholy Alliance of Religion and Medicine.*"

NOTES

1. Lewis to Don Giovanni Calabria, January 14, 1953, in *The Latin Letters of C. S. Lewis*, trans. and ed. Martin Moynihan (South Bend, IN: St. Augustine's Press, 1998), 81.

2. Lewis to Don Giovanni Calabria, March 17, 1953, in *The Latin Letters of C. S. Lewis*, trans. and ed. Martin Moynihan (South Bend, IN: St. Augustine's Press, 1998), 85.

3. C. S. Lewis, "Petitionary Prayer: A Problem Without an Answer," in *Christian Reflections*, ed. Walter Hooper (Grand Rapids, MI: Eerdmans, 1967), 150.

4. Lewis to Sister Penelope, February 15, 1954, quoted in Walter Hooper, *C. S. Lewis: Companion and Guide* (London: HarperCollins, 1996), 378.

5. Due to the kindness of Walter Hooper, a copy of this handwritten manuscript is available for others to read at the Marion E. Wade Center, Wheaton College, Illinois ("Untitled Manuscript on Prayer," Wade CSL MS-155), as well as at the Bodleian Library, Oxford.

6. See "Untitled Manuscript on Prayer," Wade CSL MS-155, 41.

7. Ibid., 4–5.

8. Ibid., 42.

9. For Lewis's description of this experience see his autobiography, *Surprised by Joy* (London: Geoffrey Bles, 1955), 39, 63.

10. See "Untitled Manuscript on Prayer," Wade CSL MS-155, 47.

11. A portion of this work (chapters 15, 16, and 17 of *Letters to Malcolm*) was first published as a slim hardcover book on December 25, 1963, by Harcourt, Brace & World in New York. This excerpt was titled, *Beyond the Bright Blur*, and on the flyleaf was the statement that this limited edition was issued "as a New Year's greeting to friends of the author and his publisher."

12. The handwritten manuscript of *Letters to Malcolm* was apparently disposed of after it was typed, but the typescript that Lewis had prepared for his publisher has survived. The original typescript is in the Bodleian Library, Oxford, and research copies are available at the Marion E. Wade Center, Wheaton College, IL, Wade CSL-MS 69 and Wade CSL-MS 70.

13. C. S. Lewis, *Letters to an American Lady*, ed. Clyde S. Kilby (Grand Rapids, MI: Eerdmans, 1967), 113.

14. Jocelyn Gibb to Lewis, June 13, 1963, quoted in Walter Hooper, *C. S. Lewis: Companion and Guide* (London: HarperCollins, 1996), 380.

15. Lewis to Jocelyn Gibb, June 28, 1963, quoted in Walter Hooper, *C. S. Lewis: Companion and Guide* (London: HarperCollins, 1996), 380.

16. C. S. Lewis, Letter 2, *Letters to Malcolm: Chiefly on Prayer* (New York: Harcourt Brace & World, 1964), 13.

17. C. S. Lewis, Letter 4, *Letters to Malcolm: Chiefly on Prayer* (New York: Harcourt Brace & World, 1964), 22.

18. C. S. Lewis, Letter 6, *Letters to Malcolm: Chiefly on Prayer* (New York: Harcourt Brace & World, 1964), 34.

19. Lewis to Jocelyn Gibb, June 28, 1963, quoted in Walter Hooper, *C. S. Lewis: Companion and Guide* (London: HarperCollins, 1996), 380. This statement by Lewis appeared virtually verbatim on the flyleaf of the British First Edition, but not on the American First.

20. Lewis to Sheldon Vanauken, April 17, 1951, *Encounter with Light* (Wheaton, IL: Wade Center, 1978), 25; and also in chapter 5 of *A Severe Mercy* (San Francisco, CA: Harper & Row, 1977).

21. Lewis's essay was originally published in *The Observer* (March 24, 1963), and later included in *God in the Dock*, (Grand Rapids, MI: Eerdmans, 1970), 184–185.

22. Lewis to Edward T. Dell, editor of *The Episcopalian* Magazine (NY), April 29, 1963, quoted in Roger Lancelyn Green and Walter Hooper, *C. S. Lewis: A Biography* (London: HarperCollins, revised and expanded edition, 2002), 422.

23. A. R. Vidler, "Religion and the National Church" in *Soundings* (Cambridge: Cambridge University Press, 1962), 254. Lewis's own copy of A. R. Vidler's *Soundings* can be read in the research library of the Marion E. Wade Center, Wheaton College, IL. The essay by Vidler, along with several others in this volume, contains brief markings by Lewis. Another one of these essays, "Christian Prayer" by John Burnaby, is specifically referenced in *Letters to Malcolm* (Letter 5 and Letter 7), and the Wade copy of this essay also has brief marginal notes made by Lewis.

24. C. S. Lewis, *Letters to Malcolm: Chiefly on Prayer* (New York: Harcourt Brace & World, 1964), 59.

25. This letter to Reverend R. Morgan Roberts has been published in *Letters of C. S. Lewis*, revised and enlarged edition Walter Hooper (London: Collins, 1988), 439; but the recipient of the letter has been mistakenly identified as Mrs. Ursula Roberts.

26. Walter Hooper, *C. S. Lewis: A Companion and Guide* (London: HarperCollins, 1996), 682.

27. Father R. E. Head, interview by Jerry Root, June 22, 1988, transcript 18, Wade Center Oral History, The Marion E. Wade Center, Wheaton College, IL.

28. See Clifford Morris, "A Christian Gentleman" in *Remembering C. S. Lewis*, ed. James Como (San Francisco, CA: Ignatius Press, 2005), 326.

29. There is a fainter echo of Joy Davidman to be found in the book's final letter (Letter 22), when Lewis discusses the resurrection of the body. He surmises that after death, perhaps while the body sleeps, the "intellectual soul" is sent to Lenten Lands. The phrase Lenten Lands is also used by Lewis in a poem he wrote for Joy's memorial

tablet, where he describes Joy's rebirth from Lenten Lands. And Douglas Gresham, Joy's son, later chose this phrase as the title of his memoir on his boyhood days with his mother and stepfather.

30. Lewis to Mary Willis Shelburne, July 6, 1963, in *Letters to an American Lady* (Grand Rapids, MI: Eerdmans, 1967), 117.

31. Lewis to Sheldon Vanauken, April 17, 1951, *Encounter with Light* (Wheaton, IL: Marion E. Wade Center, 1978), 25; and also in chapter 5 of Sheldon Vanauken, *A Severe Mercy* (San Francisco, CA: Harper & Row, 1977).

32. Tolkien to David Kolb, S. J. November 11, 1964, in *The Letters of J. R. R. Tolkien*, ed. Humphrey Carpenter (Boston, MA: Houghton Mifflin Company, 1981), 352.

33. See pages 50, 51–52, 216, and 232 in Humphrey Carpenter, *The Inklings* (Boston, MA: Houghton Mifflin Company, 1979).

34. A. N. Wilson, *C. S. Lewis: A Biography* (London: Collins, 1990), xvii.

35. C. S. Lewis, *Reflections on the Psalms* (London: Geoffrey Bles, 1958), 1. It should be pointed out that the opening section of *Reflections on the Psalms* is essentially the same as the text of Lewis's introduction to his manuscript draft on prayer. Thus, this is another example of the way in which he incorporated his early unpublished work on prayer into his later publications.

36. Peter J. Schakel, *Reason and Imagination in C. S. Lewis* (Grand Rapids, MI: 1984), 174, 176.

37. Chad Walsh, *The Literary Legacy of C. S. Lewis* (New York: Harcourt Brace, 1979), 224–225.

38. Clyde S. Kilby, *The Christian World of C. S. Lewis*, (Grand Rapids, MI: Eerdmans, 1964), 165–166.

BIBLIOGRAPHY

Carpenter, Humphrey. *The Inklings*. Boston, MA: Houghton Mifflin Company, 1979.

Dorsett, Lyle W. *Seeking the Secret Place: The Spiritual Formation of C. S. Lewis*. Grand Rapids, MI: Brazos Press, 2004.

Downing, David C. *Into the Region of Awe*. Downers Grove, IL: Inter-Varsity Press, 2005.

Ford, Paul F. "A Bibliography of C. S. Lewis on Prayer." In Paul F. Ford's Web site, http://www.pford.stjohnsem.edu/ford/cslewis/documents/bibliographies/CSL%20Prayer%20Bibliography.pdf.

———."C. S. Lewis, Ecumenical Spiritual Director." Ph.D. dissertation, Fuller Theological Seminary, Pasadena, CA, 1987.

———."C. S. Lewis's Letters to Malcolm, Chiefly on Prayer." In *Classics of Christian Spirituality*. Edited by Frank N. Magill (San Francisco, CA: Salem Press/Harper & Row, 1989), 615–621.

Green, Roger Lancelyn, and Walter Hooper. *C. S. Lewis: A Biography*. Fully revised and expanded edition. London: HarperCollins, 2002.

Head, Father R. E. Oral history interview transcript. Interview by Jerry Root. June 22, 1988, Headington, England. The Marion E. Wade Center, Wheaton, IL.

Hooper, Walter. *C. S. Lewis: A Companion and Guide*. London: HarperCollins, 1996.

Kilby, Clyde S. *The Christian World of C. S. Lewis*. Grand Rapids, MI: Eerdmans, 1964.

LeFevre, Perry D. "C.S. Lewis—Orthodox Apologetics." Chapter 6 in *Understandings of Prayer*. Philadelphia, PA: The Westminster Press, 1981.

Lewis, C. S. *Beyond the Bright Blur*. New York: Harcourt, Brace & World, 1963.

————. "The Efficacy of Prayer." In *The World's Last Night, and Other Essays*. New York: Harcourt Brace Jovanovich, 1960. Originally published in *The Atlantic Monthly* (January 1959).

————. *The Latin Letters of C. S. Lewis*. Translated and edited by Martin Moynihan. South Bend, IN: St. Augustine's Press, 1998.

————. *Letters of C. S. Lewis*. Revised and enlarged edition. Edited by Walter Hooper. London: Collins, 1988.

————. *Letters to an American Lady*. Edited by Clyde S. Kilby. Grand Rapids, MI: Eerdmans, 1967.

————. *Letters to Malcolm: Chiefly on Prayer*. New York: Harcourt, Brace & World, 1964.

————. *Letters to Malcolm* typescript (copy). Wade CSL MS-69 and CSL MS-70. The Marion E. Wade Center, Wheaton, IL.

————. "Must Our Image of God Go?" In *God in the Dock: Essays on Theology and Ethics*. Edited by Walter Hooper. Grand Rapids, MI: Eerdmans, 1970. Originally published in *The Observer* (March 24, 1963).

————. "Petitionary Prayer: A Problem without An Answer." In *Christian Reflections*. Edited by Walter Hooper. Grand Rapids, MI: Eerdmans, 1967. Originally read to the Oxford Clerical Society (December 8, 1953).

————. *Reflections on the Psalms*. London: Geoffrey Bles, 1958.

————. *Surprised by Joy*. London: Geoffrey Bles, 1955.

————. *Untitled Manuscript On Prayer*. Wade CSL MS-155. The Marion E. Wade Center, Wheaton, IL.

————. "Work and Prayer." In *God in the Dock: Essays on Theology and Ethics*. Edited by Walter Hooper. Grand Rapids, MI: Eerdmans, 1970. Originally published in *The Coventry Evening Telegraph* (May 28, 1945).

Morris, Clifford. "A Christian Gentleman." In *Remembering C. S. Lewis*. Edited by James Como. San Francisco, CA: Ignatius Press, 2005.

Schakel, Peter. "Annotations and Study Guide to *Letters to Malcolm*." Hope College, Holland, MI. http://hope.edu/academic/english/schakel/Let2malc.htm. (Last accessed August 22, 2006).

————. *Reason and Imagination in C. S. Lewis*. Grand Rapids, MI: Eerdmans, 1984.

Smilde, Arend. "Quotations and Allusions to C. S. Lewis, *Letters to Malcolm*." Arend Smilde's C. S. Lewis Pages. At http://www.solcon.nl/arendsmilde/cslewis/reflections/e-malcolmquotes.htm.

Tolkien, J. R. R. *The Letters of J. R. R. Tolkien*. Edited by Humphrey Carpenter. Boston, MA: Houghton Mifflin Company, 1981.

Vanauken, Sheldon. *An Encounter with Light*. Wheaton, IL: The Marion E. Wade Center, 1978.

———. *A Severe Mercy*. San Francisco, CA: Harper & Row, 1977.

Vidler, A. D., Editor. *Soundings: Essays Concerning Christian Understanding*. Cambridge: Cambridge University Press, 1962. Lewis Library Copy. The Marion E. Wade Center, Wheaton, IL.

Walsh, Chad. *The Literary Legacy of C. S. Lewis*. New York: Harcourt Brace, 1979.

Wilson, A. N. *C. S. Lewis: A Biography*. London: Collins, 1990.

10

An Apologist's Evening Prayer: Reflecting on C. S. Lewis's *Reflections on the Psalms*

Donald T. Williams

INTRODUCTION

"I have never been made so uncomfortable by a book," said Byron Lambert to the New York C. S. Lewis Society in 1970.[1] Whether for Lambert's reason—that it revealed his own "moral immaturity"—or because it seems to challenge doctrines held dear by a large part of Lewis's fan base, *Reflections on the Psalms*[2] has often produced such a reaction. Never one of Lewis's most popular books and deeply disturbing to many of his American Evangelical readers, *Reflections* also provokes words of deep appreciation. An anonymous early reviewer typically called it "charming and urbane," a "literary masterpiece" because it reflected Lewis's "accustomed skill."[3] James M. Houston includes *Reflections* along with *Letters to Malcolm*[4] as part of Lewis's "substantial contribution to the theology of prayer."[5] And Perry Bramlett echoes many even of the book's critics when he says that it is "full of interesting, provocative, and convincing observations as well as the genuine piety that enriches Lewis's religious works." By showing the reader "how to enjoy, appreciate, and learn from the psalms," Lewis succeeded in doing his part to keep both Bible and Psalter in the minds of Christendom.[6]

How does a book that can do so many good things also make many of its readers profoundly uncomfortable? That is the question we must try to answer.

HISTORY OF COMPOSITION

The idea for a book on the Psalms was suggested to Lewis by his friend Austin Farrer in 1957, at a time when Lewis was out of ideas for a new book and worried about his wife, Joy's, illness and his own health.[7] He wrote to Arthur Greeves from Magdalene College, Cambridge, on November 27, 1957, that "I don't think I'll ever be able to take a real walk again,"[8] referring to the effects of osteoporosis. Farrer's suggestion must have had a revitalizing effect, on Lewis's mind at least. He discussed the contents of the book with Joy and Farrer during the long vacation of 1957. In the same letter to Greeves he mentions that "I've been writing nothing but academic work except for a very unambitious little work on the Psalms, which is now finished and ought to come out next spring."[9] It was actually published on September 8, 1958. Eleven thousand copies were sold in England before publication, which was for the time an impressive number for a religious paperback. Lewis's biographer George Sayer reports that the original reviews were "tepid,"[10] but some were enthusiastic, as have been many of the references since.

A historical footnote to the composition of *Reflections* that demands special attention is the way the apparent hiatus of books of expository theology by Lewis in the decade from 1947 to 1957 has been used to propagate what Victor Reppert calls "the Anscombe legend."[11] The idea is that Lewis was so embarrassed by Elizabeth Anscombe's critique at the Oxford Socratic Club of his argument for the self-refuting character of naturalism in *Miracles*[12] that he gave up rational apologetics from then on. Reppert has given us a detailed refutation of the Anscombe legend in general terms, which we need not repeat here. But we do need to examine the way in which Lewis scholars have used *Reflections on the Psalms* in support of the legend and see if there are flaws in their arguments.

Humphrey Carpenter gives a succinct summary of the claims that have been made in this regard and how they relate to *Reflections*:

Lewis had learnt his lesson [from the debate with Anscombe]: for after this he wrote no further books of Christian apologetics for ten years . . . and when he did publish another apologetic work, *Reflections on the Psalms*, it was notably quieter in tone and did not attempt any further intellectual proofs of theism or Christianity.[13]

George Sayer, usually Lewis's most sagacious biographer, repeats the claim even more starkly: *Reflections* was Jack's "first religious work" since *Miracles* and the "humiliation" he received in the debate with Anscombe.[14] Bramlett unfortunately picks the claim up and repeats it in the widely used *C. S. Lewis Readers' Encyclopedia*: Reflections was "the first religious work since *Miracles* (1947)."[15]

Now, these claims, stated as if they were simple facts and not tendentious interpretations, are quite strange. This legend seems to grow in the telling, morphing from (at first) a limited move away from "rational apologetics" to a decade-long abandonment of "religious works," all stemming from one debate that was actually considered a draw by many of the people in attendance. Not only is the thesis implausible, but it also runs afoul of some rather inconvenient facts.

For example, accepting this account of Lewis's career and the place of *Reflections* in it would entail, to say the least, some rather peculiar interpretations of *Surprised by Joy* (1955).[16] Certainly a book that focuses on the experience that led Lewis back to faith in God qualifies as a religious work. And a book that analyzes those experiences so rigorously in terms borrowed from thinkers like Alexander, Bevan, and Otto[17] qualifies as rational, just as a book that is essentially an *apologia pro vita sua* (defense of one's life) qualifies as a work of apologetics, especially when what it sets out to explain is precisely the combination of reason and imagination—which constitutes Lewis's unique approach to Christian writing—the very same combination he had less clearly called "reason and romanticism" in his earliest Christian book, *The Pilgrim's Regress*.[18] Not only does *Surprised by Joy* not fit very well into the scenario of the Anscombe legend, but what are we to make of the essays collected in books like *God in the Dock*,[19] several of which are religious and even rational apologetics and written during this period? Not only that, but the Narnia books no less than the earlier Space Trilogy contain set pieces of rational apologetics, like the famous conversation between Puddleglum and the Green Witch in *The Silver Chair*.[20]

The truth is that C. S. Lewis's career and his books—scholarly and popular, nonfiction and fiction—are all of a piece.[21] There was development in Lewis's thinking, of course,[22] but there was no radical departure from his basic commitment to an approach to faith in which mind and heart, reason and imagination, rigorous thinking and personal piety, so often estranged in modern Christian experience, are reconciled.

If this view is correct, then we need another explanation for the apparent lull in popular expository theology in Lewis's career between *Miracles* and *Reflections on the Psalms*. We have already seen that the hiatus is in fact only apparent, but there is still a relative lack of productivity in this area between 1947 and 1957 to be accounted for. A number of factors could have contributed. There was the disruption of the move from Oxford to Cambridge to assume the new chair of Medieval and Renaissance Literature in 1954. By the end of the period in question Lewis was in declining health. Corbin Scott Carnell attributes a "falling off in Lewis's productivity and possibly in his powers" to the death of Charles Williams in 1945.[23] Certainly Lewis owed a lot to the inspiration and encouragement of his friends. The regular Thursday evening meetings of the Inklings in his rooms at Magdalene ceased in October of 1949, though the Tuesday lunch meetings at the Eagle and Child pub continued for some time afterward.[24] But the factor that probably carries the most weight, indeed, which would have been sufficient all by itself to account for everything, was the fact that this was the decade in which Lewis was working on his most time-consuming and backbreaking scholarly project, the magisterial sixteenth-century volume of *The Oxford History of English Literature*.[25]

We have already seen that Lewis wrote to Arthur Greaves in 1957 that he had been writing "nothing but academic work" except for his "unambitious little work on the Psalms."[26] His comment to Greeves was an apt summary of Lewis's feeling about the decade just past, when the bulk of the "academic work" had been his history of Sixteenth-Century English literature. It is a massive tome of 696 pages, including a thirty-three page chronological table and ninety pages of bibliography. To write it, Lewis first read everything in that bibliography. Sayer refers to the "immense amount of reading" involved because Lewis "refused to give an opinion on a book he had not read."[27] It was an all-consuming project. Lewis was engaged to write the volume in 1944; he did not finish the first draft until 1952. Revisions and preparing the bibliography took another year, and the book was finally published in the autumn of 1954.[28] Lewis frequently complained about the sheer amount of work involved, and jokingly referred to the book by the series acronym, OHEL—pronounced as if it were the expletive referring to the place of eternal punishment. Significantly, Roger Lancelyn Green reports that Lewis told him toward the end of the project that he was "longing for the day when he would be able to turn away from 'this critical nonsense and write something really worthwhile—theology and fantasy.'"[29] The fantasy would be the Narnia series; the theology included *Reflections on the Psalms*.

This may have seemed a rather long digression, but it has an important point. It is clear that, contrary to the claims of a number of commentators, we should not see the apparent gap in Lewis's production of popular theology between 1947 and 1957 as having resulted from any crisis in his thinking, nor should we see his return to that genre in *Reflections on the Psalms* as a new departure with a different emphasis and a more subdued approach. To read *Reflections* thus is to misunderstand its nature and its place in Lewis's life and in the Lewis canon. He had matured, no doubt; but the author of *Reflections* is the same Lewis with the same insistent wholeness of vision that his readers have met in the better-known works of earlier decades.

Reflections on the Psalms should therefore be read with the expectation that it will be continuous with Lewis's other works of popular theology. Lambert indeed notes that the book is "implicitly apologetic," that is, "the very difficulties that Lewis addresses... are the difficulties seized on habitually by unbelievers to throw doubt on the inspiration of the Bible."[30] It has the same strengths and weaknesses as those earlier works and is written from essentially the same point of view. Some of those views, which Lewis's more conservative Christian readers find troubling (his concept of biblical inspiration, for example), are harder to ignore here, but their exposition is consistent with positions he had hinted at earlier.[31] To that exposition we shall now turn.

SUMMARY

Lewis begins chapter I, "Introductory," by denying that *Reflections* is a work of scholarship. It is one layman sharing with others things he has found helpful in reading the Psalms. His typically self-effacing explanation for this approach is that one schoolboy can often solve difficulties for another better than the master can. But while he claims only to be "comparing notes" and disavows any intention to "instruct," it soon becomes apparent that Lewis is at least an older and more experienced schoolboy, able to help us novices with much more than just the odd trick he has picked up to get us through long division. He reminds us that the psalms are poems meant to be sung and gives us a simple but clear and helpful primer in Hebrew poetic parallelism, showing that our Lord himself had absorbed this style of speaking from his environment and from his mother, the author of the Magnificat. And Lewis lets us know that he will begin with characteristics of the psalms that many readers have found difficult, and that he will base his studies on the version Anglicans find in the Book of Common Prayer, that of Coverdale. With these preliminaries out of the way, we are ready to begin.

Chapter II deals with "Judgment' in the Psalms." Christians think of judgment in terms of a court in which they are the defendants in need of God's mercy. But often in the psalms the scenario is rather a court in which the psalmist is the plaintiff, asking for a righteous decision to protect him from his enemies. This situation reflects a common human complaint from which modern Westerners have been mostly spared: the difficulty of the "small man" getting his case heard at all, given the levels of corruption, the legions of hands out for bribes, he must go through even to get a hearing. We need to think about both concepts of judgment. Christians can benefit from the Jewish version by picturing themselves as the defendants, that is, asking if they have wronged anyone, and by remembering that being in the right and being righteous is not the same thing.

Chapter III turns to the "The Cursings," or what are technically called the imprecatory psalms. Lewis looks the problems presented by these psalms squarely in the face, with no attempt to soften the impression they can make: "In some of the psalms the spirit of hatred strikes us in the face like the heat from a furnace."[32] Examples include the blessing pronounced in the "otherwise beautiful" Psalm 137 on one who would dash a Babylonian baby's head against a stone, or even the line in the familiar Psalm 23 where God prepares a table before the psalmist in the presence of his enemies. Lewis comments, "The poet's enjoyment of his present prosperity would not be complete unless those horrid Joneses (who used to look down their noses at him) were watching it all and hating it." The "pettiness and vulgarity" of this sentiment is "hard to endure."[33]

The dilemma as Lewis sees it is that "We must not either try to explain [the cursing psalms] away or to yield for one moment to the idea that, because it comes in the Bible, all this vindictive hatred must somehow be good and pious."[34] Instead, we can understand that the writers lived in a more barbaric but less insincere age and learn to see the reality of our own hearts in those feelings they felt no need to hide. We can come to understand something of the natural result of injuring another human being: we tempt the injured person to such hatred. We can come to realize that one reason that the Jews cursed more bitterly is that they took right and wrong more seriously, and that what we think of as our greater compassion may really be a culpable absence of the capacity for indignation. And when we have factored out the forbidden hatred of the sinner, which taints them, we can still hear the Word of God in these passages teaching us something about His hatred of sin itself.

Chapter IV, "Death in the Psalms," notices the surprising lack of emphasis on—or even, perhaps, belief in—a future life in the psalms. The dead, for example, can no longer thank God or even remember him (30:10 [*sic*; actually 30:9 in KJV], 6:5, etc.). The Jews were surrounded by people who were very much concerned about the afterlife; the Egyptians could have been said to be obsessed with it. But apparently God did not want his people to be like that. He did not want them to worship him for the sake of eternal happiness but for what he is. Only after they had learned to desire him for that does a clear revelation of the next life come to them.

In chapter V Lewis turns from those elements in the psalms that he finds problematic to those which make them a sheer delight. "The most valuable thing the Psalms do for me is to express that same delight in God which made David dance."[35] And they do this "perhaps better than any other book in the world."[36] The ancient Jews, who did not yet know Christ, had less reason to love God than we do, yet they express an exuberant "appetite" for God that few of us rise to. And this tells us something about the God we both adore.

Chapter VI is entitled "Sweeter than Honey." It is a phrase the Hebrew poets applied often to the Law of God. They had almost the same enthusiasm for God's commandments as for God himself. This is an attitude modern people find hard to empathize with. How can one sincerely like prohibitions? But part of what the poet meant when he said he delighted in the law is similar to what we would mean in saying that we loved history, or English, or science. When this love goes bad it becomes Pharisaism, but the psalms can help us recover the innocent love of the Law before it was corrupted by self-righteousness. They can remind us that "The order of the Divine mind, embodied in the Divine Law, is beautiful. What should a man do but try to reproduce it, so far as possible, in his daily life?"[37]

We might have thought we were done with the "problem" psalms, but chapter VII, "Connivance," strangely returns to them. The problem here is the many psalms in which the psalmist professes to hate God's enemies. The dangers of such an attitude, as well as its apparent contradiction of the New Testament teaching that we are to love our enemies, are obvious. But we may also ask whether a society like our own in which there is no social sanction for being a scoundrel is not equally unhealthy. We can use these psalms to redress that imbalance and cause us to ask ourselves when taking a stand against evil might be our duty.

Chapter VIII examines the psalmists' attitude toward "Nature." Like other ancient peoples, the Hebrews lived close to the soil. Unlike them, they believed in creation. When nature is a created thing, she is emptied of divinity; but this frees her to function as a symbol for the Divine, as a carrier of messages from the truly Other. For, if the thunder is the voice of Zeus, it is still not a voice from beyond the world (Zeus not being transcendent in the same way a true creator God would be). Thus, by emptying nature of divinities, the doctrine of creation ironically fills her with Deity, for she is now his handiwork.

Chapter IX offers "A Word about Praising." Lewis expects that most readers will not have had the difficulty he finds in the praise psalms, especially with their constant exhortations for us to praise God. For a while, it seemed to Lewis to make God seem like a vain tyrant who liked to be surrounded by toadies. But then he noticed that it is sometimes appropriate to say that a picture or a sunset deserves or demands our admiration. We mean that admiration is the correct or appropriate response on our part to such an object. (Well-read Lewis readers will cross-reference the arguments in favor of objective value in *The Four Loves* and *The Abolition of Man*.) Lewis also noticed that all true enjoyment spontaneously overflows in praise; we are not satisfied until we have talked about the painting or the poem that moved us. Well, God is the most deserving object of all, so that to truly love him, to be truly awake and alive to him, is to praise him. We are exhorted so often to praise him not because he needs it, but because we do: it is the ultimate fulfillment of our creaturely natures.

Chapter X, "Second Meanings," introduces a new topic that will occupy Lewis until the end of the book. Christians have not tended to limit themselves to the psalms as they were presumably understood originally, but have seen second or hidden meanings in them having to do with the central truths of the Christian faith, so that the full significance of these texts is only discernible after the fact in the light of the New Testament. The modern mind is rightly suspicious of such meanings, for anyone who is clever enough can read almost anything into any writing. Nevertheless, Christians cannot just abandon the possibility that the original writers might have truly said more than they could know. Statements that turn out to be true in ways the speaker could not have anticipated sometimes happen by luck. They can also happen because the unanticipated truth is an extension of a real insight—as if a person who noticed that the higher a mountain is the longer it retains its snow should imagine a mountain so high that it never lost it. If he then discovered such mountains (for example, the Alps) in the world, the similarity between them and his imagined mountain would be more than just luck. The anticipations of Christian truths in pagan mythology (for example, the dying god) might be resemblances of this kind.

Chapter XI, "Scripture," continues the line of thought begun in chapter X. If even pagan writings can anticipate the New Testament in ways that are not merely accidental, how much more should we expect the Old Testament Scriptures to do so? For they are "inspired." This raises the question of the nature of biblical inspiration. Lewis neither rejects all accounts of the supernatural automatically like a theological liberal, nor does he accept every word of Scripture as literally true like what he calls a Fundamentalist. Imperfect human materials, including perhaps pagan legends, are "taken into the service" of the Word of God. Inspiration was a "divine pressure" on the process of retelling. The result was "God's word" as Lewis understands it:

The human qualities of the raw materials show through. Naivety, error, contradiction, even (as in the cursing psalms) wickedness are not removed. The total result is not "the Word of God" in the sense that every passage, in itself, gives impeccable science or history. It carries the Word of God; and we (under grace, with attention to tradition and to interpreters wiser than ourselves, and with the use of such intelligence and learning as we have) receive that word from it not by using it as an encyclopedia or an encyclical but by steeping ourselves in its tone or temper and so learning its overall message.[38]

If the Old Testament has been so "taken up," we cannot preclude the possibility that it could have been meant to refer to Christ. Moreover, we have Christ's own authority for taking it so.

Having laid a foundation for doing so in chapters X and XI, Lewis uses his final chapter, "Second Meanings in the Psalms," to look at the messianic references in the psalms. Psalms examined include 110, 68, 45, and 22. Christ's interpretations of the psalms were not controversial at the time in his taking them messianically, but rather in his identifying the messianic figure with Isaiah's Suffering Servant and in claiming to be both figures himself. Finally, the messianic application to Christ turns out not to be arbitrary but to spring "from depths I had not expected."[39]

ANALYSIS

Perhaps the best way of coming to understand both the strengths and the weaknesses of *Reflections on the Psalms* is to return to our initial question: why does this book make so many of Lewis's readers profoundly uncomfortable? We are not made uncomfortable by a bad book, or even necessarily by a book with which we disagree. But what if we find a trusted author who seems at points to be undermining the very things we are used to seeing him defend? And what if this book is so full of his many virtues that we cannot dismiss it as an aberration? And what if, worst of all, our problems with it are inextricably bound up with those very virtues? That qualifies as an uncomfortable reading experience indeed. While many of Lewis's readers may find this a discussion not strictly necessary, a vast number of his most devoted fans—conservative American Evangelicals, for example—will recognize the reaction just described as their own.

If what these readers see as weaknesses flow from the book's strengths, let us begin with the strengths. Lewis's whole career had established him as one of the best people in the world at performing two services that are combined in *Reflections*. First, he can teach us how to read poetry, especially kinds of poetry we are not used to, and do it without making heavy sailing of it. Think of *A Preface to Paradise Lost* and the essay on "The Alliterative Meter," two of the best examples of such instruction ever written.[40] Second, he can give us the background equipment we need to read ancient literature with understanding, as he had done superbly in *The Allegory of Love* and the lectures that were posthumously published as *The Discarded Image*.[41]

While Lewis claims not to be instructing us but only comparing notes, his notes end up being quite instructive. Lambert was justified in saying that *Reflections* reveals Lewis as "a luminous teacher of poetry," and his description of the explication of Psalm 19 is a good summary of the kind of reading that awaits us throughout the book:

In the course of showing us this Lewis has taken us on a tour of the parched Palestinian countryside, given us a lesson in cultural history, introduced us briefly to modern poetry, made a study in the psychology of religion, developed a commentary on the psalm, and, best of all, taught us how to read the rest of them.[42]

Chad Walsh concurs. In *Reflections* Lewis "rescues" the psalms for the honest reader. "It is a remarkable book, sketching out and demonstrating a fruitful approach to one of the most beautiful—and perplexing—books in the Bible."[43] In like manner C. S. Kilby sees it as an "important idea" in *Reflections on the Psalms* that the Bible has "a creative rather than an abstractive quality."[44] The psalms are poems.

Truly this is Lewis at his best. He reminds his audience—lay Bible readers—of a fact that is so obvious that many of them have forgotten it. "Most emphatically the Psalms must be read as poems; as lyrics, with all the licenses and all the formalities, the hyperboles, the emotional rather than logical connections, which are proper to lyric poetry."[45] He then in just a couple of pages has a lucid explanation of Hebrew poetic parallelism which, by comparing it with well-known passages in English poetry, gives his lay readers just enough to get on with, without burdening them with the technical details. Despite his protestations of amateur status, Lewis the professor is seen as well here as anywhere, instructing us with such gentle ease that it actually feels like we've only been comparing notes with a schoolfellow. Only a master teacher can make significant learning seem so effortless.

Lewis is equally adept at enabling us to enter the mindset of ancient people. He does this with his characteristically deft use of apt analogy. In the Christian view of judgment, the believer is in the dock needing God's mercy; in the typical presentation in the psalms, the speaker is the plaintiff wanting God to redress injustice. Every ancient temple was a slaughterhouse—but if it smelled of blood, it had also the festive smell of roast meat. Like the relentless desert sun, the Law finds us out in the most shadowy hiding places of our hearts. The publicans were the Palestinian Vichy or collaborationists. Both as a teacher of poetry and as a tour guide to lost cultures, Lewis gets us closer to being able to hear the psalms as they were meant to be heard.

A third strength of this book is the way in which Lewis's uncompromising commitment to what he understands of Christian morality and truth lead him to look without flinching at the most difficult problems facing modern readers of the Psalms. He will not allow himself to opt for easy solutions or to paint over the problems with pious language. Again we see the continuity with Lewis's earlier Christian writings. This is the Lewis of *The Problem of*

Pain, or even more so, perhaps, the Lewis of the essay "Petitionary Prayer: A Problem without an Answer."[46]

It is, however, this very strength that gives rise to perplexity, especially when Lewis is dealing with the two most intractable problems, the cursing psalms (chapter III) and those in which the psalmist expresses hatred of God's enemies (chapter VII). Surely Lewis is right to eschew easy answers: "We must not either try to explain [the cursing psalms] away or to yield for one moment to the idea that, because it comes in the Bible, all this vindictive hatred must somehow be good and pious."[47] Yet it is easy to feel that he has painted the picture worse than it is or ignored some obvious ameliorating factors.

Take for example the psalms in which the speaker professes to hate, not just evil, but evil people, and to avoid even associating with them, culminating in the declaration of 139:21-22, "Do I not hate those who hate Thee, O Lord? And do I not loathe those who rise up against Thee? I hate them with the utmost hatred; they have become my enemies" (New American Standard Bible [NASB]). Though Lewis admits that the toleration of evil in modern times is equally problematic (indeed, he rightly sees these psalms as a useful corrective to it), and though he rightly sees the danger of self-righteousness and Pharisaism in such attitudes, he also says that "this evil is already at work" in the Psalms themselves.[48] Is this conclusion not reached a bit too quickly?

Something Lewis never mentions in this discussion is the common Old Testament idiom of hatred as a metaphor for rejection. God himself says that He has loved Jacob but hated Esau (Malachi 1:2, 3). This does not mean that God felt personal animosity toward Esau, but it is a metaphorical way of stating that He had chosen Jacob and rejected Esau as the bearer of the Abrahamic covenant. The statement in Genesis 29:31 that Leah was hated is qualified and interpreted by the fact that Verse 30 has just said that Jacob loved Rachel more than Leah. To be loved less is still to be loved. The obvious meaning is that Rachel, not Leah, was Jacob's first choice, his preference. We are not necessarily required by this language to believe that he actually despised, held animosity for, treated with overt hostility, or even strongly disliked a woman who, after all, kept bearing him children. (This perspective goes far, by the way, toward explaining certain hard passages in the New Testament, such as the statement that disciples of Jesus must "hate" their father and mother.) It is clear that in biblical language hatred is often not meant literally but rather as a metaphor for rejection, sometimes (as in the case of Leah) not even an absolute rejection. To recognize this possibility certainly puts the language of the psalms in a different light.

Now, one would expect a person with Lewis's sensitivity to poetry to have noticed such a metaphorical usage, and his failure to do so is as puzzling as the readiness of a strong Christian apologist to read Scripture as not only enshrining but also encouraging moral imperfection. But there is more puzzlement awaiting us. Psalm 139 is attributed to David. What if he is speaking at this moment, not as a private person, but as the king? What if he is speaking as the one responsible to uphold right and justice in the nation? Then there is a very legitimate sense in which God's enemies are by that fact his as well.

Lewis's failure to consider adequately the possibility of an official or corporate rather than a private voice in the psalmist is possibly explained by yet another puzzling statement from the introduction. Several poets wrote the psalms at different dates. "Some, I believe, are allowed to go back to the reign of David; I think certain scholars allow that Psalm 18 . . . might be by David himself."[49] This is a strangely meek acceptance of the results of negative biblical criticism from the man who two years later would write "Modern Theology and Biblical Criticism,"[50] the classic explanation of why we should not be overly impressed by the pronouncements of the so-called "higher" critics of the New Testament. One can only guess that, while Lewis's classical training made him feel sufficiently at home in the world of the New Testament confidently to see through the pretensions of negative scholarship there, in the less familiar world of Semitic studies his characteristic deference to those known as experts made him more vulnerable. Others have since done for Old Testament criticism what Lewis did for the New Testament.[51] Had Lewis, in keeping with his own advice in "Modern Theology and Biblical Criticism," been more skeptical of the skeptics,[52] he might have thought more concretely about David's own situation in his interpretation of Psalm 139.

I am not suggesting that such considerations are capable of solving all of the problems Lewis raises. But they help a great deal, even in the cursing psalms. Lewis complains of the vulgarity of 23:5, "Thou preparest a table before me in the presence of mine enemies." But if we seriously think of this poem as coming from the mouth of David, it is easier to believe that vindication, rather than one-upping the horrid Joneses, is what is in view. Again, if 109 is by David, the enemies can be seen not just as personal enemies but as the foes of Israel and of peace, and the curses not as the mere expression of personal vindictiveness but the prophetic pronouncement of God's judgment on the unrepentant troublers of the land. There remain the blessing on infanticides of 137:9, which is much more difficult to justify, and the general dangers of making these curses our own, which Lewis rightly wrestles with. The discomfort comes not from the fact that Lewis forces us to wrestle with such problems but from the not wholly unjustified feeling that there is more to be said on behalf of the biblical writers than he allows for.

For conservative believers, unease also attaches itself to the general view of Scripture and the relationship of the reader to the authority of the Bible not only implied by these chapters but also spelled out in chapter XI. Robert Merchant summarizes Lewis's lesson on how to read the problem psalms and their "expression of pure hatred": "What shall we do with it? Toss it out? Consume it whole? No, says Lewis, don't toss it out, yet don't take it as it is. Transform it, and then it becomes delightfully nourishing."[53] But on what basis are we to transform it? On the basis of a notion of what the author *should* have said picked and chosen from other parts of Scripture? If Scripture itself is not our authority for what is right, how do we avoid the problem of a "canon within the canon"? If we ourselves have to discern that canon within the canon, have we not ourselves become the canon? Then the authority of Scripture dissolves completely. How can Lewis feel free to criticize the psalmists' morality and yet avoid these problems?

In chapter XI, "Scripture," Lewis tries to explain his view of biblical inspiration as an answer to such questions. Because he is not a modernist— one who automatically rejects as unhistorical any narrative containing the supernatural—people often assume he is a Fundamentalist, that is, one who believes that "every sentence of the Old Testament has historical or scientific truth."[54] Instead, Lewis thinks that much of the Old Testament is myth, gradually sharpening its focus until, without losing its mythical quality, it becomes history in the incarnation of Christ. He conceives of the inspiration of the Old Testament as a "Divine pressure"[55] on the process of human retellings of pagan myths, giving us eventually a story of real creation instead of pagan theogony and not completely accidental anticipations of the coming of Christ. The end result "carries" the Word of God, which we can receive from the "overall message," while still being free to question individual statements: "The human qualities of the raw materials show through. Naivety, error, contradiction, even (as in the cursing psalms) wickedness are not removed." Thus the Bible is not "truth in systematic form—something we could have tabulated and memorized and relied on like the multiplication table"[56]

Echoing Lewis's perception of Fundamentalism, Walter Ramshaw writes,

I was raised in a tradition which vigorously insisted on a doctrine of "verbal inspiration"—by which was meant that every word of Scripture had been dictated by God.... As a consequence, one was obliged to maintain that the Scriptures were accurate and correct in all respects.... It is, of course, impossible for a thoughtful person to maintain this position without indulging in prodigies of mind-bending ratiocination.[57]

This is all well and good—except that "Fundamentalists" (and their living heirs, Evangelicals, as well as conservative Roman Catholics) will feel that their position in being rejected has been horribly caricatured, since their more informed teachers have never held any such thing. The notion, for example, that "plenary inspiration" and "the mechanical dictation theory" are synonymous is simply ignorant. The so-called Fundamentalists' actual tradition as summarized in the 1978 "Chicago Statement on Biblical Inerrancy" maintains that "We must pay the most careful attention to [the Bible's] claims and character as a human production." As a result,

History must be treated as history, poetry as poetry, hyperbole and metaphor as hyperbole and metaphor, generalization and approximation as what they are, and so forth. Differences between literary conventions in Bible times and in ours must also be observed. Since, for instance, nonchronological narration and imprecise citation were conventional and acceptable and violated no expectations in those days, we must not regard these things as faults when we find them in Biblical writers. When total precision of a particular kind was not expected nor aimed at, it is no error not to have achieved it. Scripture is inerrant, not in the sense of being absolutely precise by modern standards, but in the sense of making good its claims and achieving that measure of focused truth at which its authors aimed.[58]

How Lewis would have responded to a more nuanced version of the doctrine of inerrancy than he was apparently ever exposed to we will never know. The point here is to understand that in rejecting that doctrine he is rejecting a straw man.[59] This realization must be part of a full evaluation of Lewis as a Christian apologist and teacher of the church, as well as part of a full evaluation of *Reflections on the Psalms*.

Though many of Lewis's readers are surprised by what they find in *Reflections*, it represents no real departure from Lewis's views in earlier books. There is nothing inconsistent with the view of Scripture presented here in *Miracles, The Problem of Pain*, or "Myth Became Fact."[60] His view of inspiration is noticed here because Lewis actually spells it out and because it allows him to be critical of biblical writers in unaccustomed ways. In Lewis's approach to the New Testament there is no practical difference between him and those who have a high view of Scripture. As he explained to C. S. Kilby in a personal letter, it matters more whether some events literally happened than others, and "the ones whose historicity matters are, as God's will, those where it is plain."[61] By the time of the New Testament, myth had become fact. (This of course begs for more conservative readers the question whether the first Adam might not also have been myth become fact). Thus, because he was usually focused on the New Testament, Lewis was—a believer might say providentially—protected in most of his religious writings from departing from the high road of "mere Christianity." Here he is aware that he has not quite been able to include fully all of his Fundamentalist and Roman Catholic readers. And the book suffers from it.

Nevertheless, *Reflections on the Psalms* remains a valuable part of the Lewis canon. For all the positive reasons discussed above, it succeeds in helping us read the Psalms better and with fuller understanding, even for those readers who are troubled by some of its analysis. It contributes to our understanding of Lewis's theology and helps to round out our view of his strengths and weaknesses as a Christian thinker. Best of all, it sometimes rises to an ability to help the Psalmists do what they can do so well: lead us in the worship and adoration of God. In not knowing Christ, the Old Testament writers knew less reason for loving God than we do, Lewis reminds us. "Yet they express a longing for Him, for His mere presence, which comes only to the best Christians or to Christians in their best moments." Lewis in his best moments in this book helps the psalmists to lead us into "an experience fully God-centered, asking of God no gift more urgently than His presence, the gift of Himself, joyous to the highest degree, and unmistakably real."[62]

NOTES

1. Byron C. Lambert, "Reflections on *Reflections on the Psalms*," *CSL: The Bulletin of the New York C. S. Lewis Society* 2(1) (November 1970), 2.

2. C. S. Lewis, *Reflections on the Psalms* (New York: Harcourt, Brace, & World, 1958).

3. Review of *Reflections on the Psalms*, by C. S. Lewis *Current History* 36 (March 1959), 173.

4. C. S. Lewis, *Letters to Malcolm: Chiefly on Prayer* (New York: Harcourt Brace Jovanovich, 1963).

5. James M. Houston, "The Prayer Life of C. S. Lewis," in *The Riddle of Joy: G. K. Chesterton and C. S. Lewis*, ed. Michael H. MacDonald and Andrew A. Tadie (Grand Rapids, MI: Eerdmans, 1989), 70.

6. Perry C. Bramlett, "*Reflections on the Psalms*," in *The C. S. Lewis Reader's Encyclopedia*, ed. Jeffrey Schultz and John G. West, Jr. (Grand Rapids, MI: Zondervan, 1998), 353.

7. George Sayer, *Jack: A Life of C. S. Lewis* (1988) (reprint, Wheaton, IL: Crossway, 1994), 390.

8. C. S. Lewis to Arthur Greaves, 1957, in *They Stand Together: The Letters of C. S. Lewis to Arthur Greeves (1914–1963)* (New York: Macmillan, 1979), 545.

9. Ibid.

10. Sayer, op. cit., 391.

11. Victor Reppert, *C. S. Lewis's Dangerous Idea: In Defense of the Argument from Reason* (Downers Grove, IL: Inter-Varsity Press, 2003), 15–28; cf. Reppert's article "The Lewis-Anscombe Controversy: A Discussion of the Issues," *Christian Scholar's Review* 19(1) (September 1989), 32–48.

12. C. S. Lewis, *Miracles: A Preliminary Study* (New York: Macmillan, 1947).

13. Humphrey Carpenter, *The Inklings: C. S. Lewis, J. R. R. Tolkien, Charles Williams, and Their Friends* (Boston, MA: Houghton Mifflin, 1979), 217.

14. Sayer, op. cit., 390.

15. Bramlett, op. cit., 351.

16. C. S. Lewis, *Surprised by Joy: The Shape of My Early Life* (New York: Harcourt, Brace & World, 1955).

17. Samuel Alexander, *Space, Time and Deity* (New York: The Humanities Press, 1950), Edwyn Bevan, *Symbolism and Belief* (1938) (reprint, Boston, MA: Beacon Hill, 1957), and Rudolf Otto, *The Idea of the Holy* (1917) (reprint, London: Pelican, 1959).

18. C. S. Lewis, *The Pilgrim's Regress: An Allegorical Apology for Christianity, Reason, and Romanticism* (1933) (reprint, Grand Rapids, MI: Eerdmans, 1958).

19. C. S. Lewis, *God in the Dock: Essays on Theology and Ethics*, ed. Walter Hooper (Grand Rapids, MI: Eerdmans, 1970), 13–17.

20. C. S. Lewis, *The Silver Chair* (1953) (reprint, New York: HarperCollins, 1981), 179–191.

21. For a good recent treatment of this point see William J. McClain, "C. S. Lewis and the Reflective Christian," *CSL: The Bulletin of the New York C. S. Lewis Society*, 36(3) (May–June 2006), 1–9, esp. 5–6.

22. See Donald T. Williams, *Mere Humanity: G. K. Chesterton, C. S. Lewis, and J. R. R. Tolkien on the Human Condition* (Nashville, TN: Broadman & Holman, 2006), 139f., for further discussion of this point.

23. Corbin Scott Carnell, *Bright Shadows of Reality: C. S. Lewis and the Feeling Intellect* (Grand Rapids, MI: Eerdmans, 1974), 64. See also Colin Duriez, *A Field Guide to Narnia* (Downers Grove, IL: Inter-Varsity Press, 2004), 45, who correct some of Carnell's dating.

24. Sayer, op. cit., 253; Carpenter, op. cit., 225–227.

25. C. S. Lewis, *English Literature in the Sixteenth Century, Excluding Drama* (Oxford: Oxford University Press, 1954).

26. C. S. Lewis to Arthur Greaves, 1957, op. cit., 545.

27. Sayer, op. cit., 323.

28. Ibid., 326.

29. Roger Lancelyn Green and Walter Hooper, *C. S. Lewis: A Biography* (New York: Harcourt Brace Jovanovich, 1974), 282.

30. Lambert, op. cit., 2.

31. See for example the discussion of the "fabulous" elements of the Old Testament in "Answers to Questions on Christianity," 1944; reprint in *God in the Dock*, ed. Walter Hooper (Grand Rapids, MI: Eerdmans, 1970), 57–58, or the discussion of Genesis in chapter 5 of *The Problem of Pain* (1940) (reprint, New York: Macmillan, 1967).

32. Lewis, *Reflections on the Psalms*, op. cit., 20.

33. Ibid., 21.

34. Ibid., 22.

35. Ibid., 45.

36. Ibid., 44.

37. Ibid., 59.

38. Ibid., 111–112.

39. Ibid., 129.

40. C. S. Lewis, *A Preface to Paradise Lost* (Oxford: Oxford University Press, 1942) and "The Alliterative Meter," in *Selected Literary Essays*, ed. Walter Hooper (Cambridge: Cambridge University Press, 1969), 15–26.

41. C. S. Lewis, The Allegory of Love: *A Study in Medieval Tradition* (Oxford: Oxford University Press, 1936), and *The Discarded Image: An Introduction of Medieval and Renaissance Literature* (Cambridge: Cambridge University Press, 1964).

42. Lambert, op. cit., 2.

43. Chad Walsh, *The Literary Legacy of C. S. Lewis* (New York: Harcourt Brace Jovanovich, 1979), 224.

44. Clyde S. Kilby, *The Christian World of C. S. Lewis* (Grand Rapids, MI: Eerdmans, 1964), 147.

45. Lewis, *Reflections on the Psalms*, op. cit., 3.

46. C. S. Lewis, "Petitionary Prayer: A Problem without an Answer" (1953) in *Christian Reflections*, ed. Walter Hooper (Grand Rapids, MI: Eerdmans, 1967), 142–151.

47. Lewis, *Reflections on the Psalms*, op. cit., 22.

48. Ibid., 67.

49. Ibid., 2.

50. C. S. Lewis, "Modern Theology and Biblical Criticism," 1959; in *Christian Reflections*, ed. Walter Hooper (Grand Rapids, MI: Eerdmans, 1967), 152–166.

51. See for example Gleason Archer, *A Survey of Old Testament Introduction*, revised edition (Chicago, IL: Moody Press, 1974), especially 439–443 on the reliability of the Davidic attributions in the psalm titles.

52. "I do not wish to reduce the skeptical element in your minds. I am only suggesting that it need not be reserved exclusively for the New Testament and the Creeds. Try doubting something else." Lewis, "Modern Theology," op. cit., 164.

53. Robert Merchant, *"Reflections on the Psalms," CSL: The Bulletin of the New York C. S. Lewis Society* 5(3) (January 1974), 4.

54. Lewis, *Reflections on the Psalms*, op. cit., 109.

55. Ibid., 111.

56. Ibid., 111–112.

57. Walter Ramshaw, "Reflections on *Reflections on the Psalms*," *CSL: The Bulletin of the New York C. S. Lewis Society* 11(11) (September 1980), 5.

58. "The Chicago Statement on Biblical Inerrancy," 1978; quoted from *One Faith: The Evangelical Consensus*, ed. J. I. Packer and Thomas Oden (Downers Grove, IL: Inter-Varsity Press, 2004), 50.

59. Scott R. Burson and Jerry L. Walls, *C. S. Lewis and Francis Schaeffer: Lessons for a New Century from the Most Influential Apologists of Our Time* (Downers Grove, IL: InterVarsity Press, 1998), 127, bend over too far backwards in saying that Lewis "is not challenging the doctrine of inerrancy" in *Reflections on the Psalms* and the letter to Kilby. For further evaluations of Lewis's approach to inspiration, see Wesley L. Kort, *C. S. Lewis Then and Now* (Oxford: Oxford University Press, 200), 24; and Will Vaus, *Mere Theology: A Guide to the Thought of C. S. Lewis* (Downers Grove, IL: InterVarsity Press, 2004), 32–41.

60. C. S. Lewis, "Myth Became Fact," *World Dominion* 22 (September–October 1944), 267–270; reprint in *God in the Dock: Essays on theology and Ethics*, ed. Walter Hooper, 63–67.

61. Quoted in C. S. Kilby, *The Christian World of C. S. Lewis*, op. cit., 153. For the complete text, see C. S. Lewis to Professor Clyde S. Kilby, May 7, 1959, in *Letters of C. S. Lewis*, ed. with a memoir by W. H. Lewis (New York: Harcourt, Brace and World, 1966), 286–287.

62. Lewis, *Reflections on the Psalms*, op. cit., 50, 52.

BIBLIOGRAPHY

Alexander, Samuel. *Space, Time and Deity.* New York: The Humanities Press, 1950.

Archer, Gleason. *A Survey of Old Testament Introduction.* Revised edition. Chicago, IL: Moody Press, 1974.

Bevan, Edwyn. *Symbolism and Belief,* 1938. Reprint. Boston, MA: Beacon Hill, 1957.

Bramlett, Perry C. "*Reflections on the Psalms.*" In *The C. S. Lewis Reader's Encyclopedia.* Edited by Jeffrey Schultz and John G. West, Jr. Grand Rapids, MI: Zondervan, 1998, 351–353.

Burson, Scott R. and Jerry L. Walls. *C. S. Lewis and Francis Schaeffer: Lessons for a New Century from the Most Influential Apologists of Our Time.* Downers Grove, IL: Inter-Varsity Press, 1998.

Carnell, Corbin Scott. *Bright Shadows of Reality: C. S. Lewis and the Feeling Intellect.* Grand Rapids, MI: Eerdmans, 1974.

Carpenter, Humphrey. *The Inklings: C. S. Lewis, J. R. R. Tolkien, Charles Williams, and their Friends.* Boston, MA: Houghton Mifflin, 1979.

Current History. Review of *Reflections on the Psalms*, by C. S. Lewis. 36 (March, 1959), 173.

Duriez, Colin. *A Field Guide to Narnia.* Downers Grove, IL: Inter-Varsity Press, 2004.

Green, Roger Lancelyn and Walter Hooper. *C. S. Lewis: A Biography.* New York: Harcourt Brace Jovanovich, 1974.

Hooper, Walter. Editor. *They Stand Together: The Letters of C. S. Lewis to Arthur Greeves (1914–1963).* New York: Macmillan, 1979.

Houston, James M. "The Prayer Life of C. S. Lewis." In *The Riddle of Joy: G. K. Chesterton and C. S. Lewis.* Edited by Michael H. MacDonald and Andrew A. Tadie. Grand Rapids, MI: Eerdmans, 1989, 69–86.

Kilby, Clyde S. *The Christian World of C. S. Lewis*. Grand Rapids, MI: Eerdmans, 1964.

Kort, Wesley A. *C. S. Lewis Then and Now*. Oxford: Oxford University Press, 2001.

Lambert, Byron C. "Reflections on *Reflections on the Psalms*." *CSL: The Bulletin of the New York C. S. Lewis Society* 2(1) (November 1970), 2–4.

Lewis, C. S. *The Allegory of Love: A Study in Medieval Tradition*. Oxford: Oxford University Press, 1936.

———. "The Alliterative Meter." In *Selected Literary Essays*. Edited by Walter Hooper. Cambridge: Cambridge University Press, 1969, 15–26.

———. *The Discarded Image: An Introduction to Medieval and Renaissance Literature*. Cambridge: Cambridge University Press, 1964.

———. *English Literature in the Sixteenth Century, Excluding Drama*. Oxford: Oxford University Press, 1954.

———. *God in the Dock: Essays on Theology and Ethics*. Edited by Walter Hooper. Grand Rapids, MI: Eerdmans, 1970.

———. Letter to Professor Clyde S. Kilby, 1959. In *The Letters of C. S. Lewis*. Edited with a memoir by W. H. Lewis, 286–287. New York: Harcourt, Brace and World, 1966.

———. *Letters to Malcolm: Chiefly on Prayer*. New York: Harcourt Brace Jovanovich, 1963.

———. *Miracles: A Preliminary Study*. New York: Macmillan, 1947.

———. "Modern Theology and Biblical Criticism," 1959. In *Christian Reflections*. Edited by Walter Hooper, 152–166. Grand Rapids, MI: Eerdmans, 1967.

———. "Myth Became Fact." *World Dominion* 22 (September–October 1944), 267–270. Reprint in *God in the Dock: Essays on theology and Ethics*. Edited by Walter Hooper. Grand Rapids, MI: Eerdmans, 1970, 63–67.

———. "Petitionary Prayer: A Problem without an Answer," 1953. In *Christian Reflections*. Edited by Walter Hooper. Grand Rapids, MI: Eerdmans, 1967, 142–151.

———. *The Pilgrim's Regress: An Allegorical Apology for Christianity, Reason, and Romanticism*, 1933. Reprint, Grand Rapids, MI: Eerdmans, 1958.

———. *A Preface to Paradise Lost*. Oxford: Oxford University Press, 1942.

———. *The Problem of Pain*, 1940. Reprint, New York: Macmillan, 1967.

———. *Reflections on the Psalms*. New York: Harcourt, Brace & World, 1958.

McClain, Williams J. "C. S. Lewis and the Reflective Christian." *CSL: The Bulletin of the New York C. S. Lewis Society* 36(3) (May–June 2006), 1–9.

Merchant, Robert. "*Reflections on the Psalms*." *CSL: The Bulletin of the New York C. S. Lewis Society* 5(3) (January, 1974), 1–5.

Otto, Rudolf. *The Idea of the Holy*, 1917. Reprint. London: Pelican, 1959.

Packer, J. I. and Thomas C. Oden. *One Faith: The Evangelical Consensus*. Downers Grove, IL: Inter-Varsity Press, 2004.

Ramshaw, Walter. "Reflections on *Reflections on the Psalms*." *CSL: The Bulletin of the New York C. S. Lewis Society* 11(11) (September 1980), 1–7.

Reppert, Victor. *C. S. Lewis's Dangerous Idea: In Defense of the Argument from Reason.* Downers Grove IL: Inter-Varsity Press, 2003.

———. "The Lewis-Anscombe Controversy: A Discussion of the Issues." *Christian Scholar's Review* 19(1) (September 1989): 32–48.

Sayer, George. *Jack: A Life of C. S. Lewis,* 1988. Reprint, Wheaton, IL: Crossway, 1994.

Smilde, Arend. "*Reflections on the Psalms*: Quotations and Allusions." *Notes and Reflections on C. S. Lewis,* http://www.solcon.nl/arendsmilde/cslewis/reflections/e-psalmsquotes.htm

Vaus, Will. *Mere Theology: A Guide to the Thought of C. S. Lewis.* Downers Grove, IL: Inter-Varsity Press, 2004.

Walsh, Chad. *The Literary Legacy of C. S. Lewis.* New York: Harcourt Brace Jovanovich, 1979.

Williams, Donald T. *Mere Humanity: G. K. Chsterton, C. S. Lewis, and J. R. R. Tolkien on the Human Condition.* Nashville, TN: Broadman & Holman, 2006.

Understanding C. S. Lewis's *Surprised by Joy:* "A Most Reluctant" Autobiography

Mona Dunckel and Karen Rowe

INTRODUCTION: AUTOBIOGRAPHY AS STRUCTURE AND SUBSTANCE

Most readers initially know C. S. Lewis in only one context, not realizing that during his lifetime his unusual gifts allowed him to carve out three diverse yet successful careers, what Owen Barfield, his longtime friend and fellow Inkling, has called the "three Lewises."[1] He was first a well-respected literary critic and renowned Oxford don; he was also an award-winning author of children's literature and science fiction; he was additionally a popular broadcaster and Christian apologist—ranking behind only Churchill in voice recognition on British radio during the 1940s. Because the audiences for each of Lewis's roles were so different, not many of his readers know the whole picture of his life. *Surprised by Joy*, published in 1956 only seven years before his death, reveals more the *person* of Lewis, making it distinct from the popular *persona* of Lewis created in part by the 1993 film *Shadowlands*.

Surprised by Joy is C. S. Lewis's most directly autobiographical work; it was not, however, a quickly completed text. He had begun writing during the 1940s but set it aside during the writing of his *Chronicles of Narnia*. While there are elements of autobiography in *The Magician's Nephew*, and

The Pilgrim's Regress, an earlier allegory that offers a glimpse into Lewis's life and conversion, neither offers the clear and immediate autobiographical look that *Surprised by Joy* affords, for in this book Lewis openly traces the search for joy in his own life. Since the book was written relatively late in Lewis's life, one might expect that the work would cover more of his life experiences. However, as its subtitle informs us, *Surprised by Joy* covers only the early years of Lewis's life. Perhaps because, as Lewis tells his readers in the book's Preface, that he had "never read an autobiography in which the parts devoted to the earlier years were not far the most interesting."[2] The narrative continues through his conversion at age thirty-one, and ends shortly thereafter.

While crafting his many works of fiction Lewis often tells the story of a character's journey to joy, always a process of moving beyond themselves toward undying desires, for example John in *Pilgrim's Regress*, or Orual in *Till We Have Faces.* In *Surprised by Joy*, Lewis is tracing his own journey to Joy—not an outward one, but an inward journey of thought that lead to faith. This requires Lewis to adopt a direct and personal discussion of his private life. However, there is no pride, no self-aggrandizement in the way that Lewis tells his own story. Delivered in an easy conversational tone, it creates an encounter in which Lewis, ever the private man, moves beyond his reluctance to speak about himself and shares details regarding his life. He permits himself to tell his story for two primary purposes, reasons that he identifies in the preface; first, the story will be told to respond to "requests that I would tell how I passed from Atheism to Christianity" and second, "to correct one or two false notions that seem to have got about" (p. vii). Yet while Lewis offers direct entrance to his past, it is at the same time limited access. Lewis regularly checks himself through comments that permit the reader to know that a door is being closed or a shade pulled, as in the opening line of chapter twelve, "The rest of my war experiences have little to do with this story."[3] There is no general "airing out" of all he had done or all he had been.

Lewis would describe his book as a "spiritual autobiography," although the book is not a confession like the autobiography of St. Augustine, or that of Rousseau. As Lewis scholar Bruce Edwards has written, "Lewis views himself in *Surprised by Joy* as no more or less a sinner than anyone else, [. . .] his is not a grand repentance from fleshly indulgence but a recovery of a child-like wonderment at the world and its mysteries."[4] In telling his tale, Lewis also fashions for the reader an intellectual autobiography, detailing his search for what he called "joy" and exploring the ideas, people, writings, and events that help him describe to us his conversion. Lewis limits himself and his readers to only those dealings that are truly cogent in describing his gradual movement from atheism to Christ. When describing the culmination of his passage to faith Lewis, ever shunning overstatement and drama, states simply: "Every step

I had taken, from the Absolute to 'Spirit' and from 'Spirit' to 'God,' had been a step toward the more concrete, the more imminent, the more compulsive. [. . .] I know very well when, but hardly how, the final step was taken."[5]

While David Downing has called Lewis "the most reluctant convert," one might also call him the most reluctant autobiographer. Lewis's disinclination is not merely what Bruce Edwards calls the "conventional modesty of the autobiographer who wishes to downplay the importance of his life,"[6] but his hesitancy stems also from his certainty that psychological inquiry into an author's life does not particularly illuminate any writer's text. In his own work as literary historian and as a critic, Lewis had found far too many works that substituted assumptions or recreations of the author's thinking and writing process for careful investigation of the text—what had actually been written. Lewis referred to this obsession of twentieth-century criticism as "the personal heresy": the trend of assuming that everything that a writer produces is in some way playing out of his or her own experiences, the assumption that authors can be identified with their creations. Believing that such a critical approach destroyed the inherent power and meaning of texts, Lewis totally rejected the opinion that the writer was obligated in some way to open his or her private life to the world and to the critics. This meant that in order to write about his life, Lewis was forced to go against his longstanding "distaste for all that is public, all that belongs to the collective."[7] While chronicling his conversion led Lewis to open his life to the world, he controlled the access, making available to the reader only those experiences that suited his purpose. He would speak of his life, but only in a way that furthered his defense of his faith. Even here, Lewis remains doubtful regarding the vehicle of autobiography, and his preface to *Surprised by Joy* contains this warning for readers: "The story is, I fear, suffocatingly subjective; the kind of thing I have never before and shall probably never write again. I have tried so to write the first chapter that those who can't bear such a story will see at once what they are in for and close the book with the least waste of time."[8]

CRITICAL ANALYSIS

Because *Surprised by Joy* is his spiritual autobiography, an account of those elements that were influential in bringing Lewis to his Christian faith, its content does not follow biographical conventions of the time that chronicle friendships, detailed military histories, and stories of the loves (false and true), which have made up a life. Lewis writes a biography that is filled as much with books and ideas as it is with people and events. Lewis begins *Surprised by Joy* as one might expect, with a portrait of his family and home, which served as the secure and happy base for his idyllic early years.

Central to Lewis's childhood happiness were his parents, particularly his mother. Albert Lewis, his father, had a temperament that his son describes as shaped by his Welsh heritage; his mother, Flora Hamilton Lewis, was the daughter of a clergyman. Both parents were educated and the home was one rich in books, richer for the diverse authors and genres that pleased the differing reading tastes of the two. Lewis describes his home as being full of books, from bookcases in which shelves were loaded two deep to stacks in the attic, any of which he was permitted to read. Shakespeare, Swift, Trollope, and Dickens were all authors whom Lewis investigated. He does identify one lack in his available reading material, however; there were few titles from the Romantics that Lewis himself preferred, for his parents had, in his words, "never listened for the horns of elfland."[9] A picture of Lewis as a bookish but happy child emerges, a child for whom a book was transport to worlds that he found as real and as satisfying as the physical world around him. His reading material was not always adult fare, for when Lewis describes favorite reading material from his childhood he singles out Nesbit's trilogy, *Five Children and It*, *The Phoenix and the Wishing Carpet*, and *The Amulet*. He further gives special place to the stories of Beatrix Potter, identifying them as the place where he first came to know beauty.

Another treasure of Lewis's childhood household was his brother Warren, known as "Warnie." The brothers were constant playmates, but were also much more. Lewis describes a childhood of sharing secrets and hopes with his brother as they played together. Together they created worlds, in pictures and in words, populated them and created their complete histories and geographies. When the boys grew older and Warnie was sent to school in England, Lewis recalls the long period of separation as no impediment at all to their relations. The boys merely picked up where they had left off the last time they had been together.

All changed for Lewis, however, when he was nine. His mother fell ill, was treated for cancer, and died several months later. After her death Lewis was to long for a return of the joy he had known as a child, and it is Lewis's yearning for the return of joy that becomes the key theme dominating the rest of his story. This "joy" is more than merely delight in the moment or common pleasure; it is instead a momentary and transitory experience that Edwards calls "the sublime experience of the transcendent."[10] It is the fragmentary glimpse of eternity that is only ephemerally experienced and grasped on earth. Lewis later came to understand that such joy could only be found by those who have been redeemed and restored to their Creator's image when they meet Him at the end of the ages. Like the joy experienced by the Pevensie children as they are welcomed at last into the real Narnia by Aslan himself at the climax of the final tale of *The Chronicles of Narnia*, this joy can be given only by the one who is both creator of the world and its redeemer.

STRUCTURE AND CONTENT

The title of *Surprised by Joy* is taken from the first line of a sonnet published in 1815 by Wordsworth:

Surprised by joy—impatient as the Wind
I wished to share the transport—Oh! With whom
But Thee, long buried in the silent tomb,
That spot which no vicissitude can find?

It was not uncommon for Lewis to derive his titles from the works of other authors. The title *Pilgrim's Regress* is a parody of the title of John Bunyan's well-known Christian classic *Pilgrim's Progress*. There is nothing to indicate that Lewis had the complete poem in mind when he selected his title. There is ample evidence in consideration of other titles of works and chapter titles within his books that entire lines or mere phrases could be selected and used by Lewis with no regard for the context from which they were lifted. It is probable that this is the case here for the original Wordsworth poem was written about the poet's dead daughter. The title, apart from context, seems apt for Lewis's work, however, for it is clear in the reading of *Surprised by Joy* that Lewis was ultimately surprised by that for which he had sought so long, and was surprised by the ultimate source of the joy he craved. The title of the work often gives those aware of Lewis's life pause, for it seems that he is referring to the wonderful surprise of Joy Gresham, the fan turned wife, who came into his life in 1952 and whom he wed in a civil ceremony in 1956, the year *Surprised by Joy* was published. At that time, he was apparently not considering a love-match with Joy; the ceremony was merely to allow her to remain living in England. So to ascribe the book's title to Joy Gresham is to ignore the biographical details of the author's life as well as the major concept of the book itself.

The works of other authors play an additional role in *Surprised by Joy*, for it, like *Pilgrim's Regress* before it, makes use of epigraphs. The epigraph for the book itself is the complete first line of Wordsworth's poem, but Lewis goes beyond selecting an epigraph merely for the book; each chapter has its own epigraph as well. The quotations are taken from a broad range of authors that include John Milton, George Herbert, George MacDonald, and St. Augustine. Not all of the epigraphs seem to be totally accurate quotations from the identified works. This may be in part because Lewis was using them as he remembered them; he had a profound memory for things that he had read, but his memory of the passages may not have been exact. How much attention the epigraphs should be given is debated by critics, but it appears that although they provide introductory "road signs" for the reader, they are not of critical importance to an appropriate understanding of Lewis's narrative.

Surprised by Joy may be viewed as comprised of four segments that might be subtitled: loss brings decline; reason leads to rationalism; experience fosters disillusionment; and salvation produces joy. Each stage is marked by key events in Lewis's life that serve as markers for the stages of Lewis's spiritual awareness, and these events are the "necessary elements" that Lewis includes in his narrative. The stages are by no means uniform in time. Within these events lies the story of Lewis's spiritual decline—from church attendee, to atheist, to Aristotelian idealism, through theism and finally to Christianity.[11] As one can see from chapter titles and content, the bulk of the book treats Lewis's life before World War I, for it is the events of these years before his time at Oxford that profoundly shape that which follows; it is in these first years that Lewis's quest for joy begins.

Loss Brings Decline

The earliest years of Lewis's life, those before he went to study with his beloved tutor the "Great Knock," comprise the stage of Lewis's life that can be titled *loss*. The first of the losses that marks this period is the physical loss of his brother to boarding school for much of the year. Shortly after the family had moved into Little Lea, their second home, Warren was sent to England to begin his schooling. It was the intention of Albert Lewis that his sons would have the kind of traditional British education that he assumed would create lifelong opportunities for them. While not devastated by Warren's absence, Jack did as a result of it spend increasing time alone, which continued to sharpen his imagination. This temporary seasonal loss of his brother's presence is rather minor, but alone in a large house with his afternoons to himself Lewis spent more and more time creating worlds and stories from his imagination. He describes himself as living almost totally in his imagination. Approximately a year later, Lewis would endure a second and much greater loss.

The second key loss that Lewis experienced was the loss of his mother, Flora Hamilton Lewis, who died when he was nine. Lewis and his mother had spent increasing time together after his brother Warnie had been sent off to school in England. Mrs. Lewis, who was a university graduate in mathematics, had begun teaching Jack French, Latin, and Mathematics; it was from her that he received his earliest education in logic. Early in 1908 Flora Lewis's health began to deteriorate. The diagnosis was cancer, and she died in August of the same year. Her death shattered the peaceful tranquility that had structured Lewis's childhood home and his existence. He describes the loss of his mother as beginning before her death, because her condition led to her gradual but consistent removal from Lewis's life. Lewis had always been closer to his mother than to his father, and he deeply felt her death. But the loss of his mother created another loss for Lewis as well; it created a greater separation between the boy and his father.

Albert Lewis, Jack's father, was devastated by the loss of his wife. His grief was intensified because his own father had died earlier that year, and his brother died only ten days after his wife. Lewis describes his father at this time saying, "Under the pressure of anxiety his temper became incalculable; he spoke wildly and acted unjustly."[12] Lewis describes a process of gradual disengagement by his father, and a concomitant growing closeness between the brothers. While Albert loved the boys, he was unable to relate to them. Because Albert was unable to care for the boys himself, in September of 1908, Jack was sent off with his brother to the first of the several boarding schools that he would attend. It is in his experience at one of the schools, Cherbourg, that Lewis's next loss comes.

It was during his years at Cherbourg that Lewis suffered another noteworthy loss: that of his youthful Christian faith. The process by which Lewis underwent this change was a gradual one, and he lists several things that were contributing factors. First among them was Miss C., the matron of the school. Lewis describes her as a woman who was "floundering in the mazes of Theosophy, Rosicrucianism, Spiritualism; the whole Anglo-American Occultist tradition."[13] She introduced Lewis to the objects of her search and awakened in him an obsession with the occult. The introduction to the occult mixed poorly with Lewis's practice of creating unrealistic rules for personal religious practice and constantly questioning the adequacy of his performance, especially in prayer. Together the two elements served to raise general doubts about religion and its value. Lewis identifies as additional intensifiers in his loss of faith his basically pessimistic nature and his belief that the world was only drudgery. This led him to think that if there had been a God who had created the world, it would not have been such a dreary and unpleasant place. While he states he cannot identify the specific moment at which it happened, Lewis knew that when he left his boarding school, he no longer believed in Christianity. He describes himself as happy because of his loss of faith, like John in the *Pilgrim's Regress* who, when he is told by Mr. Enlightenment that there is no Landlord, runs up the hill before him in celebratory joy. "Such a weight had been lifted from his mind that he felt he could fly." He had been made free of the rules that had circumscribed his behavior. He was now free to go his own way.

There is an additional loss that Lewis experiences during his boarding school years; he describes it as the loss of his "virtue and his simplicity."[14] During his studies at Cherbourg Lewis had come under the influence of a young teacher at the school from whom he learned to desire "glitter, swagger, distinction, the desire to be in the know."[15] This was also the time during which Lewis began to struggle with sexual temptation; the intensity of his temptations is revealed in Lewis's correspondence with Arthur Greeves. Lewis described his time at the boarding school as a period in which he had replaced humility and desirable characteristics of childlikeness with a new vulgarity. The Lewis who left boarding school was a different young man from the one who had arrived two years before. The pattern of loss had transformed Lewis's life and Lewis himself.

Finally at the end of this period Lewis loses the emotional closeness he had always shared with his brother. The break began because Jack did not share Warnie's joy in Wyvern College. Lewis describes his negative reaction to the school as "the first great disappointment my brother had ever experienced."[16] Rather than becoming one more item that cemented the brothers together, the college had become the first major separator of the two. The split was exacerbated by Warnie's difficult relationship with their father at the time. The unique closeness that he had shared with his brother had been the ultimate refuge to which Jack could turn; what had been for him the real essence of a home was now gone.

While this period of Lewis's life is one characterized by loss and by increasing spiritual barrenness it was not totally without positive experiences. This was also the time in which he first came to know Joy. As a child there were three distinct experiences that brought him glimpses of joy. The first came before he was even six years old. His brother made him a miniature forest in the lid of a biscuit tin. This gave Lewis his first glimpse of beauty and with the beauty a new perspective on nature as a whole. Lewis's second childhood experience with Joy came through Squirrel Nutkin, the Beatrix Potter book. The story stirred in him an intense sensation of "the idea of autumn"[17] so that he returned to the book just in order to reawaken the sensation, a desire that was otherworldly. The third experience with Joy came from a scrap of poetry that he discovered as he sat turning the pages of a book. He read from *Tegner's Drapa*:

I heard a voice that cried,
Balder the beautiful
Is dead, is dead—

Once this joy had been awakened, Lewis was unable to forget it. It remained a stab of sweet inconsolable want like none other he had experienced. It was a desire so real that he could, in today's vernacular, "taste it." He was not certain what it was that was the object of his desire, but he knew surely that once he saw whatever it was he would know that he had found that which he sought. Even the knowledge of joy is, however, a sort of loss, for although the longing had been awakened, Lewis had no way of quenching his desire. Lewis's early experiences with joy made him increasingly conscious over his school years of a duality in his life. There was his outer life of school and the hidden inner life in which his imagination reigned. He describes his story as a story of two distinct lives that "have nothing to do with each other: oil and vinegar, a river running beside a canal, Jekyll and Hyde."[18] The tension which came with trying to reconcile his romantic nature and the solely logical world of academics would be a constant source of struggle for Lewis until he found in his Christianity that which united his worlds and resolved the tension.

A second thing that moderated the bleakness of his early years for Lewis was the beginning and growth of his friendship with Arthur Greeves. Although the two lived near each other in Belfast, Lewis had rebuffed several overtures at friendship that Greeves had made. He finally accepted an invitation to visit Arthur who was confined at home recovering from an illness. The two became immediate friends when they found that they shared a zest for Northern mythology and that they both had known "the stab of joy." Lewis, later writing about friendship in *The Four Loves*, described true friendship as a deep and lasting relationship that is based on common interests, likes, and ideas that the friends share. In part, Lewis's description was based on the long and rich friendship that he and Greeves had known. It was through his friendship with Greeves that Lewis's interests broadened to include a love of landscapes, particularly the ordinary or "homely." Greeves, who eventually studied art in London, often walked with Lewis and talked about the landscapes that they were seeing. This must certainly account in part for Lewis's rich description of Aslan's singing forth the landscape of Narnia as well as the descriptions of the landscapes experienced by Ransom as he traveled to Malacandra and Perelandra in Lewis's space trilogy. Lewis also learned from Arthur to broaden his reading. Lewis admits that prior to his friendship with Greeves he had ignored the classic English novelists; with Arthur's encouragement, he began to read Bronte, Austen, and Walter Scott. While not a total replacement for all that he had lost, the friendship with Greeves was a key influence to come out of this period of Lewis's life.

Reason Leads to Rationalism

Lewis's period of loss and its surrounding despair and misery ended in 1914 when his father permitted his son to leave school and to begin studying with

William T. Kirkpatrick, Albert's own former tutor. Referred to as the "Great Knock" or simply "Knock" by both father and son, Kirkpatrick was as totally devoted to logic as a teacher could be and his methodology, an exaggerated Socratic dialogue by which he attempted to find truth and expose error was one to which Lewis immediately took. During his time with Kirkpatrick, Lewis developed both his thinking and his debating skills. He established patterns of thought and intellectual inquiry that he would continue to hone during his Oxford years.

Kirkpatrick did not introduce Lewis to logic and reason; he merely sharpened the skills that a young Lewis had learned from his parents. While with Kirkpatrick, Lewis rapidly advanced not only in language and literature skills, but also in his concern for his own logic and reason. He recalled with particular relish one of his tutor's comments, "When the man who had so long been engaged in exposing my vagueness at last cautioned me against the dangers of excessive subtlety."[19] While Kirkpatrick was influential in shaping Lewis's mind, he had no direct part in shaping Lewis's return to faith, for Kirkpatrick was an atheist. Kirkpatrick took Lewis no closer to the elusive joy for which he yearned, but he gave him an important foundation for his later belief. He taught Lewis that reason could never by itself bring one to truth, but that reason had to serve as the basis for any belief that was trustworthy and could rightly be defended. At the same time, Lewis's study with Kirkpatrick took him no farther from Christianity, for Lewis had lost that faith before he came to Great Bookham. Lewis did become more "reasonable" in the rejection of his childhood faith. Lewis also took on Kirkpatrick's materialism, giving up all ideas about the existence of the supernatural. Despite this he was confirmed in 1914 at the insistence of his father. Sure that his father would not understand or accept his views, Lewis went along with the confirmation although he was already an atheist.

The realism that Lewis learned under his tutor nurtured only one side of his nature. There was nothing of the Romantic or poetic in the training Lewis received at Great Bookham. That side of his nature Lewis satisfied with long walks in the countryside delighting in the "intricacy" of Surrey, a sharp contrast from his Ulster home haunts. He also continued his correspondence with Arthur, who, in his letters wrote of his concerns about Lewis's atheism. Lewis replied that his view of Christ was that he had existed but that all of the stories of miracles and the virgin birth were just like any other mythology in the world.[20] Beyond their discussions of Christianity, the two continued their search for the mythological in their study of the great Northern writers.

Experience Fosters Disillusionment

While Lewis had enjoyed the sharpening of his intellect and of his reasoning, he still longed for the Joy that he had earlier experienced. Lewis particularly hoped that in his study of the great Northern writers and composers he could again experience the Joy that they had earlier showered on him. However, he soon discovered that the study had robbed them of their influence. And in his determination to resurrect the stab he learned the fundamental paradox of Joy: "the very nature of Joy makes nonsense of our common distinction between having and wanting. There, to have is to want and to want is to have. Thus, the very moment when I longed to be so stabbed again, was itself such a stabbing."[21] The satisfaction is the desire, not the possession. What Lewis learned is that the human soul is otherworldly; it recognizes the lack inherent in its being but only by the outline of the fissure, never by what fills it. Like the sentimental saying, "Happiness is like a butterfly. You cannot snare it by trying, but turn your attention to other things, and it softly comes and lights on your shoulder," Lewis found that the harder he tried to get Joy back, the more elusive it became. However, it arrived unexpectedly when he was preoccupied with other matters. So Lewis maintained the separation of the mind and the spirit, a separation that was not mended by anything he had yet tried.

Lewis pursued joy in other places as well, returning to the occult, to which he had been introduced by the Matron at Cherbourg. He was led there by his reading of Yeats, a poet he had always enjoyed. From Yeats and the magic that he saw there, Lewis went on to investigate Spiritualism, and Pantheism, and Theosophy. He came again to a voracious appetite for things of the occult world. Nothing came of his interest, however, for Lewis describes himself as "protected first by ignorance and incapacity [. . .] also by cowardice; the reawakened terrors of childhood might add spice to my life as long as it was daylight."[22] As with everything else he pursued, the occult failed to produce the sought-after Joy.

Lewis, defended against all of Joy's counterfeits, met his match in the form of George MacDonald's *Phantastes, A Faerie Romance.* Here were the beloved elements of his favorite authors, Malory and Spenser, but infused with what Lewis called "holiness." He records that his "imagination was, in a certain sense, baptized."[23] Baptism, the physical sign of a new relationship to God, was exactly what happened to Lewis, for the Adversary had begun an active work in his life. Although Lewis accords only about ten pages to his war experiences, World War I, of course, played a part as well, no only because Lewis faced great destruction but also because he encountered Chesterton during a bout of trench fever. Finding in the writer an attractive goodness, Lewis unsuspectingly opened himself to spiritual truths argued by a sound dialectician. It was Chesterton's work in which Lewis saw God to be "unscrupulous."[24] He also formed a friendship with soldier with whom he could argue Theism and encounter a conscience, a conscience that confronted Lewis with the values he had often read about and embodied.

After the War, Lewis returned to Oxford, where as he studied Lewis worked to adopt an "intellectual new look."[25] He resolved to operate only according to "good sense," which included an intentional withdrawal from his romanticism. He did so because of several incidents in his life had caused him to perceive the romantic imaginative side of himself to be dangerous. He first had an encounter with an old Irish parson who though he had lost his faith, hypocritically kept his position in the church. The old man had a "ravenous desire for immortality,"[26] which led Lewis to abhor the whole concept of immortality. In a second experience he spent two weeks with a friend who was going mad. The man's horrible ravings, and Lewis's knowledge that his friend had dabbled in the same occult practices in which he had imbibed, seemed a warning to change his ways. Third, Lewis took up the new Psychology, which made it necessary to distinguish clearly between Imagination, Fancy, and Fantasy. Lewis pushed all of his past experiences into this philosophical mold and decided he was done with all of the romanticism of his past. Finally, in reading Bergson, Lewis came to hold a "stoical Monism" a philosophical perspective that accepted totally the necessity of the world's existence even if that world were essentially evil. He reduced Joy to what he called "an aesthetic experience," something that while "valuable" seldom occurred.

Lewis's Oxford years were the source of new friends as well as new ideas. Chief among the friends was Owen Barfield who proved to be Lewis's most dedicated friend. Lewis described Barfield as a "second friend," not like your first real friend who seems to be your alter ego, but a "man who disagrees with you about everything. [. . . Who] has read all the right books but has got the wrong thing out of every one."[27] The two men, both keen debaters, carried on through their correspondence "the Great War," an ongoing disputation about Anthroposophy, a system of early New Age-type ideas that Barfield had embraced. They debated intensely over many years. Through his friendship with Barfield, Lewis was forced to confront what his friend called the "chronological snobbery" in his thinking. This snobbery is the idea that whatever is passed or has gone out of date is false or somehow discredited. The temporocentricism that Lewis had practiced was a common position among intellectuals and academia, yet if Lewis was to be true to his own rationalism he could not make the overtly moral judgments and valuations that he commonly made.

Barfield's arguments forced Lewis to reject realism. In its place he embraced Idealism and the Aristotelian concept of the Absolute. Doing so permitted Lewis to "get all the conveniences of Theism without believing in God."[28] Lewis was two steps closer to conversion, though he did not realize it at the time. He had come to believe in necessary existence, and he now believed in an Absolute, if not in the God that he would come to know.

Redemption Produces Joy

When Lewis finished his degree, there were no teaching positions available at Oxford for which he qualified. With his father's assistance, Lewis remained for a fourth year to study English and improve his chances for a position. It was here he met Nevill Coghill who presented Lewis with a living, breathing, and brilliant Christian. Lewis was shocked to discover that this man whom he considered the most intelligent man in the class they shared was a Christian. The two often walked together and talked of literature, but it was the traits of Coghill's personal life that Lewis found particularly attractive.

Hard on the heels of this discovery was that all of his favorite authors—Spenser, Milton, Chesterton, and MacDonald—"were beginning to turn against" him.[29] Confronted by the excellence of these authors among others, especially George Herbert, Lewis recognized the depth of their ideas, and the lack of depth of those without religious slants, but was unwilling to explore the degree to which Christianity may have been responsible for that depth.

Lewis uses chapter fourteen, titled "Checkmate," of *Surprised by Joy* to describe his advancement to Christianity through a series of five events that he chronicles as chess moves by which the Creator captures him. Lewis counts as the first move his rereading of *Hippolytus*, by Euripides. Lewis states, "In one chorus all that world's end imagery I had rejected rose up before me."[30] By the next day he had thrown off his New Look and headed back into the land of romantic desire, his imagination rekindled. The second move of the adversary was intellectual and came through Lewis's reading of Alexander's *Space Time and Deity*. Alexander created a clear distinction between enjoyment and contemplation of what is enjoyed. Lewis recognized that one could not have both at the same time. He came to realize that he had been wrong in searching for Joy, and that it had been an impossible pursuit. Lewis came to the realization that the Joy that he had spent a lifetime recognizing, possessing, losing, and denying was not the thing that he wanted after all. That the longing for Joy was the main thing, the true significance of the emotion. He learned that Joy was merely an indication that "you want—I myself [Joy] am your want of—something other, outside, not you nor any state of you."[31]

This led to the third move, Lewis's recognition that this new notion of Joy fit with his philosophy of Idealism. Since our roots are in the Absolute we as mortals yearn to be reunited with the Absolute, and that Joy was rather than a deception, "the moments of clearest consciousness we had."[32]

The fourth move came during Lewis's teaching when he tried to explain to his students the notion of the Absolute that he now held. Lewis attempted, in his lecture, to make a distinction between a "philosophical 'God'" and "the God of popular religion." His distinctions crumbled as he read Chesterton's *Everlasting Man*. Chesterton, whom Lewis considered "the most sensible man alive 'apart from his Christianity,'" explained the story of Christianity in a way that made sense to Lewis. A comment made in conversation by the most cynical atheist Lewis knew that "all that stuff of Frazer's about the Dying God [. . .] It almost looks as if it had really happened once"[33] drove Lewis to carefully consider the evidence personally.

Lewis was aware that the facts required a choice, and the fifth move he describes is his moment of "wholly free choice."[34] He felt that he was shutting something out and that the choice was his, whether to open the door or to leave it closed. While he chose to open the door, he felt that not to open it would seem impossible; yet paradoxically, he still felt totally free in his choice. He describes himself as pursued by a pack of hounds; his closest friends were all part of the opposition, as were the authors he read. Lewis describes how he sat every night in his room at the college feeling the approach of a God that he had no desire to meet. It was at this point only a God who demanded his submission, who was absolute. Lewis finally bowed; "In the Trinity Term of 1929 I gave in, and admitted that God was God, and knelt and prayed: perhaps, that night, the most dejected and reluctant convert in all England."[35] The reader familiar with literature is reminded in these scenes of Francis Thompson's "Hound of Heaven."

This was, however, only a conversion to Theism, not to Christianity. To this point Lewis had only intellectually accepted the concept of God. He had recognized that there was a God, and believed that since he was God he deserved obedience. But Lewis had not yet met a personal God who had provided a way for his salvation, a fact he makes clear in the opening sentences of chapter fifteen. He also remarks that he began attending church, but only as a symbolic practice.[36] Lewis was a man who now believed in God, but who had to answer the question: Which religion was the right way to God? He continued to consider scripture, especially the gospels and felt that if ever "myth must have become fact; the Word flesh; God, Man." it was in the story of Jesus Christ.[37]

The actual event that moved Lewis toward Christianity came on September 19, 1931. After dining together Lewis and two good friends, Hugo Dyson and J. R. R. Tolkien, began to walk and talk. As they traversed Addison's Walk on the Magdalen College grounds, Lewis, in speaking about myths, told of his love for reading and studying them, but said he was sure they could not be true. Tolkien disagreed, sharing his belief that all myths originate from God, and thus reveal or reflect aspects of God's truth. Tolkien went on to explain his belief further describing Christianity as a myth that was true. He also described a God who is real, and whose dying can transform the lives of those who believe in Him. A gust of wind blew through the trees, and Lewis felt it a message from God.[38] The conversation forced Lewis back to the Gospels again to reconsider the story they told. He came to see that Christianity "is not a "religion," nor a "philosophy." It is the summing up and actuality of them all."[39]

The actual moment of Lewis's conversion is not one of great emotion; there were no fireworks, but like John, the character that he created for *Pilgrim's Regress,* Lewis came at last to the natural conclusion of the journey that had taken him far away from God to lead him at last to God. Lewis's belief in Christ came on September 22, 1931. He was riding in the sidecar of his brother's motorcycle on the way to the zoo. "When we set out I did not believe that Jesus Christ is the Son of God, and when we reached the zoo I did."[40]

And what of the joy Lewis sought? In the act of recognizing the insufficiency of himself and his own experience, he was prepared to accept that the source of Joy was God. And once he accepted the destination for which he likened Joy to be a signpost for travelers in the wood,[41] he no longer struggled to grasp it, for what he possessed was so much more satisfying. Joy became irrelevant; he lost most of his interest for it. In this sense at least, the title is rich with dual meaning: Lewis was surprised, pleasantly accosted, by Joy when he began his journey; but in the end, he is surprised, astonished by, the true nature of Joy as insufficient in itself, useful, but ultimately not the goal. Joy serves only as a temporary connection to the eternal, replaced by the fulfillment that accompanies being made whole as our relationship with God is begun. Lewis had like John in *Pilgrim's Regress* come full circle to find that what he desired was not at all what he thought he wanted, but something eternally more rich and fulfilling.

KEY CONCEPTS AND THEMES

There are several dominating concepts in the work that deserve special consideration; the first two are those of *Joy* and Imagination, which Lewis introduces in the first chapter of the book, detailing the start of his search before age six. However at that age, he only knew longing or *Sehnsucht,* the name he gives the desire as a scholar. As a child, the toy garden that his brother, Warnie, made awakens in Lewis the longing that was to lead him to Christianity by such a winding path. Lewis's treatment of *Sehnsucht* is inextricably linked with his search for Joy. But he discusses the concepts by way of Imagination first, defining the term in three distinct ways.

The first definition of Imagination is the concept that immediately comes to mind: the play of the mind, which creates alternate realities, or daydreams. In Lewis's case, as with many children, imagination took the form of enhanced persona, knights in shining armor, elegant gentlemen, and heroic actions. But then Lewis separates that almost universal kind of imagination from the imaginative activity associated with Animal-Land, the created kingdom that served as his apprenticeship in novel writing. In this way Lewis crafted an almost factual other world of talking beasts, the only part that he retained for Narnia. These strata of imagination were almost unrelated to what Lewis called the pinnacle of the quality. And it is this type of imagination that really drives the rest of Lewis's life and the autobiography that relates it. For the sources of this imagination, or the elements that best illustrate it in his life are all commonly denominated by this longing—the toy garden, the autumn created by Beatrix Potter, and the heroic poetry of Longfellow. Lewis is so intent upon the importance of this category of imagination that he tells the reader to stop reading if these three experiences do not awaken any interest in him or her. Elsewhere Lewis has commented on the commonality of certain experiences between humans, a commonality that quite often creates friendships between strangers. Thus, he invites the reader to evaluate his or her own life in response to the longing that Lewis is recounting. In this way, Lewis also invites the reader to satisfy that longing in the same way, through an encounter with Joy and its source.

Another key concept wound through *Surprised by Joy* is longing, the inevitable partner to joy and imagination. Longing. Almost everyone will admit to a desire for something, but many people will not admit readily to a desire for something unnameable or practically unknowable. Lewis, however, sees that very admission as the core of his conversion. It is the recognition that such a desire is incapable of being satisfied in this world that makes one open to a satisfaction from another. And it is the very elusive quality of that desire that makes it both easy to ignore and difficult to forget. Humans will try almost anything to squelch that desire and the memory of it, seeking satisfaction in people, places, and resources. Lewis's autobiography recounts such a seeking, first for a repetition of the prompting of that longing and then for the satisfaction of it and then for the silencing of it. For the longing was almost painful in its nature; he likens it to a stab, to an arrow of the adversary, a weapon of spiritual warfare that refuses to call a truce. Lewis's autobiography details the truth of Augustine's position that our hearts are restless until they find their rest in God, the same concept found in George Herbert's poem

"The Pulley," which details the drawing toward God of the soul constantly encountering dissatisfaction in life. Lewis's progress toward God was not the gentle motion of a pulley, but it was just as inexorable.

In *Till We Have Faces*, the main character, Orual, learns about inconsolable longing as well. Deprived of mother and fatherly affection, her home life is not unlike Lewis's own. And like Lewis she too finds solace in a sibling. Devoted to Psyche, Orual, delights in being tutored by the Fox, a grandfatherly figure who instills love of Greek culture and learning in her. Here, Orual is spared the early education ordeals of Lewis's own experience and spends her entire schooldays with the equivalent of the Great Knock, one of Lewis's most beloved teachers. But Orual fears the worship of Ungit, the fertility goddess of Glome. Her fears are vindicated when it is demanded that Psyche serve as an appeasing sacrifice. This loss of the most precious thing to her embitters Orual against the gods, a fact compounded by Psyche's own submission to the demand. Thus, Lewis sets up for Orual the conflict between reason and faith, a battle won by Psyche herself who embodies the *Sehnsucht*, which accounts for her willingness to embrace death, as she says, "The sweetest thing in all my life has been the longing—to reach the Mountain, to find the place where all the beauty came from ... my country, the place where I ought to have been born. Do you think it all meant nothing, all the longing? The longing for home? For indeed it now feels not like going, but going back. All my life the god of the Mountain has been wooing me."[42] This recognition of longing and its ultimate meaning is an action that culminates in godhood for her and redemption for Orual. Lewis must also lose his relationship with his brother and battle the reason inculcated in him by the Great Knock, but ironically finds that very rationalism a pathway to faith. As Lewis learns, the desire for Joy is actually the Joy itself, but it is irrevocably wrapped in loss. For Lewis as for Psyche and Orual, the path to Joy is through unsatisfied desire, itself the Joy.

Lewis addresses this desire for Joy in the essay "The Weight of Glory." Here he points out the truth that Joy transcends all the evidences of itself. "The books or the music in which we thought the beauty was located will betray us if we trust to them; it was not *in* them, it only came *through* them, and what came through them was longing. These things—the beauty, the memory of our own past—are good images of what we really desire; but if they are mistaken for the thing itself they turn into dumb idols, breaking the hearts of their worshippers. For they are not the thing itself."[43] Here Lewis, in 1941, recounts what he learned by 1929: trying to generate the stab of Joy is useless. For it lies not in the thing that arouses the longing; the longing is itself the Joy, the recognition that this world, this experience is not the ultimate satisfier. Though beautiful, the music of Wagner, the writing of the Norsemen, these all brought Joy though they themselves were not the entity itself. Lewis would eventually be driven to realize that Joy was only a "signpost" to God, an echo of another world that he was created to inhabit. Thus imagination fostered only the knowledge of a lack; that perception of the lack was the Joy, which the imagination existed to obtain. This to-and-fro-ness mirrors the division in Lewis's life, an outer life of books and studies and bloods and games; an inner life of beauty and desire and longing and lack.

To one who finishes the book, Lewis's warning in the preface seems more and more appropriate. One who has not felt the stab of Joy nor the longing to be wounded again would be sore pressed to see in the telling of Lewis's life more than events common to most: birth, death, schooling, job, and war. However, those who themselves will admit to being stabbed by Joy see the plan of "the Adversary" as Lewis terms Him, who is in reality the Friend of Sinners, both of author and reader alike. C. S. Lewis's autobiography *Surprised by Joy* answered the demand of readers for an account of his life and conversion. Unfortunately, for many readers it detailed the essence of the man himself, not the individual incidents many were curious about. Yet, it is the essence of a person that drives the choices he or she makes or his or her reactions to events beyond their choice. And in this, Lewis wrote the ultimate autobiography, for his work, which he admitted from the start, was not the tell-all book some wanted; instead it was the account of his conversion to Christianity, both a response to events in his life and a choice that he made. And it was this choice that served as the impetus for the majority of his work in scholarship, apologetics, and children's writing. In 2000, *Christian Reader* compiled a list of the ten best biographies or autobiographies of the twentieth century. *Surprised by Joy* tied for the top position. What more eloquent statement of the continuing value for contemporary readers could there be? *Surprised by Joy* will continue to surprise those who read in its pages the story of Lewis's successful search for joy found where he least expected it.

ADDITIONAL READING

One excellent resource for contextualizing the events Lewis touches on in *Surprised by Joy* is *The Most Reluctant Convert* by David Downing. Published in 2002, Downing's book provides an in-depth treatment of Lewis's life from the time he left home until his conversion. Downing offers complete chapters on Lewis's years of study with Kirkpatrick, his war years, and his years as a student at Oxford. In each chapter Downing seeks to trace those elements in Lewis's intellectual struggle that served to create the man who was to become one of the twentieth-century's most successful Christian apologists. Derrick Bingham's 2004 biography of Lewis, *A Shiver of Wonder*, is another recent work. More concerned with the story of Lewis's life than with merely the story of his conversion, Bingham divides his book about equally on the period up to Lewis's conversion and his life after 1931. Because he chooses to focus on Lewis as an evangelist, the volume lacks critical evaluations of Lewis's works. It does offer an intriguing list of well-known people, ranging from Margaret Thatcher to Tom Monaghan the founder of Domino's Pizza, whose lives have been touched by Lewis or his books.

More singular in its focus than Downing's biography is Alan Jacobs's *The Narnian*, a 2005 publication. Its intent is, according to the author, to "write the story of the life of a mind, the story of an imagination."[44] Jacobs considers the unique blend of morality and imagination that characterizes Lewis's works, especially his Narnia stories, to be the distinctive mark of Lewis's genius. There are several older biographies that are also especially valuable. *C. S. Lewis: A Biography* by Roger L. Green and Walter Hooper is the best overall biographical resource, although even with its 1987 revision the book is dated. Kathryn Lindskoog's *C. S. Lewis: Mere Christian*, 1988, and *C. S. Lewis* by Margaret Hannay, 1981, offer more than biographical material; readers will find both valuable overviews and thought-provoking evaluations of Lewis's major works. For those interested in other's impressions of Lewis, *C. S. Lewis at the Breakfast Table*, edited by James C. Como offers remembrances from both friends and former colleagues at Oxford and Cambridge.

For those who prefer to investigate primary sources, there are several options available. Walter Hooper has edited Lewis's diaries from 1922 to 1927 and they have been published with the title *All My Road before Me*. The book permits the reader to gain a glimpse into Lewis's everyday life and to a lesser degree into his thoughts. Another interesting volume, also edited by Walter Hooper, is *They Stand Together: The Letters of C. S. Lewis to Arthur Greeves*. This book covers experiences, thoughts, and feelings that Lewis shared with his friend during their forty-nine years of correspondence, and provides the reader with additional insights into Lewis's thinking. Another particularly rich source is *Letters of C. S. Lewis*, edited by his brother, Warren. The broad range of years covered and the wide scope of Lewis's correspondents permits candid views of his personal life and allows the reader to follow Lewis's spiritual growth through the years. Hooper has also edited a three-volume series, arranged chronologically, titled *The Complete Letters of C. S. Lewis*, published in 2007.

The two strongest volumes covering Lewis's literary criticism are Bruce L. Edwards *A Rhetoric of Reading: C. S. Lewis's Defense of Western Literacy*, 1986, and *The Taste of the Pineapple*, a collection of fourteen essays that merge consideration of Lewis's critical values and fictional principles, which Edwards edited. Although somewhat difficult to find, *The Taste of the Pineapple* is worth seeking out. Peter Schakel's *Reason and Imagination in C. S. Lewis: A Study of*

Till We Have Faces offers readers an in-depth critical interpretation of Lewis's last and most difficult fiction work. *Planets in Peril*, by David C. Downing, presents a critical study focused on the Ransom or space trilogy. Two other works by Bruce Edwards, both published in 2005, focus on the Narnian tales, *Further Up and Further In*, and *Not a Tame Lion*, and their relationship to Lewis's spiritual journey.

NOTES

1. Owen Barfield, introduction to *The Taste of the Pineapple*, ed. Bruce L. Edwards (Bowling Green, OH: Bowling Green State University Popular Press, 1988), 1.

2. C. S. Lewis, *Surprised by Joy* (New York: Harcourt, 1955), viii.

3. Lewis, *Surprised*, 197.

4. Bruce L. Edwards, "*Surprised by Joy* by C. S. Lewis: A Critical Summary and Overview" http://personal.bgsu.edu/˜edwards/surprised.html (accessed July 30, 2006).

5. Lewis, *Surprised*, 237.

6. Edwards, "*Surprised*," 2.

7. Lewis, *Surprised*, 4.

8. Ibid., viii.

9. Ibid., 5

10. Edwards, "*Surprised*," 5.

11. John Bremer, "Clive Staples Lewis 1898–1963: A Brief Biography," in *The C. S. Lewis Readers' Encyclopedia*, eds. Jeffrey D. Schultz and John G. West, Jr. (Grand Rapids, MI: Eerdmans, 1998), 24.

12. Lewis, *Surprised*, 19.

13. Ibid., 59.

14. Ibid., 70.

15. Ibid., 68.

16. Ibid., 126.

17. Ibid., 16.

18. Ibid., 119.

19. Ibid., 137.

20. C. S. Lewis, *The Letters of C. S. Lewis to Arthur Greeves (1913–1963)*, ed. Walter Hooper. (New York: MacMillan, 1979), 137–138.

21. Ibid.

22. Lewis, *Surprised*, 176.

23. Ibid., 181.

24. Ibid., 191.

25. Ibid., 201.

26. Ibid., 202.

27. Ibid., 199.

28. Ibid., 209.

29. Ibid., 213.

30. Ibid., 217.

31. Ibid., 221.

32. Ibid., 222.

33. Ibid., 224

34. Ibid., 224.

35. Ibid., 228–229.

36. Ibid., 234.

37. Ibid., 236.

38. Derrick Bingham, *A Shiver of Wonder* (Greenville, SC: Ambassador Emerald International, 2004), 127–128.

39. Lewis, *Surprised*, 236.

40. Ibid., 237.

41. Ibid., 238.

42. C. S. Lewis, *Till We Have Faces: A Myth Retold* (New York: Harcourt, 1956), 75–76.

43. C. S. Lewis, *The Weight of Glory and Other Addresses* (Grand Rapids, MI: William B. Eerdmans, 1965), 5.

44. Alan Jacobs, *The Narnian: The Life and Imagination of C.S. Lewis* (San Francisco: Harper, 2005), ix.

BIBLIOGRAPHY

Barfield, Owen. "Preface." *in The Taste of the Pineapple*. Edited by Bruce L. Edwards, Bowling Green, OH: Bowling Green State University Popular Press, 1988, 1–2.

Bingham, Derrick. *A Shiver of Wonder*. Greenville, SC: Ambassador Emerald International, 2004.

Bremer, John. "Clive Staples Lewis, 1898–1963: A Brief Biography." In *The C. S. Lewis Reader's Encyclopedia*. Edited by Jeffrey D. Schultz, and John G. West, Jr. Grand Rapids, MI: Zondervan, 1998, 9–65.

Carnell, Corbin Scott. *Bright Shadow of Reality: C. S. Lewis and the Feeling Intellect*. Grand Rapids, MI: Eerdmans, 1974.

Christopher, Joe R. *C. S. Lewis*. Boston, MA: Twayne, 1987.

Coren, Michael. *The Man Who Created Narnia: The Story of C. S. Lewis*. Grand Rapids, MI: Eerdmans, 1996.

Dorsett, Lyle W. *And God Came In*. Wheaton, IL: Harold Shaw Publisher, 1998.

Downing, David. *The Most Reluctant Convert: C. S. Lewis's Journey to Faith*. Downer's Grove, IL: IVP, 2002.

Duriez, Colin. *Tolkein and Lewis: The Gift of Friendship*. Mahwah, NJ: Hidden Spring, 2003.

Edwards, Bruce L. *"Surprised by Joy* by C. S. Lewis: A Critical Summary and Overview." http://personal.bgsu.edu/~edwards/surprised.html (last accessed July 30, 2006).

Gibb, Jocelyn. Editor. *Light on C. S. Lewis*. New York: Harcourt Brace, 1965.

Green, Roger Lancelyn, and Walter Hooper. *C. S. Lewis: A Biography.* New York: HBJ, 1974.

Jacobs, Alan. *The Narnian: The Life and Imagination of C.S. Lewis*. San Francisco: Harper 2005.

Lewis, C. S. *The Letters of C. S. Lewis to Arthur Greeves (1913–1963)*. Edited by Walter Hooper. New York: MacMillan, 1979.

————. *The Pilgrim's Regress: An Allegorical Apology for Christianity Reason and Romanticism*. Grand Rapids, MI: William B. Eerdmans, 1992.

————. *Surprised by Joy: The Shape of My Early Life*. New York: Harcourt, 1955.

————. *Till We Have Faces: A Myth Retold*. New York: Harcourt, 1956.

————. *The Weight of Glory and Other Addresses*. Grand Rapids, MI: William B. Eerdmans, 1965.

Lewis, W. H. Editor. *Letters of C. S. Lewis*. New York: Harcourt Brace, 1966.

Lindskoog, Kathryn. *C. S. Lewis: Mere Christian*. Chicago, IL: Cornerstone Press, 1997.

Myers, Doris T. *C. S. Lewis in Context*. Kent, OH: Kent State University Press, 1994.

Smallwood, Julie. *Out From Exile: C. S. Lewis and the Journey to Joy A Comparative Study of* "Surprised by Joy" *and* "Till We Have Faces." Master's thesis, Bowling Green State University, 1999.

Smith, Robert H. *Patches of Godlight: The Pattern of Thought of C. S. Lewis*. Athens, GA: University of Georgia Press, 1981.

Walsh, Chad. *The Literary Legacy of C. S. Lewis*. New York: Harcourt Brace, 1979.

White, Michael. *C. S. Lewis: Creator of Narnia*. New York: Carroll & Graf, 2005.

12

"Gifted Amateurs": C. S. Lewis and the Inklings

David Bratman

INTRODUCTION

Warren Lewis, C. S. Lewis's brother, finding that the Inklings had "already passed into literary legend," felt obliged to explain the group's nature in the memoir published in his 1966 prefaced to the edition of his brother's *Letters*:

Properly speaking it was neither a club nor a literary society, though it partook of the nature of both. There were no rules, officers, agendas, or formal elections—unless one counts it as a rule that we met in Jack [C. S. Lewis]'s rooms at Magdalen [College, Oxford] every Thursday evening after dinner. . . . The ritual of an Inklings was unvarying. When half a dozen or so had arrived, tea would be produced, and then when pipes were well alight Jack would say, "Well, has nobody got anything to read us?" Out would come a manuscript, and we would settle down to sit in judgement upon it—real unbiased judgement, too, since we were no mutual admiration society: praise for good work was unstinted, but censure for bad work—or even not-so-good work—was often brutally frank.[1]

He emphasizes, then, the Inklings as what would now be called a writers' circle: a literary society for the purpose of critiquing, rather than just listening to, manuscripts, but with the informality of a club. With the rise of interest in the works first of C. S. Lewis, then those of his colleagues in the Inklings, an awareness of this club has led to a natural curiosity among readers and scholars about it, its effect on their work, and the manner of men who were part of it. For the choice of members was important, as Warren Lewis emphasizes: "From time to time we added to our original number, but without formalities: someone would suggest that Jones be asked to come in on a Thursday, and there could be either general agreement, or else a perceptible lack of enthusiasm and a dropping of the matter. Usually there was agreement, since we all knew the type of man we wanted or did not want."[2]

C. S. Lewis shared his brother's taste for a particular type of man. He once expressed a longing "for the people who speak one's own language,"[3] and in his book *The Four Loves* he elaborates on the meaning of true friendship:

Two friends delight to be joined by a third, and three by a fourth, if only the newcomer is qualified to become a real friend. . . . Friendship arises out of mere Companionship when two or more of the companions discover that they have in common some insight or interest or even taste which the others do not share and which, till that moment, each believed to be his own unique treasure (or burden). The typical expression of opening Friendship would be something like, "What? You too? I thought I was the only one."[4]

This discovery of friendship, and its expression through sharing their writings, was the root and heart of the Inklings. The Inklings told stories, and they themselves are best explained in the form of a story, one that begins with a series of friendships. We will find out more about the nature of the men involved as the story proceeds. What stands out for most of us who encounter the background behind their remarkable journey together is that the very thing that pleased them and their readers the most, their penchant for creating wonderful mythic landscapes, was something at which they were complete amateurs. But what gifted "amateurs" they were . . . .

***

During the 1920s, C. S. Lewis made a lot of friends. Not an unusual thing for a young man in his twenties, at first a student and then a young don at the University of Oxford. What struck Lewis as unusual about his friendships was that he was a professed atheist but his friends were Christians. Of one of them, Nevill Coghill, Lewis later wrote:

I soon had the shock of discovering that he—clearly the most intelligent and best-informed man in that class—was a Christian and a thorough-going supernaturalist. There were other traits that I liked but found (for I was still very much a modern) oddly archaic; chivalry, honor, courtesy, "freedom," and "gentillesse." One could imagine him fighting a duel. He spoke much "ribaldry" but never "villeinye." . . . Had something really dropped out of our lives? Was the archaic simply the civilized, and the modern simply the barbaric?[5]

Lewis met Coghill, a theatrically inclined scion of the Irish landed aristocracy, in an English discussion class they took together in early 1923.[6] About seven years later, after they'd both become members of the Oxford English faculty, Coghill introduced Lewis to his friend from undergraduate days, Hugo Dyson. Dyson was a man of quicksilver wit.[7] Lewis was delighted to know him and arranged more meetings: "Having met him once I liked him so well that I determined to get to know him better. . . . How we roared and fooled at times in the silence of last night—but always in a few minutes buckled to again with renewed seriousness."[8] Dyson was teaching at the University of Reading, thirty miles away, but he was often in Oxford, and Lewis occasionally visited him in Reading.

By this time, all three of them had gotten to know J. R. R. Tolkien. Back in 1920, Tolkien was an alumnus of Oxford's Exeter College then writing definitions for the *Oxford English Dictionary*. Coghill, then an undergraduate and secretary of the college Essay Club, had asked Tolkien to read a paper to the club. What the puzzled but interested audience got from Tolkien was a strange warlike mythological story called "The Fall of Gondolin."[9] Coghill and Dyson in particular must have found something recognizable in this description from their fellow veteran of the recent World War:

But now Gothmog lord of Balrogs, captain of the hosts of Melko, took counsel and gathered all his things of iron that could coil themselves around and above all obstacles before them. . . . Then the engines and the catapults of the king poured darts and boulders and molten metals on those ruthless beasts, and their hollow bellies clanged beneath the buffeting, yet it availed not for they might not be broken, and the fires rolled off them. Then were the topmost opened about their middles, and an innumerable host of the Orcs, the goblins of hatred, poured therefrom into the breach; and who shall tell of the gleam of their scimitars or the flash of the broad-bladed spears with which they stabbed?[10]

Soon afterwards, Tolkien had left Oxford to teach at the University of Leeds, but by 1926 he was back in Oxford, newly appointed Professor of Anglo-Saxon. Lewis, newly appointed English tutor at Magdalen College, first spoke with him at any length at a faculty tea at Merton College on May 11, 1926. At first Lewis was not favorably impressed. "No harm in him," he wrote in his diary, "only needs a smack or so."[11] But soon events were to bring them closer together.

Lewis was on the "literature" side of the English faculty, but Tolkien wanted to promote the "language" side of the curriculum, and specifically Old Norse, which fell under the English faculty's purview. So Tolkien did a very Oxfordian, and very Tolkienian, thing: he founded a faculty club. He called it the Kolbítar or Coalbiters, after the Icelandic term for men who huddled so close to the fire that they seemed to bite the coals. Its purpose was to read Icelandic sagas and myths aloud. A variety of dons with an interest in these subjects joined in, though none knew the language as well as Tolkien did. Coghill was a member from the club's founding in early 1926. Lewis, who had a piercing love for what he called "the Northernness," was invited to join probably that fall.[12] Gradually, Lewis came around to Tolkien's view of the curriculum, and by the next year they also had become close friends. Their shared love of fairy tales and Norse myth, and their equally abundant creativity, were the keys. Lewis told his childhood friend Arthur Greeves that Tolkien was "the one man absolutely fitted, if fate had allowed, to be a third in our friendship in the old days, for he also grew up on W[illiam] Morris and George Macdonald." On another occasion Lewis went further in describing Tolkien to Greeves: "In fact he *is*, in one part of him, what we were."[13]

Tolkien was not only a philologist, but also a practicing Catholic. Lewis later said that he had been warned against both, but this friendship "marked the breakdown of two old prejudices."[14] Not only did Tolkien's mythological interests help turn Lewis to the language side, they helped turn him to Christianity. On Saturday, September 19, 1931, both Tolkien and Dyson were Lewis's guests for dinner at Magdalen. After the meal, the three walked along the path through Magdalen's river grounds, discussing myth and Christianity late into the night. Tolkien believed so strongly in the truth to be found in myth, and in Christianity as myth become fact, that he wrote a 148-line poem outlining the argument he and Lewis had had that evening. He called it *Mythopoeia* and addressed it to "Misomythus," hater of myths.[15]

Lewis was quickly ceasing to be Misomythus. The example of his Christian friends, the richness he was finding in Christian literature, and the force of rational arguments for religion had already led him to declare himself a theist. He thought over Tolkien's points, which Dyson had reinforced in his own way, and about a week later suddenly realized that he believed in Christ. "The immediate human causes of my own conversion," he called Tolkien and Dyson years later.[16]

By this time, Lewis and Tolkien were meeting frequently and regularly. "It has also become a regular custom," he wrote that November, "that Tolkien should drop in on me of a Monday morning and drink a glass. This is one of the pleasantest spots of the week."[17] Tolkien had also begun showing Lewis his creative writings. Despite his having read "The Fall of Gondolin" to the Exeter College Essay Club, Tolkien tended to keep to himself the massive private mythology he'd been constructing since the war in the form of myths, stories, epic and pastoral verse, chronologies, cosmologies, and mock histories. Very few friends saw any of it. But Lewis was one who did. Some time probably in November of 1929, the two of them stayed up late in Lewis's rooms at Magdalen talking of Norse mythology after a meeting of a society—not the Coalbiters, but some other one we know nothing of, because this was a Monday and the Coalbiters were then meeting on Wednesdays. "Who cd. turn him out," Lewis asked rhetorically, "for the fire was bright and the talk good?"[18] It might have been on this occasion, or at most a few weeks later—for Lewis wrote back to him about it on 7 December—that Tolkien lent Lewis his uncompleted epic poem, *The Lay of Leithian*. Lewis responded positively as a reader to the poem: "I can quite honestly say that it is ages since I have had an evening of such delight: and the personal interest of reading a friend's work had very little to do with it—I should have enjoyed it just as well if I'd picked it up in a bookshop, by an unknown author."[19] Not only that, he went on later to write a massive critique of it, framed in a gently humorous manner as the textual speculations of imaginary scholars studying the work as if it were a real medieval text. His judgments cover the spectrum. "Let any one believe if he can that our author gave such cacophony," he writes of one passage, and "The description of Lúthien has been too often and too justly praised to encourage the mere commentator in intruding" of another.[20] Diana Pavlac Glyer has analyzed how seriously Tolkien took this critique and how many of Lewis's suggestions he incorporated into the poem.[21]

Tolkien and Lewis took seriously their interest in sharing creative work. Some time in the early 1930s they accepted the invitation of an undergraduate named E. Tangye Lean to join a literary club he was forming at University College. Lean was, Tolkien explained, "more aware than most undergraduates of the impermanence of their clubs and fashions, and had an ambition to found a club that would prove more lasting." He hoped that having some faculty members would lend it stability. In the end, Tolkien recalled, "the club lasted the usual year or two of undergraduate societies," and soon "only [Lewis] and I were left of it." But while it lasted, the club fulfilled its purpose of reading aloud "unpublished poems or short tales," including Tolkien's poem *Errantry*. Lean called his club the Inklings.[22]

Upon or after its demise—which must have been at the time of Lean's graduation in 1933, or perhaps it was earlier, nobody knows for sure—"its name was then transferred (by C. S. L.) to the undetermined and unelected circle of friends who gathered about C. S. L., and met in his rooms in Magdalen."[23] These friends, the Inklings that we know, included Tolkien, Coghill, Dyson, and others whom Lewis had accumulated as friends over the years. They were not only all Christians, and mostly Oxford dons and lovers of myth, they were all poets—Coghill had a knack for doggerel and satirical verse, though years later he disclaimed any talent for poetry; and even Dyson, who talked a lot but wrote virtually nothing, once penned a detailed and allusion-filled pastiche of his scholarly specialty, Alexander Pope.[24] Adam Fox also became an Inkling. He had become the dean of divinity at Magdalen in 1929 and gravitated towards Lewis with whom he sat at breakfast in hall after morning services in the college chapel.[25] Fox too was a poet, whose major work would be a four-part narrative poem titled *Old King Coel.*

And so was Owen Barfield, one of Lewis's earliest college friends. They'd met in 1919, and throughout the 1920s they'd constantly visited, written each other letters about poetry and philosophical matters, and shared their poetry for intense mutual criticism, much less tactfully phrased than Lewis's gentle handling of Tolkien. In 1930 Barfield had moved to London to take up a career as a lawyer, putting his other interests mostly into abeyance for some years, but he and Lewis stayed close friends and visited each other when they could. They and some mutual friends of similar vintage took a long multiday walk every spring and called themselves the Cretaceous Perambulators. Most of the other Perambulators were not academically minded and none besides Lewis and Barfield are known to have attended Inklings, though occasionally an Inkling would walk with them.[26] Barfield later recalled that during the later 1920s he'd met with Lewis, Tolkien, and sometimes other dons, occasions he concluded were the "foregatherings that ultimately turned into the Inklings."[27] No known record of these survives, in Lewis's diary or anywhere else.

The fact is that we don't know how the Inklings began. It was a very "informal club"[28] that never kept a minute book. Our only sources are the diaries, letters, and later recollections of those who were there. Diaries and letters are not always written consistently and may not mention their authors' social lives, and recollections usually come without exact dates and are subject to the vagaries of memory. The Inklings as a group emerge into the full light of day only when the attendees had reason to mention meetings regularly. And the period of their formation in the early 1930s is one of the least documented. As a result, our knowledge of Inklings history is fitful and often misleading—flashes of light amid darkness.

Even the Inklings weren't sure how their club began. Lewis never said, so far as we know. Tolkien, though he traced the name to Lean's club, also emphasized that the group of friends "and its habit [of reading compositions aloud] would in fact have come into being at that time, whether the original short-lived club had ever existed or not."[29] Coghill, as one of the Coalbiters, unsurprisingly assumed that the Inklings grew out of that group, which after reading its way through the Icelandic canon quietly dissolved some time in the early 1930s.[30]

Scholars, too, are uncertain. One writer, Andrew Lazo, has argued for the Coalbiters' importance as a crucible for the Inklings.[31] The leading scholarly historian of the Inklings, Humphrey Carpenter, says that "the nucleus of the

Inklings when that group began to meet" was a circle consisting of the dons who'd supported Tolkien and Lewis in the curriculum dispute. It held dinner meetings called Caves.[32] Coghill attended the Caves; so did Dyson, who wasn't even an Oxford don at the time. But the Caves also included many dons who did not become Inklings, including even some women. No woman ever crossed the threshold of an Inklings meeting. Dorothy L. Sayers is often put in the list of Inklings. But though Lewis called her a friend, he also stated categorically: "Needless to say, she never met our own club, and probably never knew of its existence."[33] The opening phrase is interesting; why is it "needless to say" it? Lewis was not afraid of intellectual and formidable women—he married one, befriended others, and participated with yet more in faculty activities and formal clubs such as the Oxford Socratic Club—but the Inklings was an informal club of friends rather than a formal society of colleagues, and it was simply not the custom in the Inklings' time and place for the sexes to mix socially in friendships of such intimacy.[34]

What all these identifications of the seed or seeds of the Inklings have in common—the Monday morning glass, the sharing of *The Lay of Leithian*, the Christianity, the love of myth and the North, the Coalbiters, the Caves, the Tangye Lean Inklings—is that they all put the interaction between Lewis and Tolkien at the heart of the Inklings' beginning.

This makes sense because both Lewis and Tolkien were very clubbable men. Lewis thrived on an active social life: in his undergraduate years he'd been active in a venerable University College literary society, The Martlets; he hiked and conversed with the Cretaceous Perambulators; he was President of the Socratic Club; he held "Beer and Beowulf" evenings to entice his students into learning Old English verse; he and Hugo Dyson formed a dining club with some of their students. Even Lewis's solo friendships he tended to think of as potential social groups, as when he wishes that Tolkien could have joined him and Greeves in their childhood friendship. In *The Four Loves* he elevates this to a principle: "In each of my friends there is something that only some other friend can fully bring out. By myself I am not large enough to call the whole man into activity; I want other lights than my own to show all his facets. . . . We possess each friend not less but more as the number of those with whom we share him increases." And he cites the Inklings as an example of this.[35]

Tolkien, though a much more private (even hermetic) creative artist than Lewis, and more in need of intimate solo friendships, was equally attached to a social life among groups of friends. At school he had been part of a close-knit group of four creative and imaginative boys who sparked his desire to be a poet; as an undergraduate he, like Lewis, had belonged to college clubs and founded one of his own; as a young lecturer, he, like Lewis, had organized social gatherings with students to facilitate learning, and produced creative writing in that context; as a new don at Oxford he founded the Coalbiters.

But though the interaction between Lewis and Tolkien seems to have generated the Inklings, there seems little doubt that the friends were mostly Lewis's when they weren't friends of both, and that Lewis was the driving engine behind the group. Tolkien testifies as much: "C. S. L. had a passion for hearing things read aloud, a power of memory for things received in that way, and also a facility in extempore criticism, none of which were shared (especially not the last) in anything like the same degree by his friends."[36]

But the frequent statement that the Inklings were primarily a group of Lewis's friends, who convened at his behest, should not mislead into a conclusion that Lewis was necessarily the central figure of the group. The Inklings were a conversation that developed from a conversation between Lewis and Tolkien, and, though Lewis could be overbearing in debate, in conversation he refused to dominate. "The steady flow of ideas" among Lewis and his friends at a pub, visitor Chad Walsh later reported, "is not a one-way traffic. Lewis is as good a listener as talker, and has alert curiosity about almost anything conceivable."[37] As he wanted his tutorial students to stand up and argue back to him, he wanted his friends to do the same. The other Inklings were not satellites or wallflowers, or in any way shy or subordinate to Lewis. Tolkien was already a noted scholar of early English literature. Barfield would develop into one of the most significant linguistic philosophers of his day. Coghill was a charismatic figure who would soon become Oxford's most renowned theatrical director (an interest which, as it took up more of his time, took him away from meetings of the Inklings but not from his friendships with them). And Dyson famously could outtalk almost anybody.

Some Inklings did consider Lewis the center of the group. But "Lewis himself always pictures [Charles] Williams in that position," reports scholar Charles Moorman from their correspondence. "The importance of [Williams's] presence," Lewis elaborates, "was, indeed, chiefly made clear by the gap which was left on the rare occasions when he did not turn up. It then became clear that some principle of liveliness and cohesion had been withdrawn from the whole party: lacking him, we did not completely possess one another."[38] Some scholars, such as Robert J. Reilly and Verlyn Flieger, have emphasized the importance of Barfield, "because I believe," says Reilly, "that many of the romantic notions common to the members of the group exist in their most basic and radical form in his work."[39] He is "the less known, less popular, but most influential of all," says Flieger.[40] Barfield's influence on Lewis is well known; his influence on Tolkien is the subject of Flieger's study *Splintered Light*. Tolkien himself testified to this, as Lewis reported it to Barfield: "You might like to know that when Tolkien dined with me the other night he said *à propos* of something quite different that your conception of the ancient semantic unity had modified his whole outlook . . . 'It is one of those things,' he said, 'that when you've once seen it there are all sorts of things you can never say again.' "[41]

But if Barfield's work was an intellectual fount for the Inklings, his person was more rarely seen. "Certainly during most of the time during which the Inklings were meeting," he recalled, "I was only really on the fringe of them because I could very rarely attend."[42] A modest discounting of one's own significance was not unknown among the Inklings. Tolkien's accounts of the group's origins imply nothing of his own importance. Colin Hardie, a regular attendee in later years, would only admit that he "was an 'Inkling' of sorts, though only on the fringe of that informal group."[43]

In such a context, and with such a paucity of primary sources, one thing may be said for certain about the origin of the Inklings: it, and the other clubs such as the Coalbiters and the University College Inklings, existed in a context of incessant social activity among these young men. Many of the Inklings, as we have seen, had been friends for years, even over a decade, before the club came into existence. And other activities continued through the Inklings years. This included academic work. Lewis taught separate informal classes in collaboration with Tolkien, Coghill, and Fox at various times in the 1930s, for example. Lewis had his dining club with Dyson in the late 1940s; several Inklings spoke at the Socratic Club or belonged to the Oxford University Dante Society. Tolkien and Dyson, as fellow alumni of Exeter, hosted a private dinner there on July 26, 1933, to which they invited several fellow Inklings. It was "an excellent dinner" and "a thoroughly enjoyable evening," according to Warren Lewis. Afterward several of the party walked to Magdalen "where we strolled in the grove, where the deer were flitting about in the twilight— Tolkien swept off his hat to them and remarked, 'Hail fellow well met.' "[44] On the social context in which the Inklings met, I have written:

> In general when reading of the Inklings-to-be in the late 1920s and early 1930s, I am struck by the amount of activity in their social lives, the intensity and exuberance and fun of it all. In this they contrast with the often equally enjoyable but more subdued middle-aged Inklings of the post-World War II period. In the later period the pleasure was like a fine whiskey, not necessarily rare but to be savored, while in the earlier period it flowed like wine without a hint of melancholy.[45]

For this reason, it is probably both futile and misleading to try to fix on a single origin for the Inklings. Individual Inklings may have identified particular series of previous meetings as the seed of the club, but they disagree as to which it was, and none of them point to any particular meeting or incident as the birth of the club. This is interesting because it contrasts so startlingly with Lewis's specificity on other events, including the incidents that led to and formed his religious conversion. If the Inklings had been formed as a kind of intellectual revival meeting, somebody would have said so. One can apply to the formation of the Inklings Michael P. Farrell's comment on something that *was* an intellectual revival meeting, the early feminists' calling of the Seneca Falls Convention in 1848: "Like many circles in the early stages of development, at this point no one cared who had the idea first. Ideas emerged out of the dynamics of the interaction."[46]

Many of the best Inklings scholars, such as Carpenter and Glyer, are the most cautious about postulating the actual process by which the Inklings formed. Carpenter indeed cautions: "There is no record of precisely when" the Inklings formed, "if indeed it was a precise event and not a gradual process."[47] Tolkien's account does not establish exactly when the undergraduate club died, not does his phrasing make clear whether the Lewis circle already existed. This has not prevented other writers from proceeding boldly through the darkness. Colin Duriez, for instance, states flatly, "The fall term of that year [1933] marked the beginning of Lewis's convening of a circle of friends dubbed 'the Inklings.'"[48] George Sayer, in his generally admirable biography of Lewis, similarly states that "that autumn [1933] Jack first used the name the Inklings to describe the group that had already begun to meet in his rooms."[49] So though Duriez and Sayer agree on a rough date (which they evidently derive from Tolkien, with a certainty not attributable to this source), they disagree about whether the Inklings already existed and on whether it was formally convened by Lewis or just grew without a gavel being struck.

Sayer continues on his next page with a slightly contradictory story. Here he says that a duo of Lewis and Tolkien founded in 1929 "became a trio in 1933 by the addition of" Warren Lewis, and that "in 1934, Hugo Dyson and Dr. Robert E. Havard made it a group."[50] This sounds precise, but Sayer provides no evidence for these particular people gathering at these specific dates in this exact order.

Certainly 1933 was about the time that Warren Lewis became available to participate in the Inklings. After nineteen years in the Royal Army, he retired in December 1932 and came to live with his brother in Oxford. The closeness of the two brothers, so fundamental to their lives that it may easily be overlooked, dated back to their earliest childhoods, but this was the date at which they came permanently to live together as adults. But if Warren did join the Inklings at this time, it is curious that he makes no mention of the group in the diary that he kept regularly through 1933 and 1934, though it is full of references to seeing Barfield, Dyson, and Tolkien individually. Possibly Sayer is thinking of an occasion in early 1934 when the Lewis brothers and Tolkien spent an evening at Magdalen reading aloud the libretto of Richard Wagner's *Die Walküre*, Tolkien and C. S. Lewis in the original German, Warren Lewis in English translation. This was in preparation for an intended trip to a performance of Wagner's entire *Ring* cycle at Covent Garden, London, that summer in company with Owen Barfield and Cecil Harwood of the Cretaceous Perambulators.[51]

Whether or not he was an Inkling this early, or whether there was an Inklings to belong to at this time, Warren Lewis became another central figure in the group. If his brother was the gatekeeper,[52] Warren was the host. He "stays in my memory," one Inkling recalled, "as the most courteous [man] I have ever met—not with mere politeness, but with a genial, self-forgetful considerateness that was as instinctive to him as breathing."[53] Warren Lewis was a bit unusual among the Inklings: a military man, not in any way an academic, with no personal connection to the university, and not a poet beyond a few pieces of doggerel verse, he was nevertheless a Christian who'd returned to the church at about the same time his brother did, and he was learned in his own way. Though he did not at that time consider himself a writer, he spent the first few years of his retirement carefully compiling documents into a typescript history of his family titled *The Lewis Papers*.[54] Then he turned to his true scholarly specialty, the history of the French court in the time of Louis XIV and XV. He and Dyson and Williams, C. S. Lewis reported, "could often be heard in a corner talking about Versailles, *intendants*, and the *maison du roy*, in a fashion with which the rest of us could not compete."[55] When Warren began writing a social history of the period, and read a chapter to the Inklings, Tolkien was delighted. Authorship is catching, Tolkien noted, and added that although it was "a subject that does not interest me . . . it was most wittily written (as well as learned)."[56]

We know little of the Inklings's group activities in the late 1930s. But we do know, from Tolkien's letters, that the club was meeting for "reading things short and long aloud," including Lewis's *Out of the Silent Planet*, born out of a conversation between its author and Tolkien, and which Tolkien enthusiastically recommended to his own publisher in terms strikingly similar to Lewis's recommendation of Tolkien's *Lay of Leithian*: "I at any rate should have bought this story at almost any price if I had found it in print, and loudly recommended it as a 'thriller' by (however and surprisingly) an intelligent man."[57]

At about the same time, in June 1938, the Inklings made their one successful foray into academic politics in the tradition of the Cave, "our first public victory over established privilege," as Tolkien crowed at the time.[58] Adam Fox was elected the University of Oxford's Professor of Poetry, a five-year-term lectureship with nominal duties but high public prestige, chosen by all Oxford graduates with MAs who chose to show up on election day. Fox himself was painfully aware of his lack of either creative or scholarly credentials for the post. But Lewis stoutly maintained that Fox would preserve traditional poetry against the modernists, and wrote (anonymously) a campaign piece in the form of a Johnsonian pastiche arguing the point.[59] It is possible, though uncertain, that bad feelings in the Oxford academic community over this contributed to Lewis's own loss in the 1951 Professorship of Poetry election, his failure to be chosen for any other English professorship at Oxford, and thus his eventual departure for Cambridge in 1954.

If Lewis was disliked in some places, he made warm friends in others. He had an openhearted habit of writing fan letters to authors whose works he admired. At various times he invited authors as varied as E. R. Eddison and T. H. White to visit Oxford and meet a few readers. Twice during World War II Eddison did visit Oxford, dined with the Inklings, heard their new works, and read them his own; it is not known if White ever took up the invitation.[60] During the late 1930s, this habit brought the Inklings their most significant new member, Charles Williams. Nevill Coghill had lent Lewis a copy of Williams's novel *The Place of the Lion* in 1936. Lewis immediately added it to his small collection of "spiritual thrillers," books like David Lindsay's *A Voyage to Arcturus* carrying theological significance in the form of popular fiction. He passed it on to his brother and Tolkien, whom he reported to be "buzzing with excited admiration." And he invited the author to attend a meeting of "a sort of informal club called the Inklings ... some day next term ... [to] talk with us till the small hours."[61] Williams, an editor at the London offices of the Oxford University Press who had just been reading proofs of Lewis's scholarly study, *The Allegory of Love*, immediately replied with equal enthusiasm. Both men being averse to travel, they went through a little verbal dance of each insisting that the other come to see him. In the event they finally got together in both Oxford and London on occasion over the next few years.

At the outbreak of World War II in September 1939, the London staff of the Press was evacuated to Oxford. Williams moved with the rest, and geographic proximity at last allowed him to become a regular attendee of the Inklings. His presence invigorated the group. Lewis had what Tolkien called a "marvellous" ability to appreciate authors as wildly divergent as himself and Williams.[62] And Lewis, who delighted in nothing more than introducing his friends to one another and appreciating the richness of conversation that flowed therefrom, took particular pleasure in having Williams's distinctive character—a self-trained rather than academic scholarship, in which theology and romance were intertwined—among them.

Williams himself was less a clubbable man as Lewis and Tolkien were, and more one who built circles of disciples around himself: his Press mythology of the 1920s had had such character, and his Companions of the Co-inherence was a full-scale mystical mutual-support group. Williams joked to his wife that he was turning the Inklings into another such set of disciples,[63] but he knew well that they were not so malleable. The Inklings, and later the Oxford Dante Society which he joined in 1944 at the behest of Colin Hardie, provided an academic and scholarly rigor lacking in his other circles, and he found this bracing. Though Williams had no university degree (like Dr. Johnson he had dropped out of college for financial reasons), his scholarly work was impressive enough that Lewis and Tolkien arranged for him to give lectures and take tutorial pupils at Oxford. Williams sometimes wondered sourly if the dons were doing as much for him as they could, but he did hold dreams of gaining some regular position in the Oxford English faculty after the war.[64]

Lewis later wrote that Williams "had already become as dear to all my Oxford friends as he was to me" even before his wartime move. To this Tolkien sadly replied, "Alas no!"[65] Tolkien saw his friendship with Lewis as a personal companionship as well as part of the Inklings. At least in retrospect he disliked Lewis's imposition of Williams into it. Yet the attempts by some biographers to inflate this into a seething jealousy are certainly wrong. Tolkien, who acknowledged the narrowness of his literary sympathies, found much of Williams's work difficult, but so did the other Inklings. Lewis said that Williams labored "under an almost oriental richness of imagination"; Dyson ambiguously called his work "clotted glory from Charles."[66] "Don't imagine I didn't pitch in to C. W. for his obscurity for all I was worth," Lewis added.[67] But Williams and Tolkien certainly got along on a superficial level. Tolkien testified that if each found the other's work "impenetrable," they also each "found the other's presence and conversation delightful."[68] John D. Rateliff has carefully examined the available documentary evidence and concluded that Tolkien and Williams enjoyed each other's company and sought out occasions to meet, and that Williams, at least, appreciated what Tolkien was trying to accomplish in *The Lord of the Rings*.[69] If Tolkien's and Lewis's one-on-one weekly morning meetings, which had lasted at least a decade, were replaced by tripartite meetings during the war years, as was apparently the case, they were still richly productive ones: Tolkien read to his fellows from *The Lord of the Rings*, which was warmly approved, and Williams read his essay on *The Figure of Arthur*. Tolkien found their meetings "enjoyable" even when discussing authors he didn't care for, and of one such meeting wrote that he could "recollect little of the feast of reason and flow of soul, partly because we all agree so."[70]

The war years are well documented for the Inklings in frequent letters by the principal members to family members separated from them by the exigencies of the time. Lewis wrote weekly to his brother, Warren, while the latter was on active military duty for the first year of the conflict, including detailed accounts of meetings. Williams wrote regularly to his wife, Florence (who stayed in London for most of the war), and discussed his daily life, though rarely giving specifics of the Inklings. And in the summer of 1943, Tolkien's 18-year-old son Christopher was called up for military duty. Christopher already knew some of the Inklings, and his father discussed meetings in frequent letters to him. There are still gaps for periods when letters were not being written—there is little record of the Inklings for 1941 and none whatever for 1942, though they must have been meeting regularly—but enough record survives to allow a rich picture of their activities.

Lewis's occasional references to the Inklings in 1930s letters had implied that meetings were irregular and scheduled far in advance, but his letters to his brother show the group meeting weekly on Thursdays in November 1939 and January–February 1940, so regularly that the absence of a meeting one week is specially noted. So when Lewis writes to his brother in April 1940 of "the first weekly Inklings," he evidently means the first weekly meeting after an interterm break, rather than the first regular weekly meeting ever as some scholars have taken him to mean.[71]

Nor did the Inklings always meet on Thursdays. The day of the week changed frequently according to their convenience, though the location during this period was always Lewis's rooms at Magdalen College. In September 1943, for instance, they were meeting on Tuesdays, but Williams was assigned to fire-watch duty on Tuesday nights, preventing him from going to Magdalen. He asked Lewis to change the evening.[72] At other times during the war the Inklings are reported as meeting on Wednesdays and Fridays—though there is a persistent difficulty with the sources of defining exactly what counts as an Inklings meeting. When Williams writes to his wife, as he does frequently, that he "shall probably go to Magdalen to-night," it is no more than an assumption that his destination was the Inklings, and less than certain that he actually did attend. Even when reporting attendance, all sources often omit naming the club. Lewis sometimes calls them "the usual party."[73]

The membership of the Inklings slowly altered during this period. Coghill ceased attending meetings; Fox left Oxford altogether. Others came in to enrich the group. Most significant of them was Robert E. Havard, Lewis's physician and eventually Tolkien's as well. A letter by Lewis written in 1940 describes him as a new attendee, though one who had "been bidden all along." Havard's own recollection was that he became Lewis's physician in 1935 and began attending the Inklings soon afterwards, but here as elsewhere his memory of chronology is not always reliable.[74] Havard was a quiet member, but one who contributed greatly to the atmosphere and ethos of the group. Charles L. Wrenn, who assisted Tolkien in teaching Anglo-Saxon, attended some of the first recorded meetings in 1939 and 1940, then departed Oxford for a post in London and reappeared after the war. Lord David Cecil, an Oxford English don with a bent towards nineteenth-century realist writers, and more highbrow aesthetic principles than Lewis's "everyman" view, would seem an unlikely Inkling, but as an astute literary historian he recognized literary history in the making and attended occasional meetings. In later years, Cecil mused over whether he'd been present at the birth of an Oxford "school" of writers.

The Inklings invited guests. E. R. Eddison was warmly welcomed twice. Roy Campbell, a noted poet who came to Oxford to seek Lewis and company out, was rewarded by an invitation to an Inklings meeting. "If I could remember all that I heard in C. S. L.'s room last night it would fill several airletters," a delighted Tolkien wrote to his son.[75]

A large number of significant works were read in manuscript at Inklings meetings during these years—Lewis's *Perelandra*, *That Hideous Strength*, *The Screwtape Letters*, and *The Problem of Pain* (plus its clinical appendix contributed by Dr. Havard); large parts of Tolkien's *The Lord of the Rings*; Williams's last novel, *All Hallows' Eve*, and some of his plays and nonfiction; Warren Lewis's social history of eighteenth-century France, *The Splendid Century*. "They owe a good deal to the hard-hitting criticism of the circle," says C. S. Lewis.[76] Indeed, comparison of early drafts of *The Lord of the Rings* and *All Hallows' Eve* with the final texts demonstrates how extensive alteration and improvement could be. Glyer writes of *All Hallows' Eve* and its abandoned first draft, *The Noises that Weren't There*, "The key difference between the two novels is structural rather than stylistic. The fragment *The Noises that Weren't There* is largely an extended explanation of concepts. . . . *All Hallows' Eve* uses the same underlying ideas, and even some of the same characters and scenes, in the service of the story. In the new novel, narrative portions are increased, conversations and explanations are decreased, and the pace of the plot is much improved."[77]

When two of the books read during these years, Lewis's *The Problem of Pain* and Williams's *The Forgiveness of Sins*, were published in 1940 and 1942 respectively, readers found dedications reading in both cases simply, "To the Inklings."[78] Thus the world at large began to be aware of the existence of a group by this name. One of the first enquirers was Lewis's former pupil Dom Bede Griffiths. To him, Lewis identifies the Inklings by their denominational affiliations, and says that they meet "theoretically to talk about literature, but in fact nearly always to talk about something better."[79] What that "something better" might be is suggested by the topics of those two books, both published in the Christian Challenge series from Geoffrey Bles's Centenary Press, both of them deep considerations of knotty theological problems that might well arise in the course of discussions of literature. It is suggested by the deep spiritual and theological resonance, and the Christian underpinnings, of the novels of all three major Inklings. It is suggested by the discussions and actual arguments that the Inklings broke into: the problem of damnation and the goodness of God (which led to the other Inklings agreeing in frustration that "Williams is eminently combustible"), and what Lewis called "a furious argument about cremation."[80] In this context it is worth remembering that Lewis had taken the unlikely step of inviting Havard, his doctor, to a club of dons in the first place because of his quick discovery that Havard, like himself, would rather discuss ethics and philosophy than influenza.[81]

The Inklings loved what Lewis called "the cut and parry of prolonged, fierce, masculine argument,"[82] or at least they claimed to. One night when Barfield attended and read a play on Jason and Medea, the group had what Tolkien called "a most amusing and highly contentious evening, on which (had an outsider eavesdropped) he would have thought it a meeting of fell enemies hurling deadly insults before drawing their guns." Barfield was less amused, if his recollections of reading a play about Medea refer to this occasion.[83] But it would be a mistake to see the Inklings as a debating society akin to the Socratic Club. On the basics—Christianity, and the importance of myth and pure storytelling in literature—they were in agreement. Lewis says that your friend may disagree with you, but "of course he shares your interests; otherwise he would not become your friend at all."[84] And wit as well as argument ruled at their meetings. In addition to their own works read for appreciation and criticism, the Inklings read Amanda M'Kittrick Ros's eccentric novel *Irene Iddesleigh* purely for laughs; and seven years later Lewis's pupil John Wain "won an outstanding bet by reading a chapter" of it aloud "without a smile."[85] Dyson, if his avatar Arry Lowdham in Tolkien's *The Notion Club Papers* can be believed, was a particularly rich source of quips. Here the Notion Club discusses the feasibility of travel to the distant stars:

"Rockets are so slow [said Guildford]. Can you hope to go as fast as light, anything like as fast?"

"I don't know," said Frankley. "It doesn't seem likely at present, but I don't think that all the scientists or mathematicians would answer that question with a definite *no*."

"No, they're very romantic on this topic," said Guildford. "But even the speed of light will only be moderately useful. ... You'll have to plan for a speed greater than light; much greater, if you're to have a practical range outside the Solar System. Otherwise you will have very few destinations. Who's going to book a passage for a distant place, if he's sure to die of old age on the way?"

"They still take tickets on the State Railways," said Lowdham.[86]

The Notion Club Papers was an incomplete novel Tolkien worked on in the late 1940s and read to the Inklings. If *That Hideous Strength* is Lewis's Charles Williams novel, this one is Tolkien's, suggesting that he was far more favorably impressed by Williams's approach to myth than he later let on. The story tells of a group of men who receive intimations of myth through dreams and language. These men are Oxford dons; some of them resemble individual Inklings; and their club is a literary reading and discussion club very like the Inklings. Indeed, though the content of *The Notion Club Papers* reflects Tolkien's personal concerns, the style of the story probably conveys the flavor of an actual Inklings meeting better than Carpenter's valiant but stiff attempt to reconstruct one from written statements.[87]

These had been the peak years for the Inklings. But Charles Williams died suddenly on May 15, 1945, just after the end of World War II in Europe. The Inklings were devastated at the loss of their friend. Warren Lewis wrote,

One often reads of people being "stunned" by bad news, and reflects idly on the absurdity of the expression; but there is more than a little truth in it. I felt just as if I had slipped and come down on my head on the pavement. . . . The blackout has fallen, and the Inklings can never be the same again. I knew him better than any of the others, by virtue of his being the most constant attendant. I hear his voice as I write, and can see his thin form in his blue suit, opening his cigarette box with trembling hands. These rooms will always hold his ghost for me. There is something horrible, something *unfair* about death, which no religious conviction can overcome. "Well, goodbye, see you on Tuesday Charles" one says—and you have in fact though you don't know it, said goodbye for ever. He passes up the lamplit street, and passes out of your life for ever. . . . And so vanishes one of the best and nicest men it has ever been my good fortune to meet.[88]

The Inklings had already begun planning a Festschrift, a volume in Williams's honor, to mark his planned peacetime departure for London, and now offered it as a memorial, with the royalties sent to his widow. The book was published in 1947 with the title *Essays Presented to Charles Williams*. Five Inklings and Dorothy L. Sayers offered essays on literary and historical topics, all of them related to conversations they'd had with Williams at the Inklings or elsewhere.

The postwar Inklings had a different flavor from the group's earlier period. Part of this change was due to the loss of Williams. John Wain believes that "the group had begun to spiral downward from the time Williams died."[89] Williams had been, in Farrell's sociological terminology, the "charismatic leader," the one who "has a personal vision of some sort, and [who] lends to the group a sense of mission that transcends ordinary life."[90] Part of it may have been due simply to the members becoming older. And part of it was due to the increasing fame of the Inklings. New members who joined the group—Gervase Mathew, a lecturer in Byzantine studies; R. B. McCallum, a political scientist who later became Master of Pembroke College; Colin Hardie, a Classics don at Magdalen; and C. E. Stevens, a historian also at Magdalen—were distinguished scholars, but their interest in creative writing was minimal. Like Dyson, they preferred conversation, and readings of original work apparently trailed off in the postwar years. The Lewis brothers were great enthusiasts for Tolkien's *The Lord of the Rings*, but others disliked the book or found that readings interfered with their desire to talk. Hardie had become C. S. Lewis's friend through their shared interest in Dante which expressed itself in wartime readings of the *Divine Comedy* together, and Hardie attributes his own conversion from the modernist "Progressive Element" to Christianity to this influence.[91] Hardie's own contributions to readings tended to be scholarly papers which others found unintelligible. Warren Lewis, in the privacy of his diary, confessed that he found Mathew gossipy and McCallum pompous. They may have been among those who, Carpenter says, tended to have "invited themselves to be Inklings,"[92] but new members were not entirely unwelcome. Stevens was one Magdalen don whom C. S. Lewis had found particularly entertaining at college meetings, and formally proposed his election to the club in October 1947.[93]

Nor were all the new members senior dons. Lewis occasionally invited promising students to the Inklings, though at least in some cases he issued the invitation only following graduation. Both of his students who later became his biographers were among these: Roger Lancelyn Green never attended an evening Inklings due to personal obligations and the late development of his friendship with Lewis, but he drank with them frequently, and George Sayer managed to attend a few meetings. John Wain, medically invalided from military service, was a pupil of Lewis's during the war. He thrived under Lewis's scholastic regimen, and his obvious critical acumen earned him an invitation to the Inklings on his graduation in 1946. Wain attended often for two or three years, delighting in being accepted as an equal among his seniors, but feeling alienated from their political conservatism and love of fantasy. He went on to be a teacher, critic, creative writer, and defender of English literary traditions as Lewis had been, but within the very different context of a younger generation.

Christopher Tolkien, a few months older than Wain but still an undergraduate in the late 1940s due to the interruptions of war service, also became a regular Inkling. At his demobilization in October 1945, his father informed him that the Inklings proposed to consider him a permanent member.[94] He attended regularly, sometimes reading aloud chapters of his father's *Lord of the Rings*, suitable preparation for a man who would become best known as his father's literary executor.

In the postwar period, the Inklings always met on Thursday evenings, usually in Lewis's rooms at Magdalen but sometimes in the rooms at Merton College that Tolkien had acquired when he changed colleges in 1945. They met so regularly that meetings were even held on rare occasions when Lewis was absent. A new Inklings institution began at this time, as well: the ham supper. Various Inklings were used to dining together at an inn, restaurant, or pub prior to the meeting. During the postwar years when rationing was tight in Britain, American admirers of Lewis's writing began sending him parcels of goods, especially of food, which he would distribute among the Inklings. "His method," recalls Wain, "was to scatter the tins and packets on his bed, cover them with the counterpane, and allow each of us to pick one of the unidentifiable humps; it was no use simply choosing the biggest, which might turn out to be prunes or something equally dreary."[95] One such American, Dr. Warfield M. Firor of Johns Hopkins Medical School, specialized in sending hams. Lewis would have these prepared by the Magdalen College cook and served at private dinners to which he would invite selected Inklings. Colin Hardie became the designated carver at each such "red letter Inkling."[96]

Descriptions of Thursday Inklings of the postwar years in Warren Lewis's diary vary from "very pleasant" and "capital" through "drouthy though pleasant" to "slack and halting" and "mere noise and buffoonery."[97] The dislike of some Inklings for readings in general and for readings of *The Lord of the Rings* in particular, Tolkien's resulting disillusion and withdrawal from readings, and his gradually increasing dislike of Lewis's recent writings, may have played a role in the Inklings' decline. But it could equally have been that there was no proximate cause: the group had simply had its day. "One after another, people fell away," writes Wain,[98] though Warren Lewis's diary shows no obviously steady decline. Weekly meetings seem to have drifted to a halt by the end of 1949, and this date is often taken as the cessation of the Inklings.[99] But it is more likely that the end of the Inklings was gradual rather than precise. There are records of occasional ham suppers in the early 1950s, so it is possible that Inklings meetings, too, occasionally continued up to the end of 1954, when Lewis left the University of Oxford for that of Cambridge.

Throughout their lives, members of the Inklings met together in settings other than club meetings and ham suppers. Over the years, the context of literary and professional clubs was gradually succeeded by one of college dinners, expeditions to country inns, and vacations together—the Lewis brothers took, at separate times, Tolkien, Dyson, and Havard with them on vacations to Malvern. And they met at pubs during the daytime. Various Inklings had a number of regular pubs, especially in the early years, but it seems—especially from Tolkien's letters to his son—that Tuesday noon meetings at the Eagle and Child coalesced about 1943 out of convivial gatherings of the Lewis brothers, Tolkien, and Williams in whichever local pub was not out of beer. The King's Arms in Holywell, the White Horse next to Blackwell's in Broad Street, the Mitre hotel bar in the High Street, and—when Havard or another driver could take them there—the Trout Inn at Godstow outside Oxford, were all frequent Inklings meeting places. But their favorite was the Eagle and Child, a pub in St. Giles high street which they called the Bird and Baby, the Bird, or the B&B. Its signal virtues were the friendly landlord, a private parlor where the Inklings could talk undisturbed, and homemade cider of which C. S. Lewis was especially fond.

These informal gatherings seem to have opened up to a larger group around the end of the war. These meetings were rarely referred to as "Inklings" at all; they just consisted of a group of people who overlapped with the Inklings. Though many B&B regulars attended the Thursday evening meetings, others did not even know about the evening group. Contrary to popular impression—and contrary, in particular, to the sign hanging in the pub today—the Inklings did not read their manuscripts in the pub. That activity was reserved for evening Inklings in college; the pub mornings were for broader general conversation.

Though the Inklings welcomed visitors to the pub sessions, Lewis tried to keep their location a secret. He wrote in 1947 of his wartime meetings with Williams: "From [1939] until his death we met one another about twice a week, sometimes more: nearly always on Thursday evenings in my rooms and on Tuesday mornings in the best of all public-houses for draught cider, whose name it would be madness to reveal."[100] The following year, when Chad Walsh visited from America to research *C. S. Lewis: Apostle to the Skeptics*, Lewis made him promise not to name "a certain small, sedate pub . . . so that the ravenous public will not storm it for the delectable cider that is its specialty."[101] But it was too late for secrets: even before Walsh arrived, recent Oxford graduate Bruce Montgomery, under the pen name Edmund Crispin, published his mystery novel *Swan Song*. In Chapter 8, his detective sits in the Bird and Baby and observes, "There goes C. S. Lewis. . . . It must be Tuesday."[102] The pub meetings had become an Oxford institution.

A third meeting, if it may be called such, went on for a few years in the late 1940s and early 1950s when Lewis was spending much of his time at the Bodleian reading sixteenth-century literature for his volume in the Oxford History of English Literature series. The nearest convenient pub was the King's Arms, and here Lewis would often meet with the Tolkiens, Dyson, and Green.[103]

The Bird and Baby pub sessions continued on long after the original Inklings had faded away. When Lewis took a chair at the University of Cambridge in 1954, and began spending weeknights in term there, Tuesdays were changed to Mondays to better fit his schedule. The Bird and Baby, which had changed ownership, was remodeled in the early 1960s eliminating the private parlor, and the meetings were moved to the Lamb and Flag across the street. After Lewis's death in 1963 a few members tried to keep them going, but they were not the same without him. "He was the link that bound us all together," says Havard. "When he was no longer able to meet us, the link was snapped, and regular meetings came to a swift end, although many friendships remained."[104] McCallum formally pronounced the epitaph: "When the Sun goes out there is no more light in the solar system."[105]

***

So the Inklings, after a sixteen- to twenty-year run as a writers' group, and after over forty years as a collection of friends, passed into history. What they have left behind them are their books. Scholars studying the works of Lewis, Tolkien, and Williams have had to address these questions: To what extent did their close personal association over many years affect their work? To what extent is it significant in discussing their work?[106]

Chad Walsh considered the question of Williams's influence in his pioneering study of Lewis published in 1949. Showing a detached skepticism that would not characterize all his successors, he wrote, without much elaboration, "Much of the influence that Williams had on Lewis was of the intangible sort that comes when two friends sit together over their mugs of cider and talk about anything that pops into their heads."[107]

After the publication of *The Lord of the Rings* in 1954–1955 it became common for scholars, especially in America, to study the three (or four, if including Barfield) major Inklings together, emphasizing common features and assuming that they are best studied in the light of each other's work. The pioneering studies were two doctoral dissertations that appeared in 1960, both emphasizing the Inklings as authors of fiction with common features of religious depth. Marjorie Evelyn Wright declares that their

cosmologies have much in common. Each is set in a remote, mysterious land . . . The forces of evil (wraiths, monsters, witches, headless monarchs) are always physical characters such as can be met and defeated in battle; and whenever evil threatens, there arises a company—a group of people—especially suited to do battle with it. . . . The myths of these three authors satisfy the requirements for living myth: they are set in eternal mobility, and they invite further development.[108]

Robert J. Reilly is even more dogmatic: "Four contemporary writers fall naturally into an ideological group ... Much of their work, both critical and creative, is best seen as ... an attempt to reach religious truths by means and techniques traditionally called romantic, and an attempt to defend and justify these techniques and attitudes of romanticism by holding that they have religious sanction."[109]

Other scholars followed, notably Charles Moorman, whose 1966 study *The Precincts of Felicity* dubbed the Inklings, with the outlying additions of T. S. Eliot and Dorothy L. Sayers, "the Oxford Christians," to "suggest a shared outlook and to connote both an academic and a religious point of view common to them all." He concludes that they "most certainly can be described as a literary group and perhaps in days to come as a movement."[110] Moorman's scholarly goal is to show their common use of St. Augustine's model of the city. It takes some strain to find an Augustinian City of God in Tolkien's intensely rural fiction, but Moorman does his best. In the next few years, Robert J. Reilly's study was published as a book, more books by other authors and collections of essays on the Inklings began to appear, and The Mythopoeic Society, an organization studying the Inklings together on the premise that they are all creators of myth, was founded.

The surviving Inklings were aware of these scholarly conclusions, and vehemently disagreed. This had never been their intent. Clyde S. Kilby explains that the Inklings were "primarily a friendship. The last thing they anticipated was the forming of a 'school.' The Inklings as an organization is more our conception after the fact than it ever was a reality."[111] The scholars made the Inklings sound as if they had a conscious, polemic purpose, and that their works are in some degree interchangeable. Neither of these things, the Inklings held, was true. Warren Lewis called Moorman's "a silly book."

To begin with he dubs the Inklings "The Oxford Christians" which strikes a wrong note at the outset by suggesting an organized group for the propagation of Christianity, whilst in fact the title is justified only in the most literal sense, i.e. that we nearly all lived in Oxford and were all believers. His thesis is that in the Inklings a kind of group mind was at work which influenced the writing of every Inkling, and this he supports by assertions which seem to me very shaky. ... I smiled at the thought of Tollers [Tolkien] being under the influence of Moorman's group mind, and think of sending him the book.[112]

"If he did," writes John D. Rateliff, "the explosion which must surely have resulted has left no surviving evidence."[113] Tolkien had seen many misinterpretations of the intentions of his fiction, which both irritated and alarmed him. Among these were assumptions that his purposes and spirit were essentially identical with Lewis's and Williams's. Rateliff notes Tolkien's "innate antipathy towards being labeled or pigeon-holed in any way or indeed written about at all," suggesting that the rise of Inklings criticism is one reason Tolkien began distancing himself from his fellows in the 1960s, going so far as to claim of Williams, "I didn't even know him very well."[114] On the surface this contradicts their documented friendship, but it's fair applied to Tolkien's appreciation of Williams's work.[115] And after a biography of Williams was published in 1959, Tolkien came to learn how extensive Williams's intellectual life had been outside the Inklings.

Lewis too, before his death, had a chance to weigh in on this subject. When John Wain published a memoir in 1962 describing the Inklings as "a circle of instigators, almost of incendiaries, meeting to urge one another on in the task of redirecting the whole current of contemporary art and life," referring to its "unexpected alliances" with people like Sayers and Campbell, and even calling it a "corporate mind,"[116] Lewis was moved to protest. "The whole picture of myself as one forming a cabinet, or cell, or coven, is erroneous. Mr. Wain has mistaken purely personal relationships for alliances."[117] Wain apologized, but insisted that he had a point. "This was an embattled period of Lewis's life, and if these friends didn't offer essential support, if they were not in some sense 'allies,' what were they?"[118]

In the 1970s the scholarly consensus began to come up with a different answer: they weren't a coterie of instigators, they weren't allies, they had no common purpose, they were just a group of Lewis's miscellaneous friends, nothing more. The Inklings themselves said, or had begun to say, that they were an "undetermined and unelected circle of friends who gathered about C. S. L." (Tolkien), "simply a group of C. S. L.'s wide circle of friends who lived near enough to him to meet together fairly regularly" (Havard), "simply, a group of individuals, friends of Lewis who acquired the habit of dropping into his rooms on one evening a week" (Barfield).[119] This view was popularized by biographer Humphrey Carpenter. He devotes a chapter of his study *The Inklings* to claiming that seeking for what Moorman had called a shared outlook and a common point of view was what Lewis had told Moorman that hunting down their mutual influence was: "chasing after a fox that isn't there."[120] Claiming that disparities far outweighed commonalities in their religious and literary views, in their treatment of fantasy, and in their dislike of modernism, and discarding the idea that their friendship was a literary ginger group or a university clique, Carpenter concludes: "They were Lewis's friends: the group gathered round him, and in the end one does not have to look any further than Lewis himself to see why it came into being."[121] In a sense this takes us back to Chad Walsh's comments about Williams's influence on Lewis being due to sheer proximity, but it fails to ask how Lewis made these particular friends, and why he asked them to join him in the Inklings.

Carpenter's assumptions that the Inklings were wildly disparate men, and that their writings were unrelated, have been accepted by subsequent scholars. For instance, Verlyn Flieger declares that "Tolkien was distinct from both Lewis and Williams, far more unlike than he was like them." She cites Carpenter in denying that "their shared Christianity . . . their informal membership in the Inklings . . . [and] superficial similarities in their use of fantasy as a mode of expression" amount to a justification "to lump them together as writers with a common religious purpose and whose writing had a common religious bias."[122] Similarly, Jared Lobdell insists that the Inklings wrote entirely different types of fiction, and that their common factors are superficial. Lobdell even suggests that their works are not even really fantasy, though they have its atmosphere and flavor. Like Flieger, he cites Carpenter to counteract "the myth of the Inklings (or 'Oxford Christians') as a unified group designedly providing a radical and reactionary alternative to the evils of modernity."[123]

Neither the similarities seen by Wain nor the differences cited by Carpenter are entirely imaginary. How do we reconcile these wildly disparate interpretations? Havard provides a clue in discussing his and Lewis's different routes to Christianity: "Our differences laid the foundation of a friendship that lasted, with some ups and downs, until his death nearly thirty years later."[124] Diana Pavlac Glyer uses the key word in this quote to cut the knot altogether. She offers an antisynthesis, finding that the Inklings' closeness lay in their differences. Those differences provided them with something to talk about, and with flint to strike sparks off each other. They demonstrated disparity within community. Applying to the Inklings theoretical studies of writers' groups and of the nature of influence, Glyer shows that while similarities in the work of two authors may be pure coincidence or simply the result of shared values, even the most intense influences need not lead to similarities. By criticisms and comments, by actual suggestions for rewriting (such as Lewis's critique of Tolkien's *Lay of Leithian*), and by "sheer encouragement" (as Tolkien said of what Lewis's friendship had most meant to his writing),[125] the Inklings brought each other to write things they would not otherwise have written, and in ways they would not otherwise have written them. But this did not necessarily bring their work closer together. Thus, Tolkien accepted some of Lewis's suggestions regarding his poem, but this made it a more successfully Tolkienesque poem, not a Lewisian one. Glyer amasses evidence to show how closely the Inklings worked together over many years, how many creative works and scholarly projects they collaborated on, and how many acknowledgments they leave to each other in the pages of their works, to demonstrate these influences.[126]

A simpler synthesis of the opposing views may be found in the basic observation that both similarity and distance are relative. Increasingly detailed, "close-up" study of the work of the individual Inklings has magnified their differences in the eyes of these precise observers such as Flieger and Lobdell. The broader overviews of earlier years, by contrast, magnified the Inklings' similarities. In a sufficiently broad sense, the Inklings did have compatible goals. The similarity of those goals becomes evident when compared with the quite different goals of their contemporaries. Flieger says that the Inklings' "use of fantasy as a mode of expression" shows only "superficial similarities," but those similarities look a lot deeper when contrasted with the modernist symbolical realism of such writers as D. H. Lawrence, proclaimed the greatest novelist of the day by F. R. Leavis, its most influential critic. Apart from the psychological use of myth by such authors as James Joyce and T. S. Eliot, a very different type of writing than the Inklings did, "fantasy as a mode of expression" was severely in critical disfavor. A few critics such as Edmund Wilson had a grudging admiration for the medieval satires of James Branch Cabell, but the past fantasists Lewis and Tolkien had grown up on, writers such as George MacDonald and William Morris, had fallen off the critical map, and contemporaries such as David Lindsay and E. R. Eddison had never gotten on it. Even John Wain, a much younger man than the leading critics of the Inklings's day, saw no point to fantasy. "It presents no picture of human life that I can recognize," he says, with astonishing lack of perception, of *The Lord of the Rings*.[127] Wain scoffs at MacDonald and Morris as the Inklings' "literary household gods," and describes the "almost forgotten" Eddison's work as "seem[ing] to me to consist of a meaningless proliferation of fantastic incident."[128] Wain's own novels are conservative modern realism. "I think," Lewis once remarked sadly to Wain, "you and I had better have an agreement not to read each other's fiction."[129]

What the writers admired by the Inklings all had in common, Wain says, is that "they *invented*."[130] Lewis agreed that the virtues of romance as a literary form, and the importance of narrative, were high literary principles for the Inklings. "The problems of narrative as such—seldom heard of in modern critical writings—were constantly before our minds."[131] Here, too, the Inklings were greatly at odds with a contemporary literary culture where one of the leading novelists, E. M. Forster, acknowledges only with great reluctance, "Yes—oh dear, yes—the novel tells a story."[132] Their shared Christianity—despite a wide variety in doctrine and in pastoral styles—and their willingness to express these beliefs through their fiction also set the Inklings apart in an age of secularism. So did their quietist political conservatism and little-England insularity in an age of Marxism and other forms of leftist political activism and international solidarity. Though the Inklings's own attitudes—as critics and readers—toward modernism varied greatly, their position as writers forms a little cluster outside the mainstream. Only when one looks more closely do they break strongly apart.

What Wain saw, because he was close enough personally to the Inklings to observe them well, but far enough away in philosophy to view them at a distance, was that relative closeness compared to the general literary culture. No wonder the Inklings felt beleaguered and sought such allies as they could find. Lewis could sound almost belligerent in his opposition to literary modernism, as in his declarations that Williams's Taliesin cycle was among the twentieth century's great poetry and that *The Lord of the Rings* was one of its great novels.[133] Even today, with the Inklings more read and more respected than ever, such declarations can meet with critical scorn.[134]

Within the Oxford academy, as well, the Inklings stood apart. Today the Inklings are considered the embodiment of mid-twentieth century Oxford: their homes and haunts are tourist attractions, and their memory is cherished as a colorful glimpse of past Oxford. But that is not how it seemed at the time. Many of their colleagues thought that they were wasting their time or lowering the dignity of the scholarly profession with popular theology books and fairy tales. Some have speculated that accumulated hostility against Lewis was the reason he never received an Oxford professorship.[135]

Some critics did boldly stand up to champion the Inklings. T. S. Eliot quietly praised Williams's work. W. H. Auden was a noted advocate of both Williams and Tolkien, not minding the obloquy that these tastes brought him. Edmund Fuller places the three major Inklings together as writers of "the consciously projected, controlled literary fantasy" in his 1962 critique of modern fiction, *Books with Men Behind Them*.[136] This title means to evoke approximately what Lewis does in *The Abolition of Man* when he advocates the education of "men with chests." Fuller gives his praise to literature that he sees as strong-minded, with a clear moral sense. What he means by "a man," he says, "is one who has ripened some ordered, rational, and balanced vision of life and of the nature of his kind. His work should not be considered just the container of his vision, it *is* the vision."[137] The Inklings' ability to meet this challenging goal sets them among the few writers whose works Fuller believes worthy of survival. After nearly half a century, and after many reprints and secondary studies, one can conclude that Fuller was right about them.

Similarity and distance are not only relative, however. They are also functions of personal standards, and here Lewis and Tolkien have different yardsticks. Tolkien calls Lewis "a very impressionable, too impressionable man" and writes of him being "bowled over" by Williams.[138] He declares proudly that Lewis had said to him, "Confound you, nobody can influence you anyhow. I have tried but it's no good," a perspective confirmed by Lewis's own famous comment, "No one ever influenced Tolkien—you might as well try to influence a bandersnatch."[139] These are obvious signs that Lewis, as a writer, saw literature as a web of mutual influence much more than did Tolkien, who as a writer preferred to plow his own furrow. Lewis tried to increase influence (in the sense of increasing similarity) while Tolkien backed away from it, even disliking seeing his own influence, let alone Williams's, on Lewis. The resulting dance between them became awkward over time.

Carpenter claims that "Tolkien and Williams owed almost nothing to the other Inklings, and would have written everything they wrote had they never heard of the group."[140] This is certainly not true of Tolkien. Many scholars, emphasizing Tolkien's testimony that what Lewis and the Inklings offered him was encouragement, have observed that without them, he would never have finished *The Hobbit* or *The Lord of the Rings* at all.[141] That makes the Inklings essential to almost the entire fictional oeuvre published in the author's lifetime. The most that can be said is that the work Tolkien did complete was not, at least not obviously, written in a different way because of the Inklings' role—though even then it is hard to be sure that, for instance, the experience of a shared social life among Christian friends did not reinforce the deep-rooted Christian morality in *The Lord of the Rings*. Barfield's effect on Tolkien's linguistic philosophy cannot be ignored. And there remains *The Notion Club Papers*, discussed earlier, as Tolkien's incomplete Williams novel.

Something similar could be said of Williams: though, as Carpenter notes, he had completed much of his life's work before he came to Oxford, he did create important works, of which *All Hallows' Eve* and *The Forgiveness of Sins* are only the most prominent, under the Inklings's tutelage and encouragement. Williams found exile in Oxford very lonely, and the Inklings were among his few intellectual stimulations. "They are good for my mind," he told his wife, though he added that "all enjoyments depend on your centredness."[142]

But where in a sense Tolkien and Williams each stand alone, and are read very differently in the context of the Inklings than they are by themselves, Lewis's fiction almost demands a literary context of friends and influences. His novels are all reactions to books he had read, starting with *The Pilgrim's Regress* as a calque on Bunyan, through *Till We Have Faces* as a novelization and Christian reenvisaging of Apuleius, with *The Chronicles of Narnia* containing inspirations from a mixture of children's fiction by MacDonald, Tolkien, and Roger Lancelyn Green, and the Ransom trilogy as an astonishing anthology of an H. G. Wells style science fiction novel, a George MacDonald fantasy, and a Charles Williams contemporary weird fiction tale. Besides the specifically Williamsian style and plot of *That Hideous Strength*, the example of Williams's novels, his "spiritual thrillers," seems to have what encouraged Lewis in the first place toward the idea of similarly expressing theology through fiction. With typical generosity, though from other perspectives it might look more like appropriation, Lewis models the character of Ransom in this book on Williams, throws in a mysterious reference to Tolkien's lost realm of Númenor in the conversation between Ransom and Merlin, and might be inspired to create the disparate but united community at St. Anne's by the disparate but united community of the Inklings. This grew, in the author's mind if not within the subcreation, from the cameo appearances of a loose community of Ransom's understanding friends in *Perelandra*, which includes the narrator (presumably Lewis himself), the doctor friend Humphrey (an in-joke reference to Robert Havard), and the anthroposophist called "B." (for Barfield).[143] By adding that Ransom in *Out of the Silent Planet* is a philologist, which was Tolkien's profession, one could identify an anthology of the three major Inklings in one character. But it would be misleading to identify Ransom as being "really" Williams, or Tolkien, or a combination of them, or anybody else.

Any literary circle is significant only if its effect extends beyond its own time. The work of the Inklings continues and will continue to be read, but what of their influence on subsequent literature and the literary environment? There are, of course, literally hundreds of novels—many of them weakly imitative—luring the reader with blurbs declaring themselves to be "in the tradition of Tolkien" or "for the reader who loves Narnia," but there is much more than that. Some less obviously imitative writers are influenced by the Inklings in the deeper ways that the Inklings themselves were influenced by their inspirations and by each other. Among contemporary fantasists, one can point to Ursula K. Le Guin, who in her Earthsea books is one of the few authors to have "absorbed Tolkien, comprehended him, and gone on in her own direction,"[144] and Tim Powers, who points to Williams and Lewis as among his prime inspirations.

More broadly than this, the Inklings played an important role in a recasting of twentieth, and perhaps twenty-first, century literature toward the mythic. The Inklings were in a sense modernists, mediating myths and romances for the twentieth century as canonical modernists like Joyce and Eliot in their very different ways also did. But they also created a species of postmodernism. Not the skeptical, cynical, self-questioning, always aware of its status as a text breed of postmodernism, but the love of fantasy, the mythic, and the numinous, that opposes the idealized modernism of Leavis, the relentless insistence on social relevance and hard realism. The Inklings's approach, as Tolkien puts it, "is founded upon the hard recognition that things are so in the world as it appears under the sun; on a recognition of fact, but not a slavery to it."[145] Their work becomes more relevant to our time by refusing to be tied exclusively to it. Though they did not set out as a movement to accomplish any such thing, such has been their effect.

NOTES

1. Warren Lewis, "Memoir of C. S. Lewis," in *Letters of C. S. Lewis*, ed. Warren Lewis, rev. Walter Hooper (London: Fount, 1988), 33–34.

2. Ibid.

3. C. S. Lewis, to A. K. Hamilton Jenkin, November 4, 1925, in *Collected Letters*, Vol. I, ed. Walter Hooper (London: HarperCollins, 2000), 653.

4. C. S. Lewis, *The Four Loves* (New York: Harcourt, Brace & World, 1960), 92, 96.

5. C. S. Lewis, *Surprised by Joy: The Shape of My Early Life* (New York: Harcourt, Brace & World, 1956), 212–213.

6. C. S. Lewis, *All My Road Before Me: The Diary of C. S. Lewis, 1922–1927*, ed. Walter Hooper (San Diego, CA: Harcourt Brace Jovanovich, 1991), 189–191.

7. The adjective is Warren Lewis's. He describes Dyson as "a man who gives the impression of being made of quick silver: he pours himself into a room on a cataract of words and gestures, and you are caught up in the stream—but after the first plunge, it is exhilarating." *Brothers and Friends: The Diaries of Major Warren Hamilton Lewis*, ed. Clyde S. Kilby and Marjorie Lamp Mead (San Francisco, CA: Harper & Row, 1982), 97.

8. C. S. Lewis, to Arthur Greeves, July 29, 1930, in *Collected Letters*, I:918.

9. J. R. R. Tolkien, *The Letters of J. R. R. Tolkien*, selected and ed. Humphrey Carpenter with the assistance of Christopher Tolkien (Boston, MA: Houghton Mifflin, 1981), 445–446; Daniel Grotta, *The Biography of J. R. R. Tolkien: Architect of Middle-earth* (New York: Grosset & Dunlap, 1978), 60–61.

10. J. R. R. Tolkien, *The Book of Lost Tales*, ed. Christopher Tolkien (Boston, MA: Houghton Mifflin, 1983–1984), 2:176.

11. Lewis, *All My Road*, 393.

12. Lewis, *Surprised by Joy*, 75; Andrew Lazo, "Gathered Round Northern Fires: The Imaginative Impact of the Kolbítar," in *Tolkien and the Invention of Myth: A Reader*, ed. Jane Chance (Lexington: University Press of Kentucky, 2004), 218.

13. C. S. Lewis, to Arthur Greeves, February 4, 1933, and January 30, 1930, in *Collected Letters*, II:96, 1:880.

14. Lewis, *Surprised by Joy*, 216.

15. J. R. R. Tolkien, "Mythopoeia," in *Tree and Leaf*, 2nd ed. (London: Unwin Hyman, 1988), 97–101. Lewis's account of the occasion is in two letters to Arthur Greeves, September 22, 1931, and October 18, 1931, in *Collected Letters*, I:969–970, 976–977.

16. C. S. Lewis, to Dom Bede Griffiths, December 21, 1941, in *Collected Letters*, II:501.

17. C. S. Lewis, to Warren Lewis, November 22, 1931, in *Collected Letters*, II:16.

18. C. S. Lewis, to Arthur Greeves, October 17–December 3, 1929, in *Collected Letters, I*:838. George Sayer, *Jack: A Life of C. S. Lewis* (Wheaton, IL: Crossway Books, 1994), 250, dates this evening as December 3, 1929, which is actually the date that Lewis wrote this part of the letter. Lazo (p. 219) dates it by implication as 25 November, but Lewis says it happened "one week," not "last week."

19. Humphrey Carpenter, *The Inklings: C. S. Lewis, J. R. R. Tolkien, Charles Williams, and Their Friends* (Boston, MA: Houghton Mifflin, 1979), 30.

20. C. S. Lewis, "C. S. Lewis's Commentary on the Lay of Leithian," in *The Lays of Beleriand*, by J. R. R. Tolkien, ed. Christopher Tolkien (Boston, MA: Houghton Mifflin, 1985), 315–316.

21. Diana Pavlac Glyer, *The Company They Keep: C. S. Lewis and J. R. R. Tolkien as Writers in Community* (Kent, OH: Kent State University Press, 2006), chapter 5.

22. J. R. R. Tolkien, to William Luther White, September 11, 1967, *Letters*, 387; J. R. R. Tolkien, *The Treason of Isengard*, ed. Christopher Tolkien (Boston, MA: Houghton Mifflin, 1989), 85.

23. Tolkien to White, September 11, 1967, *Letters*, 388.

24. J. R. R. Tolkien, to W. H. Auden, August 4, 1965, *Letters*, 359; Nevill Coghill, "Men, Poets and Machines," *Poetry Review* 56 (1965): 136; Warren Lewis, *Brothers*, 99.

25. Adam Fox, "At the Breakfast Table," in *Remembering C. S. Lewis: Recollections of Those Who Knew Him*, ed. James T. Como (San Francisco, CA: Ignatius Press, 2005), 184–185.

26. Tolkien did so in 1937 and Dyson in 1940. Carpenter, *The Inklings*, 57n; C. S. Lewis to Warren Lewis, April 11, 1940, in *Collected Letters, II*:382.

27. Owen Barfield, "The Inklings Remembered," *The World & I*, April 1990, 548. Barfield names Colin Hardie as an attendee of these gatherings. It is improbable that Lewis knew Hardie well before Hardie became a fellow of Magdalen in 1936. It is possible that Barfield has him confused with his elder brother W. F. R. Hardie, who was a friend of Lewis in the 1920s and who figures often in his diary; Lewis, *All My Road*, 465.

28. Lewis used this description of the Inklings several times. "A sort of informal club," letter to Charles Williams, March 11, 1936, in *Collected Letters*, ed. Walter Hooper (London: HarperCollins, 2004) 2:183; "a small informal literary club," letter to Warfield M. Firor, March 12, 1948, in *Collected Letters, II*:838; "a very informal club," "Wain's Oxford," letter, *Encounter*, January 1963, 81.

29. Tolkien to White, September 11, 1967, *Letters*, 388.

30. Grotta, *The Biography of J. R. R. Tolkien*, 79; Carpenter, *The Inklings*, 57.

31. Lazo, "Gathered Round Northern Fires," 210–215.

32. Carpenter, *The Inklings*, 56, 162.

33. Lewis, "Wain's Oxford," 81.

34. Lewis discusses this problem in *The Four Loves*, 105–111, in the middle of his chapter on "Friendship." He sees the segregation as primarily the result of the

differing education and work of men and women in his culture, and their consequent differing expectations of friendship. True friendship between individual men and women is not impossible, but close friendship must be kept separate from a sexually mixed social life, in his view, or it will dilute the intensity of friendship in both sexes.

35. Lewis, *Four Loves*, 92.

36. Tolkien to White, September 11, 1967, *Letters*, 388.

37. Chad Walsh, *C. S. Lewis: Apostle to the Skeptics* (New York: Macmillan, 1949), 17.

38. Charles Moorman, *The Precincts of Felicity: The Augustinian City of the Oxford Christians* (Gainesville: University of Florida Press, 1966), 29n; C. S. Lewis, "Preface," in *Essays Presented to Charles Williams* (Grand Rapids, MI: Eerdmans, 1966), xi.

39. Robert J. Reilly, *Romantic Religion: A Study of Barfield, Lewis, Williams and Tolkien* (Athens: University of Georgia Press, 1971), 11.

40. Verlyn Flieger, *Splintered Light: Logos and Language in Tolkien's World*, 2nd ed. (Kent, OH: Kent State University Press, 2002), xxi.

41. Carpenter, *The Inklings*, 42.

42. Shirley Sugerman, "A Conversation with Owen Barfield," in *Evolution of Consciousness: Studies in Polarity*, ed. Shirley Sugerman (Middletown, CT: Wesleyan University Press, 1976), 10.

43. Colin Hardie, "A Colleague's Note on C. S. Lewis," *Inklings-Jahrbuch* 3 (1985): 177.

44. Warren Lewis, *Brothers*, 106–107.

45. David Bratman, "Hugo Dyson: Inkling, Teacher, *Bon Vivant*," *Mythlore* 21, no. 4, whole no. 82 (Winter 1997): 25.

46. Michael P. Farrell, *Collaborative Circles: Friendship Dynamics & Creative Work* (Chicago: University of Chicago Press, 2001), 224. My thanks to Diana Pavlac Glyer for leading me to this book in general and this quotation in particular.

47. Carpenter, *The Inklings*, 67.

48. Colin Duriez, *Tolkien and C. S. Lewis: The Gift of Friendship* (Mahwah, NJ: HiddenSpring, 2003), 75.

49. Sayer, *Jack*, 249.

50. Sayer, *Jack*, 250.

51. Warren Lewis, *Brothers*, 145–146. Tickets were not obtained and the trip was apparently cancelled (see Lewis, *Collected Letters, II*:137–140), but Lewis and Tolkien may have gone on a later occasion (Carpenter, *The Inklings*, 56n).

52. The technical sociological term; see Farrell, *Collaborative Circles*, 84–85.

53. John Wain, *Sprightly Running: Part of an Autobiography* (New York: St. Martin's, 1963), 184.

54. Now held by the Marion E. Wade Center, Wheaton College, Illinois.

55. Lewis, "Preface," vi.

56. J. R. R. Tolkien, to Christopher Tolkien, April 13, 1944, in *Letters*, 71; Warren Lewis's book became *The Splendid Century: Some Aspects of French Life in the Reign of Louis XIV* (New York: William Sloane, 1953).

57. J. R. R. Tolkien, to Stanley Unwin, February 18, 1938, and March 4, 1938, in *Letters*, 29, 34.

58. J. R. R. Tolkien, to Stanley Unwin, June 4, 1938, in *Letters*, 36.

59. [C. S. Lewis], "From Johnson's *Life of Fox*," *Oxford Magazine* (June 9, 1938): 737–738. Excerpts from this rare article are reprinted in Walter Hooper, *C. S. Lewis: A Companion & Guide* (New York: HarperCollins, 1996), 658–659, and John Wain, *Professing Poetry* (London: Macmillan, 1977), 17–18. The excerpts are not in the U.S. edition of Wain's book (New York: Viking, 1978). See also Fox, "At the Breakfast Table," 186–187.

60. Exchanges between Lewis and Eddison are in C. S. Lewis, *Collected Letters, II*:535–537, 552–554; for White, see Joe R. Christopher, "Letters from C. S. Lewis in the Humanities Research Center, The University of Texas at Austin: A Checklist," *CSL: The Bulletin of the New York C. S. Lewis Society* 133 (November 1980): 1–7.

61. Lewis, to Williams, March 11, 1936, *Collected Letters, II*:183–184.

62. J. R. R. Tolkien, to Dora Marshall, March 3, 1955, in *Letters*, 209.

63. Charles Williams, to Florence Williams, March 5, 1940, in *To Michal from Serge: Letters from Charles Williams to His Wife, Florence, 1939–1945*, ed. Roma A. King, Jr. (Kent, OH: Kent State University Press, 2002), 50–51.

64. Charles Williams, to Florence Williams, October 14, 1944, and February 21, 1945, in *To Michal*, 227, 249–250.

65. Lewis, "Preface," viii; Carpenter, *The Inklings*, 120.

66. Lewis, to Griffiths, December 21, 1941, *Collected Letters, II*:501.

67. C. S. Lewis, to Owen Barfield, December 22, 1947, *Collected Letters, II*:819.

68. Tolkien, to Marshall, March 3, 1955, *Letters*, 209.

69. Rateliff points to, among other things, an occasion when Tolkien phoned Williams to suggest they visit Lewis in hospital together; and Tolkien's admiration of a perceptive comment Williams made on *The Lord of the Rings*. John D. Rateliff, " 'And Something Yet Remains to be Said': Tolkien and Williams," *Mythlore* 12, no. 3, whole no. 45 (Spring 1986), 49, 52.

70. Carpenter, *The Inklings*, 121; J. R. R. Tolkien, to Christopher Tolkien, November 7–8, 1944, *Letters*, 102.

71. C. S. Lewis, to Warren Lewis, December 3, 1939, and April 28, 1940, *Collected Letters, II*:302, 404; Hooper, *C. S. Lewis*, 123; Kilby and Mead in Warren Lewis, *Brothers*, 182–183n.

72. Charles Williams, to Florence Williams, September 27, 1943, unpublished, Marion E. Wade Collection.

73. For example, Charles Williams, to Florence Williams, August 30, 1940, in *To Michal*, 89; C. S. Lewis, to Warren Lewis, November 24, 1939, and January 28, 1940, *Collected Letters, II*:297; 2:336.

74. C. S. Lewis, to Warren Lewis, February 3, 1940, *Collected Letters, II*:343; Robert E. Havard, "Philia: Jack at Ease," in Como, *Remembering C. S. Lewis*, 349–350. Havard describes a boat trip with Lewis (353–356) for a date when Lewis was actually out of town lecturing (*Collected Letters, II*:259, 271). He places a visit from Dr. Warfield M. Firor during the war (359–360) when it was actually in July 1949 (Hooper, *C. S. Lewis*, 52; Lewis, *Collected Letters, II*:922n).

75. J. R. R. Tolkien, to Christopher Tolkien, October 6, 1944, *Letters*, 95.

76. Lewis, "Preface," v.

77. Glyer, *The Company They Keep*, chapter 4. The early fragment of *All Hallows' Eve* was serialized under the title *The Noises that Weren't There*, *Mythlore* 2, no. 2, whole no. 6 (Autumn 1970), 1–721; 2, no. 3, whole no. 7 (Winter 1971), 17–23; 2, no. 4, whole no. 8 (Winter 1972), 21–25. The earliest drafts of *The Lord of the Rings* are found in the posthumous Tolkien volume *The Return of the Shadow*, ed. Christopher Tolkien (Boston, MA: Houghton Mifflin, 1988).

78. When the first volume of *The Lord of the Rings* was published in 1954, a dedication to the Inklings also appeared, in a foreword omitted from later editions. The dedication is reprinted in J. R. R. Tolkien, *The Peoples of Middle-earth*, ed. Christopher Tolkien (Boston, MA: Houghton Mifflin, 1996), 25, and Wayne G. Hammond and Christina Scull, *The Lord of the Rings: A Reader's Companion* (Boston, MA: Houghton Mifflin, 2005), lxix.

79. Lewis, to Griffiths, December 21, 1941, *Collected Letters, II*:501.

80. C. S. Lewis, to Warren Lewis, November 5, 1939, and February 25, 1940, *Collected Letters, II*:283, 358. Carpenter tries to recreate the latter in his imaginary meeting, 146–147.

81. Havard, "Philia: Jack at Ease," 350.

82. Lewis, "Preface," xi.

83. J. R. R. Tolkien, to Christopher Tolkien, November 24, 1944, *Letters*, 103; Barfield, "The Inklings Remembered," 549; Grotta, *The Biography of J. R. R. Tolkien*, 93.

84. Lewis, *Surprised by Joy*, 199.

85. Warren Lewis, *Brothers*, 197. See also C. S. Lewis, *Collected Letters, II*:294n.

86. J. R. R. Tolkien, *The Notion Club Papers*, in *Sauron Defeated*, ed. Christopher Tolkien (Boston, MA: Houghton Mifflin, 1992), 167.

87. Carpenter's reconstruction is part 3, chapter 3 of *The Inklings*, 127–152. Barfield, "The Inklings Remembered," 549, is impressed by its realism.

88. Warren Lewis, *Brothers*, 182–183.

89. Wain, *Sprightly Running*, 185.

90. Farrell, *Collaborative Circles*, 85.

91. Hardie, "A Colleague's Note on C. S. Lewis," 177, 180.

92. Carpenter, *The Inklings*, 186.

93. Warren Lewis, *Brothers*, 212.

94. Carpenter, *The Inklings*, 205.

95. Wain, *Sprightly Running*, 184.

96. Warren Lewis, *Brothers*, 218.

97. Warren Lewis, *Brothers*, 216, 218, 217, 218, 193.

98. Wain, *Sprightly Running*, 185.

99. Carpenter, *The Inklings*, 226.

100. Lewis, "Preface," viii–ix. This statement gave rise to the belief, not supported by the documentary evidence, that the Inklings had always met on Thursdays, and that pub meetings were always at the same location in the war years.

101. Walsh, *C. S. Lewis*, 15.

102. Edmund Crispin, *Swan Song* (New York: Avon, 1981), 62.

103. Roger Lancelyn Green, "Recollections," *Amon Hen* 44 (May 1980), 7–8.

104. Havard, "Philia: Jack at Ease," 353.

105. Hooper, *C. S. Lewis*, 703.

106. The following is heavily indebted—an economic metaphor whose importance she notes herself—to the study of the Inklings' influences in Glyer, *The Company They Keep*, chapters 2 and 8.

107. Walsh, *C. S. Lewis*, 136.

108. Marjorie Evelyn Wright, *The Cosmic Kingdom of Myth: A Study in the Myth-Philosophy of Charles Williams, C. S. Lewis, and J. R. R. Tolkien*. Ph.D. Dissertation, University of Illinois, 1960. Abstract in *Dissertation Abstracts* 21 (1960–1961), 3464.

109. Robert J. Reilly, *Romantic Religion in the Work of Owen Barfield, C. S. Lewis, Charles Williams, and J. R. R. Tolkien*. Ph.D. Dissertation, Michigan State University, 1960. Abstract in *Dissertation Abstracts* 21 (1960–1961), 3461.

110. Moorman, *The Precincts of Felicity*, 15n, 138.

111. Clyde S. Kilby, *Tolkien & the Silmarillion* (Wheaton, IL: Harold Shaw, 1976), 67.

112. Warren Lewis, *Brothers*, 268.

113. Rateliff, "And Something Yet Remains to be Said," 50.

114. Rateliff, "And Something Yet Remains to be Said," 50; Henry Resnick, "An Interview with Tolkien, Date: March 2, 1966," *Niekas* 18 (Spring 1967), 40.

115. Carpenter prints at 123–126 a poem by Tolkien, beginning "Our dear Charles Williams," which Carpenter summarizes as saying that "if Williams's ideas did not appeal, then the man himself (he found) was undeniably charming." A typescript of the poem at the Marion E. Wade Center contains a cover letter by Raymond Hunt, Williams's bibliographer, dated "received with Margaret Douglas's letter of December 3, 1943." Douglas was a woman in Oxford who did typing for Williams; she presumably prepared the typescript, and the cover letter implies that both she and Williams had read the poem.

116. Wain, *Sprightly Running*, 181, 183, 185.

117. Lewis, "Wain's Oxford," 81.

118. Wain, letter, *Encounter*, January 1963, 82.

119. Tolkien, to White, September 11, 1967, *Letters*, 388; Havard, qtd. in Carpenter, *The Inklings*, 161n; Barfield, in Sugerman, "A Conversation with Owen Barfield,"9.

120. Carpenter, *The Inklings*, 154; C. S. Lewis, to Charles Moorman, May 15, 1959, *Letters of C. S. Lewis*, 481.

121. Carpenter, *The Inklings*, 171.

122. Flieger, *Splintered Light*, xix–xx.

123. Jared Lobdell, *The Scientifiction Novels of C. S. Lewis: Space and Time in the Ransom Stories* (Jefferson, NC: McFarland, 2004), 1, 25, 169.

124. Havard, "Philia: Jack at Ease," 350.

125. J. R. R. Tolkien, to Dick Plotz, September 12, 1965, *Letters*, 362. See also p. 227.

126. Glyer's chapters 6 and 7 discuss the Inklings's collaborations and scholarly interchanges. These are surprisingly extensive, including many memorial pieces, and reviews of each other's works. Two Inklings edited periodicals which may be considered Inklings "house journals." R. B. McCallum was on several occasions editor of *The Oxford Magazine*, a publication written by and for the community of Oxford dons. J. A. W. Bennett, a prominent medievalist, Lewis's successor in his Cambridge professorship, and an occasional Inkling, was editor of the scholarly journal *Medium Aevum* in 1957–1981. Many Inklings contributed to both these periodicals.

127. John Wain, "John Wain," *Contemporary Authors Autobiography Series* 4 (1986), 329.

128. Wain, *Sprightly Running*, 182.

129. Wain, "John Wain," 329. Wain as a literary polemicist, however, owes a lot to Lewis in style and in reverence for tradition, as he generously admitted in some admiring comments on his old tutor. As Wain discovered when he read *Surprised by Joy*, this makes him a kind of honorary grandson of W. T. Kirkpatrick, the tutor who had taught Lewis the virtues of rigorous argument. See *Sprightly Running*, 138–139.

130. Wain, *Sprightly Running*, 182.

131. Lewis, "Preface," v.

132. E. M. Forster, *Aspects of the Novel* (New York: Harcourt, Brace & World, 1927), 26.

133. Williams's two volumes "seem to me . . . to be among the two or three most valuable books of verse produced in the century," Lewis, "Preface," vi–vii. "I have little doubt that [*The Lord of the Rings*] will soon take its place among the indispensables," Lewis, "Tolkien's *The Lord of the Rings*," in *On Stories and Other Essays on Literature*, ed. Walter Hooper (New York: Harcourt Brace Jovanovich, 1982), 90.

134. This point is discussed in regard to Tolkien in T. A. Shippey, *J. R. R. Tolkien: Author of the Century* (Boston, MA: Houghton Mifflin, 2001), especially in the Afterword, 305–328.

135. Douglas A. Anderson, " 'An Industrious Little Devil': E. V. Gordon as Friend and Collaborator with Tolkien," in *Tolkien the Medievalist*, ed. Jane Chance (London:

Routledge, 2003), 24; Christopher W. Mitchell, "Bearing the Weight of Glory: The Cost of C. S. Lewis's Witness," in *The Pilgrim's Guide: C. S. Lewis and the Art of Witness*, ed. David Mills (Grand Rapids, MI: Eerdmans, 1998), 7–8.

136. Edmund Fuller, *Books with Men Behind Them* (New York: Random House, 1962), 135.

137. Fuller, *Books with Men Behind Them*, 5–6.

138. J. R. R. Tolkien, to Anne Barrett, August 7, 1964, *Letters*, 349; Tolkien, to Plotz, *Letters*, 362.

139. Resnick, "An Interview with Tolkien," 40; Lewis, to Moorman, *Letters of C. S. Lewis*, 481.

140. Carpenter, *The Inklings*, 160.

141. Glyer discusses this in chapters 2–3.

142. Charles Williams, to Florence Williams, August 30, 1940, *To Michal*, 89–90.

143. C. S. Lewis, *Perelandra: A Novel* (New York: Macmillan, 1965), 28–32 (in chapters 2–3). These and other references in the Ransom trilogy are discussed by Joe R. Christopher, in *C. S. Lewis* (Boston: Twayne, 1987) and Martha C. Sammons, *A Far-Off Country: A Guide to C. S. Lewis's Fantasy Fiction* (Lanham, MD: University Press of America, 2000).

144. Brian Attebery, *The Fantasy Tradition in American Literature: From Irving to Le Guin* (Bloomington: Indiana University Press, 1980), 162.

145. J. R. R. Tolkien, "On Fairy-Stories," in *Tree and Leaf*, 51.

BIBLIOGRAPHY

Anderson, Douglas A. "'An Industrious Little Devil': E. V. Gordon as Friend and Collaborator with Tolkien." In *Tolkien the Medievalist*. Edited by Jane Chance. London: Routledge, 2003, 15–25.

Attebery, Brian. *The Fantasy Tradition in American Literature: From Irving to Le Guin*. Bloomington: Indiana University Press, 1980.

Barfield, Owen. "The Inklings Remembered." *The World & I* (April 1990): 548–549.

Bratman, David. "Hugo Dyson: Inkling, Teacher, *Bon Vivant*." *Mythlore* 21, no. 4, whole no. 82 (Winter 1997): 19–34.

Carpenter, Humphrey. *The Inklings: C. S. Lewis, J. R. R. Tolkien, Charles Williams, and Their Friends*. Boston, MA: Houghton Mifflin, 1979.

Christopher, Joe R. *C. S. Lewis*. Boston, MA: Twain, 1987.

———. "Letters from C. S. Lewis in the Humanities Research Center, The University of Texas at Austin: A Checklist." *CSL: The Bulletin of the New York C. S. Lewis Society* 133 (November 1980): 1–7.

Coghill, Nevill. "Men, Poets and Machines." *Poetry Review* 56 (1965): 136–147.

Como, James T. Editor. *Remembering C. S. Lewis: Recollections of Those Who Knew Him*. San Francisco: Ignatius Press, 2005. First published in 1979 by Macmillan as *C. S. Lewis at the Breakfast Table, and Other Reminiscences*.

Crispin, Edmund. *Swan Song*. New York: Avon, 1981 [1947].

Duriez, Colin. *Tolkien and C. S. Lewis: The Gift of Friendship*. Mahwah, NJ: Hidden-Spring, 2003.

Farrell, Michael P. *Collaborative Circles: Friendship Dynamics & Creative Work*. Chicago: University of Chicago Press, 2001.

Flieger, Verlyn. *Splintered Light: Logos and Language in Tolkien's World*, 2nd edn. Kent, OH: Kent State University Press, 2002.

Forster, E. M. *Aspects of the Novel*. New York: Harcourt, Brace & World, 1927.

Fox, Adam. "At the Breakfast Table." In *Remembering C. S. Lewis: Recollections of Those Who Knew Him*. Edited by James T. Como. San Francisco: Ignatius Press, 2005, 179–188.

Fuller, Edmund. *Books with Men Behind Them*. New York: Random House, 1962.

Glyer, Diana Pavlac. *The Company They Keep: C. S. Lewis and J. R. R. Tolkien as Writers in Community*. Kent, OH: Kent State University Press, 2006.

Green, Roger Lancelyn. "Recollections." *Amon Hen* 144 (May 1980), 7–8.

Grotta, Daniel. *The Biography of J. R. R. Tolkien: Architect of Middle-earth*. New York: Grosset & Dunlap, 1978.

Hammond, Wayne G., and Christina Scull. *The Lord of the Rings: A Reader's Companion*. Boston, MA: Houghton Mifflin, 2005.

Hardie, Colin. "A Colleague's Note on C. S. Lewis." *Inklings-Jahrbuch* 3 (1985), 177–182.

Havard, Robert E. "Philia: Jack at Ease." In *Remembering C. S. Lewis: Recollections of Those Who Knew Him*. Edited by James T. Como. San Francisco: Ignatius Press, 2005, 349–367.

Hooper, Walter. *C. S. Lewis: A Companion & Guide*. New York: HarperCollins, 1996.

Kilby, Clyde S. *Tolkien & the Silmarillion*. Wheaton, IL: Harold Shaw, 1976.

Lazo, Andrew. "Gathered Round Northern Fires: The Imaginative Impact of the Kolbítar." In *Tolkien and the Invention of Myth: A Reader*. Edited by Jane Chance. Lexington: University Press of Kentucky, 2004, 191–226.

Lewis, C. S. *All My Road Before Me: The Diary of C. S. Lewis, 1922–1927*. Edited by Walter Hooper. San Diego: Harcourt Brace Jovanovich, 1991.

———. "C. S. Lewis's Commentary on the Lay of Leithian." In *The Lays of Beleriand*, by J. R. R. Tolkien, edited by Christopher Tolkien, 315–329. Boston, MA: Houghton Mifflin, 1985.

———. *Collected Letters*, Vol. 1, Edited by Walter Hooper. London: HarperCollins, 2000.

———. *Collected Letters*, Vol. 2, Edited by Walter Hooper. London: HarperCollins, 2004.

———. *The Four Loves*. New York: Harcourt, Brace & World, 1960.

———. "From Johnson's *Life of Fox*." *Oxford Magazine*, June 9, 1938: 737–738.

———. *Letters of C. S. Lewis*. Edited by Warren Lewis, rev. and enlarged by Walter Hooper. London: Fount, 1988.

———. *Perelandra: A Novel.* New York: Macmillan, 1965 [1943].

———. "Preface." In *Essays Presented to Charles Williams*, v–xiv. 1947. Grand Rapids, MI: Eerdmans, 1966.

———. *Surprised by Joy: The Shape of My Early Life.* New York: Harcourt, Brace & World, 1956.

———. "Tolkien's *The Lord of the Rings.*" In *On Stories and Other Essays on Literature.* Edited by Walter Hooper. New York: Harcourt Brace Jovanovich, 1982, 83–92.

———. "Wain's Oxford." Letter. *Encounter*, January 1963, 81.

Lewis, Warren. *Brothers and Friends: The Diaries of Major Warren Hamilton Lewis.* Edited by Clyde S. Kilby and Marjorie Lamp Mead. San Francisco: Harper & Row, 1982.

———. "Memoir of C. S. Lewis." In *Letters of C. S. Lewis.* Edited by Warren Lewis, rev. Walter Hooper. London: Fount, 1988, 21–46.

———. *The Splendid Century: Some Aspects of French Life in the Reign of Louis XIV.* New York: William Sloane, 1953.

Lobdell, Jared. *The Scientifiction Novels of C. S. Lewis: Space and Time in the Ransom Stories.* Jefferson, NC: McFarland, 2004.

Mitchell, Christopher W. "Bearing the Weight of Glory: The Cost of C. S. Lewis's Witness." In *The Pilgrim's Guide: C.S. Lewis and the Art of Witness*, Edited by David Mills. Grand Rapids, MI: Eerdmans, 1998, 3–14.

Moorman, Charles. *The Precincts of Felicity: The Augustinian City of the Oxford Christians.* Gainesville: University of Florida Press, 1966.

Rateliff, John D. " 'And Something Yet Remains to be Said': Tolkien and Williams." *Mythlore* 12, no. 3, whole no. 45 (Spring 1986), 48–54.

Reilly, Robert J. *Romantic Religion: A Study of Barfield, Lewis, Williams and Tolkien.* Athens: University of Georgia Press, 1971.

———. *Romantic Religion in the Work of Owen Barfield, C. S. Lewis, Charles Williams, and J. R. R. Tolkien.* Ph.D. Dissertation, Michigan State University, 1960. Abstract in *Dissertation Abstracts* 21 (1960–1961), 3461–3462.

Resnick, Henry. "An Interview with Tolkien, Date: March 2, 1966." *Niekas* 18 (Spring 1967), 37–43.

Sammons, Martha C. *A Far-Off Country: A Guide to C. S. Lewis's Fantasy Fiction.* Lanham, MD: University Press of America, 2000.

Sayer, George. *Jack: A Life of C. S. Lewis.* Wheaton, IL: Crossway Books, 1994.

Shippey, T. A. *J. R. R. Tolkien: Author of the Century.* Boston, MA: Houghton Mifflin, 2001.

Sugerman, Shirley. "A Conversation with Owen Barfield." In *Evolution of Consciousness: Studies in Polarity.* Edited by Shirley Sugerman. Middletown, CT: Wesleyan University Press, 1976, 3–28.

Tolkien, J. R. R. *The Book of Lost Tales*, 2 vols. Edited by Christopher Tolkien. Boston, MA: Houghton Mifflin, 1983–1984.

———. *The Letters of J. R. R. Tolkien*. Selected and edited by Humphrey Carpenter with the assistance of Christopher Tolkien. Boston, MA: Houghton Mifflin, 1981.

———. *The Notion Club Papers*. In *Sauron Defeated*. Edited by Christopher Tolkien. Boston, MA: Houghton Mifflin, 1992, 143–327.

———. *The Peoples of Middle-earth*. Edited by Christopher Tolkien. Boston, MA: Houghton Mifflin, 1996.

———. *The Return of the Shadow*. Edited by Christopher Tolkien. Boston, MA: Houghton Mifflin, 1988.

———. *The Treason of Isengard*. Edited by Christopher Tolkien. Boston, MA: Houghton Mifflin, 1989.

———. *Tree and Leaf*, 2nd edn. London: Unwin Hyman, 1988.

Wain, John. Letter. *Encounter*, January 1963, 81–82.

———. "John Wain." *Contemporary Authors Autobiography Series* 4 (1986), 314–332.

———. *Professing Poetry*. London: Macmillan, 1977.

———. *Sprightly Running: Part of an Autobiography*. New York: St. Martin's, 1963.

Walsh, Chad. *C. S. Lewis: Apostle to the Skeptics*. New York: Macmillan, 1949.

Williams, Charles. *The Noises that Weren't There*. 3 parts. *Mythlore* 2, no. 2, whole no. 6 (Autumn 1970): 17–21; 2, no. 3, whole no. 7 (Winter 1971): 17–23; 2, no. 4, whole no. 8 (Winter 1972): 21–25.

———. *To Michal from Serge: Letters from Charles Williams to His Wife, Florence, 1939–1945*. Edited by Roma A. King, Jr. Kent, OH: Kent State University Press, 2002.

Wright, Marjorie Evelyn. *The Cosmic Kingdom of Myth: A Study in the Myth-Philosophy of Charles Williams, C. S. Lewis, and J. R. R. Tolkien*. Ph.D. Dissertation, University of Illinois, 1960. Abstract in *Dissertation Abstracts* 21 (1960–1961): 3464–3465.

SPECIAL BIBLIOGRAPHIES

Selected Published Material for the Study of the Inklings

Major Published Primary Sources of the Inklings

Lewis, C. S. *Collected Letters, 3* vol. to date. Edited by Walter Hooper. London: HarperCollins, 2000; 2004, 2007.

———. *Letters of C. S. Lewis*. Edited by Warren Lewis, revised and enlarged by Walter Hooper. London: Fount, 1988.

Lewis, Warren. *Brothers and Friends: The Diaries of Major Warren Hamilton Lewis*. Edited by Clyde S. Kilby and Marjorie Lamp Mead. San Francisco: Harper & Row, 1982.

Tolkien, J. R. R. *The Letters of J. R. R. Tolkien*. Selected and edited by Humphrey Carpenter with the assistance of Christopher Tolkien. Boston, MA: Houghton Mifflin, 1981.

Williams, Charles. *To Michal from Serge: Letters from Charles Williams to His Wife, Florence, 1939–1945*. Edited by Roma A. King, Jr. Kent, OH: Kent State University Press, 2002.

Important Memoirs by the Inklings

Barfield, Owen. "The Inklings Remembered." *The World & I*, April 1990, 548–549.
———. *Owen Barfield on C. S. Lewis*. Edited by G. B. Tennyson. Middletown, CT: Wesleyan University Press, 1989.
Como, James T. Editor. *Remembering C. S. Lewis: Recollections of Those Who Knew Him*. San Francisco: Ignatius Press, 2005. First published 1979 by Macmillan as *C. S. Lewis at the Breakfast Table, and Other Reminiscences*. Includes pieces by John Wain, Adam Fox, Gervase Mathew, George Sayer, Roger Lancelyn Green, Robert E. Howard, and James Dundas-Grant.
Havard, Robert E. "Professor J. R. R. Tolkien: A Personal Memoir." *Mythlore* 17, no. 2, whole no. 64 (Winter 1990), 61.
Lewis, C. S. "Preface." In *Essays Presented to Charles Williams*. Grand Rapids, MI: Eerdmans, 1966 [1947], v–xiv.
Lewis, Warren. "Memoir of C. S. Lewis." In *Letters of C. S. Lewis*. Edited by Warren Lewis, rev. Walter Hooper. London: Fount, 1988, 21–46.
Wain, John. "John Wain." *Contemporary Authors Autobiography Series* 4 (1986), 314–332.
———. *Sprightly Running: Part of an Autobiography*. New York: St. Martin's, 1963.

Biographies of the Inklings (excluding C. S. Lewis)

Blaxland de Lange, Simon. *Owen Barfield: Romanticism Come of Age: A Biography*. London: Temple Lodge, 2006.
Bratman, David. "Hugo Dyson: Inkling, Teacher, *Bon Vivant*." *Mythlore* 21, no. 4, whole no. 82 (Winter 1997), 19–34.
———. "R. B. McCallum: The Master Inkling." *Mythlore* 23, no. 3, whole no. 89 (Summer 2001), 34–42.
Carpenter, Humphrey. *The Inklings: C. S. Lewis, J. R. R. Tolkien, Charles Williams, and Their Friends*. Boston, MA: Houghton Mifflin, 1979.
———. *Tolkien: A Biography*. Boston, MA: Houghton Mifflin, 1977.
Cranborne, Hannah. Editor. *David Cecil: A Portrait by His Friends*. Stanbridge, England: Dovecote, 1990.
Duriez, Colin. *Tolkien and C. S. Lewis: The Gift of Friendship*. Mahwah, NJ: Hidden-Spring, 2003.
Garth, John. *Tolkien and the Great War: The Threshold of Middle-earth*. Boston, MA: Houghton Mifflin, 2003.
Hatfield, Alice Mary. *Charles Williams: An Exploration of His Life and Work*. New York: Oxford University Press, 1983.

Hatziolou, Elizabeth. *John Wain: A Man of Letters*. London: Pisces, 1997.

Hooper, Walter. *C. S. Lewis: A Companion & Guide*. New York: HarperCollins, 1996. Includes biographical sketches of the Inklings.

Nichols, Aidan. "Gervase Mathew." In *Dominican Gallery: Portrait of a Culture*. Leominster, England: Gracewing, 1997, 268–303.

West, Richard C. "W. H. Lewis: Historian of the Inklings and of Seventeenth-Century France." *Seven: An Anglo-American Literary Review* 14 (1997), 74–86.

Literary Studies of the Inklings as a Group

Duriez, Colin, and David Porter. *The Inklings Handbook: A Comprehensive Guide to the Lives, Thought, and Writings of C. S. Lewis, J. R. R. Tolkien, Charles Williams, Owen Barfield, and Their Friends*. St. Louis: Chalice Press, 2001.

Fredrick, Candice, and Sam McBride. *Women Among the Inklings: Gender, C. S. Lewis, J. R. R. Tolkien, and Charles Williams*. Westport, CT: Greenwood Press, 2001.

Fuller, Edmund. *Books with Men Behind Them*. New York: Random House, 1962.

Glyer, Diana Pavlac. *The Company They Keep: C. S. Lewis and J. R. R. Tolkien as Writers in Community*. Kent, OH: Kent State University Press, 2006.

Hillegas, Mark R. Editor. *Shadows of Imagination: The Fantasies of C. S. Lewis, J. R. R. Tolkien, and Charles Williams*. Carbondale: Southern Illinois University Press, 1969.

Knight, Gareth. *The Magical World of the Inklings*. Longmead, England: Element Books, 1990.

Moorman, Charles. *The Precincts of Felicity: The Augustinian City of the Oxford Christians*. Gainesville: University of Florida Press, 1966.

Reilly, Robert J. *Romantic Religion: A Study of Barfield, Lewis, Williams and Tolkien*. Athens: University of Georgia Press, 1971.

Urang, Gunnar. *Shadows of Heaven: Religion and Fantasy in the Writing of C. S. Lewis, Charles Williams, and J. R. R. Tolkien*. Philadelphia, PA: Pilgrim Press, 1971.

Selected Studies of Barfield, Tolkien, and Williams as Individual Writers

Adey, Lionel. *C. S. Lewis's "Great War" with Owen Barfield*. Victoria, B.C.: University of Victoria, 1978.

Ashenden, Gavin. *Charles Williams: Alchemy and Integration*. Kent, OH: Kent State University Press, 2006.

Cavaliero, Glen. *Charles Williams: Poet of Theology*. Grand Rapids, MI: Eerdmans, 1983.

Diener, Astrid. *The Role of Imagination in Culture and Society: Owen Barfield's Early Work*. Berlin: Galda & Wilch, 2002.

Flieger, Verlyn. *Splintered Light: Logos and Language in Tolkien's World*, 2nd edn. Kent, OH: Kent State University Press, 2002.

Flieger, Verlyn, and Carl F. Hostetter. Editors. *Tolkien's Legendarium: Essays on The History of Middle-earth*. Westport, CT: Greenwood Press, 2000.

Howard, Thomas. *The Novels of Charles Williams*. New York: Oxford University Press, 1983.

Huttar, Charles A. and Peter Schakel. Editors. *The Rhetoric of Vision: Essays on Charles Williams*. Lewisburg, PA: Bucknell University Press, 1986.

Kocher, Paul H. *Master of Middle-earth: The Fiction of J. R. R. Tolkien*. Boston, MA: Houghton Mifflin, 1972.

Shippey, T. A. *The Road to Middle-earth*. Revised and expanded edn. Boston, MA: Houghton Mifflin, 2003. (Tolkien)

Sugerman, Shirley. Editor. *Evolution of Consciousness: Studies in Polarity*. Middletown, CT: Wesleyan University Press, 1976. (Barfield)

Index

About the Editor and Contributors

THE EDITOR

BRUCE L. EDWARDS is Professor of English and Associate Dean for Distance Education and International Programs at Bowling Green State University in Bowling Green, Ohio, where has he been a faculty member and administrator since 1981. He has published several books on Lewis, most recently, *Not a Tame Lion: The Spiritual World of Narnia* (Tyndale, 2005) and *Further Up and Further in: Understanding C. S. Lewis's The Lion, the Witch and the Wardrobe* (Broadman and Holman, 2005). These are volumes in addition to two scholarly works, *A Rhetoric of Reading: C. S. Lewis's Defense of Western Literacy* and *The Taste of the Pineapple: Essays on C. S. Lewis as Reader, Critic, and Imaginative Writer.* For many years he has maintained a popular Web site on the life and works of C. S. Lewis (http://www.pseudobook.com/cslewis). During his academic career he has served as Fulbright Fellow in Nairobi, Kenya (1999–2000); a Bradley Research Fellow at the Heritage Foundation in Washington, DC (1989–1990); as the S. W. Brooks Memorial Professor of Literature at The University of Queensland, Brisbane, Australia (1988); and as a Fulbright-Hays Grant Recipient to Tanzania (2005). Bruce and his wife, Joan, live in Bowling Green, Ohio. Edwards is General Editor of this four-volume reference set on C. S. Lewis.

THE CONTRIBUTORS

GREG M. ANDERSON is Senior Pastor of the International Community Church in suburban London, England, where he has served for eleven years. During the 2003–2004 school year he was Visiting Assistant Professor of Communication at Wheaton College in Illinois. He holds a Master of Divinity from Princeton Seminary and a Master of Sacred Theology from Yale University. His Ph.D. in Communication Studies with a minor in Religious Studies is from the University of Minnesota. He has presented papers on C. S. Lewis at the National Communication Association, Oxbridge, 2005, and at the Belmont C. S. Lewis Conference, Nashville, TN, November, 2005. He has also lectured frequently on Lewis at the London Institute of Contemporary Christianity.

DAVID BRATMAN holds a Master of Library Science degree from the University of Washington and has worked as a librarian at Stanford University and elsewhere. He is the editor of *The Masques of Amen House* by Charles Williams (Mythopoeic Press, 2000). He has written biographical articles on Hugo Dyson and R. B. McCallum of the Inklings for the journal *Mythlore*. He has contributed articles on Tolkien's work to *Mythlore, Mallorn, The Tolkien Collector*, and the books *Tolkien's Legendarium* (ed. Verlyn Flieger and Carl F. Hostetter, Greenwood Press, 2000) and *The Lord of the Rings, 1954–2004* (ed. Wayne G. Hammond and Christina Scull, Marquette University Press, 2006). He writes "The Year's Work in Tolkien Studies" for the annual *Tolkien Studies*. His guide to the lives and works of the Inklings is in press as an appendix to *The Company They Keep: C. S. Lewis and J. R. R. Tolkien as Writers in Community* by Diana Pavlac Glyer (Kent State University Press, 2006). He is a contributor to the forthcoming *J. R. R. Tolkien Encyclopedia* (ed. Michael D. C. Drout, Routledge, 2006). He reviews books on the Inklings for *Mythprint*, the monthly bulletin of The Mythopoeic Society, for which he served as editor from 1980 to 1995.

MONA DUNCKEL is Professor at Bob Jones University where she serves as chair of the Social Studies Department. She earned a B.A. in History and an M.A. in teaching English from Michigan State University. She received her doctorate in English from Bowling Green State University. Her current research interests include the Rhetoric of Holocaust Museums, and the role of railroads in the development of European colonial holdings in Africa. She has presented papers at conferences across the United States and is a willing speaker about Lewis to groups of adults or children.

PHILIP HARROLD is Associate Professor of Church History at Winebrenner Theological Seminary, University of Findlay, Findlay, Ohio. He received his Ph.D. from the University of Chicago, Divinity School, under the direction of Martin E. Marty. His primary areas of scholarly interest and publication are the history of American Christianity, with emphasis in revivalism and awakenings, late nineteenth-century Protestant modernism, religion in higher education, and, most recently, the Emerging Church movement.

JOEL D. HECK has served Concordia University at Austin as Vice President of Academic Services since 1998. He teaches courses in Old Testament and the life and writings of C. S. Lewis. He has also served as a pastor, high school teacher, author, and as a conference speaker. He holds a Doctor of Theology from Concordia Seminary, St. Louis. He is the author or editor of eight books, most recently a book on C. S. Lewis's educational philosophy. Published in 2006 by Concordia Publishing House, *Irrigating Deserts: C. S. Lewis on Education* received a Marion E. Wade Center research grant. He is currently working on a book dealing with the intellectual history of Oxford and Cambridge during the Lewis years (1952–1963). Dr. Heck spent the fall of 2004 in Oxford, working with Walter Hooper on Volume III of Lewis's *Collected Letters*.

WAYNE MARTINDALE (Ph.D., University of California, Riverside) is Professor of English at Wheaton College, Illinois. Along with his most recent book, *Beyond the Shadowlands: C. S. Lewis on Heaven and Hell* (2005), he has contributed the following to Lewis studies: coeditor of *The Quotable Lewis*, editor of *Journey to the Celestial City: Glimpses of Heaven from Great Literary Classics*, author of many articles on C. S. Lewis and contributor to *Lightbearer in the Shadowlands: The Evangelistic Vision of C. S. Lewis, Reading the Classics with C. S. Lewis*, and *The C. S. Lewis Readers' Encyclopedia*. He regularly teaches classes on Lewis and, along with his wife, Nita, has led student groups to Lewis sites in England and Ireland.

MARJORIE LAMP MEAD is Associate Director of the Marion E. Wade Center, Wheaton College, Illinois. She has a B.A. in English Literature and an M.A. in Biblical and Theological Studies, both from Wheaton College (thesis topic: *Making Sense of the Universe: Dorothy L. Sayers and the Way of the Intellect*). Her primary Lewis-related publications include *A Reader's Guide through the Wardrobe* (coauthored with Leland Ryken), *Brothers and Friends: The Diaries of Major Warren Hamilton Lewis* (coedited with Clyde S. Kilby), *C. S. Lewis: Letters to Children* (coedited with Lyle W. Dorsett), as well as numerous contributions to *The C. S. Lewis Readers' Encyclopedia*. She is also Managing Editor for *SEVEN: An Anglo-American Literary Review*, a journal published annually by the Wade Center on its authors. The Marion E. Wade

Center is a major research library and archive of writings by and about seven British authors including C. S. Lewis (the other six writers are Owen Barfield, G. K. Chesterton, George MacDonald, Dorothy L. Sayers, J. R. R. Tolkien, and Charles Williams).

VICTOR REPPERT is adjunct professor of philosophy at Glendale Community College in Arizona. He is the author of *C. S. Lewis's Dangerous Idea: In Defense of the Argument from Reason* (Inter-Varsity Press, 2003), and numerous academic papers in journals such as *Christian Scholar's Review, International Journal for Philosophy of Religion, Philo,* and *Philosophia Christi.*

KAREN ROWE is Professor of English at Bob Jones University where she has taught undergraduate composition and literature classes for almost twenty years. She has a B.A. in English and an M.Ed. in Teaching English from Bob Jones University, and a Ph.D. in English with a specialization in Rhetoric and Writing from Bowling Green State University in Bowling Green, Ohio. Her dissertation identified the inscriptions on the frames of Pre-Raphaelite artist William Holman Hunt's paintings as explanatory rhetoric.

MICHAEL TRAVERS is Professor of English at Southeastern College at Wake Forest (Wake Forest, NC). He earned a B.A. (Hons.) and an M.A. from McMaster University (Hamilton, Ontario, Canada) and the Diploma in Education, Post-Baccalaureate from the University of Western Ontario; he earned his Ph.D. at Michigan State University (1981). His publications include articles on the literature of the Bible in such journals as *Grace Theological Journal, The Journal of the Evangelical Theological Society, Faith and Mission,* and *The Westminster Theological Journal,* and two books: *The Devotional Experience in the Poetry of John Milton* (Edwin Mellen, 1988) and *Encountering God in the Psalms* (Kregel, 2003). He has also contributed articles to the *Dictionary of Biblical Imagery* (IVP, 1998) and the *Dictionary for Theological Interpretation of the Bible* (Baker Academic, 2005).

DONALD T. WILLIAMS is Professor of English and Director of the School of Arts and Sciences at Toccoa Falls College, in Toccoa Falls, Georgia. He holds a B.A. in English from Taylor University, an M.Div. from Trinity Evangelical Divinity School, and a Ph.D. in Medieval and Renaissance Literature from the University of Georgia. He is the author of five books: *The Person and Work of the Holy Spirit* (Broadman, 1994), *Inklings of Reality: Essays toward a Christian Philosophy of Letters* (Toccoa Falls College Press, 1996), *The Disciple's Prayer* (Christian Publications, 1999), *Mere Humanity: G. K. Chesterton, C. S. Lewis, and J. R. R. Tolkien on the Human Condition* (Broadman, 2006), and

Credo: An Exposition of the Nicene Creed (Chalice Press, 2007). He has also contributed essays, poems, and reviews to such journals as *Christianity Today, Touchstone, The Journal of the Evangelical Theological Society, Philosophia Christi, Theology Today, Christianity and Literature, Christian Scholar's Review, Mythlore, SEVEN, Christian Educator's Journal, Preaching,* and *Christian Research Journal.*